C000124613

Soldiers' Lives through History
The Ancient World

Soldiers' Lives through History
Dennis Showalter, Series Editor

The Ancient World
Richard A. Gabriel

The Middle Ages
Clifford J. Rogers

The Early Modern World
Dennis Showalter and William J. Astore

The Nineteenth Century
Michael S. Neiberg

The Twentieth Century
Robert T. Foley and Helen McCartney

Soldiers' Lives through History ⌔

THE ANCIENT WORLD

✳ ✳ ✳

Richard A. Gabriel

Soldiers' Lives through History
Dennis Showalter, Series Editor

GREENWOOD PRESS
Westport, Connecticut • London

Library of Congress Cataloging-in-Publication Data

Gabriel, Richard A.

 The ancient world / Richard A. Gabriel.

   p. cm. — (Soldiers' lives through history)

 Includes bibliographical references and index.

 ISBN 0–313–33348–3 (alk. paper)

 1. Soldiers—History—To 1500.   2. Armies—History—To 1500. 3.
Military art and science—History—To 500.   4. Military history,
Ancient.   I. Title.

 U29.G22   2007

 355.009'01—dc22   2006029538

British Library Cataloguing in Publication Data is available.

Library of Congress Catalog Card Number: 2006029538
ISBN: 0–313–33348–3

First published in 2007

Greenwood Press, 88 Post Road West, Westport, CT 06881
An imprint of Greenwood Publishing Group, Inc.
www.greenwood.com

Printed in the United States of America

The paper used in this book complies with the
Permanent Paper Standard issued by the National
Information Standards Organization (Z39.48–1984).

10 9 8 7 6 5 4 3 2 1

For Suzi, always,
and for John and Ann Moriarty, dear friends,
and Gerry Gagne, the smartest man I know.

✴ ✴ ✴

CONTENTS

PART II:

ANCIENT ARMIES

★ ★ ★

SERIES FOREWORD

The song "Universal Soldier" has been a staple of peace rallies since the 1960s. Written by Buffy Sainte-Marie and performed by Donovan Leitch in 1965, when it became popular, the song indicts the soldier as war's agent, unlike most other songs of its type, which cast the soldier as war's victim: "He knows he shouldn't kill / And he knows he always will...."

The killing, of course, goes on apace. Sometimes it will be by neighbors once thought of as friends, as in Rwanda during the 1990s. Sometimes it will be by bureaucratic utopians who see the path to the future obstructed by Jews in Hitler's Germany— or by class enemies in Stalin's Russia—or by people who wear glasses in Pol Pot's Cambodia. Sometimes it will be by zealots who expect to gain paradise by dying while killing others, like the Crusaders of the Middle Ages, or today's Jihadis.

Historians are currently engaged in a debate on the existence of a "Western way of war," which distinguishes the West from the rest of the world, and arguably defines Western civilization as well. Underlying that debate, and structuring it, is the question of whether there is a distinctively Western soldier. Victor Davis Hanson writes eloquently of free men voluntarily committing themselves to conquer or die in order that they might return to the homes they saved. Critics such as John A. Lynn in *Battle: A History of Combat and Culture* assert the cultural specificity of approaches to war in both Western and global contexts. The ancient Greeks, for example, sought quick decisions because of particular values emphasizing individual worth and independence. Nineteenth-century Europe's concept of the decisive battle was influenced heavily by a Romantic high culture as opposed to specific military factors, such as rapid-firing weapons and mass armies.

This series, Soldiers' Lives through History, is the first to address comprehensively the cutting-edge experiences of the Western soldier from his initial appearance at the beginning of history to his latest avatars in Vietnam and the Middle East. Richard Gabriel's volume on the soldiers of the ancient world notes that the first archaeological evidence of organized war is in present-day Iraq. Thousands of years later the wheel has turned a full circle. The authors of each volume, Richard A. Gabriel; Clifford J. Rogers; Dennis Showalter and William J. Astore; Michael S. Neiberg; and Robert T. Foley and Helen McCartney, address not only "the face of battle," but also its frameworks. The soldiers' civil origins, their emotional and intellectual makeup, their daily lives in peace and war, and above all their reactions to facing death and dealing it–these are the kinds of themes developed in all five volumes of the series. The authors' intentions are to facilitate understanding of one of history's fundamental questions: Why do humans fight wars? That question's continuing relevance is made plain everywhere, in television and in newspapers, on the Internet, in video games, and not least in the cemeteries where bugles still sound over those who gave all in war and to war. Did they do so as heroes, fools, perpetrators—or perhaps a little of all three, structured by individual factors defying collective analysis?

In this series, Greenwood Press takes a major step in providing substance to the issue of the soldier's identity and the soldier's place in Western civilization. One point that Hanson and his critics share is an agreement that war making in the West has evolved away from any class or caste restrictions on participation. War has been every man's business—and, increasingly, the business of women as well. Most men and women who will read these books have known someone who was a solider, have soldiers in their family trees, and have the potential to be soldiers themselves. In that sense, this series is about all of us: the heirs and successors of the Universal Soldier.

Dennis Showalter

⚹ ⚹ ⚹

INTRODUCTION

It is no easy task to try to synthesize the historical material relevant to soldiers, warfare, and armies in the ancient world, a period that extends from at least 4000 B.C.E. to 450 C.E. and, in the view of some historians, all the way to 1453 C.E., the year that the last great imperium of the ancient world, Constantinople, succumbed to the armies of the Muslim Turks. If one is to have any chance of success—and at the same time present the material in a manner that the reader will find sufficiently enjoyable and informative—some points of focus are required to serve as a means of organizing the material. I have chosen two such foci: first, the various elements that comprised the military life of the ancient soldier; and second, the various armies in which the ancient soldier served.

The book is therefore divided into two parts, the first addressing military life and the second addressing the ancient armies themselves. Part I, "Military Life," presents twenty-one chapters, each one addressing some significant aspect of military life in the ancient world. These chapters include

+ the origins of war
+ the physical condition of the soldier
+ recruitment
+ manpower and size of the armies
+ rations
+ soldiers' equipment
+ camp life
+ discipline and punishment
+ weapons

- defensive equipment, armor, helmets, and shields
- the chariot
- the cavalry
- logistics and transport
- the strategic range of the armies
- tactics
- military staffs
- siegecraft and artillery
- death and wounding
- infection and disease
- injury
- military medical care.

I have approached each of these chapters cross-culturally, that is, drawing examples from several cultures, armies, and time periods within each chapter in order to provide the reader with as comprehensive an understanding as possible and to avoid the usual "Western-centric" perspective too common in analyses of ancient warfare. (A note about inclusive language: I have sometimes used male pronouns and terms such as *manpower* because in almost all cases, soldiers in the ancient world were male.) I have attempted to present the material from the point of view of the common soldier and not, as so often happens, from the perspective of generals or important personages, who, truth be told, rarely experienced the hardships and difficulties attendant to the military life of the everyday soldier. Having been an infantryman myself, I can attest that things are always more difficult to achieve in battle than most academics or generals make them out to be.

Part II, "Ancient Armies," seeks to present a detailed description of eighteen major armies of antiquity. Again, the approach is cross-cultural, and the armies examined range from ancient Sumer to Persia to India and China. These chapters are arranged roughly in chronological order. Within each chapter I have endeavored to place the army within the historic-cultural context that gave it rise and to explain its organization, weapons, tactics, and the other military capabilities that proved its combat power. The armies included are those of Sumer and Akkad, Egypt, the Mitanni, the Hittites, the Canaanites, the Philistines, the Israelites, Assyria, China, India, Classical Greece, Persia, Alexander the Great, the Successors to Alexander, Republican Rome, Carthage, the Barbarians, and the Roman Empire.

The book also provides a timeline in order to put some of the events, inventions, and developments into more context. There are nineteen illustrations to help the reader visualize some of the equipment, armor, transport, and formations that ancient soldiers used, carried, and fought in.

The book was written for the information and enjoyment of general readers as well as for researchers at the collegiate level. No claim is made that the information contained in any given chapter is complete, only that it is sufficiently comprehensive to inform at a certain level and to stimulate the reader to want to know more. To facilitate this objective, I have included detailed footnotes and source materials in each of the chapters of part I as well as a short list of suggested readings in each chapter of part II. It is my hope that the reader who harbors a genuine interest in the military history of antiquity will find these materials an adequate starting point for further inquiry and research.

✳ ✳ ✳

TIMELINE

500,000 B.C.E.	*Homo erectus* produces the first stone tools
100,000 B.C.E.	*Homo sapiens* invents the first long-range weapon, the fire-hardened, wooden-tipped spear
10,000 B.C.E.	Humans learn how to herd wild animals
9000 B.C.E.	Sheep become the first pastoral animal to be domesticated by humans
8300 B.C.E.	First archaeological evidence of planting of wild cereals in Mureybet, Syria; "earliest town in the world" founded at Jericho
8000 B.C.E.	First evidence of head surgery
7500 B.C.E.	First use of pressure flaking, making longer one-piece blades possible and leading to reaping and skinning knives and, eventually, to the dagger
6500 B.C.E.	First evidence of organized violence among humans occurs at Jeban Sahaba in the Sudan; first rock painting of humans killing humans evident in Transcaucasia
6000 B.C.E.	Cattle, goats, and dogs domesticated; first evidence of harvesting of wild grains at Byblos

5500 B.C.E.	First large-scale irrigation to support agriculture at Catal Huyuk in Anatolia
5000 B.C.E.	First evidence of settled agriculture; planting of domesticated cereal grains; humans stabilize their food supply, bringing an end to the hunter-gatherer way of life they have known for 800,000 years; cities are now possible
4500 B.C.E.	Sling invented at Catal Huyuk in Anatolia
4000 B.C.E.	Beginning of the Bronze Age in the Middle East and southeastern Europe; first fortified towns appear; sling, dagger, mace, and bow are common weapons; emergence of large urban societies in Egypt, Mesopotamia, and the Indus River valley in India
4000–3000 B.C.E.	War is now an important social institution characteristic of all major cultures of the world
3500–2200 B.C.E.	Empire of Sumer and Akkad in Mesopotamia; first Sumerian war between Lagash and Umma in 2525 B.C.E.
3200 B.C.E.	Upper and Lower Egypt unified under Namer; first dynastic period begins and lasts 700 years; Egypt establishes the world's largest irrigation system to support agriculture
2750 B.C.E.	Babylonians are first to diagnose mental illness in soldiers as being a curse from the gods
2686 B.C.E.	Period of the Old Kingdom in Egypt; age of the pyramids; first evidence of military staffs
2500 B.C.E.	First evidence of soldiers wearing helmets found in Death Pits of Ur; Sumerians introduce the chariot, the first military use of the wheel; the chariot, the composite bow, the sickle sword, the penetrating axe, body armor, the helmet, the neck collar, the battering ram, and the scaling ladder are all invented in Mesopotamia; killing power of weaponry greatly increased
2500 B.C.E.	Sumerians invent the first military medical corps
2500 B.C.E.	Hittites migrate from the lower Danube to Anatolia
2325–? B.C.E.	Sargon the Great of Akkad conquers Sumer and establishes an empire; his grandson, Naram Sin (2254–2218 B.C.E.) introduces the composite bow to warfare
2200–1750 B.C.E.	Period of the Xia Dynasty in China
2158–2000 B.C.E.	Third Dynasty of Ur produces the world's first military medical text
2050–1786 B.C.E.	Middle Kingdom period in Egypt; borders are expanded before country collapses into civil war; Hyksos invade in 1750 B.C.E. and occupy Egypt for almost two hundred years; invaders introduce the chariot to Egypt

2000 B.C.E.	First evidence of the field pack in Egypt
1850 B.C.E.	The Kahun Papyrus, the oldest Egyptian medical text, appears
1728–1686 B.C.E.	Reign of Hammurabi
1700 B.C.E.	First evidence of the field boot, introduced by Aryan invaders of India
1600 B.C.E.	Mitanni establish themselves as a new kingdom in Syria; first to exploit the horse as an instrument of war and introduce the horse-drawn, spoked-wheel chariot; introduced the *maryannu* sociomilitary system of warfare, which spread throughout the Middle East
1600 B.C.E.	Indo-European migration from central Asian steppes begins
1580–960 B.C.E.	Period of the New Kingdom in Egypt; Hyksos driven out; Eighteenth Dynasty established by Amenhotep I (1570–1546 B.C.E.); imperial expansion completed under Thutmose III, the "Napoleon of Egypt"
1500–1200 B.C.E.	Archaic Age of Greece; siege of Troy; *Iliad* as oral poem first performed
1500–900 B.C.E.	Emergence of the Canaanites on the Palestine land bridge; adoption of *maryannu* military system of the Mitanni
1479 B.C.E.	Thutmose III of Egypt defeats Canaanites at Megiddo
1450–1180 B.C.E.	Rise of the Hittite empire under Suppiluliumas and his son Muwatallis
1400 B.C.E.	First weapons fashioned of iron appear in India
1300 B.C.E.	Kizwadana people of Armenia are first to make iron implements in the West
1275 B.C.E.	Ramses II of Egypt introduces the oxcart as a military logistics vehicle; defeats the Hittites at the battle of Kadesh
1275–1225 B.C.E.	Israelite exodus from Egypt
1225–1200 B.C.E.	Successful Israelite invasion of Canaan under Joshua
1200 B.C.E.	Iron Age begins in the Middle East and southeastern Europe
1200 B.C.E.	Philistines defeated by Ramses II during an attempt to invade Egypt; settlement in lower Canaan; introduction of the straight iron sword and circular shield with Argive grip; conflict with Israelites begins; introduction of the Argive shield and grip to classical Greek warfare
1200–1000 B.C.E.	Invasion by unknown peoples destroys Archaic Greece
1200–1050 B.C.E.	Period of the Judges in Israel; Gideon defeats the Midianites, and Deborah defeats Sisera, the Canaanite king

1200–700 B.C.E.	Indo-European invasion and conquest of India; the Rig-Veda and the *Mahabharata* are written; chariot introduced to Indian warfare; first evidence in India of the use of prosthetic limbs for the wounded
1150–1100 B.C.E.	Period of the Shang Dynasty in China
1100–256 B.C.E.	Period of the Zhou Dynasty in China
1053 B.C.E.	Philistines defeat Israelites at Aphek and take control of most of Canaan; defeated by Solomon in 960 B.C.E. and assimilated into Israelite society
1025–1005 B.C.E.	Kingdom of Saul; Saul killed by Philistines at the battle of Mount Gilboa
1005–961 B.C.E.	David establishes the kingdom of Israel
961–921 B.C.E.	Kingdom of Solomon in Israel; military recruitment and a logistics system are rationalized; new chariot armies are created
921–587 B.C.E.	Period of the Hebrew kings; ends with deportation by Assyrians; Philistines are deported as well
890–612 B.C.E.	Rise of the Assyrian empire; Tukulti-Ninurta II introduces mounted cavalry teams for the first time; single mounted horsemen appear fifty years later
853 B.C.E.	Battle of Qarqar; first use of cavalry in battle; first use of camel cavalry by Gingibu the Arab in the same battle; later, Assyrians are the first to use the chariot as a platform for mounted infantry
814 B.C.E.	Rise of Carthage
771–464 B.C.E.	Spring and Autumn period in China; civil war among seven states; introduction of the bronze sword, crossbow, and laminar armor to Chinese warfare
700 B.C.E.	Vedic social order in India collapses; it is replaced by sixteen states constantly at war with one another
612 B.C.E.	Assyria empire destroyed by Persians
600 B.C.E.	Elephant first used as an instrument of warfare; replaces chariot as a major combat arm in India
600–338 B.C.E.	The age of Classical Greece; Peloponnesian War; Persian invasion; bronze cuirass replaced by linen
546–323 B.C.E.	Rise of the Persian Empire; Cyrus II the Great comes to the throne of Persia; introduces universal military training for all Persians; introduces scythed chariot and mobile siege towers; first use of naphtha throwers; Cyrus dies in battle in 529 B.C.E.

544–496 B.C.E.	Sun Tzu writes *The Art of War* in China
525 B.C.E.	Cambyses defeats the Egyptians at the battle of Pelusium
500 B.C.E.	First appearance of mounted cavalry in China; cavalry does not become common for another two hundred years
500 B.C.E.	Indians introduce the Wootz process for making steel
500–28 B.C.E.	Period of the Roman Republic
481 B.C.E.	Xerxes attempts to invade Greece
464–221 B.C.E.	Period of the Warring States in China
401 B.C.E.	Xenophon writes the *Anabasis*
400 B.C.E.	Ironworking for military purposes introduced in China; iron swords first used at the battle of Guiling in 353 B.C.E.
394–386 B.C.E.	Corinthian War rages
390 B.C.E.	Iphicrates introduces *peltast* light infantry to Greek warfare
382–336 B.C.E.	Philip II of Macedon introduces the fortified camp, artillery, and cavalry as a combat arm of decision to Greek warfare; improves logistics with the introduction of the horse to replace the oxcart
357 B.C.E.	Stymphalian Aenas writes the first comprehensive work in Western literature on military theory
356–323 B.C.E.	Period of Imperial Greece led by Alexander the Great
340–290 B.C.E.	Roman wars against the Samnites; Romans acquire the *pilum*, the scutum shield and the military sandal from the Samnites
334 B.C.E.	Alexander crosses the Hellespont to invade Persia
331 B.C.E.	Alexander defeats Darius at Arbela; all Persia falls to Alexander
323–280 B.C.E.	Wars of the Successors rage; Antagonids rule Greece, Ptolemies rule Egypt, and Seleucids rule southwest Asia
323–168 B.C.E.	Reign of the Successors
321 B.C.E.	Chandragupta Maurya establishes the Mauryan empire in India
300 B.C.E.	Age of Steel begins; Roman army adopts chain mail from the Celts
281–275 B.C.E.	Pyrrhus's wars with the Romans; introduction of the elephant as an element in Western warfare
264–241 B.C.E.	First Punic War

222 B.C.E.	Pyrrhus introduces the double and articulated phalanx to Greek warfare at the battle of Sellasia
220–206 B.C.E.	Rule of the Han Empire in China
218–201 B.C.E.	Second Punic War; Hannibal invades Italy
216 B.C.E.	Battle of Cannae
204 B.C.E.	Romans replace the maniple with the cohort and adopt the *gladius* as the main weapon of the infantry
202 B.C.E.	Scipio Africanus defeats Hannibal at Zama, bringing the Second Punic War to an end
197 B.C.E.	Rome invades Greece; Pyrrhus defeated at the battle of Cynoscephalae
149–146 B.C.E.	Third Punic War; Carthage destroyed
100 B.C.E.	Marius reforms the Roman army; military training introduced and logistics improved
63 B.C.E.–14 C.E.	Gaius Julius Caesar Octavianus, known to history as Caesar Augustus, defeats Mark Antony in civil war and founds the Roman Empire
58–52 B.C.E.	Caesar conquers Gaul and invades Britain
58 B.C.E.–445 C.E.	Period of attempted barbarian invasions of Roman empire
48 B.C.E.	Civil war between Caesar and Pompey; Pompey defeated at the battle of Pharsalus
44 B.C.E.	Julius Caesar assassinated; civil war begins
9 C.E.	Romans defeated by Arminius at the battle of the Teutoburg Forest, forcing Roman influence back across the Rhine
9–450 C.E.	Period of Imperial Rome; *lorica segmenta* introduced; Roman medical corps invents the tourniquet and surgical clamp
235–297 C.E.	Rome suffers through sixty years of civil strife, during which sixteen emperors are assassinated
284–305 C.E.	Emperor Diocletian divides Roman Empire into two administrative districts
378 C.E.	Goths defeat Romans at the battle of Adrianople; eastern frontiers of the empire are breached beyond repair
450 C.E.	Rome defeats Attila the Hun at the battle of Chalons; the Roman armies are now completely barbarized; the Western Roman Empire ceases to exist

PART I

✸ ✸ ✸

Military Life

One

✳ ✳ ✳

ORIGINS OF WAR

War is the legacy that the ancient world bequeathed to the modern one. There is little evidence of war before the emergence of the world's first complex human societies. War is a social invention that required specific conditions to bring it about. Because war has been omnipresent from the very beginning of man's *recorded* history, about 4000 B.C.E., it is sometimes assumed that war must have been present even before that. But when war as a social institution is placed in historical perspective, it is obvious that it is among the most recent of human social inventions.

The first evidence of a hominid culture that used tools emerged 500,000 years ago, in the Olduvai Gorge stone culture in Africa. The honor of initiating the Stone Age to the first use of tools goes to *Homo erectus*, our direct, though not most immediate, ancestor. Four hundred thousand years later, *Homo sapiens* and their now extinct cousins, the Neanderthal people, created a more advanced stone culture with a wider range of tools, including the first long-range weapon, the spear. It is this later period that serves as a baseline from which to study the emergence of warfare. Otherwise, we would have to admit that for more than 98.8 percent of its time on this planet, the human species lived without any evidence of war whatsoever.

Using the Stone Age cultures of *Homo sapiens* and the Neanderthal as a starting point, some remarkable facts emerge about the development of war. Humans required 30,000 years to learn how to use fire and another 20,000 years to invent the fire-hardened, wooden-tipped spear; spear points came much later. Sixty thousand years later, humans invented the bow and arrow. It required another 30,000 years for humans to learn how to herd wild animals, and yet another 4,000 years to domesticate goats, sheep, cattle, and the dog. At about the same time, there is the first evidence of the harvesting of wild grains, but it took another 2,000 years for humans to transplant wild grains to fixed campsites and still another 2,000 years to learn how to plant domesticated strains of cereal grain. It is only after these developments, around 4000 B.C.E., that warfare made its appearance as a major human social institution. Seen in historical perspective, human beings have known war for only about 6 percent of the time since the *Homo sapiens* Stone Age began.[1]

Once warfare became established, however, it developed more quickly than any other social institution that we can find. In less than a thousand years, humans brought forth the sword, sling, dagger, mace, bronze and copper weapons, and fortified towns. The next thousand years saw the emergence of iron weapons, the chariot, the standing professional army, military academies, general staffs, military training, permanent arms industries, written texts on tactics, military procurement, logistics systems, conscription, and military pay. By 2000 B.C.E., war had become an important social institution in almost all major cultures of the world.[2] War can be defined as a level of organized conflict that involves forces of some size, rooted in the larger society's organizational structure, applying a killing technology with some degree of organization and expertise. Without these conditions, one might find murder, small-scale scuffles, raids, ambushes, and so on, but not warfare. War requires the systematic, organized, societal application of orchestrated violence. For the first 95,000 years after the *Homo sapiens* Stone Age began, there is no evidence at all that humans engaged in organized conflict on any level, let alone on any level requiring organized group violence. The first evidence of truly organized violence on some scale occurs sometime around 6500 B.C.E., at Jeban Sahaba in the Sudan. The skeletal remains of fifty-nine people, including women and children, suggest that they were killed by repeated arrow wounds and spear thrusts.[3] It is unclear if these people were killed in a raid or ambush or were simply executed. What is certain is that an organized force of some size was necessary to carry out the killing. A Neolithic site in Transcaucasia reveals the first rock painting of the period that seems to show a small, armed squad attacking and killing other men with bows and arrows. While it required another 1,500 years for humans to reach a level of organized violence that could be unequivocally identified as war, it seems clear that by 6000 B.C.E., humans had already learned to used organized groups to kill other humans. Yet, it is not surprising that for most of the Stone Age, humans lived without even small-scale organization for killing each other, considering how they lived for all but the last few hundred years of that age.[4]

For all but the last 10,000 years, humans lived as hunter-gathers organized into small groups of twenty to fifty persons. Most of the members of these groups were related by blood or marriage, much like an extended family. These groups traveled constantly in small migratory bands, following the seasonal migration of the game, and assembled as clans on a seasonal basis as the normal migration of the wild herds brought them together. But it is unlikely that these clan groups had any social organization of any kind. Certainly they had not yet evolved into tribes. Under these conditions, organized conflict of any sort was a rare occurrence. The small size of the groups alone would have militated against it. The average hunter-gatherer group had within it not more than six or seven armed adult males, and the need to hunt and feed their families would have made it impossible for them to serve primarily as warriors. The constant movement of the group made it unlikely that they would come into contact with other groups, except on rare occasions. The only weapon capable of being used in war was the spear, and there is no evidence that humans ever used it to kill other humans during this period.[5]

For humans to abandon seasonal migrations required an expansion and stability of their food supply and a more certain way to obtain migratory game. The expansion of the food supply came first. At Mureybet in Syria, around 8300 B.C.E., there appears the first archaeological evidence of the planting of wild cereals.[6] Later, humans moved from harvesting wild grains to transplanting them to more stable home camps. Humans were on the threshold of creating the tribe. Mureybet appears as the first stable, small village made possible by the rudimentary cultivation of cereal grains. At about the same time (8350 B.C.E.), the "earliest town in the world" came into being at Jericho in

Pictorial evidence of man fighting against man is as old as the Neolithic age, as this painting from Spain reveals. Courtesy of the Perry Casteneda Library.

Palestine, the world's first large-scale, permanent human settlement. The people of Jericho had mastered the secret of seed corn and the technology of irrigation to plant and grow it, supporting a population of about 2,500 people.

The first evidence of humans' ability to domesticate animals on some scale also appears around 6000 B.C.E. Byblos offers the first evidence of the domestication of sheep, goats, and cattle and of the use of the trained dog as a helper. Five hundred years later, at Catal Huyuk in Anatolia, we find the first large-scale irrigation to support agriculture. The number of dwellings within the town, about 1,000, suggests that the population of Catal Huyuk was about 6,000 people, twice the size of Jericho's population. By 5000 B.C.E., humans had succeeded in stabilizing and expanding their food supply to a degree that could support human groupings in the thousands, with agriculture bringing to an end the hunter-gatherer way of life that humans had known for more than 800,000 years. Large, stable populations permanently tied to specific places made possible the evolution of the tribe. Tribal societies, with their larger populations, adequate food supply, and the corresponding deemphasis on hunting, were able to produce a class of hunters who evolved into a new class of warriors, whose claims to social role and status were based less on their hunting prowess than on their ability to fight and kill other warriors in defense of the tribe. For the first time in human experience, there arose a social group whose specific function and justification was its ability to kill other human beings.[7]

Once the warrior caste came into being, it would have been a matter of only a few generations before anyone could remember when there had been no warriors at all. Within a short time the new social institution would have seemed as normal a part of society as cattle herders and farmers. Once the military technology became available, these new warriors and the tribal social orders that created them were able to fight wars of much greater scope and lethality than had previously been the case. But the presence of a warrior caste by itself did not mean that it would have had to develop into an organized force for large-scale warfare. Most early war was highly ritualized, with low levels of death and injury, much as combat between other species of animals is. To move from ritualized combat to genuine killing required a change in human psychology. When and how Neolithic tribes transitioned from ritual to real warfare is unknown. What is certain, however, is that they did make the transition. The late Neolithic age (6000–5000 B.C.E.) witnessed an advance in the development of new weapons that was, until then, unparalleled in human history. It was but a short time before these weapons were used in large-scale warfare.

The major weapons of this period were the bow and arrow, the mace, the spear, the dagger, and the sling.[8] The fire-hardened spear had been around for thousands of years, and its major improvement in the Neolithic period was the use of stone, flint, and obsidian spear points. Flint and obsidian spear points required pressure flaking when chipping the point from the larger stone. Pressure flaking made possible spear and arrow points that were flat on two sides, reducing weight and increasing penetration. Pressure flaking also made possible longer, one-piece blades, an innovation first applied to reaping and skinning knives before giving rise to the dagger. This new technology first appeared between 7500 and 6800 B.C.E. at Cayonu in Syria[9] and spread widely and rapidly throughout the Middle East.[10]

The dagger made an excellent short-range weapon, and as soon as man developed metal technology to increase the length of the blade, the sword followed. The mace, with a stone head affixed to a wooden handle, could easily cave in a man's skull. The handle also increased the accuracy and striking momentum of the weapon when thrown. The bow had been in existence for millennia, but aside from the use of flat arrowheads, there appear to have been no improvements in its composition or strength until much later, when the Sumerians introduced the composite bow. The bow was easy to fashion and use and could kill from a distance, capabilities which probably made it the basic killing weapon of the Neolithic warrior.

An important innovation was the sling.[11] Evidence for its existence appears at Catal Huyuk between 5500 and 4500 B.C.E. Here we also find the first evidence of shot made from sunbaked clay, the first human attempt to make a specific type of expendable ammunition. The sling represented a great leap in killing technology. Even an average slinger could throw shot over a range of 200 yards. Small shot could be delivered on a trajectory almost parallel with the ground over ranges of 1 to 100 yards, while larger stones could be fired howitzer-like over greater ranges.[12] All these weapons, except the sling, have developmental histories that point to their original invention as weapons of the hunt. The sling may have been the first weapon designed primarily to kill humans since its hunting function is marginal at best.

But weapons are useless without tactics to direct their employment in battle. The most basic tactics are the line and column and the ability to approach in column and move into line. Tactics, of course, require commanders, which implies at least some rudimentary military organization. The importance of tactics in the development of war is suggested by H. Turney-High, who argues that evidence of simple tactical formations is the definitive characteristic that constitutes a "military horizon" separating fighting from genuine war.[13] While the Neolithic period may have witnessed the first use of such tactics in fighting among humans at war, it is likely that they were originally developed long before as techniques of the hunt.

Just prior to 4000 B.C.E., there appears the first evidence of fortified towns. The classic and much earlier example is Jericho. While other towns of the period show some degree of fortification, mostly ditches and mud walls, or, as at Catal Huyuk, houses abutting one another so that the outside walls of the dwellings constitute a wall around the whole settlement, only Jericho reflects a type of military architecture that would be readily recognizable by a modern soldier. Jericho's walls enclosed an area of ten acres and ran to a length of 765 yards. The walls were ten feet thick and thirty feet high. A twenty-eight-foot tower with a base thirty-five feet in diameter, enclosing a doorway in its middle, was its most striking feature. A population of 2,500 people could field about 600 adults to defend the wall, or one soldier per yard of wall.[14] Jericho's walls seem to have been built in stages sometime between 8000 and 7000 B.C.E. The emergence of fortified sites in the late Neolithic period seems evidence enough of warfare conducted on some significant scale.

The connection between the development of agriculture and warfare has been long noted by scholars, such as Quincy Wright in his study of 633 cultures. Wright notes that even before the establishment of agriculture as the dominant form of economic and social organization, peoples who were *partially* agriculturalized demonstrated a greater tendency toward war, while the higher agriculturalists were the most warlike of all.[15] The post-Neolithic period, or Bronze Age, saw a great explosion in the spread of these large-scale agricultural societies and with it the spread of warfare conducted on a large scale.

The spread of agriculture set the stage for the emergence of large urban societies. The first of these societies appeared almost simultaneously around 4000 B.C.E. in Egypt, Mesopotamia, and the Indus River valley in India. This period saw the development of new weapons—the chariot, the composite bow, the sword, the axe, the penetrating axe, mail armor, the helmet, the battering ram, scaling, and later, stronger fortifications—that increased the scale and lethality of war. Supporting social and psychological structures struck deep roots so that within a mere 1,000 years the humans of the Bronze Age could not imagine a way of life without warriors and warfare. Warrior kings and large armies became routine aspects of life, when only a millennium earlier, they were unimaginable. Agricultural efficiency produced an explosion in population, providing the raw human material for war on a large scale. Humans stood on the brink of yet another revolution, this one in the area of metal technology. As humans entered the Bronze Age (4000 B.C.E.), it is unlikely that they realized that they were about to give birth to yet another social invention, one that they would bequeath to every generation yet to be born: Mankind was about to give life to war.

NOTES

1. For an analysis of weapons development from the Stone Age to the present, see Richard A. Gabriel, "Armaments," in *Italian Encyclopedia of Social Science* (Rome: University of Rome, 1990).

2. These states included Sumer, Egypt, Vedic India, and China.

3. Arther Ferrill, *The Origins of War: From the Stone Age to Alexander the Great* (New York: Thames and Hudson, 1985), 23–24.

4. James Mellaart, *The Neolithic of the Near East* (New York: Charles Scribner, 1975), 198.

5. Of all the evidence compiled on Neanderthal man by archaeologists, the only hint of conflict comes from a single skeleton with a small hole in its pelvis that *may* have been made by a spear.

6. For a discussion of the Mureybet site and its importance to agriculture, see Mellaart, *Neolithic of the Near East*, 45–50, 54, 68–71.

7. At least in the early stages of development, the ability of the new warrior caste to influence policy seems strongly controlled by a social structure that left power in the hands of civilian "peace chiefs." Only later do warriors seem to have acquired the ability to dominate policy. See Christian Feest, *The Art of War* (New York: Thames and Hudson, 1980), 16–20.

8. Ferrill, *Origins of War*, 19.

9. Mellart, *Neolithic of the Near East*, 63.

10. Ibid., 102.

11. For the history of the sling, see Manfred Korfmann, "The Sling As a Weapon," *Scientific American* 229, no. 4 (1973): 34–42.

12. Ibid., 39.

13. H. Turney-High, *Primitive War: Its Practice and Concepts*, 2d. ed. (Columbia: University of South Carolina Press, 1971), 26–28.

14. Gwynne Dyer, *War* (New York: Crown, 1985), 15–16. Dyer draws on Mellaart's figures for his description.

15. Qunicy Wright. *A Study of War*, 2nd ed. (Chicago: University of Chicago Press, 1965), 63.

Two

✳ ✳ ✳

THE SOLDIER

There is a tendency among people in the modern world to regard themselves as unique because their lives are happening to them for the first time. The claim to historical uniqueness is, of course, false. Human beings have been unchanged in their essentials for more than 100,000 years. Those who lived in the ancient world (4000–450 B.C.E.) loved and feared the same things we do, especially when it came to that organized violence that was war itself. The brain structures required for conceptual thought, language, and cultural learning had already been in place at least 100,000 years before the beginning of the age of antiquity, and they have not changed since. Humans have been humans for a very long time, and those who believe the humans of antiquity to be less intellectually agile and creative need only gaze on the pyramids to know how false that idea is.

PHYSICAL APPEARANCE AND AGE SPAN OF SOLDIERS

The inhabitants of the ancient world were physically smaller than we are but psychologically identical. The average age of death was about 44 years, an age that remained unchanged in the West from the beginning of the Bronze Age to the introduction of antibiotics in the middle of the twentieth century.[1] About one-third of children in the ancient world died before age five, a mortality rate that also remained mostly unchanged until very modern times, even in the industrial West.[2] The health of individuals would, of course, vary from place to place, depending on a number of variables. People in ancient times suffered from many of the same ills as their descendants. Anemia, tuberculosis of the bone and lung, syphilis, cancer, and poor dentition are all in evidence among ancient corpses. Various forms of malaria and other diseases caused by waterborne parasites were also present, as they still are today in much of the Middle East and Asia.[3] In ancient times, virulent outbreaks of disease—plague, smallpox, measles—sometimes reduced whole sections of countries into uninhabited wastelands. And yet, in the midst of all this, there arose some of the greatest civilizations—Sumer, Egypt, India, China, Hatti, Israel, Persia, Greece, and Rome—ever fashioned by human effort. War, too, had its place along with its practitioner, the ancient soldier.

The ancient soldier was shorter and weighed less than his modern counterpart, varying in average height from 5.4 to 5.7 feet, or about the same height as the average adult male in the nineteenth-century industrial West.[4] The primary determinant of height in humans is nutrition. Averages, however, hide interesting variations. We learn from Caesar that the average Gaul was seven inches taller than the Roman soldier and that Tacitus was impressed by the "large frames" of the Germans.[5] Thutmose III, the "Napoleon of Egypt," was only five feet tall, three inches shorter than the average Egyptian, while his son Amenhotep II was taller than six feet.[6] Battles in the ancient world involved mostly close combat, where physical size and strength of the soldier provided an advantage. Gilgamesh of Sumer and Goliath of the Philistines are both portrayed as taller, broader, and stronger than average. The Talmudic Midrash of the Israelites tells of instances where Jewish recruits were rejected by the Roman army as being too short.[7] If we may believe Vegetius, the Roman army had a minimum height requirement for its legionnaires so that the average Roman soldier of the Imperial period (first to fourth centuries C.E.) was taller than the average Roman civilian.[8] In antiquity a medium-framed soldier of 5.7 feet weighed about 145 pounds, an almost ideal height and weight to make maximum use of the caloric content of his diet.

COMPOSITION OF ANCIENT ARMIES

The age of military service varied somewhat among the armies of antiquity for which we have evidence. In the Israelite and Egyptian armies the age at which a male became eligible for military service was twenty years. This is interesting in that in both societies the age at which a male became a full member of the community was considerably less. In Egypt a male was considered an adult at thirteen years, women even younger. The average age of first pregnancy onset for Egyptian women in antiquity was only thirteen years.[9] Hittite and Mycennaean males became warriors at seventeen years of age, and the age at which males were eligible to serve in the army of the Roman Republic was also seventeen. During the Roman imperium the eligible age was eighteen, although many recruits seem to have been at least twenty. It was not, however, uncommon for officers and warrior kings to take their sons with them on campaigns at younger ages. We find Cornelius Scipio on campaign with his father at sixteen and Hannibal with his father in Spain at age ten. Assyrian kings usually took their young sons with them on military campaigns, befitting the experience required of a future warrior king.

With the average life span in antiquity being only forty-four years, taking males into military service in late adolescence provided soldiers who were at the peak of their physical strength and endurance, elements important to surviving military life.

How long a person served in the military varied considerably from country to country. Egyptian conscripts under the Old Kingdom served only when there was a campaign to be fought, the army being mostly a feudal levy. By the New Kingdom, however, Egypt's army was a large conscript force commanded by a professional officer corps. In these circumstances, one in every ten men was drafted into military service in both peacetime and war, where they served for two years. Soldiers of the legions of Republican Rome were called to the colors as required and served until the need had passed. During the Imperial period, all Roman soldiers were professionals who enlisted for six-year terms. In Sumer, Hatti, China, and India, most soldiers were conscripts brought to service as the need arose and remaining there until no longer needed.

By contrast, most armies of the ancient period possessed officer corps of professional quality, many of whom served for most of their active lives. The professionalism of these cadres was a consequence of their high social status in warrior societies. In Egypt the officer corps was a professional cadre created by and commanded by pharaoh in his role as warrior king. In Sumer, all kings were first warriors, as were their nobles. The same was true in Assyria, Hatti, and Mycennaean Greece. The Mitanni and Vedic Indians were professional warrior nobilities that imposed themselves on native cultures, where their continued ability to rule depended on their military prowess. Rome's centurionate, although technically not officers but noncommissioned officers, was a thoroughly professional military elite, although it lacked any status as nobility.

The armies of antiquity were mostly led by experienced and talented officers whose ability to devise and execute sophisticated tactical designs and command large formations of troops stands as proof of their professional skills. That the ancient soldier could execute these designs with effective results reflects the quality of the ancient soldier in applying his trade. The battle tactics of ancient armies were as sophisticated and demanded as much discipline under stress as do modern tactics, if not more, given the inability of commanders to communicate with their troops once engaged. The soldiers of conscript armies like India, China, and Egypt often performed superbly on the battlefield.[10] The notion that ancient armies, officers, and soldiers were somehow primitive is false and probably derives from the Western experience with primitive armies and commanders in the Middle Ages lasting until at least the turn of the nineteenth century.[11]

The officer corps of ancient armies were drawn from the aristocracy, and we might correctly assume that they were at least as educated and literate as the general social elite from which they came. Many of the military histories of the ancient world that have come down to us were written by soldiers: Polibius, Xenophon, and Josephus to name but three of the most famous. Literacy and the ability to do basic mathematics were absolute requirements for commerce in ancient times and were even more important to armies. Most officers and noncommissioned officers of the period were functionally literate. In Roman times, only literate recruits were accepted into the army. Where literacy was lacking, it was supplied by professional scribes assigned to the army by the king. The armies of Egypt, India, China, and Assyria all had professional corps of scribes that acted as record keepers and administrators. Most ancient kings were taught to read and write, if only to be able to conduct their civic and religious functions. Some, like Thutmose III of Egypt, wrote poetry, while others, like Sargon II of Assyria, were genuine scholars. Sargon spoke and wrote Akadian *and* ancient Sumerian, the latter learned so that he might study the texts of ancient battles, to which he often appended commentaries. The association of illiteracy with military service is probably once more a result of the West's experience with the kings and generals of the Middle Ages, who, indeed, often were illiterate. Charlemagne was illiterate and could barely write his name; surviving samples of his signature more resemble a child's drawing than the handwriting of a genuinely literate hand.[12]

Because the ancient soldier was psychologically and physiologically identical to today's soldier, he was subject to the same fears and sufferings that have always accompanied military life in whatever age. He reacted to his environment in the way soldiers always have. He felt the physiological arousal and stress of his experiences, especially the sights and sounds of battle, and, like today's soldiers, was subject to psychiatric collapse. A soldier's life in antiquity was a hard one, and a lack of sleep, physical exhaustion, insufficient nutrition, and the impact of the elements—heat, freezing cold, bone-soaking rain, the terror of the dark, and the general discomfort of living out doors, often with poor equipment—all took their toll on the ancient soldier's body and mind.

THE HARSH REALITIES OF THE ANCIENT WORLD

Life in the ancient world was harsh, and the ancient soldier was exposed to sickness and death as a matter of common occurrence from his earliest childhood. A third of all live births were dead by age six. By age sixteen, almost 60 percent of all live births would have already died. By age twenty-six, that number would have increased to 75 percent. By age 40, 90 percent of all live births would have already died. Very few, perhaps not more than 3 percent, would live to see age 60.[13] There were no hospitals in antiquity, and families witnessed the deaths of their relatives, parents, children, and siblings as a matter of course.

The brutality of the political establishments in antiquity was often publicly displayed. During Hammurabi's reign in Babylon, the great lawgiver could gaze from his palace window and see corpses floating down the Tigris. Assyria made a fetish of public displays of brutality, sometimes skinning people alive or impaling them at public gatherings. Public crucifixion, a Carthaginian invention, was the common punishment for military officers who failed in battle. Egyptian reliefs portray the pharaohs bashing in the skulls of their enemies—so commonly, in fact, that one of pharaoh's official titles was "Smasher of Foreheads." Among the Israelites the Old Testament tells of one slaughter after another of the population of whole towns by Joshua. The punishment for withholding loot in the Israelite army was burning alive.[14] In all armies of antiquity the slaughter of innocent populations was commonplace. In his campaign against the Germans in 55 B.C.E. Caesar slaughtered an entire people, some 430,000, in an act of calculated political butchery. Even the Romans were appalled; one senator called the slaughter "unquestionably the most atrocious act of which any civilized man has ever been guilty."[15] The ancient soldier was exposed to death and slaughter to a degree rarely seen in modern times, with the exception of the genocides carried out by the Nazis, Turks, and Rwandans.

The battles of antiquity in which the ancient soldier took part were different from modern battles in one very important respect: the distance at which killing was done. Since the practical use of gunpowder in the seventeenth century, killing in most battles has been accomplished at a considerable distance from the victim. Modern rifles easily kill at 500 yards, a range at which one cannot clearly see the effect of the bullet striking the body. Except for the recoil of the rifle against one's shoulder and the sound of the discharge, there is no physical contact with the victim. To be sure, infantrymen were armed with the bayonet, but in modern wars, instances of hand-to-hand combat are very rare indeed.[16] In ancient battles, by contrast, the soldier was *always* in close physical contact with the person he killed. Richard Heckler, in his book, *In Search of the Warrior Spirit*, describes the killing experience of the ancient soldier correctly when he says, "The ancient warrior met his foe in direct struggle of sinew, muscle, and spirit. If flesh was torn or bone broken, he felt it give way under his hand … he felt the pulse of life and the nearness of death under his fingers. He also had to live his days remembering the man's eyes whose skull he crushed."[17]

The impact of battle was felt directly on the *physical senses* of the ancient soldier to a much greater degree than battle usually is experienced by the modern combatant. Engaged in violent hand-to-hand combat, the ancient soldier could *hear* the pitiful screams of the wounded and dying; *smell* the stench of blood, entrails, and gore, even as he tried to gain purchase on a ground made slippery with blood, urine, and feces, the latter secreted by soldiers' bodies seized with fear; *feel* the blade of his sword or spear push through the soft flesh of his opponent and suddenly stop as it struck bone and hear the sound of air rushing from the body cavity as the weapon was withdrawn; *taste* the salt of his own sweat as it ran down his face into his eyes and mingled with the taste of the bits of sticky blood and flesh that struck him whenever he opened a wound in his adversary; and *see* the terrible results of the slaughter around him, in which he was an integral participant. Sometimes, when a town was sacked, a civilian population put to the sword, or an enemy army slain to a man where it had surrendered, the assault on the ancient soldier's senses went on for hours at a time. At Cannae Carthaginian, troops massacred more than 78,000 Roman soldiers packed so tightly together that they could not raise their weapons in defense. The slaughter went on for five hours before the last Roman was slain. The ancient soldier was affected by the sensory slaughter of battle to a degree mostly unknown in the modern world.

Livy provides us with a description of the aftermath of the battlefield at Cannae that adequately captures the horror of the ancient battlefield:

> On the following day, as soon as it dawned, they set about gathering the spoils and viewing the carnage, which was shocking, even to enemies. So many thousands of Romans were lying, foot and horse promiscuously, according as accident had brought them together, either in battle or flight. Some, whom their wounds, pinched by the morning cold, had roused, as they were rousing up, covered with blood, from the midst of the heaps of the slain, were overpowered by the enemy.
>
> Some too they found alive with their thighs and hams cut, laying bare their necks and throats, bid them drain the blood that remained in them. Some were found with their heads plunged into the earth, which they had excavated; having thus, as it appeared, made pits for themselves, and having suffocated themselves by over-whelming their faces with the earth which they threw over them.
>
> A living Numidian, with lacerated nose and ears, stretched beneath a lifeless Roman who lay upon him, principally attracted the attention of all; for when the Roman's hands were powerless to grasp his weapon, turning from rage to madness, he had died in the act of tearing his antagonist with his teeth.[18]

PSYCHOLOGICAL EFFECTS OF BATTLE ON ANCIENT SOLDIERS

It is not surprising that the ancient soldier was as subject to psychiatric collapse as the modern soldier, who, for the most part, fights under far less stressful conditions in modern war than the ancient soldier did. Even so, rates of psychiatric casualties in modern wars are amazingly high. In every war in the twentieth century the chances of a soldier becoming a psychiatric casualty were greater than the chances of being killed by enemy fire.[19] The American Army in World War I admitted 158,994 soldiers to hospital who were unable to continue in service due to psychiatric reasons. In World War II, 1,393,000 soldiers suffered psychiatric symptoms serious enough to debilitate them for some period of time. Some 504,000 of these in the U.S. Army alone were permanently lost to the fighting effort. In Vietnam, 12.6 percent of the combat force suffered psychiatric symptoms serious enough to remove them from their units for some period. In the 1982 invasion of Lebanon the Israeli Defense Force suffered a psychiatric casualty rate 150 percent greater than its killed-in-action rate. And in Iraq (2005) the American psychiatric casualty rate is almost twice that of the rate at which American soldiers have been killed in action.

The long-term psychological consequences of exposure to intense battle can be gauged somewhat by the fact that more than 1.5 million soldiers who served in Vietnam suffered from some degree of post-traumatic stress disorder. One can only imagine what psychological effects exposure to intense hand-to-hand combat had on the ancient soldier. It is clear from surviving accounts, however, that the ancients were aware of psychiatric collapse due to the stress of battle. In a letter written almost 3,000 years ago, an Egyptian combat veteran, Hori, writes to an inexperienced officer about what combat is like: "You determine to go forward.... Shuddering seizes you, the hair of your head stands on end, your soul lies in your hand."[20] In 480 B.C.E., Leonidas, the commander of the Spartan force at Thermopolae, recognized that some of his troops were so frightened that they might break and dismissed them from the field because "they had no heart for the fight and were unwilling to take their share of the danger."[21] When the battle began, one of the Spartan soldiers, Aristodemus, "finding his heart failed him," remained in the rear and did not join the fight. Plutarch notes that in the Roman siege of Syracuse in 211 B.C.E., a number of the soldiers defending the city "were struck dumb with terror," an example of a psychiatric condition called *surdomutism*.[22] Polibius, the Greek historian and Roman general, records that some Roman soldiers injured themselves (self-inflicted wounds) so as not to have to fight. Sophocles's drama *Ajax* tells the story of a soldier driven mad with war who slaughters a herd of sheep in the delusion that they are enemy soldiers.

The ancients were aware of the psychological effects of combat on the soldier. The earliest explanation for mental illness is found in Babylon in 2750 B.C.E., where madness was seen as a punishment from the gods.[23] The Old Testament attributes madness to divine sanction. The Greeks of the Classical Age (700–500 B.C.E.) were the first to attribute mental illness to physical and emotional causes and to invent the dualism that characterizes psychiatry to this day.[24] Both Greek and Roman physicians recognized and treated traumatic symptoms of battle stress. Greek physicians treated soldiers suffering from combat shock at the Aesculapian temples with techniques similar to modern abreaction, the process of getting soldiers to express repressed emotions and experiences.[25] Roman military hospitals had psychiatric wards, and great care was given to the psychological environment of recovering wounded patients.[26] The Israelites were the first to practice a form of psychiatric screening, commonplace in modern armies, more than 3,000 years ago, in which certain categories of conscripts were removed from the combat formations prior to battle.[27]

What modern studies of psychiatric collapse tell us is that it is not so much the fear of being killed as the fear of having to kill another human being that prompts the mind to rebel with such ferocity that it will do almost anything, including injuring itself or the body, to keep from killing.[28] Like most other mammals, humans have an innate revulsion to killing their own kind. The critical variable seems to be distance. The closer the engagement in which a soldier must kill, the greater the revulsion to the killing and the greater the likelihood that the soldier will suffer psychiatric effects.[29] This seems true of all but some 2 percent of soldiers exposed to close combat. These remain unaffected by the slaughter. Most of these "two-percenters," however, already showed clinical symptoms of mental illness before engaging in battle.[30] The armies of the ancient world must have been full of psychically damaged soldiers, for to be a soldier then required killing human beings at very close range indeed.

In describing the life of the soldier in the ancient world we ought never to lose sight of the fact that his stock in trade was killing and that killing often had terrible effects on the soldier's mind. The personal nature of combat in the ancient world—looking another human being closely in the eye, making a decision to kill him where he stood, and then striking him with a weapon while watching him die before your eyes—is perhaps the single most basic, primal, and traumatic experience of close-order combat. To understand this is to understand the most central fact of the life of the ancient soldier. All else is commentary.

NOTES

1. James Mellaart, *The Neolithic of the Near East* (New York: Charles Scribner, 1975), 132.

2. It is only since the age of antisepsis and vaccination, both dating only from the last third of the nineteenth century, that the death rate for children began to decline, and then only in the West.

3. Egypt, for example, is still plagued by epidemics of snail fever caused by parasites from a snail living in the irrigation canals.

4. Jonathan P. Roth, *The Logistics of the Roman Army at War* (264 B.C.–A.D. 235) (Boston: Brill, 1999), 9.

5. Richard A. Gabriel, *The Great Armies of Antiquity* (Wesport, CT: Praeger, 2002), 265.

6. Richard A. Gabriel, *Great Captains of Antiquity* (Westport, CT: Greenwood Press, 2001), 19–20.

7. Roth, *Logistics*, 9; see also Dio Cassius *History of Rome* 75.2.4.

8. Roth, *Logistics*, 9–10.

9. Richard A. Gabriel, *Warrior Pharaoh* (New York: Iuniverse, 2001), 8. See also, by the same author, *The Military History of Ancient Israel* (Westport, CT: Praeger, 2003), 113.

10. For an analysis of a number of battles in the ancient period that demonstrate both the sophistication of battle tactics and the competence of the ancient soldier, see Richard A. Gabriel and Donald W. Boose, Jr., *The Great Battles of Antiquity: A Strategic and Tactical Guide to Great Battles That Shaped the Development of War* (Westport, CT: Greenwood Press, 1994); for a

more recent and comprehensive treatment of the same subject, including the ancient armies of the non-Western world at that time, see Richard A. Gabriel, *Empires at War: A Chronological Encyclopedia*, 3 vols. (Westport, CT: Greenwood Press, 2005).

11. Gabriel, *Empires at War*, vol. 1.

12. Ibid., chapter 20.

13. John Dominic Crossan, *The Historical Jesus: The Life of a Mediterranean Jewish Peasant* (San Francisco: Harper Collins, 1991), 141.

14. Gabriel, *Military History of Ancient Israel*, 118.

15. Gabriel, *Empires at War*, vol. 1, chapter 14.

16. Dave Grossman, *On Killing: The Psychological Cost of Learning to Kill in War and Society* (Boston: Little, Brown, 1995), 121–129.

17. R. S. Heckler, *In Search of the Warrior Spirit* (Berkeley, CA: Atlantic Books, 1989), 93.

18. Livy, *The War With Hannibal*, trans. Aubrey De Selincourt (London: Penguin Books, 1965), 151–152.

19. Richard A. Gabriel, *No More Heroes: Madness and Psychiatry in War* (New York: Hill and Wang, 1987), 72–77.

20. Gwynne Dyer, *War* (New York: Crown, 1985), 22.

21. Max Hastings, *The Oxford Book of Military Anecdotes* (New York: Oxford University Press, 1985), 18.

22. Ibid., 38.

23. Gabriel, *No More Heroes*, 98.

24. For more on this point, see Richard A. Gabriel, *Military Psychiatry: A Comparative Perspective* (Westport, CT: Greenwood Press, 1986).

25. Richard A. Gabriel and Karen S. Metz, *A History of Military Medicine*, vol. 1, *From Ancient Times to the Middle Ages* (Westport, CT: Greenwood Press, 1992), 151–152.

26. Ibid., 165–166.

27. Gabriel, *Military History of Ancient Israel*, 91.

28. Grossman, *On Killing*, chap. 3.

29. Ibid.

30. Gabriel, *No More Heroes*, 87.

Three

✳ ✳ ✳

RECRUITMENT

FACTORS AFFECTING MILITARY RECRUITMENT

How did ancient armies recruit soldiers? Methods of military recruitment in the ancient world varied widely and were influenced by at least three factors: (1) the degree of national integration of the society as a whole; (2) the size of the population relative to military and economic requirements; and (3) the social structure and its values, particularly as the latter defined military service as deriving from or conferring high social status. These factors determined the nature of the general social order, and an army is a reflection of the social order that gives it life. Limitations evident in the larger social order profoundly affected recruitment patterns and other military practices.

National Strength

National integration is the degree to which a centrally organized political authority can impose its will on other competing centers of power and authority within the society. Old Kingdom Egypt (2686–2160 B.C.E.), for example, was a collection of powerful feudal lords (*nomarchs*) who raised their own armies from their feudal estates.[1] The national authority, Pharaoh, and the soldiers raised from his estates were not sufficiently powerful to compel the obedience of the *nomarchs*. Under these circumstances a national conscript army was impossible. Soldiers were retainers of the feudal lords, and Pharaoh was dependent on them.[2] Over time, however, the power of the king increased, and by the Middle Kingdom (2040–1624 B.C.E.) Egypt had a national army recruited by national conscription and led by Pharaoh and a professional officer corps. One in

every 100 men was called to some kind of military service at age twenty.[3] Examples
of ancient armies that had national recruitment systems were New Kingdom Egypt,
Assyria, China during the period of the Warring States (464–221 B.C.E.), and Persia.

Size of Population

The size of a state's population relative to its military manpower requirements was
also an important factor in the recruitment system. Societies like Israel, Classical
Greece, and the Gauls of Caesar's day were societies that were always critically short
of population relative to their economic needs. Manpower called to military service
was unavailable to work the land and manage the economy. The solution was part-
time militia armies, in which all able-bodied adult males had an obligation to perform
military service. Some societies (Gauls) called men to service only in times of war[4];
others (Classical Greece, Israel) required one year of active service and several years
(often twenty years) in reserve units, which could be called up regularly for training
(Israel)[5] or when war was imminent (Classical Greece).[6] Assyria, too, was always short
of manpower to fulfill its military and economic requirements. The Assyrian solution
was unique in that it used almost all of its native manpower for military service through
national conscription, relying on captured slaves and deportations of entire peoples to
meet the nation's economic manpower requirements while Asssyrian men served in the
army.[7] It was for this reason that Sargon II deported the Twelve Tribes of Israel and
resettled them on the Assyrian-Iranian border.

Social and Value Structures

The nature of the social and value structures of ancient societies also influenced
patterns of manpower recruitment. Societies like India, Mitanni, Hatti, the Philistines,
and Homeric Greece were warrior societies in which noble warrior castes ruled and
reserved participation in war to themselves. In a manner not unlike the medieval
European knights, only the warrior castes in these societies were permitted to engage
in combat, with the result that there was no need to recruit military manpower
from outside the caste.[8] Other warrior societies, like the German and Gothic tribes
encountered on the Roman frontiers in the first century C.E., regarded all adult males
as members of the warrior caste so that every military-age male was required to fight in
defense of his people. In these circumstances, conscription was universal.

Regardless of the method by which ancient armies raised *military* manpower, most
ancient societies had great need for manpower to construct and maintain public works.
The great River Valley Empires (Sumer, Assyria, and Egypt) could survive only with
the help of large-scale irrigation systems of canals, dikes, and cisterns that required
great numbers of workers to maintain.[9] The great Land Empires (Hatti, Mitanni, India,
China, and Persia) had need for fortifications, bridges, and religious temples constructed
and maintained by human labor.[10] Almost every state in the ancient period had a system
of corvée labor, that is, labor required from its population for public works, defense, and
religious projects. Corvée labor was a fact of life during this period, even in states whose
armies did not rely on conscription. Often, corvée labor was recruited through the same
system as were soldiers, with the least-quality recruits being sent to do construction

work.[11] The construction battalion remained a mainstay of military life until very modern times. Sometimes, as in Imperial Rome and ancient Egypt, the military itself oversaw and directed construction projects. The importance of corvée labor to ancient societies is evident in the fact that the pyramids, the Great Wall of China, the Temple of Solomon, and the Hanging Gardens of Babylon were all constructed with corvée labor.

TYPES OF RECRUITMENT PRACTICES

Feudal Organizations

It is possible to distinguish several types of military recruitment practices among ancient armies. The first was recruitment by feudal lords, who provided military contingents to the national leader or "high king." Examples are the Hittites, the Chinese during the Warring States period, the Mitanni, and Vedic India. The Hittites never maintained a national organization for military service, and the common citizen was usually not called to military service. The army comprised two types of people: the liegeman, a minor noble with tenants, and the "man of the weapon," who received land from the high king in return for military service. Both types of landed nobles provided themselves and retainers for war.[12] Hittite society comprised powerful, independent barons bound by oaths of loyalty to the high king to provide manpower for war, not unlike a similar arrangement in feudal Europe.

The Chinese possessed a similar system of recruitment, although on a much larger scale. Every level of Chinese society was organized for war, each clan (zi) living within a walled town and providing one fighting man per family under command of the clan chief. A feudal warrior aristocracy was imposed on this base so that each vassal provided certain amounts of military manpower and equipment. Some of these fiefs were so large that they could provide 30,000 infantry and 3,000 chariots each.[13] Vedic India and the Mitanni both had professional warrior castes that monopolized the waging of war. The nobles of both countries possessed fortified feudal estates and had subvassals beneath them who owed military service to them.[14] There was no conscription, and military service was monopolized by a warrior class based on land tenure and traditions. The Mitanni called this the *maryannu* system and exported its chief features to the Canaanites and Philistines, both of which reorganized their societies on this basis.[15]

Tribal Militias

Another form of recruitment was the tribal militia found in societies with a strong sense of ethnic, racial, or national identity but with an insufficient population to maintain a standing army of significant size. Examples are the Israelites, Germans, and Goths. The Germans and Goths were tribal societies ruled by warrior aristocracies based on military prowess and blood lineage. The social order comprised clans and clan leaders who led their kinsmen in battle. The entire military-age male population was subject to military service in time of threat, and leadership in war, with an elected war chief, was not the same as leadership in peace, when the civilian *hunno* presided over the tribal council.[16] The Israelites began as a militia army while still on their desert march, and every male age twenty or over was subject to military service. Recruitment was accomplished by the tribes, and soldiers fought under their own tribal commanders.[17] Sometime around 1050 B.C.E., Saul, the first king of the Israelites, created a small, 2,000-man-strong permanent standing military cadre to lead the conscript militias in battle. Under Solomon (961–921 B.C.E.), the army of Israel was organized along traditional Canaanite lines, the same system used for organizing corvée labor. There was now a small standing force augmented by a larger tribal force, part of which came on active service for one month a year, officered by professional, not tribal, commanders. All Israelite males were subject to annual military or corvée service, the number being determined by the king. The city-states of Classical Greece also maintained militias, where all able-bodied men were expected to serve and to remain in the reserve until age forty-nine.[18] A similar militia arrangement for recruitment was found in pre-Republican Rome (753–510 B.C.E.), where each family and tribe provided a certain number of soldiers to fill out the national army, called the *legio*. The pre-Republican legion numbered 3,000 infantry and 300 cavalry.[19]

Large-Scale Conscription

Only a handful of states in the ancient world were capable of large-scale conscription and recruitment of military manpower. National conscription systems required a high degree of bureaucratic organization of the larger society to a degree where almost all important aspects of the society were subject to some degree of governmental direction. Only a few states of the ancient world reached this level of organization and used it to recruit manpower for both military and corvée service. The Egypt of the New Kingdom (1552–1069 B.C.E.) was so thoroughly organized by government that it constructed and maintained a 700-mile-long irrigation system and sustained an army of conscripts of more than 100,000 men, led by a cadre of professionally selected and trained officers. Every adult male over the age of twenty was subject to military (or corvée) service, and one of every ten men was inducted annually.[20] Organized on a feudal basis, Chinese armies also practiced conscription on a national basis when faced with foreign invasion. Chinese field armies often comprised 100,000 soldiers, with the national army sometimes reaching almost one million men.[21] Assyria, too, sustained its military might by national conscription, but its relatively small national manpower pool forced the Assyrians to rely on allies to fill out its force. Nonetheless, Assyrian field armies routinely were comprised of 50,000 soldiers.[22]

Persia had a vast army comprising mostly national conscripts augmented by tribal allies. Cyrus the Great instituted universal military service for all males, and Strabo reports in his *Geography* that all Persian males underwent ten years of military training before enlisting into national service.[23] These conscripts formed the bulk of the regular army. In addition, each *satrap*, or governmental district, was responsible for raising its own local force, often from clans or tribes in the area. The Persian national army was commanded by a professional officer corps. By the Magadha period (sixth century B.C.E.), the warrior caste of Vedic India had expanded considerably beyond the narrow warrior groups that the Vedics had imposed on Indian society, with the result that the armies of this time, although led by the traditional warrior caste, were expanded enormously by the use of caste conscripts.

PROFESSIONAL, COMPOSITE, AND
MERCENARY ARMIES

There are only a few examples of truly professional armies in the ancient world, by which one means an armed force raised, equipped, maintained, and commanded by a national political authority. Only three—Sumer, the army of Philip of Macedon, and Imperial Rome—are examples of genuine, professional armies in the ancient period. Sumer was a land of powerful city-states, each ruled by a king who raised, supplied, and paid a professional army. There is no evidence that the general population was subject to regular *military* service, even in time of war, although there is convincing evidence that the civilian population was subject to regular *corvée* labor.[24] The professional armies of the Sumerian states were between 800 to 1,000 strong and were supplied with weapons from central arms depots. Soldiers in these armies were charioteers, archers, and phalanx spearmen, military specialties that required a high degree of training.[25] Philip II of Macedon conquered Greece and destroyed the armies of the independent city-states, replacing them with a genuine national army paid and supplied from the national treasury.[26] Philip's army was an armed force of full-time professionals serving mostly for life, or as long as the money held out. It was Philip's army that became the centerpiece of the army of Alexander the Great, who transformed it into a composite force of professional Greek soldiers and units supplied by tribal and national allies. The most renowned professional army of antiquity was the army of Imperial Rome. Augustus transformed the old Republican armies of the Roman civil wars into legions comprising full-time, professional soldiers, trained, maintained, and equipped by the Roman state. Soldiers served for six-year terms and were retired after twenty-five years with pensions and land grants. The Roman army of this period was the most sophisticated, organized, disciplined, and provisioned military force in the ancient world, and no army surpassed it in these qualities until the mid-nineteenth century.

Most large armies of antiquity were really composite armies in the sense that they often supplemented their conscripted soldiery with contingents of allied and tribal forces. Often, these allied contingents fell below the level of military expertise and performance expected of the main army but served important military roles nonetheless. Roman armies, for example, routinely hired German and Numidian cavalry, while tribal units comprised as much as 20 percent of the Persian army. Alexander's armies had Persian, Baluchi, and Indian contingents within them, while Hittite armies comprised any number of primitive tribesmen hired for the occasion. Chinese armies employed so many units of "barbarians" that they eventually adopted some barbarian weapons and tactics and made them standard in their armies.

The only example in antiquity of an army recruited *entirely* from among mercenary soldiers was the army of Carthage. Carthaginian society was dominated by a commercial culture that preferred to hire soldiers rather than subject its own citizens to military service. Carthaginian agents were a common sight in the ancient world as they hired individuals, and even whole contingents of specialized troops, from foreign kings. During their Spanish campaigns the Carthaginians hired entire tribal armies. Command of the Carthaginian forces, including its tribal elements, was always reserved to generals from Carthage itself. The mercenary and multinational nature of Carthaginian field armies made tactical organization and employment very difficult indeed, testimony to the brilliance of Carthaginian commanders like Hannibal and Hasdrubul. To insure excellence in command, Carthaginian officers who failed on the battlefield were often crucified in Carthage's main square.

The adult males of the populations of most states in antiquity were likely to find their way into military service or corvée labor at some time in their lives. It should not be overlooked that in many cases, military service offered a much better life than an existence of backbreaking agricultural labor or slavery. Soldiers, after all, had value to the state authorities, feudal lords, or military castes that employed them and were likely to be treated humanely, for the most part. In times of famine the army was fed first, even as it took the food from the mouths of the general population. Booty and plunder were sources of wealth not available to the nonsoldier. The military establishments of Egypt, Assyria, Persia, and Rome as well as others provided the common citizen a vehicle of upward mobility in a world where few other opportunities for advancement were available. It is not surprising, then, to find that by the first century c.e., less than 10 percent of the Roman army comprised Italians; most soldiers were voluntarily recruited from Rome's provinces and occupied territories. Ancient Egypt, too, had many troop commanders who were not Egyptians, as did the Persians and Assyrians. The *Midrash* tells of Jews in Palestine who sought service in the Roman army. Even in modern times, military service serves as a vehicle of upward mobility and economic advancement. A majority of the U.S. Army in 2004 was recruited from the poorest counties of the poorest states in the country, and more than 40 percent of its soldiers were members of minority groups. It should come as no surprise that the armies of the ancient world might have served the same purpose for exactly the same kind of recruits.

NOTES

1. Robert J. Wenke, *Patterns of Prehistory: Man's First Three Million Years* (New York: Oxford University Press, 1980), 468; see also Leonard Cottrell, *The Warrior Pharaohs* (New York: Putnam, 1969) for a good account of the Egyptian army during the Early Dynastic and Middle Kingdom periods.

2. Wenke, *Patterns of Prehistory*.

3. Alan Schulman, *Military Rank, Title, and Organization in the Egyptian New Kingdom* (Berlin: Bruno Hessling Verlag, 1964).

4. J.F.C. Fuller, *Julius Caesar: Man, Soldier, and Tyrant* (New Brunswick, NJ: Rutgers University Press, 1965), 95.

5. *Cambridge Ancient History*, vol. 2, part 2 (Cambridge: Cambridge University Press, 1975), 588–591. For an excellent account of the Israelite army during this period, see Chaim Herzog and Mordechai Gichon, *Battles of the Bible* (Jerusalem: Steimatzky's Agency, 1978).

6. Thucydides; see also Robert Laffont, *The Ancient Art of Warfare*, vol. 1, *Antiquity* (New York: Time-Life Books, 1968) and Hans Delbrück, *History of the Art of War within the Framework of Political Theory*, vol. 1, *Antiquity* (Westport, CT: Greenwood Press, 1975).

7. H.W.F. Saggs, "Assyrian Warfare in the Sargonid Period," *Iraq* 25, part 2 (1963), 134; see also Georges Contenau, *Everyday Life in Babylon and Assyria*, trans. K. R. Maxwell-Hyslop and A. R. Maxwell-Hyslop (London: Edward Arnold, 1954), 41–42.

8. For more on the caste system and recruitment and warfare in ancient India, see Sarva Daman Singh, *Ancient Indian Warfare* (Delhi: Motilal Banarsidass, 1997) and V. R. Ramachandra Dikshitar, *War in Ancient India* (Delhi: Motilal Banarsidass, 1987).

9. For the distinction between River and Land empires as it affected the development of armies, see Richard A. Gabriel, *Empires at War: A Chronological Encyclopedia*, vol. 1, *From Sumer to the Persian Empire* (Westport, CT: Greenwood Press, 2005).

10. Ibid.

11. Georges Roux, *Ancient Iraq*, 3rd. ed. (New York: Penguin Books, 1964), 87–88.

12. O. R. Gurney, *The Hittites* (Baltimore: Penguin Books, 1952), 84. See also Trevor Bryce, "The Warrior," in *Life and Society in the Hittite World* (New York: Oxford University Press, 2002), chap. 6; also Richard H. Beal, "Hittite Military Organization," in *Civilizations of the Ancient Near East*, ed. Jack. M. Sasson (Peabody, MA: Hendrickson, 1995), 545–555.

13. C. J. Peers and Angus McBride, *Ancient Chinese Armies: 1500–200 B.C.E.* (London: Osprey, 1990), 7–8.

14. Richard A. Gabriel, *The Great Armies of Antiquity* (Westport, CT: Praeger, 2002), 87–89.

15. Steven Weingartner, "Chariots Changed Forever the Way Warfare Was Fought, Strategy Conceived, and Empires Built," *Military Heritage* 4 (August 1999), 18–27.

16. Peter Wilcox and Rafael Trevino, *Barbarians against Rome* (London: Osprey, 2000), 54–58.

17. Richard A. Gabriel, *The Military History of Ancient Israel* (Westport, CT: Praeger, 2003), 29–30, 32, 35–37.

18. Ibid., 176.

19. A good history of early Italian military systems is found in Peter Connolly, *Greece and Rome at War* (Englewood Cliffs, NJ: Prentice-Hall, 1981), 90–126.

20. Alan Schulman, *Encyclopaedia Britannica*, 15th ed., s.v. "History of Egyptian Civilization."

21. Edmund Balmforth, "A Chinese Military Strategist of the Warring States: Sun Pin" (PhD dissertation, Rutgers University, 1979), 54–55, 85–86.

22. Saggs, "Assyrian Warfare," 145.

23. Strabo *Geography* 15.3.18–19.

24. Gabriel, *Great Armies*, 51.

25. Robert L. O'Connell, *Of Arms and Men: A History of War, Weapons, and Aggression* (New York: Oxford University Press, 1989), 35.

26. Richard A. Gabriel, *Great Captains of Antiquity* (Westport, CT: Greenwood Press, 2001), 95.

Four

✴ ✴ ✴

MANPOWER

ANCIENT ARMY SIZES

How large were the armies of the ancient world? While the armies of the Late Bronze Age (2000–1500 B.C.E.) were significantly larger than those which emerged at the beginning of the Early Bronze Age (3000–2500 B.C.E.), they were small compared to the armies that fought in the Iron Age (1250 B.C.E.). The Persians, for example, routinely deployed field armies that were ten times larger than anything seen the Bronze Age. A Chinese field army that fought at the Battle of Chengpu (632 B.C.E.) comprised 700 chariots supported by 52,000 infantry.[1] Two centuries later, a unified China could put one million soldiers in the field in a supreme national effort.[2] During the Early Bronze Age, Sargon II of Akkad could mobilize an army perhaps as large as 5,400 soldiers. But an army of this size required a major national effort on the part of all Sargon's vassals and could not be deployed in the field for very long.[3]

Even the smaller states of the Late Bronze Age could field armies much larger than Sargon's. The Hittites and Mitanni, both major states of the period, could deploy only comparatively small armies. The Hittites, for example, could only deploy 17,000 soldiers at the battle of Kadesh in 1275 B.C.E., and this included almost all of their allies.[4] It is unlikely that the king of Hatti could have put more than 10,000–12,000 men in the field by himself. While the size of the fully deployed army of the Mitanni (1480–1335 B.C.E.) is unknown, a reasonable guess would place it somewhere around 10,000 men. By the Late Bronze Age, however, armies were growing much larger.

Two factors restricted the size of Early Bronze Age armies. The first was the lack of national administrative mechanisms of political and social control. By the Iron Age, these had been developed almost to modern levels of efficiency so that larger numbers of recruits could be called to military service with considerably less disruption of the domestic economy. The second was the replacement of bronze with iron as the basic metal for war. Bronze is a combination of copper and tin and was very expensive to manufacture because tin was very rare in the Middle East. Archaeological evidence shows that tin could only be found in significant quantities in Bavaria, Afghanistan, and Cornwall, England, from where it had to be imported at great expense. The cost of bronze weapons was a significant limitation on the number of troops that could armed with them by a state. The discovery and utilization of iron, a metal commonly available almost everywhere, reduced the cost of weapons considerably so that more soldiers could be equipped at reasonable cost. The result was an increase in the size of Iron Age armies.

Examples of Iron Age armies are instructive. The Egyptian army in the time of Ramses II (1279–1212 B.C.E.) numbered over 100,000 men when the garrisons of military fortresses are included.[5] The army comprised largely conscripts, with one in ten adult males being called to some kind of national service, including corvée labor. An Egyptian field army was organized into divisions of 5,000 men each and could be deployed individually or as a combined force of several divisions.[6] At the battle of Kadesh (1275 B.C.E.) between the Hittites and the Egyptians, the first ancient battle for which we have reliable manpower figures, the Egyptians deployed a four-division force of 20,000 men against the Hittite army of 17,000.[7]

The Assyrian army of the eighth century B.C.E. was composed of 150,000–200,000 soldiers and was the largest standing military force the Middle East had witnessed to this time.[8] An Assyrian combat field army numbered approximately 50,000 men, with various mixes of infantry, chariots, and cavalry.[9] The Assyrian army was equal in size to five modern U.S. Army divisions or eight Russian Army field divisions. When arrayed for battle, the Assyrian army occupied an area 2,500 yards across and 100 yards deep. It was also the first army of the ancient world to be entirely equipped with iron weapons. There were weapon armories strategically placed throughout the empire, in which iron weapons and other equipment were stored. The armory at Dur-Sharrukin (Fort Sargon) alone contained 200 tons of iron weapons, helmets, and armor.[10]

As large as the Assyrian army was for its day, it was surpassed by the national army of Persia that appeared 300 years later. Darius's army in the Scythian campaign numbered 200,000 soldiers, and the force deployed by Xerxes against the Greeks comprised 300,000 men and 60,000 horsemen.[11] One analysis of Xerxes's army suggests that when support troops are included, the army included more than one million men.[12] Even at the end of the empire, the Persians could deploy very large forces. In 331 B.C.E., just before Alexander destroyed it at the battle of Arbela, the Persian army under Darius fielded 300,000 infantry, 40,000 cavalry, 250 chariots, and 50 elephants.[13]

Philip of Macedon had bequeathed his son Alexander a professional army of 32,000 soldiers organized into four divisions of 8,192 soldiers each, a military instrument far too small to achieve Alexander's dream of empire. Alexander quickly expanded the old army to 60,000, and during his campaign in India, at the battle of Jhelum (Hydaspes River) in 326 B.C.E., Alexander's army had grown to 120,000 infantry and 50,000 cavalry through the enlistment of entire tribes of central Asian soldiers.[14]

During the Roman Republic, Rome could put armies into the field that exceeded 80,000 men, although this required a supreme effort, such as in the war against Hannibal. At the battle of Cannae (216 B.C.E.) Hannibal destroyed the Roman army, killing 78,000 men. The Roman response was to raise another army. The imperium that replaced the Roman Republic in the first century C.E. had a standing army of 350,000 soldiers, all full-time professionals, augmented by almost as many tribal allies and militias brought into Roman military service for various periods of time. Rome routinely could field armies of 40,000 men with little effort.

The barbarian armies—Gauls, Germans, and Goths—that fought the Romans during Caesar's time and in the early days of the Roman Empire often produced very large armies. In Caesar's day the population of Gaul was between fifteen and twenty million divided into 300 or so tribes.[15] In 58 B.C.E. Caesar attacked the Helvetii and killed 238,000 men, women, and children. Two years later, he trapped a German tribe at the junction of the Moselle and Rhine rivers, killing 430,000 Germans.[16] The habit of these tribes of bringing their families with them to the battlefield, thus exposing them to slaughter, accounts for these horrendous casualty figures. Nonetheless, even if only one-third of the casualties were soldiers, the figures suggest a very large tribal army.

The average German tribe comprised about 35,000–40,000 people, and there were twenty-three different tribes living in the area between the Rhine and the Elbe rivers.[17] An individual tribe could raise 5,000–7,000 warriors. When assembled in coalition, the German armies easily could exceed 60,000 men. If we are to believe Eunapius, the army of Goths that crossed the Danube in 376 B.C.E. prior to the battle of Adrianople consisted of 200,000 warriors. This is surely an exaggeration. But if the number of people in the tribe was this large, then at least 50,000–60,000 of them were warriors.[18]

Probably the largest armies in the ancient world during the Iron Age were the armies of China during the fifth to fourth centuries B.C.E. and the armies of India during the Magadha state ascendancy (fifth to fourth centuries B.C.E.) and the period of Chandragupta (324–300 B.C.E.) that came after it. With the entire agricultural and urban populations of China organized down to the clan level for corvée labor, it was an easy task for Chinese rulers during the Warring States period to mobilize armies of 400,000 men. Documents of the time tell of armies approaching one million men, although this number is certainly somewhat exaggerated.

We can be more certain of the size of the Indian armies. After the battle of the Jhelum River (Hydaspes) in 326 B.C.E., Alexander advanced inland and attempted to cross the Ganga River. When Alexander's scouts reported the size of the Indian force awaiting him on the opposite bank, his army mutinied and refused to cross. As recorded by Plutarch, the combined Indian armies of the kings of Gandaritai and Praisai awaiting Alexander comprised 80,000 cavalry, 8,000 war chariots, 6,000 fighting elephants, and 200,000 infantry.[19] During the Maurayn period Megasthenes, the Greek ambassador at the court of Chandragupta, recorded the strengths of the armies of some of the states comprising the Mauryan realm. His figures appear in Table 4.1.[20] In times of national crisis the Mauryan king could call on the military resources of any or all of the states of the imperial realm. Armies of the size that China and India could deploy during the Iron Age were not seen again in the West until at least the time of the American Civil War.

Table 4.1
Military Strengths of Mauryan States

State	Elephants	Cavalry	Infantry
Mauryan	8,000–9,000	30,000	600,000
Calingas (Kalinga)	700	1,000	60,000
Modubae	400	4,000	50,000
Andraec (Andhra)	1,000	2,000	100,000
Magallae	500	—	—
Chrysei	300	800	30,000
Odomoboerae	16,000	5,000	150,000
Pandae	500	—	150,000
Gangaridae (Vanga)	700	1,000	60,000

Only in both Bronze Age and Iron Age Greece do we find armies that remained relatively small. In the *Iliad* the poet never tells us the size of the Mycenaean army besieging Troy, but the often quoted figure of 10,000 men is surely inaccurate. More likely, the army numbered less than 5,000 men, if that.[21] Mycenaean society comprised warrior clans, in which individual combats, not engagements of masses of troops, were the practice. It is likely that few of the clans could put as many as 2,000 warriors in the field at any time, and an assembly of the clans would hardly produce an army of 12,000–14,000 at the maximum. It would, however, have been impossible for the Bronze Age Greeks to logistically sustain an army of this size in the field since Mycenaean armies seem to have had no quartermasters or sutlers to supply the army on a regular basis.[22]

The Iron Age armies of Classical Greece were products of relatively small city-states whose populations, even at maximum use, could not produce very many soldiers. Even Israel under Ahab at the battle of Ai could put 30,000 men into the field, while at the battle of Marathon the Greeks were able to field only 10,000 men against the Persians. Thucydides recorded that at the start of the Peloponnesian War in 431 B.C.E., Athens had a population of 100,000 free men and 140,000 slaves and aliens[23] but could only raise 13,000 hoplites, 16,000 older garrison soldiers, 1,200 mounted men, and 1,600 archers in a maximum effort in which the survival of the country was at stake.[24] When the security situation stabilized a decade later, Thucydides reported that Athens returned to her usual military practices and could only muster 1,300 hoplites and 1,000 horsemen. In addition, it could draw on 1,400 recruits. Most of the Athenian army in 420 B.C.E. were not Athenians at all, but metics (non-citizens; a commercial class) and aliens.[25] Battles between the city-states of the Greek Classical period usually involved no more than 20,000 men on both sides and, more often, involved combined forces of less than 10,000 soldiers. As products of their respective social orders, warrior clans and city-states, the armies of both Bronze and Iron Age Greece never reached the size or level of military sophistication and capability of other armies of these periods.

ARMY GROWTH FACTORS

The growth in the size of armies in the Iron Age was almost exponential when compared to the armies of the previous era. What made this growth possible? First, the populations of Iron Age states were generally much larger than during the Bronze Age, perhaps as a function of more productive agricultural techniques that allowed more and better nutrition and thus a healthier population. Second, the ability of government to organize and control the social order grew in scope and sophistication and permitted greater governmental control over all aspects of social life, including recruitment for corvée labor and military service. States had developed the bureaucratic mechanisms to govern territory of imperial dimension and to do it efficiently. Third, the introduction of iron weapons greatly reduced the cost of equipping a soldier so that even small states could afford to maintain larger armies. While iron seems to have made its appearance in the Middle East sometime around 1200 B.C.E., and even earlier in India, bronze remained the primary metal for military weapons until 900 B.C.E. or so, when iron replaced it on a large scale.[26] Fourth, the professional officer corps of the major states of the Iron Age had acquired the experience and ability to command and control larger military establishments so that larger armies could be employed and supplied effectively. As a consequence of these factors, the armies of the Iron Age were of greater size than anything the world had seen to that point.

Napoleon is supposed to have remarked that "in war, quantity conveys a quality all its own." The armies of the Iron Age were truly modern with respect to their size. With the collapse of the Roman imperium and its large armies in the fourth century C.E., only a few states were able to maintain large military establishments until well into the nineteenth century—and none of them were in the West. The composite armies of Islam were quite large, as were the armies of China and India. In the West it was Napoleon who reintroduced the large conscript army. But even this was an exception. With Napoleon's defeat Europe returned to the practice of retaining relatively small standing armies buttressed by large conscript reserve forces that could be called to service to meet a national emergency, a pattern that survives into the beginning of the twenty-first century.

NOTES

1. Frank A. Kierman and John K. Fairbank, eds., *Chinese Ways in Warfare* (Cambridge, MA: Harvard University Press, 1974), 2.

2. Edmund Balmforth, "A Chinese Military Strategist of the Warring States: Sun Pin," (PhD dissertation, Rutgers University, 1979), 58.

3. Gwynne Dyer, *War* (New York: Crown, 1985); see note 21 for an estimate of the size of Sargon's army.

4. Arther Ferrill, *The Origins of War: From the Stone Age to Alexander the Great* (New York: Thames and Hudson, 1985), 58.

5. The strength of the Egyptian army is based on an extrapolation of the figures provided by Robert J. Wenke, *Patterns of Prehistory: Mankind's First Three Million Years* (New York: Oxford University Press, 1980), 486.

6. Ferrill, *Origins of War*, 58.

7. Ibid.

8. Ibid., 70.

9. Trevor N. Dupuy, *The Evolution of Weapons and Warfare* (New York: Bobbs-Merrill, 1980), 10.

10. Robert Laffont, *The Ancient Art of Warfare*, vol. 1, *Antiquity* (New York: Time-Life Books, 1968), 45.

11. These figures are taken from Plato's account of the war and are considerably less than the numbers offered by Herodotus, who gives the size of the Persian army at 2,641,640 men.

12. See Sir Percy Sykes, *A History of Persia*, vol. 1 (London: Macmillan, 1958), 196–198.

13. Laffont, *Ancient Art of Warfare*, 38–39.

14. Gurcharn Singh Sandhu, *A Military History of Ancient India* (Delhi: Vision Books, 2000), 187.

15. J.F.C. Fuller, *Julius Caesar: Man, Soldier, and Tyrant* (New Brunswick, NJ: Rutgers University Press, 1965), 95.

16. Richard A. Gabriel and Donald W. Boose, Jr. *The Great Battles of Antiquity: A Strategic and Tactical Guide to Great Battles That Shaped the Development of War* (Westport, CT: Greenwood Press, 1994), 355.

17. Ibid., 415; see also Walter A. Goffart, *Barbarians and Romans, A.D. 418–584: The Techniques of Accommodation* (Princeton, NJ: Princeton University Press, 1980) for a more comprehensive examination of German tribal society.

18. Timothy Newark, *The Barbarians: Warriors and Wars of the Dark Ages* (London: Blandford Press, 1985), chap. 2; see also Hans Delbrück, *History of the Art of War within the Framework of Political History*, vol. 2, *The Germans* (Westport, CT: Greenwood Press, 1975), 307.

19. Sandhu, *Military History*, 199.

20. Ibid., 223.

21. Thomas D. Seymour, *Life in the Homeric Age* (New York: Biblo and Tannen, 1963), 586–587.

22. Ibid., 571.

23. Thucydides 2:13; see also Delbrück, *History of the Art of War*, vol. 1, 39.

24. Ibid.

25. Ibid.

26. Jane C. Waldbaum, "From Bronze to Iron: The Transition from the Bronze Age to the Iron Age in the Eastern Mediterranean," *Studies in Mediterranean Archaeology* 54 (1978): 39, Table IV.I.

Five

✳ ✳ ✳

RATIONS

FOOD

What did the ancient soldier eat? During peacetime, soldiers were usually stationed within fortified towns or permanent military garrisons. Some of these garrisons, like Dur Sharrukin in Assyria, Manchester, England, and Cologne, Germany, eventually became large cities themselves. Soldiers stationed in towns or garrisons usually consumed a diet that was not very different from that of the townspeople and farmers of the region where these garrisons were located. Most food consumed by the garrisons was grown and provided by the local merchants and farmers, who sold it to the military. Once out of garrison and on campaign, however, the diet of the soldier changed. Much of the movement to the battlefield occurred within the borders of the soldier's country or imperium, that is, along interior lines of communication and supply. Depots containing stored food were located along strategic routes of advance to supply the army as it marched to the battlefield. Assyria, Persia, and Rome required the governors of provinces through which the army passed to provide it with rations for as long as the army remained within the governor's jurisdictional boundaries. Merchants and sutlers usually followed the armies, providing them with additional goods and services, including food.

Once beyond the homeland's borders or away from the ships, the soldier was dependent on whatever rations he could carry or could be carried with the army in its supply train, the "iron rations" of an army in the field. These rations could be supplemented with whatever food could be foraged from the enemy's stores and fields, one reason why the traditional campaign season often coincided with the harvest season. Whether requisitioned in supply depots or carried by the soldier or the army's quartermaster, the ability to preserve foods so they would not spoil and could be transported or stored for several months was crucial to the successful nutritional support of all ancient armies. Not surprisingly, military field rations mostly comprised those foodstuffs that could be preserved for a long time.

FOOD PRESERVATION

The quartermasters of the ancient armies were experts in the preservation of food. After the collapse of the ancient societies, the knowledge of food preservation for military rations was mostly lost and not rediscovered by modern armies until the nineteenth century, when it began to be preserved in tins and other methods of storage.[1] Cereal grains, the main ration of all armies throughout all periods of antiquity, could be stored for as long as ten years if kept in sacks stacked in a manner to permit air to circulate around the stacked bundles.[2] Grain could also be stored loose if kept dry and turned regularly. Exposure to rain or extreme humidity, however, could cause deadly fungi to contaminate the grain. One of these fungi, ergot, produced hallucinations; others were poisonous. Carried as loose grain in the packs of the soldier, however, cereals could easily keep for the duration of any campaign. Baked into bread, grain could last for about a week. Baked into biscuits or rebaked into hardtack, grain rations lasted for months.

Meat and fowl were also preserved. Salted meat and fish kept for months, as did smoked beef, ham, or fowl. A favorite ration of the Egyptian army was smoked gooseflesh. Pork and beef jerky kept for years. It is likely that it was the Egyptians who first discovered the secret of salt preservation, but we cannot be certain. Salting meat preserved it for as long as two years,[3] but salted meat had to be soaked in water for a few hours before it could be reasonably cooked and consumed. Soaking required water that may have been needed for drinking, and soaking drew the nutrients out of the meat so that while a meal of boiled salt beef filled the soldier's stomach, it provided little in the way of nutrients.[4] However, it did provide the soldier with salt. A soldier requires about a half-ounce of salt a day to remain healthy. The body requires salt to retain water and maintain its electrolyte balance. In high-temperature, low-humidity climates, as most of the Middle East is, a lack of salt could be fatal. Modern armies operating in these climates provide their soldiers with daily salt tablets.

Pickling was another way of preserving meat, and we find references to it in Sumer, where ox joints were pickled for transport and sale.[5] Vegetables could also be pickled, and olives, beets, and carrots (bulb vegetables) were commonly preserved in this manner. Most pickling was done with vinegar and salt. Vinegar is an excellent source of vitamin C and eight important amino acids.[6] Vinegar is also an antiscorbutic, that is, a preventive for scurvy. In modern times, naval crews were fed sauerkraut, sliced cabbage in vinegar, to prevent scurvy. Ancient armies frequently drove herds of cattle and sheep along with them to provide their soldiers with meat on the hoof.

Vegetables could also be preserved by drying. The pulse vegetables—beans, lentils, peas (plants with edible seeds)—were easily preserved in this way and lasted for years. Dried beans have been a staple of armies for thousands of years. Dried pulse vegetables could be ground to make a thick flour, from which the soldier could make a soup. Some of the bulb vegetables, onions and garlic, kept well for months without any preservation at all if they were kept dry. Others—beets, carrots, radishes—usually were pickled. Leafy green vegetables could not be preserved at all and were foraged in the field if they were to be had.

Fruits were easily preserved by drying in the sun. Sometimes dried fruit was pressed into large blocks for easier handling and transport or pressed around a string that could be hung from the soldier's belt. Pressed blocks of fruit could be sliced and passed out to the troops as they marched along.[7] Pressing fruit required that the pits be removed. These pits were an excellent source of fuel when firewood was scarce, as it often was on the march or in the desert.

The ancient soldier was supplied with various vegetable and animal oils to supplement his diet. Vegetable oils—olive, sesame, sunflower, balsam, radish, linseed—could be stored for long periods without spoiling. An Indian oil, ghee, was made by skimming off the oil from melted butter while leaving the solids behind. It kept for very long periods, even in the warmest and most humid climates.[8] Besides being consumed as food, oils could also be used as fuel for lamps and for cleansing the skin after bathing.[9]

Two staples of the ancient armies, wine and beer, also were preserved for use as military rations. Some armies, the Sumerians and Egyptians, preferred beer, while others, Romans, Assyrians, Hittites, and Germans, preferred wine. Sealed properly in jars or wooden casks, wine could be kept for years. Even when transported in leather skins, wine still keeps for weeks. Beer, on the other hand, tends to spoil rather quickly, often within a few days. Most beers were produced from grain, often in the form of bits of bread mixed with water to make a thick mush, and could be made quickly. It is likely that beer was not usually transported in the supply train because of its tendency to spoil but was made on the spot whenever the army was encamped for more than a few days.

FOOD PRODUCTION IN ANCIENT TIMES

All regions of the ancient world produced sufficient foodstuffs to sustain large populations and armies. The most widely consumed foods of the ancient world were the cereal grains: wheat, barley, emmer, rye, oats, and millet.[10] It was only late in the ancient period that rice was imported from India and China, where it had been a staple for centuries. In the West and Middle East, wheat, barley, and emmer were the most commonly used grains for making bread and were the primary source of carbohydrates in the ancient soldier's diet. Cereals were usually prepared in the form of bread, porridge, or biscuits. The pulse crops—beans, peas, lentils, and soybean—provided the primary source of protein, although meat also provided protein. The major sources of vitamins were fruits and green vegetables, including leeks, cucumbers, and lettuce. It was the Sumerians who invented shade gardening, a technique where small gardens were shaded by date palms to lessen the heat of the sun and break the force of the wind.[11] Otherwise, it would have been impossible to grow leafy green vegetables in the hostile climates of the Middle East and India. Bulb vegetables—radishes, onions, garlic, beets, and turnips—were also cultivated in shade gardens. The oils extracted from these plants were also a valuable source of vitamins. A variety of fruit—olives, grapes, figs, sycamore figs, pomegranates, dates, apples, pears, plums, and cherries—were widely cultivated and, because they could be easily preserved, were an important part of the military diet. The plants grown for food in Eurasia constituted 90 percent of the normal diet of both soldier and civilian in the ancient period: bread, beer, wine, oil, fruits, and vegetables. The remaining 10 percent of the ancient diet was meat from animals and other products derived from them: milk, cheese, ghee, and eggs.[12]

Sometime during the ninth millennium B.C.E., sheep became the first pastoral animal stock to be domesticated. Sheep were the primary source of fiber and the most common pastoral resource during all periods of antiquity.[13] Next came goats, and around the sixth millennium B.C.E., cattle were domesticated in Anatolia. The pig was domesticated soon after and remained a major source of meat until the Late Bronze Age, when, for unknown reasons, it was no longer consumed in large quantities in Egypt and Canaan. The chicken was first domesticated in China during the Neolithic period but did not become a major food source until circa 600 B.C.E.[14] The Egyptians, however, had discovered the bird almost a thousand years earlier, when it was brought back to Egypt by one of Thutmose III's military expeditions. Known to the Egyptians as the Bird of Babylon, it was valued more for its egg-laying ability than its flesh. Heretofore Egyptians ate only the eggs of wild birds, which usually nested only once or twice a year, making eggs very expensive and available only to the wealthy. With the coming of the chicken to Egypt, eggs became cheaply available and became a staple of the Egyptian military diet.[15] The goose was also widely available, and smoked gooseflesh was a staple of the soldier's rations in Egypt.

THE ANCIENT SOLDIER'S DIET AND NUTRITION

The daily nutritional demands of the human body expressed in terms of the calories necessary to sustain health and activity vary with both age and weight. Caloric requirements peak in late adolescence, decline, and then remain constant until middle age. Most ancient soldiers entered military service around age twenty, when their caloric needs were already reduced; most left service before their caloric needs increased again. The average soldier of the ancient period was about five feet seven inches in height and weighed about 145 pounds, somewhat shorter and lighter than a modern soldier. In addition, long periods of reduced physical activity while in garrison permitted the soldier to take on extra weight. Stored body fat provides caloric energy at the rate of 1,600 calories per pound of body fat.[16] When these factors are considered, the ancient soldier required approximately 3,000 calories a day in order to keep him healthy and in fighting trim, or about 25 percent less than the 3,500–4,000 calories the American military estimates is required for the modern soldier.[17]

Protein is needed in addition to calories to sustain tissue, create body fluids, and balance the nitrogen levels of the body. Salt, too, is needed to cause the body to retain fluids. The water requirement for troops in desert conditions where temperatures are high and humidity is low is estimated by the U.S. Army to be nine quarts a day. Trained soldiers can get along on less, perhaps six quarts a day, and if we are to believe the Persians, they got along on just two quarts a day.[18] In cooler climates with more shade it is not unreasonable to expect a soldier to consume only two to three quarts of water daily.

The soldier's diet in the ancient period seems to have provided him with sufficient calories, certainly the minimum of 3,000 per day. A typical diet of the time included at least seven items: (1) grain prepared as bread, porridge, biscuit, or hardtack; (2) meat, including pork, mutton, and beef (pork seems to have been the most commonly consumed meat, often in the form of salt pork or bacon, tasty and long-lasting items ideal for military field rations); (3) vegetables, beans, peas, and lentils, usually boiled but sometimes crushed into a crude flour to make soup (green leafy vegetables were eaten if they could be foraged); (4) milk from goats and cows, including cheese and butter or ghee; (5) oil, including olive, sesame, sunflower, and linseed oil; (6) salt on a daily basis for health and flavoring food; and (7) liquids, usually water, wine, or beer. A liter of wine with 12 percent alcohol provides 700 calories and is antiscorbutic. Beer is high in B-complex vitamins and was a good source of carbohydrates. These seven food items were most likely available to the soldier when in garrison or sometimes while marching through his own country, where they could be provided by pre-positioned depots or obtained from cities along the route of march. Once in the field, the soldier's diet changed considerably and was not nearly as extensive.

The caloric value of each of the above food items can be calculated to provide a general idea of the amount of energy each provided to the soldier. The standard grain ration in the ancient world was between two and three pounds of raw grain per soldier per day. Ground into flour and mixed with water and salt, this produced about 1.8 pounds of bread, an amount that provided the soldier with 1,950 calories, or about two-thirds of his daily requirement.[19] Flour heated and ground by machine during the Civil War required the removal of the grain kernel, a primary source of calories, with the result that flour prepared in this way provided only about 650 calories per pound.[20] Rice, the staple of Chinese armies, provided about 1,200 calories per pound, roughly equivalent to the other cereal grains. The caloric content remains the same whether the grain is prepared as bread, porridge, or biscuit.

Meat is particularly high in calories, and even a small portion is of considerable caloric benefit to the soldier. Thus three ounces of mutton produced 317 calories; of salt pork, 400 calories; of roasted beef, 245 calories; of pork, 340 calories; of chicken, 200 calories; and of gooseflesh, 175 calories. Three ounces of meat is a very small portion, and it is likely that the soldier ate more than this at a sitting, even when in the field. The American soldier of the Civil War was given either twenty ounces of beef per day or twelve ounces of salt pork.[21]

Vegetables provided calories, although they were more important for providing vitamins. Eight ounces of beans or lentils a day provided 350 calories, and the Civil War soldier was issued three times that amount for his daily vegetable ration. Two ounces of cheese provided 90 calories, eight ounces of goat's or cow's milk provided 160 calories, and 1.5 ounces of olive oil provided 350 calories. A half-liter of wine or beer provided 350 calories. Dried fruits greatly enhanced the soldier's diet. A dried fig provided 50 calories, a date 25 calories, and an apple 150 calories. If mixed with honey to make a jam, an additional sixty calories is gained.[22] It is very likely that the ancient soldier consumed somewhat greater quantities than the minimum amounts calculated here when he had opportunity to do so.

The caloric value of the soldier's diet in the ancient period, at least while in garrison, provided more than the minimum of 3,000 calories a day considered adequate for a soldier to remain healthy and active. This can be compared with the diet of the American Civil War soldier in 1861. The mandated ration for a Federal soldier during this time included twenty ounces of fresh or salted beef or twelve ounces of salted pork, more than a pound of white flour, a vegetable (usually dried beans), and a ration of coffee (sometimes four pints a day), sugar, vinegar, and salt.[23] A pound of white flour provided about 650 calories, while twelve ounces of salt pork provided 1,020 calories and twenty ounces of salted beef provided 1,400 calories, or a total of between 1,800 and 2,000 calories a day, far fewer than was afforded the ancient soldier by his diet. When on the march, some armies, most notably the Romans, Assyrians, and Indians, had excellent logistics trains that could transport large quantities of much the same food that the soldier consumed in garrison. Almost all the other armies of the period, however, relied on much less capable quartermaster trains, foraging, and the soldier carrying his own "iron rations." Except in garrison, where central cooking and bakery facilities existed, the soldier prepared his own food in the field over an open fire, cooking meat on an iron spit and bread or porridge either on an iron plate, a hot flat stone, or in his mess kit or pot.

Only a few examples of "iron rations" as recorded in ancient texts have come down to us. There is the complaint of Egyptian soldiers on campaign in Canaan that all they received for breakfast was "sour milk, salted fish, and hard bread." Higher-ranking soldiers, the king's messenger, and the standard bearer were provided with better fare. One text from Old Kingdom Egypt instructs that these men receive "good bread, ox meat, wine, sweet oil, olives, fat, honey, figs, fish, and vegetables."[24] Avidius Cassius, a rebellious Roman officer during the reign of Marcus Aurelius in 175 c.e., ordered his troops to carry nothing on the march except "*laridum ac buccellatum atque acetum*," or "bacon fat, hard biscuit, and sour wine."[25] A surviving Indian text from around 1000 b.c.e. lists the supplies that a commander must gather inside a fortress to resist a siege. These include "great stores of grass, wood, water, rice, and wheat, sesame, beans, vetches, and cereals and medicines, including ghee, fresh butter, oil, honey, sugar and salt…."[26] Western sources also record examples of the military diets of some different peoples. Livy notes that when Perseus the Macedonian provided rations for his Gallic auxiliaries, he gave them wine and grain but had to give them "animals" as well, suggesting that they ate meat in the field.[27] The Roman historian Appian tells us that the Germans and Numidians "lived on herbs or grass" and that the Numidians drank only water, not wine.[28] Caesar says that the British diet was mostly dairy products and meat.[29] But Boudicca, queen of the Britons, tells us something different: "The Romans cannot bear up under hunger and thirst as we can … they require kneaded bread and wine and oil, and if any of these things fail them, they perish; for us, on the other hand, any grass or root serves as bread, the juice of any plant as oil, any water as wine."[30]

The Roman use of hardtack biscuits or *buccelatum* (literally, "mouthfuls") as a field ration is well documented, as are *cibaria cocta*, or "cooked rations," usually meaning dried meat, vegetables, and fruit. Prepared rations eliminate the need for cooking on the march, reducing the need to carry or gather firewood and for stopping to eat, thus increasing the rate of march. The Roman soldier carried a canteen of *posca*, a sour wine turned almost to vinegar (*acetum*) mixed with water. Posca was an excellent liquid ration in that the *acetum* provided vitamin C, calories, and helped reduce the usually bad taste of local water supplies. The highly acidic content of *acetum* killed harmful waterborne bacteria, which often caused intestinal illness. Unlike most peoples of the Middle East, who preferred sweet wines, the Romans preferred strong, harsh wines. When the New Testament records the story of the Roman legionnaire at the foot of the cross giving Jesus "vinegar on a sponge" to quench his thirst, it suggests that the soldier was tormenting the victim. In fact, the legionnaire offered Jesus a sponge soaked in *posca* from his own canteen in an act of mercy. But to the Middle Eastern palate, the *posca* tasted like vinegar, leading to the notion that the legionnaire was tormenting, not comforting, the victim.[31]

The *Iliad* provides a description of the Mycenaean diet of the Homeric warriors laying siege to Troy. The Greek warriors ate mostly cattle and goat meat roasted on a spit and served in round, pita-like, unleavened flat bread cooked on an iron plate.[32] The bread was made from parched barleycorn, a hard grain that could also be crushed to make porridge. The first mention of leavened bread in Greek literature is in Xenophon's *Anabasis* (401 B.C.E.).[33] (Leavened bread is found in Old Kingdom Egypt 2,000 years earlier.) Beans and chickpeas were also consumed by the Greeks, as was cheese and goat's milk. Cow's milk was considered by the Greeks to be unhealthy. Cattle were slaughtered and eaten as soon as they were killed, and there is no evidence of dried meat, salted fish, or dried fruit. Indeed, there is no mention of any kind of preserved rations.[34]

In general, then, the diet of the ancient soldier of most armies of the period provided him with sufficient calories and other nutrients to remain at least as healthy and strong as other citizens of his society. The ancient soldier seems to have been fed even better in garrison than the average civilian, and his diet was certainly more varied. It is remarkable that although ancient quartermasters had no scientific knowledge of nutrition, most military diets nevertheless provided sufficient quantities of all the nutritional components of which we are aware today. It is telling that on average the Roman soldier lived at least five years longer than the average Roman citizen, a fact attributed, in some part, to his superior diet.[35]

With the end of the ancient world around 450 C.E. the ability of armies to feed their troops sufficiently declined. The use of bread and dried vegetables as military staples was common through World War I, when canned food rations began to make a regular appearance. These foods were prepared by mechanical techniques requiring high temperatures to kill harmful bacteria, techniques which also reduced the nutritional quality of the rations considerably. It seems fair to say that no army from the Middle Ages to the Civil War provided their troops with rations as nutritionally sufficient or as varied as did the armies of the ancient world.

NOTES

1. Napoleon was the first of the modern commanders to experiment with meat preserved in tins, followed closely by the British in the Crimean War. Northern forces in the Civil War had tinned beef. Very often, the meat spoiled in the tin and was inedible. Other times, the meat developed bacteria, such as botulism, that was deadly if consumed.

2. Jonathan P. Roth, *The Logistics of the Roman Army at War (265 B.C.–A.D. 235)* (Boston: Brill, 1999), 185.

3. J. I. Robertson, Jr., *Tenting Tonight: The Soldier's Life* (Alexandria, VA: Time-Life Books, 1984), 85.

4. Ibid.

5. H.W.F. Saggs, *The Might That Was Assyria* (London: Sidgwick and Jackson, 1984), 166.

6. Roth, *Logistics*, 8.

7. Jane M. Renfrew, "Vegetables in the Ancient Near Eastern Diet," in *Civilizations of the Ancient Near East*, vol. 1, ed. Jack M. Sasson (New York: Scribner, 1995), 201.

8. A. L. Basham, *The Wonder That Was India: A Survey of the Culture of the Indian Sub-continent Before the Coming of the Muslims* (New York: Grove Press, 1959), 195.

9. Renfrew, "Vegetables"; see also Thomas D. Seymour, *Life in the Homeric Age* (New York: Biblo and Tannen, 1963), 216.

10. Victor W. von Hagen, *The Ancient Sun Kingdoms of the Americas: Aztec, Maya, Inca* (Cleveland, OH: World Publishing, 1961), 444.

11. Renfrew, "Vegetables," 193.

12. Ibid.

13. Ibid., 192.

14. Brian Hesse, "Animal Husbandry in the Human Diet in the Ancient Near East," in *Civilizations of the Ancient Near East*, vol. 1, ed. Jack M. Sasson (New York: Scribner, 1995), 213.

15. Richard A. Gabriel, *Lion of the Sun* (New York: Iuniverse, 2003), 110.

16. Roth, *Logistics*, 12.

17. Ibid., 8.

18. Donald W. Engels, *Alexander the Great and the Logistics of the Macedonian Army* (Berkeley: University of California Press, 1978), 125.

19. Ibid., 125.

20. Roth, *Logistics*, 51.

21. Ibid.

22. Irma S. Rombauer and Marion Rombauer Becker, *The Joy of Cooking* (New York: Penguin Books, 1993), 175.

23. Robertson, *Tenting Tonight*, 85.

24. Renfrew, "Vegetables," 202.

25. Roth, *Logistics*, 52.

26. Sarva Damn Singh, *Ancient Indian Warfare* (Delhi: Motilal Banarsidass, 1997), 132.

27. Livy 44.26.6.

28. Appian *Celtic Wars* 1.3.

29. Julius Caesar *Gallic Wars* 5.14.

30. Dio Cassius 62.5.5–6.

31. Graham Webster, *The Roman Imperial Army of the First and Second Centuries* A.D., 3rd. ed. (Totowa, NJ: Barnes and Noble Books, 1985), 263.

32. Seymour, *Life in the Homeric Age*, 232.

33. Ibid., 233.

34. Ibid., 214.

35. Richard A. Gabriel and Karen S. Metz, *A History of Military Medicine*, vol. 1, *From Ancient Times to the Middle Ages* (Westport, CT: Greenwood Press, 1992), 165.

Six

✳ ✳ ✳

EQUIPMENT

A soldier needs much more than his weapons to be an effective fighter. Fighting, after all, can only be accomplished after the soldier has arrived on the battlefield, often after a grueling march of several weeks or even months in the field. During these times it is the soldier's other equipment that makes the difference in the quality of his life and whether or not he arrives on the battlefield fit to do combat. A soldier weakened by fatigue, thirst, malnutrition, sore feet, sunburn, illness, and injury cannot fight well and will have made the journey to the battlefield only to suffer defeat.

FOOTGEAR

Among the most important items of the ancient soldier's personal equipment was footgear. Long marches over hot sand or rocky terrain could easily cause injury. The need to carry heavy loads required strong support for the foot. Good shoes and boots also helped reduce injuries caused by mules, horses, donkeys, camels, and oxen, all animals used in the baggage trains of ancient armies, stepping on the soldier's feet. The evolution of military footgear seems to follow a pattern of climate and terrain. In general, nations whose armies fought mostly in hot desert climates used sandals, while countries whose armies were required to fight in cold, mountainous, or rocky terrain developed the field boot for better protection. India, China, Sumer, and Egypt developed the sandal very early, while it was the Vedic invaders, the Mitanni, and the Hittites who seemed to have been the earliest users of the boot.

Sumerian reliefs dating to 2200 B.C.E. show Narim-Sin, the ruler of Akkad, wearing military sandals[1]; pre-Vedic Indian soldiers (1700 B.C.E.) also wore sandals.[2] The sandals of the Egyptian soldier (2000 b.c.e.) were made of woven reeds, papyrus, or thin animal skin and did not wear well in military use. Early accounts of Egyptian expeditions recount that "the asses were laden with sandals," suggesting that the sandals wore out quickly and had to be constantly replaced while on the march.[3] Replacement footwear was an important logistical item for the early Egyptian armies. During the New Kingdom (1550 b.c.e.) the Egyptians replaced the reed sandal with a new design with a thick leather sole held to the foot by an additional third strap running around the heel that held the sandal more securely to the foot, permitting the soldier to run without fear of losing his sandal. The Egyptian sandal added leather sidepieces so as to become like a genuine shoe. It was during the New Kingdom period that Egypt broke out of its geographic isolation, sending its armies into the hills and mountains of Palestine, Syria, and Hatti, all areas of rough terrain that required better footgear for Egyptian soldiers to function well.

With some variation in design the sandal continued to be the basic footgear of many ancient armies until the end of the ancient period in 450 c.e. Chinese crossbowmen wore wooden-soled, open-toe sandals or clogs because of their light weight instead of the heavy boots of the spear and halberd infantry. Crossbowmen had to be agile and fast to survive, while spear and halberd infantry fought in phalanx with little need for rapid movement. Indian infantry wore sandals until the end of the ancient period.[4] The warriors of the *Iliad* wore leather sandals. During the winter these sandals (*pedila*) were stuffed with felt or fur for warmth.[5] The famous Warrior Vase of the Mycenaean period (1200 b.c.e.) shows warriors wearing leather sandals woven with leather thongs up to the top of the ankle.[6] The cavalry of Philip II and Alexander also wore sandals laced with thongs above the ankle. The Persian cavalry used a tie-shoe with a soft leather sole, perhaps because it permitted the cavalryman to better feel his mount and obtain greater control over the animal at a time when spurs and stirrups were unknown. The armies of Republican Rome wore open sandals. With the coming of the Roman Empire in the first century c.e. the armies were required to fight in all types of terrain, with the result that the army developed a sturdier sandal that evolved into genuine field boots called *caligai*. The Roman sandal was heavy, tough, and thick, with a sole made of several layers of leather for a total thickness of about three-quarters of an inch. The sole was studded with hobnails for better traction. The upper was cut of one piece and sewn up at the heel; the front laced up for a good fit. In winter they could be stuffed with cloth or fur for warmth.[7]

The earliest military field boot for which we have evidence seems to have made its appearance sometime around 1700 c.e. and probably was introduced by the Aryan invaders of central Asia who overran India and parts of the Middle East and became the Hyksos, Mitanni, and Hittites. It is worth noting that these invaders were horse-raising peoples who introduced the two-wheeled war chariot to the area. One might suspect that the combination of chariot riding and the climate from which they came were stimuli for the use of boots instead of sandals. Indian texts describe the Aryan invaders as wearing leather and felt boots common to central Asia as well as trousers and long, quilted coats.[8] These boots were impractical in the hot climate of India. Nonetheless, their early association with great warriors was so strong that Indian charioteers and cavalrymen continued to wear them until the end of the ancient period.[9] The boot probably spread throughout the Middle East as a result of the spread of the Mitanni *maryannu* chariot system, with its chariot-borne warrior, that greatly influenced the development of chariot warfare in Canaan, Syria, and among the Philistines.[10] Hittite warriors are usually portrayed in reliefs as wearing leather boots. Infantry guards-men wore boots that reached to the mid-calf and had turned up toes. Boots worn by charioteers were only ankle high and seem to have had a flatter sole, perhaps for greater stability when riding on the chariot platform.

The Assyrian army (850 B.C.E.) was the first to improve on the field boot. The Assyrian soldier wore a knee-high, leather jackboot with thick leather soles, complete with hobnails on the sole to improve traction. The boot also had thin plates of iron sewn into the front to protect the shin.[11] The high boot provided good ankle support for troops who regularly had to traverse rough terrain and served as excellent protection in cold weather, rain, and snow. Another Assyrian innovation in military footwear was the long stocking worn under the boot. Other reliefs show Assyrian units in open sandals with their legs covered with knee-high socks for warmth and protection of the shin. The Assyrian boot reduced foot injury and was one of the primary reasons why the Assyrian army was able to move easily over rough terrain in all kinds of weather. A similar boot was used by the Urartu of Kurdistan and Iran, and Chinese soldiers of the Shang Period (1100 B.C.E.) are portrayed as wearing heavy, knee-high boots that were probably of indigenous design.

CLOTHES

Of great importance to ancient soldiers were their clothes, and once more, climate and terrain influenced the design and material of clothing. The primary material from which military clothes were made was wool. Early Sumerian reliefs show that sheepskin, too, was sometimes used for military kilts.[12] Germanic tribes of first-century C.E. Europe sometimes wore animal skins as clothing.

The sheep was the most common domesticated animal in the ancient world throughout the entire period of antiquity, so it is hardly surprising that wool was the most common material for clothing. In Egypt, however, the sheep was considered ceremonially unclean, although mutton was widely consumed by the common people of the country. The Egyptian climate was hot, and the woolen clothes worn by the neighboring Philistines, Canaanites, and Israelites in Palestine were uncomfortable. In Egypt, flax was the primary material for making linen cloth. Linen could be woven as fine as sheer gauze (a favorite with women) or as heavy as canvas for boat sails and rope. Linen is a very strong fiber and could even be used to make textile armor. Egypt exported linen to other countries. In seventh-century B.C.E. Greece we find linen tunics being used in war, as burial shrouds, and in the manufacture of lamellar armor made of strips of linen glued together to make plates.[13] The Greek word for "tunic" is borrowed from the Phoenician word, *linen*, suggesting that it was the Phoenicians who traded the cloth with Greece after obtaining it from Egypt.[14]

Indian common soldiers were clad mostly in cotton, the staple fiber for clothing manufacture in India for millennia. The professional officers (*Ksatriyas*) often wore garments made of linen with a girdle of *munja* grass and a cloak. The underwear of the *Ksatriyas* was made of deerskin. Some elite units continued to wear the woolen quilted coats, long trousers, and leather boots that were originally introduced by the Aryan invaders.[15] The earliest mention of cotton in the Middle East is found in the annals of the Assyrian king Sennacherib (704–681 B.C.E.), who describes one of the plants set in his park around Nineveh as a "wool bearing tree." The text also tells us that "they plucked the wool-bearing tree and wove it into cloth."[16] Herodotus records that Indian military contingents wearing cloth from the "wool tree" served in the Persian army at the battle of Platea in 479 B.C.E.[17] The first date of cotton cultivation in Egypt is 370 B.C.E.[18] Cotton was widely used in China, and the quilted cotton jacket served as armor for light infantry units.[19] Chinese aristocrats and officers wore silk gowns, while the common infantry soldier was often outfitted in little more than a knee-length tunic made of hemp cloth tied at the waist with rope or a belt.[20]

Clothing Styles

The styles of military clothing varied widely from country to country. Indian soldiers wore skirts or kilts (*paridhana* or *vasana*) made of lengths of cotton cloth draped loosely around the body and fastened at the waist, with the body being uncovered above the waist. Sometimes another length of cloth draped shawl-like over the shoulder (*uttariya*) was worn as an upper garment. In the cold season a third garment (*pravara*) was worn like a cloak.[21] The early Egyptian soldier wore a short, pleated, linen kilt called a *shendo'ot* with no shirt. By the New Kingdom (1500 B.C.E.) the Egyptian soldier wore a sleeveless body shirt which offered much better protection from the sun. Reliefs of Hittite guardsmen on Anatolian monuments show these soldiers wearing a short woolen kilt, the upper body being either left uncovered or covered with armor.[22] Egyptian portrayals of Hittite troops at the battle of Megiddo appear to show the Hittites wearing long, one-piece uniforms from neck to mid-thigh. O. R. Gurney has suggested that these may have been lighter-weight summer uniforms[23] used in hot climates; others have suggested that they may have been a kind of great coat fashioned in one piece of heavy wool that was carried in the baggage train and could be retrieved and donned quickly when needed.[24] The Philistines had spent considerable time in the land of the Hittites before moving south to settle in Palestine and were outfitted much like the Hittites in woolen kilts. Mycenaean soldiers wore only loincloths or small trunks[25] and sometimes fought naked; all the clothing mentioned in the *Iliad* was made of wool.[26] Later, Greek hoplites wore cotton or linen tunics under their armor. Celtic and German tribesmen wore woolen trousers and heavy cloaks. Persian cavalrymen wore woolen trousers, a long-sleeved tunic reaching to the knee, and a sleeved cloak (*kandys*) worn on the shoulders to leave the arms free.[27] Roman troops wore a linen undershirt next to their skin covered with a short-sleeved woolen tunic that came to the mid-thigh and was fastened at the waist with a belt. Undershorts with drawstrings for sizing were standard issue. During operations in cold climates Roman soldiers wore leather trousers (*bracae*) that reached just below the knee.[28] A long, heavy, woolen cloak served as the soldier's main protection against the elements and was also used as his bedroll or blanket.

CARRYING EQUIPMENT

The ancient soldier carried considerably more on the march than his shield, helmet, and weapons. Rations, cooking pot, canteen, tools, bedroll, extra clothing and shoes, and palisade stakes were all part of the soldier's personal equipment. Some sort of backpack must have been a common item, but we have very little evidence that it was. There is only a single Egyptian relief showing what appears to be a soldier's pack.[29] More common are references to "carrying poles," the earliest dating to 2000 B.C.E. in Egypt in a text where the commander, Henu, tells how he issued carrying poles to his soldiers during the march in Punt.[30] There are no surviving examples of Egyptian carrying poles. We might surmise that it was a length of forked stick about five feet long that could be balanced on the soldier's shoulder with one hand. Various items of equipment could either be lashed to the space between the fork or hung from the pole's end in the manner of a hobo carrying his kit. Chinese and Indian reliefs show soldiers carrying heavy loads, but there is no discernible evidence of backpacks or carrying frames, even though we might reasonably assume that they existed.

The most complete description of the equipment carried by the ancient soldier and the means to carry it comes down to us from Vegetius, Frontius, and Josephus and their descriptions of the Roman soldier. There were four elements to the Roman soldier's equipment: (1) clothing and weapons (*arma*); (2) personal equipment, including cooking gear (*vas*); (3) tools, including an axe, spade, saw, sickle, and rope (*instrumenta*)[31] (each legionnaire also carried two *pila muralia*, rectangular double-pointed stakes used for constructing a palisade around the camp at night); and (4) rations (*cibus*).[32] The soldier's personal equipment included a carrying pole, a leather satchel, a string bag for food, a metal canteen, a mess kit, a cloak, an extra tunic, and an undershirt and shorts. In cold weather, leather trousers and extra shoes would be included.[33]

Types of Packs

The Roman soldier's pack was called a *sarcina*, and the Romans developed an effective method of carrying their equipment that served as well as a modern backpack. The Romans used a wooden carrying pole with a fork in it, probably quite similar to the Egyptian carrying pole described earlier. A little board (*tabella*) was fixed between the forks, and a crossbar was lashed to the top of the pole. The soldier's equipment was packed and tied into a cloth bundle or placed in his leather satchel and lashed to the *tabella*. A bundle of extra clothes, shoes, and underwear was then wrapped in the soldier's cloak like a roll and tied to the crossbar. Other equipment—canteen, pots, tools, and so on—could be hung from

A typical Roman soldier in full kit. Courtesy of the Library of Congress.

the crossbar as well. The helmet was slung around the neck with a strap so that it rested on the soldier's chest. The entrenching stakes and, perhaps, the soldiers *pilum* (javelin) were lashed lengthwise along the length of the carrying pole, and the whole load balanced like a fulcrum on the soldier's shoulder. This arrangement, however, did little to lessen the weight of the pack pressing on the shoulder. To balance the weight more evenly, Roman soldiers carried their shields slung over their backs held with leather straps, with the upper edge of the shield reaching just above the neck. When the carrying pole was balanced on the shoulder, most of the weight of the pack fell on the edge of the shield, distributing it over the soldier's back and transferring much of the weight from his shoulders.[34]

It may be reasonably estimated that soldiers in Alexander's army and the Roman army routinely carried between sixty and seventy-five pounds on their backs: Vegetius reports that the Roman soldier's equipment weighed forty-three pounds, not counting his weapons,[35] and the armor and weapons of the Roman soldier weighed an additional thirty-two pounds. By comparison, American troops during the Normandy invasion carried eighty-two pounds of weapons and equipment, while Napoleon's soldiers at Waterloo carried seventy pounds, and the British soldiers who stormed Bunker Hill attacked uphill carrying eighty pounds on their backs.[36] Requiring the soldier to carry his equipment and weapons considerably reduced the logistical burden of the army and increased its rate of march substantially. With soldiers carrying one-third of the load that would normally be carried by pack animals, an army of 50,000 men required 6,000 fewer pack animals than it would have needed, along with another fewer 240 animals to haul the feed for the others.[37]

PROTECTION FROM WEATHER AND THE ELEMENTS

Ancient soldiers usually mounted their campaigns from late spring to early fall, with much of their activity taking place in the heat of the summer, when thirst, heat, and dust were their greatest enemies. From early times (2000 B.C.E.) leather bottles served as water canteens for many ancient armies. The leather exterior covered either a clay bottle or another animal skin. Canteens made of boiled leather, leather boiled to make it soft and then shaped into the form of a canteen, were not uncommon in the Orient. Canteens could hold two quarts of water, barely sufficient to keep a soldier going in moderate temperatures and not enough for activity in high temperatures.

The blazing sun of the Middle East, Asia, and India could easily incapacitate a soldier in a matter of hours. Metal weapons, helmets, and armor often could not be worn because they became heated to the point that they were too hot to touch.[38] Intense heat accompanied by low humidity increases the body's evaporation of fluids and causes the skin to chap and develop sores. Blindness caused by reflected sunlight was also a major problem, especially in the desert, where the lightly colored sands reflected light like a mirror.[39] An army on the move creates a tremendous amount of dust, which, if inhaled, can make breathing difficult. To deal with some of these conditions, the ancient soldier was issued oil (olive, sesame, linseed, or palm) to rub on his skin and protect it from the sun by keeping the skin moist.[40] Egyptian troops sometimes wore small cones of beeswax mixed with oil on their heads, allowing the sun to melt the cone so that the oil would run down over their heads and upper bodies. Umbrellas were known, but their use seems to have been confined to the nobility and high-ranking officers.[41] Interestingly, the design of these parasols seems to be almost identical, regardless of the army that used them.[42]

None of the surviving reliefs and portrayals of which I am aware seem to show how common soldiers protected themselves from the sun. Egyptian reliefs, for example, always show their troops in kilts with no upper body shirt, a condition that would have been ruinous to the health of the troops if they indeed did march this way in the Egyptian sun. Perhaps the shirts were discarded just before battle. But soldiers are very pragmatic beings and are quick to discard equipment (and ignore instructions) that are not practical, even as they invent simple means to increase their comfort and survival. The ancient soldier had at his disposal a number of means to protect himself in harsh environments. A wet cloth placed on the head helped keep the body's temperature down and prevent sunburn. The Egyptian soldier's military-issue wig may have served the same purpose. It is not difficult to imagine that the light bedroll made of woven reeds might have been suspended from a stick to provide shade. Burnt wood or charcoal from a cooking fire rubbed under the eyes would reduce the reflection of the sun and reduce blindness. A wet cloth wrapped or held over the mouth and nose offered some protection against the dust. Xenophon tells us that in cold weather an ointment made from hog's lard, sesame, bitter almonds, and turpentine helps protect against frostbite when rubbed on the body.[43] All these remedies were probably used by the common soldier but do not appear in the surviving reliefs and portrayals produced to glorify the victories of generals and kings. The life of the common soldier was very much different indeed.

BEDDING AND TENTS

The ancient soldier slept mostly on the ground using either a woven reed mat (Egypt), a cotton blanket (India), or his woolen cloak (Rome) for his bedding and blanket. Usually, armies carried tents in their baggage trains that could accommodate a small group of soldiers. Egyptian tents were small, round-topped tents that accommodated a small number of men, perhaps a squad of ten in cramped accommodations.[44] In all probability, Egyptian tents were made from heavy linen, a fabric with a wide weave that permitted air to pass through easily. Assyrian tents came in two varieties. The tents of the ordinary soldiers and officers resemble modern Bedouin tents, with open fronts to catch the cool breezes. The sidewalls of the tents were kept up by guy ropes helped by a three-branched internal support, often cut from a tree.[45] The tents used by the king and high-ranking officers and officials were larger and rectangular and had rounded roofs with a section that could be opened to the sky. Often, these tents were protected by canvas screens around them. The tents of ancient armies were most commonly fabricated of leather, linen, wool, and goat's hair; cotton may have been used later, as was certainly the case with camel hair after 1000 B.C.E., when the camel was turned to military use.

The tents of the Roman army were made from the best-quality leather, were ten Roman feet square, and had openings in front and in back.[46] Each tent accommodated an eight-man squad (*contubernium*). The tent could be rolled up into a sausage-shaped bundle and carried on the squad's mule, which also carried its grain mill, palisade stakes, tools, and sacks of grain rations.

NOTES

1. Nigel Stillman and Nigel Tallis, *Armies of the Ancient Near East: 3000 to 539* B.C.E. (Sussex, UK: Flexiprint, 1984), 127.

2. A. L. Basham, *The Wonder That Was India: A Survey of the Culture of the Indian Subcontinent Before the Coming of the Muslims* (New York: Grove Press, 1959), 211.

3. Henu, "Myrrh, Soldiers, Wells," in *Ancient Records of Egypt: Historical Documents from the Earliest Times to the Persian Conquest*, vol. 2, *The Eighteenth Dynasty*, trans. and ed. James Henry Breasted (Chicago: University of Chicago Press, 1906), 215–217.

4. Richard A. Gabriel and Donald W. Boose, Jr., *The Great Battles of Antiquity: A Strategic and Tactical Guide to Great Battles That Shaped the Development of War* (Westport, CT: Greenwood Press, 1994), 173.

5. Thomas D. Seymour, *Life in the Homeric Age* (New York: Biblo and Tannen, 1963), 170.

6. Steven Weingartner, "The Saga of Piyamaradu," *Military Heritage* 3 (October 2001): 86.

7. John Warry, *Warfare in the Classical World: An Illustrated Encyclopaedia of Weapons, Warriors, and Warfare in the Ancient Civilisations of Greece and Rome* (London: Salamander Books, 1980), 135.

8. Basham, *Wonder That Was India*, 211.

9. Ibid.

10. Richard A. Gabriel, *The Military History of Ancient Israel* (Westport, CT: Praeger, 2003), chap. 2.

11. Georges Contenau, *Everyday Life in Babylon and Assyria* (London: Edward Arnold, 1954), 144; for details on the Assyrian boot, see also Robert Laffont, *The Ancient Art of Warfare*, vol. 1, *Antiquity* (New York: Time-Life Books, 1968), 45.

12. Laffont, *Ancient Art of Warfare*, 35.

13. Seymour, *Life in the Homeric Age*, 152.

14. Ibid.

15. Basham, *Wonder That Was India*, 211.

16. H.W.F. Saggs, *The Might That Was Assyria* (London: Sidgwick and Jackson, 1984), 165.

17. Basham, *Wonder That Was India*, 48.

18. Victor W. von Hagen, *The Ancient Sun Kingdoms of the Americas: Aztec, Maya, Inca* (Cleveland, OH: World Publishing, 1961), 445.

19. Gabriel, *Great Battles*, 173.

20. Ibid.

21. Basham, *Wonder That Was India*, 210.

22. J. G. Macqueen, *The Hittites and Their Contemporaries in Asia Minor* (Boulder, CO: Westview Press, 1975), 103.

23. O. R. Gurney, *The Hittites* (New York: Penguin Books, 1962), 88–89.

24. Macqueen, *Hittites and Their Contemporaries*, 103.

25. Weingartner, "Saga of Piyamaradu," 81.

26. Seymour, *Life in the Homeric Age*, 152.

27. Sir John Hackett, *Warfare in the Ancient World* (New York: Facts on File, 1989), 85.

28. Graham Webster, *The Roman Imperial Army of the First and Second Centuries* A.D., 2nd ed. (New York: Barnes and Noble Books, 1979), 121.

29. Stillman and Tallis, *Armies*, 100.

30. Henu, "Myrrh, Soldiers, Wells," 216.

31. Josephus *Jewish War* 3.55.

32. Jonathan P. Roth, *The Logistics of the Roman Army at War (264 B.C.—A.D. 235)* (Boston: Brill, 1999), 72.

33. Marcus Junkelmann, *The Legions of Augustus: The Roman Soldier in an Archeological Experiment* [in German] (Mainz, Germany: Philipp von Zabern, 1986), 199.

34. Roth, *Logistics*, 75–76.

35. Ibid., 72.

36. Richard A. Gabriel, *The Culture of War: Invention and Early Development* (Westport, CT: Greenwood Press, 1990), 96–99.

37. Richard A. Gabriel and Karen S. Metz, *From Sumer To Rome: The Military Capabilities of Ancient Armies* (Westport, CT: Greenwood Press, 1991), 26.

38. Donald W. Engels, *Alexander the Great and the Logistics of the Macedonian Army* (Berkeley: University of California Press, 1978), 101.

39. Ibid., 102.

40. Oil was needed to keep the hide shields supple; they would shrink and crack in the desert heat if not kept moist.

41. Stillman, *Armies*, 153.

42. Ibid., 154.

43. Xenophon, *The Persian Expedition*, trans. Rex Warner (Baltimore: Penguin Books, 1972), 193.

44. Stillman, *Armies*, 201.

45. Ibid., 202.

46. Webster, *Roman Imperial Army*, 169–170.

Seven

THE CAMP

The armies of the ancient world often undertook military campaigns that took them beyond their own state borders over relatively long distances. These long marches required the development of the marching or field camp, where the army stopped for the night for rest and nourishment before moving on in the morning. This type of camp can be distinguished from the battle camp, a stronger redoubt constructed once the enemy was detected in a movement to contact and when battle was imminent. Armies rarely offered battle immediately on learning the location of the enemy force, permitting several days—and sometimes even weeks—during which the encampment could be strengthened and made more secure. Castrametation is the art of constructing camps.

TYPES OF CAMPS

The need for a strongly fortified encampment arose from the fact that unlike the field camp, the battle camp was expected to play an important role in the forthcoming battle. A well-fortified encampment gave the army commander a strong defensive position from which to fight, if he found himself outnumbered, or from which to foray in the offensive if conditions appeared favorable. A strongly fortified camp could also serve as a rallying point for an army that had been mauled on the battlefield, a place to gather and regroup one's forces or, if need be, to offer a final resistance. It was the tactical role of the battle camp that determined its design and degree of fortification.

Whenever an army laid siege to a city or town, the battle camp would be transformed into a siege camp to accommodate the army for a long period. In these circumstances the fortifications of the battle camp were extended and greatly improved. The Assyrians, for example, usually surrounded their marching and battle camps with wooden stakes; their siege camps, however, were fortified with brick walls fashioned on the spot and equipped with tall guard towers. At the siege of Massada, which lasted almost three years, Roman camps became functioning towns, complete with housing for workmen, barracks for troops, and entertainment houses for the soldiers. Indian siege camps were so large and full of people and buildings that they resembled small cities and often accommodated hundreds of thousands of people within their walls.[1] Several Roman siege camps transformed themselves over time into permanent garrisons, which then developed into full-fledged cities. Cologne, Germany, and Manchester, England, are examples of such cities.

Military camps in antiquity ranged from the simple to the complex, depending on the sophistication of the armies that constructed them and the ability of their logistics trains to transport materials for construction. Some armies, like those of India, China, and Assyria, routinely incorporated large numbers of construction workers, tools, and construction materials in their logistics trains. Sargon of Assyria (721–705 B.C.E.) took along thousands of workmen in his campaign against the Urartu, using them to construct camps, roads, and bridges along his route of advance.[2] The Egyptian, Alexandrian, and Roman armies, by contrast, required their own soldiers to construct whatever encampments and fortifications were needed. Besides resting the troops and animals, the main purpose of encampments was to provide security against surprise attack.

Early Roman armies did not usually construct fortified encampments, but their experience with the surprise attacks of tribal armies quickly led them to adopt the fortified camp as a necessary element of any military march. It takes considerable time, however, to construct an encampment adequate to hold a 5,000-man legion and its 1,200 animals, to say nothing of its other equipment. The time for construction is necessarily deducted from the time the army can march, with the result that Roman armies often could not move very far in a single day. If the tactical situation required it, however, the encampment could be abandoned, often with the baggage, and the army made to move quickly, sometimes twenty-five miles a day.

The importance of the encampment in the military thinking of ancient commanders is testified to by a number of surviving texts instructing the army's advanced scouts on how to select a proper campsite. One Indian text dating from 700 B.C.E. tells us that "generally thickly wooded spots were selected for the disposition of troops. The best ground for entrenching horses is a level plain with no rocks and covered only with a few trees, and not muddy; for chariots, a well-laid road, devoid of sand or mud, trees, shrubs, etc.; for elephants, one without mud or having a layer of sharp gravel; and for infantry and others, one free from all defects, but with available supplies of drinking water. It should be broad and free from thorns."[3] Officers in charge of locating, surveying, and overseeing the construction of encampments were important officials in all ancient armies.

Egypt

The earliest portrayals of military encampments among ancient armies are Egyptian and date to Ramses II's victory at the battle of Kadesh (1275 B.C.E.). The reliefs found at Ramses's Luxor temple show an example of a battle camp. The shape of the camp is rectangular, its perimeter walls fashioned by large leather shields standing upright and lashed together. The camp is oriented so its main entrance faces east, the direction from which the sun rises. The Egyptians believed that the sun god rose from the land of the dead every morning; his arrival was accompanied by religious worship in the military camp each morning. At the center of the camp is Pharaoh's tent; the tents of other officers and officials are located nearby. Other areas are set aside for horses, chariots, food kitchens, and medical treatment. Donkeys, mules, and oxen are shown in the baggage area. Despite the clamor of the camp, Ramses's pet lion dozes serenely in the sun.

In the left-hand corner Ramses can be seen sitting on his portable throne inside his command tent. Behind him are two figures, each holding a long pole. Atop one of these poles is the hieroglyph for a flame or burning brazier. Atop the other pole is the hieroglyph for a covered brazier, which produces smoke. These two devices were used by the commander to exercise command and control over the movement of the camp. When the army was encamped during the night, the flame burned brightly in the brazier atop Pharaoh's tent. When it was time to gather and move the army in the morning, the brazier was covered, and a steady smoke rose from the brazier atop the pole. As the army moved, the smoke provided a guide to the rest of the army along the route of march.[4] It was these two Egyptian signal devices that were recorded in the Old Testament as the "pillars of smoke and fire" that led the Israelites in their trek across the desert.[5] The Roman historian Curtius, writing more than 1,000 years later, records in his *History of Alexander* how Alexander the Great, having learned of this means of waking, moving, and stopping the army while in Egypt, adopted the device for his army. Curtius says that Alexander "set up a pole on top of the general's tent which could be clearly seen from all sides, and from this lofty signal, visible to all alike, was watched for, fire by night, smoke by day *(ignis noctu fumus interdieu)*."[6]

It is also intriguing that there are remarkable similarities between the Tabernacle that the Old Testament tells us was constructed by the Israelites in the desert and Ramses's military camp at Kadesh. Not only do the dimensions and configuration of the Tabernacle conform to the layout of the Egyptian camp, but Yahweh's portable tent is of the same dimensions and layout as Pharaoh's command tent. Like Pharaoh's war tent, the Tabernacle may have served as a mobile military headquarters for the Israelites.[7] There is some evidence that Israelite units may have served at one time as part of Pharaoh's elite guard, a position which would have permitted their commanders to become familiar with the Egyptian war camp and which they may have copied once they left Egypt.[8]

Assyria

Assyrian camps depicted in reliefs are well fortified. They are oval in shape and surrounded with a wooden palisade of tall, pointed stakes that, like Alexander's and the Roman armies, were probably carried by the army. The stakes appear too long and thus too heavy to have been carried by the individual soldier and probably were transported in the baggage train. Ashurnasirpal II (883–859 B.C.E.), was probably the first Assyrian monarch to use this type of camp on a regular basis.[9] This camp is almost certainly not a marching camp for it is too well fortified, with lower mud brick walls and even guard towers, features that are not portable. Most likely, the portrayal is of a siege camp. The interior of the camp is divided into quarters, with a single main road running from back to front connecting the two main gates. The top left quarter depicts the king's religious shrine attended by a priest standing across from the royal chariot. The bottom left quarter shows baggage animals and horses at rest next to a covered battering ram and soldiers cooking in a tent. The division of the camp and the complexity of the happenings within it testify to the organizational complexity of the Assyrian army on campaign.

Persia

The Persian military camp was well organized, although it seems not to have been fortified. Xenophon, in describing the marching camp of Cyrus the Great, tells us that the king pitched his tent in the middle of the camp and arranged everyone else in outward-reaching concentric circles. Next to his tent, Cyrus placed his bodyguards and the cooks ("breadmakers and saucemakers"). Around the king, bodyguard, and cooks were the knights and charioteers, placed deep inside the camp because "they encamp without having any of the weapons with which they fight ready at hand, but they need a lot of time for arming.... "[10] The knights are the heavily armored, spear-bearing infantry called the Immortals. To the left and right of the knights were the "targeteers" (probably javelineers) and archers. Surrounding the entire encampment "like a wall" were the hoplite heavy infantry with their spears and great shields, who slept in shifts and maintained a guard all night long. The archers and javelineers also slept in shifts to stand ready to reinforce the hoplites if the camp came under an attack.[11] Cyrus required that all his officers post their insignia on their tents so that they could be found easily by messengers. The separation of the armed units in separate circles, Xenophon tells us, also made it easier for Cyrus to assess the condition of the troops and their weapons at a glance. The most important reason for the arrangement was "that if someone were to attack during the night or day, the attackers would fall upon his camp as into an ambush."[12] They would meet a defense in depth with Cyrus's best units having time to arm and counterattack. Given that Cyrus often fought tribal armies until meeting his death at Cunaxa in 401 B.C.E., the prospect of a surprise night attack against his encamped army was not something that could be dismissed as unlikely.

India

The Indian *Epics* (1100–600 B.C.E.) provide us with a detailed description of Indian military camps. The camp was usually quadrangular in shape, furnished with four entrances, six roads, and nine internal divisions or areas.[13] A deep ditch was dug around the entire encampment, and guards were stationed at regular intervals.[14] A system of passes was employed to ensure that only authorized personnel passed through the camp's gates.[15] Pits were dug along likely avenues of approach and were covered to make traps. Like the Viet Cong's *punji* traps, sharpened sticks, nails, and thorns were placed in the pits to impale the victim. To prevent surprise attack or enemy reconnaissance, "forest men" were posted "in circular arrays" outside the camp to watch for the approach of the enemy and to sound the alarm if necessary. Reconnaissance units of cavalry patrolled outside the camp day and night to detect any enemy presence.[16] Within the encampment itself, specified areas were assigned for tents and housing, the baggage train, religious shrines, the camp hospital (to include veterinary physicians for the animals), animal corrals, officers' quarters, workmen's quarters, supply depots, and an area for the commander's tent and those of his staff. Indian troops began the day with morning formations and prayers.[17]

Greece and Carthage

While the nature of Achaean town fortifications made of Cyclopean walls is well known, we have only one description of an Homeric-era field camp. The *Iliad* tells of a camp surrounded by walls equipped with towers accessed by a single gate at the left of the camp.[18] A trench dug a short distance from the wall surrounded the camp. But the *Iliad*'s description of the fighting that took place around the camp, where a single thrown stone broke open the gate, where an assailant pulls at the battlements with his hands, and where an attacker strikes a defender in the "tower" with a thrusting spear, suggests that the Achaean "camp" described in the *Iliad* was little more than a mere wooden breastwork.[19] Warfare in the West was considerably more primitive than warfare in the Middle East or East at this time, and this primitivism is clearly reflected in the construction of the Achaean camp.

Five hundred years later, during the classical period of Greek warfare (700–350 B.C.E.), the armies of the Greek city-states still did not construct regular camps while on the march, perhaps because the distances from their home bases to the agreed-on site of the battlefield made such camps seem superfluous since a surprise attack was not possible and was considered dishonorable in any event. The armies of the Greek city-states lacked a formal command structure, an organized logistics system, and were comparatively small, all factors mitigating against the ability and need to construct battle camps. It was Philip II of Macedon who seems to have introduced the fortified battle camp to the Greek practice of war. Like the Romans, who adopted many Greek military practices, the encampments of Philip and Alexander were regularly fortified with a ditch and palisade, the latter constructed of sharpened stakes carried by the soldiers or in the baggage for precisely this purpose.[20] Philip's armies and those of Alexander were far more mobile and much faster moving than the earlier hoplite armies and possessed a strong cavalry arm. Trained as they were in the forced march (even at night), these armies were quite capable of surprise attack. So, too, were the armies of the Persians whom they fought. The result was an appreciation of the need for security on the march that only a well-planned and fortified field camp could afford.

The costs of not preparing a proper camp could be very high. Livy describes the camp of the Carthaginians facing Scipio in 203 B.C.E.: "The winter camp of the Carthaginians ... was almost entirely of wood. The Numidians, especially, were living in reed huts, mostly under thatch, scattered about quite irregularly, some of them having even been chosen on their own initiatives and without orders...."[21] The camp had no straight roads running through it and only a few gates. Scipio's troops blocked the exits and set the camp on fire. Livy tells us that "many [Carthaginians] were burned to death half asleep in their beds; many more were trampled to death in the narrow gateways in their wild rush to escape.... The flames devoured the whole camp in a single conflagration."[22] Forty thousand Carthaginian soldiers perished in the fire.

Rome

No such catastrophe ever befell a Roman army because the Romans were expert at the art of castrametation. A fortified camp was constructed every night while the army was on the march and again prior to battle. A camp for two 5,000-strong legions, the size of a Roman consular army, required land about 800 meters square, preferably on raised clear ground close to a river or stream for a source of water. Surveyors moving ahead of the main body selected the campsite. They marked out the site of the commander's tent (*praetorium*). This area also held the senior officers' tents and the headquarters (*principia*). From this point, two principal streets, one across the front of the headquarters area, the *via principalis*, and one at right angles to it, the *via praetoria*, were laid out forming a T shape, with the *principia* facing the enemy. The legion tents were arranged in long rectangles with an intersecting main street (*via quintana*). The main streets were eighteen meters wide, the secondary roads were fifteen meters wide, and the others between tent sections were six meters wide. Approximately 220 men could be packed comfortably on each acre of land. Each tent holding a squad was always located in the same place relative to the other tents in the maniple, each maniple was always located in the same place relative to the cohort, and each cohort was always located in the same place relative to the legion so that each unit and all men knew just where to go when pitching camp. This made encampment and breaking camp faster. The camp had four exits, each of which was fortified and angled to the opening in the camp rampart to make an attack on the gates more difficult. The main gate, the *porta praetoria*, was at the top of the camp at the end of the main street, the *via praetoria*. A second gate was located directly opposite at the other end of the same street, the *porta decumana*. Two additional gates were located at each end of the *via principalis*. Adequate space for wagons and animals was allotted within the walls of the camp, although sometimes they were located outside in an annex close by.[23]

As the army approached the campsite, cavalry units would deploy in a screen, behind which half the heavy infantry would deploy in full battle dress to repel any attack. The other half of the legion was set to work on the camp's rampart. Polibius tells us that in a marching camp, when the enemy was not in the area, a V-shaped ditch (*fastigata*) about one meter deep and one meter across was dug, behind which the dirt and turf were piled to make a vertical rampart (*punica*). Atop this packed earthen rampart were planted two-meter-long wooden palisade stakes, *pila muralia*, carried with the legion.[24] Vegetius, writing during imperial times, says that when in the vicinity of the enemy or when battle was expected, the ditch around the camp was dug three meters across and two meters deep.[25] On a rampart with a 3,000-meter perimeter, 40,000–50,000 sharpened palisade stakes allowed thirteen to sixteen stakes per meter.[26] Sentinels were posted at key points around the perimeter, and centurions regularly checked to insure that the sentries were always awake. The punishment for sleeping on guard duty was the *fustuarium*, being beaten to death with stones or cudgels by the comrades whom the sentry had endangered.

Tribes

Tribal armies like the Germans, Gauls, and Goths usually traveled with their entire populations and baggage in wagons and used the wagon *laager* as a fortified camp. This amounted to little more than concentric circles of wagons placed close to one another so as to narrow any gaps. Within the *laager* were gathered the women, children, animals, and the army's baggage. The *laager* served as a base from which to launch attacks at the enemy in the open or as a redoubt to gather stragglers or to fight a final battle.[27]

Within a century of the collapse of the Roman order (about 450 B.C.E.) Europe was overrun and settled by tribal peoples whose knowledge of warfare was decidedly primitive by any standard in the ancient world. The rise of the Franks and Charlemagne brought with it the supremacy of the mounted horseman and the demise of disciplined infantry. The art of castrametation was lost during this period. No Western army constructed a military encampment equivalent to Roman standards of size, organization, hygiene, supply, and protection until at least 1870.

NOTES

1. A. L. Basham, *The Wonder That Was India: A Survey of the Culture of the Indian Sub-continent Before the Coming of the Muslims* (New York: Grove Press, 1959), 135.

2. Richard A. Gabriel and Donald W. Boose, Jr., *The Great Battles of Antiquity: A Strategic and Tactical Guide to Great Battles That Shaped the Development of War* (Westport, CT: Greenwood Press, 1994), 110–111.

3. V. R. Ramachandra Dikshitar, *War in Ancient India* (Delhi: Motilal Banarsidass, 1987), 243–244.

4. Richard A. Gabriel, *The Military History of Ancient Israel* (Westport, CT: Praeger, 2003), 75.

5. Ibid.

6. Quintus Curtius Rufus, *The History of Alexander* (New York: Penguin Books, 1984), 96.

7. Michael M. Homan, "The Divine Warrior in His Tent: A Military Model for Yahweh's Tabernacle," *Bible Review* 6 (December 2000): 24.

8. Gabriel, *Military History of Ancient Israel*, 96–98.

9. Nigel Stillman and Nigel Tallis, *Armies of the Ancient Near East: 3000 to 539 B.C.E.* (Sussex, UK: Flexiprint, 1984), 202.

10. Xenophon, *Cyropaedia*, trans. Wayne Ambler (Ithaca, NY: Cornell University Press, 2001), .

11. Xenophon *Cyropaedia* 8.5.11–13.

12. Xen. *Cyr.* 8.5.14.

13. Dikshitar, *War in Ancient India*, 244.

14. Sarva Daman Singh, *Ancient Indian Warfare* (Delhi: Motilal Banarsidass, 1997), 151.

15. Basham, *Wonder That Was India*, 135.

16. Dikshitar, *War in Ancient India*, 244.

17. Ibid., 245.

18. Thomas D. Seymour, *Life in the Homeric Age* (New York: Biblo and Tannen, 1963), 608.

19. Ibid.

20. Donald W. Engels, *Alexander the Great and the Logistics of the Macedonian Army* (Berkeley: University of California Press, 1978), 17.

21. Livy, *The War with Hannibal* (Baltimore: Penguin Books, 1965), Bk. 30, Ch. 3.

22. Ibid., Ch. 4.

23. Peter Connolly, *Greece and Rome at War* (Englewood Cliffs, NJ: Prentice-Hall, 1981), 135–137. Connolly's description of the Roman camp most closely follows the description of Polybius.

24. Graham Webster, *The Roman Imperial Army of the First and Second Centuries* A.D., 3rd. ed. (Totowa, NJ: Barnes and Noble Books, 1985), 173.

25. Ibid. The description most closely follows Vegetius.

26. Connolly, *Greece and Rome*, 135.

27. See Gabriel, *Great Battles of Antiquity*, 449–457 for a description of the battle of Adrianople, where Fritigern, fighting from a wagon *laager*, defeated the Roman army.

Eight

✳ ✳ ✳

DISCIPLINE AND PUNISHMENT

Military service in the ancient world could quickly turn harsh, and even deadly, if the soldier ran afoul of military authorities. Like modern armies, ancient armies had codes of discipline that set out penalties for infractions of laws governing military life. These rules and regulations governed behavior that would be familiar to a modern soldier and addressed such issues as desertion, being absent without leave (AWOL), obeying one's superiors, proper care of equipment, and sleeping on guard duty. Other more serious offenses—rape, looting, murder, mutiny, and so on—were also addressed by these codes. The expected rules of behavior were the subject of official military education. In India, for example, soldiers were instructed in the proper code of military ethics and were held strictly accountable for its provisions.[1] The Hittite *Oath of the Soldier* is very specific as to what is expected of the soldier and spells out the punishments that might befall the soldier who breaks his oath.[2] The Roman army's oath of service was not as detailed as regards punishment, stressing more the soldier's obligations to public authorities, as do modern military oaths. The solemn oath sworn by the Roman soldier was called the *sacramentum*, from which the English word *sacrament* is derived.

CODES OF ANCIENT LAW

Except for tribal armies (Germans, Goths, Achaeans, Israelites, and so on), the military organizations of most ancient armies were highly structured and organizationally complex, characteristics that brought into being the need for codes of law to govern them. The degree to which an army possessed these characteristics was a reflection of the larger society from which it sprang. These societies were not lawless by any means, and all were governed by systems of law and the concomitant means to apply the law. Law in ancient societies was seen to be a gift of some deity. Since most kings were seen to be divine or the sons of the divine, royal promulgations of law were held to be of divine audience. Law was therefore seen to be gift of the gods to regulate the behavior of human beings in order to achieve certain ends. These might include showing humans how to serve the gods (Assyria), how to create a just society (Egypt), how to live a religious life (Israel), how to gain virtue (India), or how to serve the objectives of the secular state (Rome).

Ancient systems of law, then, were neither arbitrary nor capricious nor based solely on the whims of the monarch or his officials. As Egyptian, Indian, and Hittite texts clearly reveal, the purpose of law was justice.[3] Moreover, officials of the king had an obligation to enforce the law fairly and without prejudice.[4] In the Hittite king's instructions to his military governors the governor is told that "he must not decide it in favor of his superior, he must not decide it in favor of his brother, his wife, or his friend; no one shall be shown any favor. He must not make a just case unjust; he must not make an unjust case just. Whatever is right, that shall he do."[5] It was the Egyptians who gave us the first written treatises where ethics, justice, and law were morally connected and affirmed so that even the kings had moral and legal responsibilities for which they could be held accountable.[6] We find a similar idea expressed in the ancient Sumerian legend of *Gilgamesh*, where the hero must submit himself to the assembly of free men to account for his actions.[7]

The punishments for infractions of military rules might strike the modern reader as draconian, and in some cases they were indeed. Many modern armies, however, retain elements of a similar draconianism in their provisions for the death penalty for desertion, cowardice, and mutiny. In practice, however, such terrible punishments could not have been applied very frequently. Soldiers were expensive to conscript or hire and train, and it gained the army little to execute the soldier if another course could be found. Moreover, experienced combat soldiers who would fight were even more valuable. Modern studies of soldiers in battle found that only a small percentage, perhaps no more than 15–20 percent, actually fired their weapons. Most were too frightened. The number of aggressive combat soldiers willing to take the fight to the enemy is very small, perhaps under 5 percent.[8] A good fighter was too valuable a military asset to execute without very grave cause. Moreover, punishment applied in a manifestly unjust manner did little for maintaining discipline for the victim's comrades might become enraged or sullen, conditions that could lead to mutiny or, as has happened in all armies since time immemorial, even modern armies, the assassination of officers.[9] An army that was abused by its commander or officers was likely to be unreliable in that it perceived no value in taking risks and fighting bravely for its leaders.[10]

The purpose of military discipline and punishment is to insure the good order of the army as a fighting force; it is a means, not an end. It is instructive that ancient armies seem mostly to have provided for some sort of court or hearing before which the accused could present his case. Alexander the Great, for example, convened assemblies of his officers to judge cases, Egyptian pharaohs had legal officers and staffs, the Assyrians had special officers *(tartans)* to administer justice in the armies, the Romans used courts of senior centurions or tribunes to hear disciplinary cases, and Indian armies had philosopher-priests to help judge cases. The purpose of these hearings was fairness, to communicate to the troops that they would not be treated arbitrarily when charged with an offense. To treat soldiers unjustly, even as an occasional lesson in discipline to the others, was not an admirable quality of an ancient commander any more than of a modern one.

TYPES OF PUNISHMENT

That said, it is nonetheless interesting to examine the punishments that were inflicted by ancient armies on the soldier who violated military regulations. A Hittite soldier who violated his oath of service could be deafened, blinded, or slain.[11] The Code of Hammurabi (1728–1686 B.C.E.) levied a punishment of death on any soldier who was ordered on campaign and refused to go.[12] The same code imposed the death penalty on the soldier's superiors ("sergeant or captain") if they treated the soldier poorly by appropriating his household goods or forcing him into service by false contracts.[13] While a soldier was serving on active service as a conscript, none of his property or land could be sold while he was away.[14] For all the elements of harshness that attend it, Hammurabi's Code attempts to strike the same balance found in Egyptian legal codes between severe punishments for serious offenses and just treatment of the soldier in general.

Egypt

Beating seems to have been the most common punishment in the armies of Egypt. In a letter written sometime in the thirteenth century B.C.E. an Egyptian soldier wonders why he and his comrades (conscripts) are always being beaten.[15] A letter written two centuries later describes the lot of a typical conscript on arriving in the military camp: "He is brought while a child [twenty years old was the age of military service in Egypt] to be confined in the camp. A searing beating is given his body, an open wound inflicted on his eyebrows. His head is split open with a wound. He is laid down and he is beaten like papyrus."[16] This is a description of a conscript's initiation into military life, or "boot camp." Beatings of recruits were a common part of the initiation into military life in Western armies until World War I, as they were in the Soviet Army until its demise in 1988.[17] Horemheb, a professional soldier who became pharaoh (1323–1295 B.C.E.), punished a soldier who was stealing hides from the local population by "beating him a hundred blows, opening five wounds, and taking from him by force the hides which he took."[18] The "opening of wounds" probably refers to cutting of the skin so that the soldier would suffer additional pain for some time after the beating. In order to keep soldiers from stealing from the royal estates, Seti I (1294–1279 B.C.E.) ordered that anyone caught would have his ears cut off; anyone working on the estate caught stealing would be impaled on a stake.[19] Ramses II was furious at the chariot commanders who had abandoned him during the battle of Kadesh, almost costing him his life. He ordered the cowardly officers brought before him and personally beheaded them in full view of the assembled army.[20]

India

The armies of India largely comprised members of a single caste whose purpose in life was to fight just wars as part of a moral life. All officers were instructed in the ethics of war and the proper conduct of a soldier. India seems to have been the first country to develop such an ethic to regulate the conduct of soldiers in wartime.[21] Like the *bushi* or samurai of much later Japan, observing the code of war was an integral part of the soldier's life. And like the samurai, shame was more feared than death. A defeated Indian general was not usually subjected to physical punishment. Instead, "he has to exchange his soldier's dress for that of a woman, much to his shame and chagrin. Mostly those men put themselves to death to avoid such disgrace."[22] The laws of warfare in India called for punishments ranging from social ostracism to death. A soldier who deserted his comrades in battle "should be done to death with sticks or stones. Or he might be rolled in a mat of dry grass and burnt to death."[23]

Persia

Xenophon served as a mercenary soldier in the army of the Persian king, Cyrus the Great, and described the punishments employed by both Persian and Greek commanders in their armies. Xenophon himself once ordered a man to be beaten who had refused to carry his wounded comrade and had attempted to bury him alive to avoid having to do so. What is interesting is that the man was given a hearing and permitted to offer a defense. Xenophon remarked that perhaps a harsher punishment might be warranted but that the army could not afford to lose a soldier given the circumstances in which it found itself.[24] Xenophon's description of Clearchus offers us a different view of a Greek field commander: "Clearchus was a man to be obeyed. He achieved this result by his toughness. His punishments were severe ones and were sometimes inflicted in anger.... With him punishment was a matter of principle, for he thought that an army without it was good for nothing; indeed, it is reported that he said that a soldier ought to be more frightened of his own commander than of the enemy...."[25] Frederick the Great of Germany was said to have subscribed to the same dictum.

Xenophon tells us that Cyrus himself was a strict disciplinarian and that "his punishments were exceptionally severe."[26] Cyrus's punishments included blinding, amputation of hands and feet, and beheading as the ultimate penalty.[27] Xenophon says that ultimately, however, Cyrus was a fair judge and often granted the accused a fair hearing, in one case assembling his officers to seek a verdict regarding charges of treason against one of his officers.[28]

Alexander the Great and Macedonia

The system of military law and punishment in the army of Alexander the Great lacked any written codification that applied equally to all. Instead, the customs and traditions that regulated the behavior of the Macedonian tribal society continued unchanged in the imperial armies, including the unrestricted prerogative of the king to inflict harsh penalties for minor offenses. Alexander once had one of his officers flogged because he speared a wild boar that Alexander himself wanted to hunt.[29] The traditional Macedonian method of execution, stoning, was employed by Alexander, as were torture by fire and hanging.[30] In many cases, however, Alexander provided the accused with a hearing by an assembly of officers, also a Macedonian tradition. In one case Alexander suspended the rule that the accused's male family members also be subject to the same penalty as the accused if he was found guilty. When Cleander and his men had been found guilty by the officers' assembly on charges of committing atrocities, Alexander sentenced them to death along with 600 of Cleander's troops responsible for carrying out his barbarous orders[31] in what may have been a case of finding that soldiers have a responsibility not to execute illegal orders. The unwritten tribal law based in custom and tradition carried out by the tribal chief that characterized Alexander's system of military discipline and punishment was Homeric in content and practice and was the same system found among the Achaean Greeks as portrayed in the *Iliad* 1,000 years earlier.[32]

In Achaean times, written formal laws did not exist, justice and infractions being defined only by custom, tradition, and precedent. Most crimes and misdemeanors were private matters and not offenses against the state, calling for resolution by private quarrels and combats. Even murder was not, strictly speaking, a public crime; it was a private wrong against the murdered man, his family, and his clan or tribe. The murderer might withdraw from his land only to escape vengeance, not to escape legal prosecution. Similar legal systems exist today in Iraq and Afghanistan.

Other Greek City-States

The tribal nature of the Macedonian system of military punishment did not extend to the other Greek city-states. During the Classical period (500–350 B.C.E.) Greek city-states, with their hoplite citizen militia armies, used a much different system. The civilian system of justice that guaranteed the accused a hearing before an assembly of citizens, the presentation of evidence, and a secret ballot to determine guilt or innocence was the same as that used by the military. As a practical matter, Greek soldiers were drawn from the politically enfranchised classes and fought short wars led by elected commanders, conditions that made a separate and different system of justice for Greek citizen-armies unnecessary and unlikely.

Rome

Rome also valued its civilian traditions of law and legal institutions and found them too valuable to abandon, even when the citizen-armies of the Roman Republic were replaced by the armies of the imperium, armies mostly filled by non-Romans. Soldiers charged with crimes were entitled to a hearing to defend themselves against the charge. Minor offenses were usually heard by a board of centurions of the accused's maniple or cohort.[33] More serious charges were heard by senior officers or tribunes, elected officers, part of whose responsibility was to look after the welfare of the troops.[34] Punishments in the Roman army included fines, extra work details, confinement to camp, being forced to eat barley instead of wheat for rations, and forced to bivouac beyond the protective walls of the camp. After their defeat at Cannae the legions who fought poorly there were forced to camp outside the walls and eat barley rations for a full year.[35]

The most feared Roman military punishment was the *fustuarium*. Reserved for the most serious offenses, a soldier found guilty by court martial was led before his comrades and touched with a cudgel by a centurion, at which point his comrades commenced to beat the guilty man to death. Among the more serious offenses for which the *fustuarium* was applied were sleeping on guard duty (and thus endangering the entire camp), stealing from one's comrades, bearing false witness, attempting to avoid combat by self-inflicted wounds (a serious problem later in the empire), and being convicted of the same offense three times.[36] Desertion was a particularly serious crime punishable by death. The Romans never stopped trying to apprehend deserters so that whenever Rome signed a treaty with anyone, it always contained a provision that any Roman deserters be returned to Roman authorities. The *fustuarium* was also used to punish soldiers who acted cowardly in battle. When an entire unit of soldiers performed in a cowardly manner, they were subject to decimation. The tribunes assembled the legion and led forward those guilty of leaving the ranks. The accused were lined up, and 10 percent of the unit was selected at random to be stoned or beaten to death. The rest, like the survivors at Cannae, were forced to eat barley instead of wheat and required to pitch their tents outside the protective walls of the legion encampment.[37]

As harsh as Roman punishments for military infractions could be, they were applied uniformly, mostly justly, and with a strict regard for legal procedure, including the rights of the accused to a hearing and evidence. Rome, after all, gave the West its system of civil law; that it would have an appropriate regard for military law is not surprising. Whenever an army was in the field, however, these procedures could be exercised quickly and punishment meted out immediately. To bring an end to a mutiny in his army in Spain, Scipio had the mutineers arrested, tried, and executed all in a single day. The condemned were brought naked before the troops, bound to stakes, scourged, and beheaded.[38] By way of a harsher comparison, Carthaginian officers who performed poorly in battle were crucified in front of their troops; senior officers were executed in this manner in Carthage's public square.

NOTES

1. Sarva Daman Singh, "Ethics of War," in *Ancient Indian Warfare* (Delhi: Motilal Banarsidass, 1997), chap. 8; see also V. R. Ramachandra Dikshitar, "The Laws of War," in *War in Ancient India* (Delhi: Motilal Banarsidass, 1987), chap. 2.

2. James B. Pritchard, "The Soldier's Oath," in *Ancient Near Eastern Texts Relating to the Old Testament*, trans. W. F. Albright (Princeton, NJ: Princeton University Press, 1955), 353–354.

3. Pritchard, "The Hittite Laws," *Ancient Near Eastern Texts*, 186–196; see also Singh, *Ancient Indian Warfare*, and Dikshitar, *War in Ancient India*, as noted above. For an examination of Egyptian law, see Richard A. Gabriel, "The Dawn of Conscience," in *Gods of Our Fathers: The Memory of Egypt in Judaism and Christianity* (Westport, CT: Greenwood Press, 2002), chap. 1.

4. Gabriel, *Gods of Our Fathers*.

5. Pritchard, "Instructions for the Commander of the Border Guards," *Ancient Near Eastern Texts*, 211.

6. Gabriel, *Gods of Our Fathers*, 11.

7. Pritchard, "Sumerian Myths and Epic Tales," *Ancient Near Eastern Texts*, 37–50.

8. Dave Grossman, *On Killing: The Psychological Cost of Learning to Kill in War and Society* (Boston: Little, Brown, 1995), 50.

9. See Richard A. Gabriel and Paul L. Savage, *Crisis in Command: Mismanagement in the Army* (New York: Hill and Wang, 1978), 43–46 for an analysis of the "fragging" of officers during the Vietnam war.

10. Grossman, *On Killing*, 50.

11. Pritchard, "The Soldier's Oath," 354.

12. Pritchard, "The Code of Hammurabi," *Ancient Near Eastern Texts*, 176.

13. Ibid.

14. Ibid.

15. Pritchard, *Ancient Near Eastern Texts*, 476.

16. "A Soldier's Lot," in *The Literature of Ancient Egypt: An Anthology of Stories, Instructions, and Poetry*, ed. William Kelly Simpson (New Haven, CT: Yale University Press, 1972), 216–217.

17. See Richard A. Gabriel, "Morale and Discipline," in *The Antagonists: A Comparative Combat Assessment of the Soviet and American Soldier* (Westport, CT: Greenwood Press, 1984), chap. 5 for an analysis of the torment often suffered by new conscripts in the Soviet Army.

18. "Horemheb Delivers the Poor from Oppression, 1315 B.C.E.," in *Ancient Egypt*, ed. Jon E. Lewis (New York: Carroll and Graf, 2003), 165.

19. Ibid., 167.

20. Richard A. Gabriel and Donald W. Boose, Jr., *The Great Battles of Antiquity: A Strategic and Tactical Guide to Great Battles That Shaped the Development of War* (Westport, CT: Greenwood Press, 1994), 82. For an excellent analysis of law, crime, and punishment in ancient Egypt, see Joyce A. Tyldesley, *Judgement of the Pharaoh: Crime and Punishment in Ancient Egypt* (New York: Peartree, 2002).

21. Singh, "Ethics of War."

22. Dikshitar, *War in Ancient India*, 79.

23. Ibid.

24. Xenophon, *The Persian Expedition*, trans. Rex Warner (Baltimore: Penguin Books, 1972), 256–258.

25. Ibid., 131.

26. Ibid., 92.

27. Ibid.

28. Ibid., 81.

29. Quintus Curtius Rufus, *The History of Alexander* (New York: Penguin Books, 1984), 190.

30. Ibid., 142.

31. Ibid., 238.

32. See Thomas D. Seymour, *Life in the Homeric Age* (New York: Biblo and Tannen, 1963), 87–93 for an examination of law and punishment in the Homeric age.

33. Peter Connolly, *Greece and Rome at War* (Englewood Cliffs, NJ: Prentice-Hall, 1981), 139.

34. Ibid.

35. Ibid., 140.

36. Ibid., 139.

37. Ibid., 140.

38. Livy, *The War with Hannibal* (Baltimore: Penguin Books, 1965), 28, 30:29.

Nine

WEAPONS

As humans entered the Bronze Age, they kept with them a number of weapons from the previous Neolithic period. Among these were the bow and arrow, mace, spear, dagger, sword, and sling. These weapons constituted the main armament of the early armies of the Bronze Age. The invention of bronze metal manufacture did little to add to the killing power of Neolithic weapons. The dagger, for example, could now be cast of bronze and lengthened to make the first sword, but neither the dagger nor the sword played a significant role in Bronze Age warfare, taking their place behind the spear and the axe. Bronze spear points could now be cast with sockets and affixed more securely than the old obsidian spear points, but this provided no significant advantage in combat. Metal technology had no effect at all on the construction and manufacture of the bow, and although the bronze arrowhead had greater penetrating power than the ebony, obsidian, or fire-hardened wooden point, the arrow's effectiveness in war depended more on the nature of the target (armored or unarmored) than the arrowhead itself.

EARLIEST WEAPONS

Metal technology did permit the introduction of two important new weapons, the socket axe and the sickle sword, the effectiveness of which depended directly on the ability to cast metal into required shapes. Neither weapon, however, really revolutionized Bronze Age warfare. Indeed, the most important and revolutionary weapons of the period, the composite bow and the chariot, were manufactured of wood and did not depend on metal technology at all. For almost 1,500 years after the invention of metal technology, there is no compelling evidence that armies utilized any metal weapons in the conduct of war, no doubt because the armies of the period (4000–2500 B.C.E.) found the weapons of the Neolithic period quite sufficient as killing instruments.[1]

The earliest archaeological representation of war, the Tablet of Narmer,[2] dates to 3100 B.C.E. and shows that the Egyptians used the simple bow, mace, ebony-tipped arrow, and obsidian spear point almost 1,000 years after the Bronze Age and metal technology had begun. Egypt's armies continued to use these same weapons until the seventeenth century B.C.E., when the Hyksos invasion forced the introduction of new ones, some of them manufactured of bronze.[3] Until this time, only the simple cutting axe with a bronze blade represented a new weapon dependent on metal technology, and it was not significantly more effective, if at all, than the old stone or obsidian axe.

The Bronze Age is normally dated from 4000 to 1200 B.C.E., at which date the Iron Age is held to have begun. The first evidence of metal technology appeared around 4000 B.C.E. in Anatolia and Mesopotamia, when the technique of combining melted copper with 10–12 percent tin to make bronze was invented. It is likely, though not certain, that bronze manufacture may have begun even earlier in India.[4] It took about 1,000 years for bronze manufacture in Mesopotamia to spread to the rest of the Middle East, where by 2600 B.C.E., it became common throughout the area. The impact of the new technology on warfare varied widely, however, its military use being dictated by factors other than the technology itself. In Mesopotamia, where warfare between rival city-states was endemic, metal weapons assumed an immediate importance. The constant warfare in the region accelerated the rate of weapon development and accounted for a large number of weapon innovations introduced by the Mesopotamian states of this period. Elsewhere, in Egypt, for instance, metal technology had only a marginal impact on war, and the rate of weapon innovation was slow. The point is that metal technology per se did not compel the development of new weapons any more than the invention of lasers in the modern age compelled their use as weapons. The use to which any technology is put is the result of human choice as it is influenced by larger social, economic, and political forces, not by the technology itself.

Another reason why the introduction of metal technology did not produce a weapon explosion was the cost of manufacture. While copper was relatively available and cheap, the tin required to make bronze was scarce and expensive. Most tin in the Near East was found in the form of alluvial placers produced by the large rivers.[5] Because Egypt and Mesopotamia were located on large rivers, both were able to exploit their tin deposits to manufacture bronze weapons on a large scale. Most other states could not. The Hittites were able to obtain tin from Bohemia, while India obtained its tin from Afghanistan. Later, Phoenician traders even exploited tin deposits on the Cornish coast of England. But the supply of tin was never adequate for large-scale weapon production, and the cost of manufacture was high, while the skills required were not common. All these factors remained major limitations on the size of the armies that could be economically equipped by the states of the Near East until the end of the period.

Early Metal Technology

The Iron Age marked the first true revolution in metal weapon technology. The discovery of iron manufacture is often attributed to the Hittites sometime around 1300 B.C.E., when the Hittite king Huttusilis III sent an iron dagger as a gift to the king of Assyria.[6] The actual invention of the process of producing iron blooms to obtain raw iron which could then be hammered into shape is attributed to a tribe living in Kizawadana in the Armenian mountains, who may have passed the secret to the Mitanni.[7] There is, however, substantial evidence that iron making may have occurred in central India in the fourteen century B.C.E.[8] Of greater importance is that the Indians seem to have made iron *weapons* in the form of double-edged daggers, socketed axe heads, flat axes, spearheads, and arrowheads at this early date.[9] Whenever iron was first manufactured in the Near East, it was not widely used for weapons until around 900 B.C.E., bronze remaining the preferred metal for weapons because it was much easier to melt and cast.[10] It was not until the time of Sargon II of Assyria (721–705 B.C.E.) that we encounter an army that was mostly equipped with iron rather than with bronze weapons.[11]

It is important to understand that the military advantage of iron did not lie in its physical properties. Iron weapons are much more difficult to manufacture, requiring repeated heating and hammering to fashion the required shape. Iron cannot be easily cast into shape or sockets, resurrecting the age-old problem of how to securely affix points to arrows, spears, and swords that had plagued early Bronze Age weapons makers. Iron does hold an edge somewhat better than bronze, but iron rusts, where bronze does not, both dulling the edge and weakening the weapon's strength. This is why far more bronze than iron weapons have survived the ages. The importance of iron to ancient warfare lies in the fact that while tin was rare and expensive, iron was commonly available almost everywhere. The plentiful supply of iron made it possible to produce large amounts of cheap, reliable weapons. No longer was it only the larger and richer states that could afford enough weapons to equip a significant military force; now almost anyone could. The result was a dramatic increase in the number of weapons, the size of armies, and the scale of warfare.

Weapons fashioned of steel began to make their way into Europe and the Near East sometime around 300 B.C.E. Steel involves the use of higher melting temperatures, now made possible by the introduction of the funnel bellows to rush forced air over the heated ore, drawing off more carbon from the melted metal. This process—the Wootz process—appears to have originated in India sometime around the fifth or sixth century B.C.E.[12] and may have made its way to the Near East and West as a consequence of Alexander's campaigns having increased commercial contacts with India. Curtius tells us that Alexander was given 100 talents of Indian steel as a gift.[13] By the time of the Second Punic War, the armies of Rome and Carthage were both equipped with steel weapons, and steel has remained the metal of choice for weapons of war ever since.[14]

TYPES OF WEAPONS

The Mace

The oldest known weapon for which we have archaeological evidence is the mace. Originating in the Neolithic period as an improvement on the simple club, the mace remained the most commonly used close-range battlefield weapon in antiquity from 4000 to 2500 B.C.E. The mace was so important a weapon in ancient Egypt that it became the very symbol of pharaonic authority. The Palette of Narmer (3100 B.C.E.) depicts the pharaoh striking his enemies with the mace. The mace remained the primary battlefield weapon in Egypt until the Hyksos invasions of the seventeenth century B.C.E. Mace heads were fashioned of solid copper and bronze, but the most common type used a stone head with a hollow cut in the base into which the handle could be inserted. The head was further secured by leather wrappings. The mace disappeared from the battlefields of Sumer around 2500 B.C.E., when the Sumerians invented the helmet. Constructed of two millimeters of copper worn over four millimeters of leather cap underneath, the Sumerian helmet was sufficient to neutralize the mace as a killing weapon. To fracture the skull under a helmet of this sort requires a force of 810 foot-pounds. A mace weighing 1.8 pounds can only be swung at a speed of sixty feet per second by a human arm to generate 101 foot-pounds of energy on impact, quite insufficient to fracture the protected skull or to render the soldier unconscious.[15] The Egyptians continued to fight without the helmet for almost another millennium, with the result that Egyptian military physicians became expert on treating head fractures.[16]

The Spear

The spear had its origins in the pre-Neolithic age as a weapon of the hunt. By Neolithic times the fire-hardened wooden tip had been replaced by the bone or obsidian point. The appearance of the bronze spear point added little to the killing power of the spear. For more than 1,500 years, and even longer in Egypt, bronze spear points were affixed to the shaft by inserting the blade spine, sometimes with a bent tang at its base, into a split in the shaft and affixing the blade with leather lashings. This arrangement actually reduced the penetrating power of the spear insofar as its impact routinely drove the spear blade back into the shaft, dissipating energy and causing the shaft of the spear to split. It was not until the introduction of the cast, socketed spear blade that could be affixed to the shaft with rivets that the spear became a reliable combat weapon. While the timing is uncertain, it is likely that the socketed spear blade made its first appearance in Sumer/Akkad sometime around 2250 B.C.E. Similar spear blades are found in pre-Aryan India (pre-1700 B.C.E.) in the highly developed Indus Valley culture.

The spear quickly became the primary weapon of ancient armies and remained so until sometime around 300 B.C.E., when the legions of Republican Rome adopted the steel sword (*gladius*) and became the first army in antiquity to use the sword as its primary weapon. The dominance of the spear for more than 2,000 years shaped the tactical deployment of ancient armies more than any other weapon. If men were to fight effectively, they had to fight in groups. If soldiers armed with the spear were to fight effectively in groups, they had to arrange themselves in close-order formation, thereby giving rise to the infantry phalanx. The first recorded instance of a phalanx of spearmen appeared in Sumer in 2500 B.C.E.[17] Paradoxically, it was the unwieldy nature of the spear in meeting an attack from any direction than the front that required soldiers to fight in closely packed formations if they were to protect themselves from assault from the flanks. Thus the spear produced the phalanx, which remained the basic infantry formation in all armies of antiquity for more than two millennia.

The spear came in all lengths, depending on its tactical function. The short spear, or javelin, was meant to be thrown and found wide use among Alexandrian, Persian, and Roman cavalry. Indian, Chinese, and Assyrian cavalrymen used both the javelin and the lance, a long spear used for stabbing. Infantry spears were sometimes very long. The Macedonian *sarissa* was thirteen feet long and had to be wielded with two hands. It was designed to be used in packed phalanx, with the phalanx itself used not so much as an attack formation, but as a "hedgehog" to deny the enemy important space on the battlefield while the cavalry acted as the arm of decision. In this role the phalanx became a platform for maneuver of the cavalry.

The Roman legions carried the *pilum*, a short, weighted spear with a thin, pointed, metal rod extending from a wooden shaft. The *pilum* was hurled just before the sword-wielding legionnaires closed with the enemy. While some *pilae* no doubt found their mark in enemy bodies, their primary purpose was to render the enemy unable to use his shield effectively. When the *pilum* struck the enemy shield, its metal rod bent, making it impossible to remove the spear from the shield and making the shield very difficult to use against the Roman sword attack. Greek hoplite infantry, although fighting in phalanx, used short, seven-foot spears *(dory)* for stabbing at close range. Homeric, Indian, and Mycenaean wars were often characterized by individual combats between individual spear-bearing warriors rather than group fighting.[18] Achaean warriors seemed to have carried one long spear and one shorter one. The latter was initially thrown at one's opponent. If it missed, the combat continued with the long spears.[19] India and China seemed to have developed a wide variety of spear points.

Axes

Among the most effective close-order weapons in ancient armies was the axe, and its evolution over 1,500 years of warfare offers an excellent example of the search for a new weapon to deal with the advances in body and head armor. The availability of bronze blades potentially increased the penetrating power over the old stone or copper axe blades. However, the problem of how to affix the blade to the shaft remained. The usual solution was to split the shaft and secure the blade with rivets and lashings. This produced an unreliable weapon, one prone to having its blade fly off in mid-stroke or coming loose on impact. Once again, it was the Mesopotamians who solved the problem by introducing the bronze-cast socket and blade in one piece, the socket axe. A socket axe first appears on the Stele of Vultures, and early Sumerian kings are portrayed holding the new weapon.[20] The Egyptians did not adopt the socket axe until its introduction by the Hyksos in the seventeenth century B.C.E. The socket axe appeared in India around 1400 B.C.E.[21] The old axes worked well against troops without armor, but by the dawn of the second millennium, effective body armor was becoming standard equipment among most armies of world, Egypt and India being exceptions.

The evolution of the axe tended toward making the blade narrower in order to concentrate energy on impact in the smallest possible area to improve the penetrating power of the blow. Both the size and shape of the older types of axe blades worked to distribute the force of the blow over too wide an area, thus reducing the power of the blade to penetrate. The Sumerians hit on the solution of making the axe slightly heavier and narrowing the blade so as to reduce the impact area to less than one-half inch and the wound area to one and three-quarters inches.[22] The results were dramatic. The new axe could generate 77.5 foot-pounds of impact energy against existing body armor that required only 66 foot-pounds to penetrate.[23] The result was the socketed penetrating axe, one of the most devastating close-combat weapons of the Bronze and Iron ages. For 2,000 years it remained the only close-combat weapon that could defeat protective body armor, and it conveyed a prodigious advantage on the armies that possessed it. It seems to have dawned on the weapon designers of both the Chinese and Indian armies to combine the axe and the spear into a single weapon that could both hack and slash, the forerunner of the halberd made famous by the Swiss infantry armies of the sixteenth century C.E.

Swords

Among the more interesting short-range weapons of the ancient soldier was the sickle sword. Invented by the Sumerians around 2500 B.C.E., this weapon originally derived from the axe and not the dagger.[24] The length of the weapon as portrayed on the Stele of Vultures is relatively short, suggesting that its most primitive origins may have been the common agricultural sickle used to harvest grain. By the dawn of the third millennium (3000 B.C.E.), metal technology made it possible to produce long sword blades; the problem of affixing them securely to the handle remained for another 1,000 years. In Sumer the sickle sword quickly gave way to the more effective penetrating socket axe, while in Egypt it remained a major weapon until the dawn of the Iron Age. The Egyptian sickle sword became longer and heavier over time, and for 1,000 years the Egyptians used the sickle sword effectively against unarmored enemies. It superseded the mace as the symbol of pharaonic authority. The sickle sword became a basic weapon for all the armies of the Near East, including the Israelites and Canaanites. It was not, however, a weapon of the armies of the Far East and was not used by the Philistines, Mycenaeans, Achaeans, or Romans. When the Bible speaks of someone being "smoted by the edge of the sword," the reference is to the sickle sword.

The sword was never a major weapon of most ancient armies until the second century B.C.E., when the *gladius* became the standard weapon of the Roman legions. The problem of affixing the blade securely to the handle, the success of the penetrating axe, and the preeminence of the spear utilized in packed formations of combatants all worked against the development of the sword. Dense formations were not well suited to swordplay in that they afforded little room for the individual infantryman to maneuver. All ancient armies after the seventeenth century B.C.E. carried the sword, but in none was it a major infantry weapon; rather, it was used when the soldiers' primary weapons (axe and spear) were lost or broken or when combat formations broke down in the swirling general melee of combat, forcing the soldier to use the sword as a last resort. For the sword to emerge as a major infantry weapon required a change in battle formations from the densely packed phalanx to a looser formation with built-in spaces between men to allow the soldier adequate room to wield his sword against individual targets. But the looser formation required a higher degree of training and

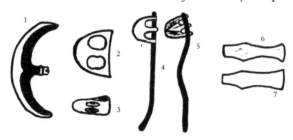

Various types of battle axes used in ancient armies: (1) epsilon axe, (2) eye axe, (3) duckbill axe, (4) tang axe, (5) socket axe, and (6, 7) two types of lugged axe heads. Courtesy of Richard Gabriel.

discipline than most ancient armies were capable of producing. The Roman army produced the first open infantry formations in the ancient armies, the famous maniple formation arranged in checkerboard (quincunx) fashion. With the change in tactics Rome abandoned the spear and produced the first soldier in history whose primary weapon was the sword.

The *gladius* was introduced to the Roman army as a result of its experience in Spain during the Second Punic War. Rome had encountered Hannibal's excellent Spanish infantry armed with the *gladius hispaniensis*, or Spanish sword. Although its origins are Spanish, by the first century B.C.E. the *gladius* had

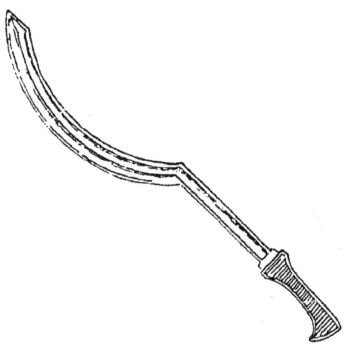

The sickle sword. Courtesy of Richard Gabriel.

undergone enough changes at Roman hands to make it an entirely new weapon.[25] It was forged from high-grade steel, which made it highly reliable in combat. The problem of affixing the blade to the handle had also been solved, further increasing reliability. The *gladius* was slightly less than two feet long, with a blade three inches wide rising to a slight spine in the middle and weighing just under two pounds. The weapon was meant to be a stabbing weapon, not a chopping one, and Roman soldiers were trained again and again to stab and not chop. Stabbing, of course, permits the soldier to strike while keeping his body mostly covered with his shield. Raising the arm to chop exposes the soldier's body to a far greater degree. In the hands of the highly trained Roman legionnaire this weapon became the most deadly of all weapons produced by ancient armies, and it killed more soldiers than any other weapon in history until the invention of the firearm.[26]

Of interest is the sword used by the Sherden, one of the Sea Peoples that attacked Egypt in the eleventh century B.C.E., only to be defeated and settled in Palestine, where they became known to history as the Philistines. The Sherden, however, entered Egyptian military service as elite guards to Pharaoh. One reason for their military value may have been their use of the long, straight sword. The sword was thirty-eight inches long and very narrow, its raised spine blade ending in a very sharp, needle-like point. The sword's design suggests that it was used for a very specific purpose, which appears to have been killing charioteers in close combat. The sword's length gave the Sherden warrior superior "reach" to get at his target while on foot and below the enemy charioteer. The sharp point could easily penetrate leather, lamellar, and, perhaps, even thin (two millimeters) bronze scale armor. Striking from below, the needle-like point could find a seam or slide under the overlapping scales of the charioteer's armor coat.

Used as "chariot runners," supporting infantry surrounding Pharaoh in a chariot fight, the Sherden served as an elite battle guard, using their long swords to strike down any charioteer who tried to attack the king.[27]

Bows

The primary long-range weapons of the ancient armies were the bow and the sling. The bow was probably at least 6,000–10,000 years old by the dawn of the Bronze Age, and it may well have been man's first attempt at constructing a composite tool. The bow underwent three stages of development beginning with the simple bow, followed by the compound bow, and culminating in the composite bow. The bow remained a primary instrument of war among most armies of the world of antiquity. Exceptions were Western armies, most notably the Achaeans, Greeks, and Romans. Both Greece and Rome, of course, had knowledge of the bow but did not grant it a large role in battle.[28] The armies of Troy and the Minoans in Crete possessed the composite bow and seemed to have used it extensively.[29] The composite bow was the primary weapon of the Indian noble warrior. In China the emphasis on large formations of spear and sword infantry reduced the bow to a minor role. Its resurrection in the form of the crossbow around 500 B.C.E. increased its importance to Chinese armies, but only because the crossbowman could maneuver far better than the bowman and could fight as an individual instead of in a group. The bow played a large role among the Persians, whose archers were famous for their range and accuracy. As a weapon of war, the range, rate of fire, and penetrating power of the composite bow easily outperformed the rifle at least until Napoleonic times and, perhaps, even later.

The simple bow was constructed of a single piece of wood powered with a gut or leather bowstring. It produces most of its power when the bowstring is drawn back away from the ends of the bow. As the bow is drawn, however, the ends move farther and farther away from the center, a movement that weakens its power. A simple bow of the fourth millennium required thirty or forty pounds to draw to full length and could fire an arrow between 100 and 150 yards that would easily penetrate an unprotected body. Evidence from an Egyptian graveyard of 2000 B.C.E. revealed the remains of soldiers shot through the skull with ebony-tipped arrows fired by the simple bow.[30]

Ancient armorers attempted to increase the killing power of the bow by varying its shape. The double convex bow appeared in Egypt around the middle of the third millennium. Constructed of a single piece of wood, the double convex bow was shaped like cupid's upper lip, an arrangement that brought the ends of the bow closer to the center to increase its pull weight. The compound bow was a significant improvement in bow design. It was constructed of two pieces of wood glued or bound with hide at the center. The bow could be shaped like a double concave bow or like a triangle. The compound bow increased the pull weight of the weapon by 10 percent.[31]

The decisive evolution of the bow came in its composite form. The first evidence of the composite bow appears on the victory stele of Naram Sin (2254–2218 B.C.E.), the grandson of Sargon I of Akkad. Yigael Yadin notes that the bow on the stele shows the two distinct marks of the composite bow: (1) it is about ninety centimeters in length, much shorter than the simple or compound bow, and (2) its arms recurve toward and then away from its center.[32] The composite bow was constructed of wood, horn, and the tendons of oxen, all carefully laminated together. The laminated layers gave the bow greater strength and recoil power, and its recurved shape positioned the ends of the bow as close to its center as possible when at full extension.

The composite bow was a mixed military blessing. It could easily outrange the simple and compound bows and deliver long-range fire against the enemy, but unless the target was unarmored or unprotected by a shield, the composite bow could usually not penetrate the armor of the day. The composite bow produced greater power from a shorter draw, a characteristic that made the horse archer possible, but this power was partially offset by the great strength needed to draw the bow. It was the usual practice in the West to draw the bow to the breast, while in the East, among the Persians and the Indians, the technique was to draw the bowstring fully to the ear.[33] The composite bow was smaller and could be more easily carried, but it was a very difficult and expensive weapon to manufacture with any consistency, requiring, in Egypt at any rate, at least nine months to manufacture. Its composition made the weapon very susceptible to moisture and humidity, which rendered it useless. Egyptian tombs show portrayals of bowmen carrying their fragile bows in what look like violin cases.[34] While the simple bow could be put to military use with little selection or training of archers, the composite bow required that archers be selected for strength. Even then, it required a long time to train the archer in the use of the weapon. Strength and endurance were important for the archer of the composite bow. Modern archery experts note that fatigue is a great factor affecting range and accuracy. After ten to twelve arrows fired at maximum pull, even a professional archer can no longer perform well.[35]

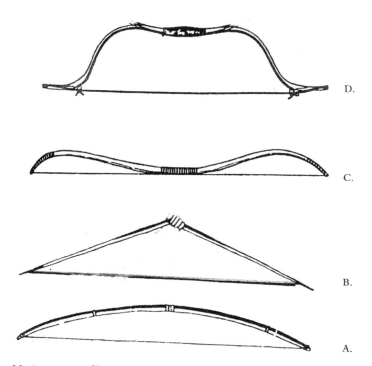

Various types of bows used in ancient armies: (A) simple curved bow, (B) triangle bow, (C) double convex bow, and (D) composite bow. Courtesy of Richard Gabriel.

It is likely that Sargon I of Akkad introduced the composite bow to Mesopotamian warfare. Advances in armor probably had rendered the old, simple bow ineffective, touching off the search for a more powerful weapon, the composite bow. Once introduced, archer formations would have been quickly equipped with it. Sargon's reign of fifty years would have provided sufficient time for these developments so that by the time of Naram Sin the composite bow had become important enough to be portrayed as a weapon of the king. Within 500 years the weapon had spread to most other armies of the period. India developed the weapon independently, and in China it may have been adopted from the barbarian tribes. It was probably the Hyksos invaders who introduced the composite bow to Egypt, where it had appeared among the Mitanni and Canaanites a century earlier. Arming the charioteer with the new weapon served to combine its lethality with increased battlefield mobility. It was the Assyrians who first took advantage of the weapon's small size and powerful snap-draw by putting it in the hands of a mounted horseman, giving birth to the new combat arm of archer cavalry. Persian armies were quick to adopt this innovation so that large units of cavalry were armed with the composite bow. Greek hoplite armies usually had no archer units, although there is evidence of a unit of Scythian archers armed with the composite bow during the Peloponnesian Wars.

The most common use of the bow in ancient armies was as a weapon of indirect fire in support of infantry on the battlefield or in siege operations. It could also be used by charioteers in chariot-to-chariot engagements (aimed fire) or when pursuing shattered infantry forces to their deaths. Usually, however, large groups of archers were positioned behind the main bodies of contesting armies and fired in salvo to rain down a hail of arrows on the enemy. Archers were not placed at the flanks, a position that would have made them vulnerable to attack by cavalry, chariots, or light infantry. Placing archers in front of the main army as a screen would have made them vulnerable to massed fire from the archers behind the enemy army. The need to use both hands to operate the bow also meant that the shield could not be used for protection. It was common to have either a large shield standing on the ground from behind which the archer fired or to have another soldier, a shield bearer, with him, using the shield to protect the archer.

How effective was archery fire? A composite bow can fire a 553-grain arrow 250 yards at a thirty to thirty-five degree angle in about 5.8 seconds into a crosswind of less than eight miles an hour. At that range an experienced archer can place almost 100 percent of his arrows within a fifty by twenty yard target box. At 300 yards, however, accuracy drops off to where only 50 percent of the arrows fall within the target box. As the target moves closer (as the infantry phalanx closes) from 200 to 100 yards, accuracy remains at about 50 percent. The angle of the plunging arrow, however, is severely acute, almost vertical, so that the number of hits on enemy soldiers drops off drastically.[36] Still, these rates of accuracy were much higher than those for the muzzle-loading musket of the eighteenth century. Field tests of these muskets conducted by the armies of the time showed that, on average, of 200 rounds fired at a fifty-foot wooden square from 250 yards, only 16 percent would hit anywhere in the target area. Of these, only 1.5 percent of the rounds could be relied on to actually hit a soldier.[37] Compared with archery fire in ancient armies, the rifle fire of eighteenth-century armies was largely ineffective.

Slings

Next to the spear and bow, the sling ranks among the oldest weapons used by ancient armies, probably appearing sometime in the seventh millennium B.C.E.[38] The sling could hurl a variety of lead and clay shot varying in weight from one to ten ounces and in size from a small plumb to a tennis ball.[39] Heavier shot could be lobbed into enemy formations at distances up to 200 yards; smaller shot could be fired along an almost flat trajectory like a bullet at ranges up to seventy-five yards. Short-range shot was often made of lead and cast in the shape of a plumb to increase its penetrating capability. Xenophon noted that this shot inflicted terrible wounds, and the wide head and tapered tail allowed the tissue of the wound to close behind the missile, making extraction from the body very difficult. Vegetius tells us that the Roman standard for certifying a slinger as combat qualified was his ability to hit a man-sized target at 600 feet, a feat Vegetius suggests could be accomplished with regularity.[40] The sling required a high degree of training and experience to hit any target at any range, a fact that encouraged ancient armies to hire professional slingers as auxiliaries rather than try to develop their own. As a combat weapon, however, the sling was far less effective than Vegetius, Xenophon, and the story of David and Goliath would suggest. Besides the high degree of training required to use slingers effectively, slinger units had to be deployed in mass, which increased their own vulnerability to sling and archery counterfire. Moreover, slinger units had no defensive weapons with which to protect themselves from close attack by chariots, infantry, or cavalry. Finally, slinger units were usually much smaller in relation to the other combat arms deployed on the battlefield and were never decisive as to the battle's outcome. Most often, slingers were used at the beginning of the battle to lob shot into packed infantry formations and then retired from the field to await the outcome of the battle.

NOTES

1. Richard A. Gabriel and Karen S. Metz, *From Sumer to Rome: The Military Capabilities of Ancient Armies* (Westport, CT: Greenwood Press, 1991), 48.

2. Yigael Yadin, *The Art of Warfare in Biblical Lands in the Light of Archaeological Study*, vol. 1, trans. M. Pearlman (New York: McGraw-Hill, 1963), 123–127.

3. Richard A. Gabriel, "Egypt," in *Empires at War: A Chronological Encyclopedia*, vol. 1, *From Sumer to the Persian Empire* (Westport, CT: Greenwood Press, 2005), chap. 3.

4. V. R. Ramachandra Dikshitar, *War in Ancient India* (Delhi: Motilal Banarsidass, 1987), 129–130. The issue, of course, is very much unsettled.

5. *Encyclopaedia Britannica*, 15th ed., s.v. "Metallurgy."

6. Sarva Daman Singh, *Ancient Indian Warfare* (Delhi: Motilal Banarsidass, 1997), 98.

7. Ibid.

8. Gurcharn Singh Sandhu, *A Military History of Ancient India* (Delhi: Vision Books, 2000), 69.

9. Ibid.

10. Jane C. Waldbaum, "From Bronze to Iron: The Transition from the Bronze Age to the Iron Age in the Eastern Mediterranean," *Studies in Mediterranean Archaeology* 54 (1978): 39, Table IV.I.

11. Arther Ferrill, *The Origins of War: From the Stone Age to Alexander the Great* (New York: Thames and Hudson, 1985), 67.

12. Singh, *Ancient Indian Warfare*, 102.

13. Quintus Curtius Rufus, *The History of Alexander* (New York: Penguin Books, 1984), 9.8.1.

14. Except for cannon, which continued to be made mostly of bronze until at least the American Civil War, when rifled steel cannon made their first appearance.

15. Gabriel, *From Sumer to Rome*, 57.

16. For a detailed examination of Egyptian military medicine in the ancient period, including their skill in dealing with fractured skulls, see Richard A. Gabriel and Karen S. Metz, *A History of Military Medicine*, vol. 1, *From Ancient Times to the Middle Ages* (Westport, CT: Greenwood Press, 1992), chap. 3.

17. Robert L. O'Connell, *Of Arms and Men: A History of War, Weapons, and Aggression* (New York: Oxford University Press, 1989), 34–35.

18. Thomas D. Seymour, *Life in the Homeric Age* (New York: Biblo and Tannenn, 1963), 578, 631–632.

19. See Steven Weingartner, "The Saga of Piyamaradu," *Military Heritage* 3 (October 2001): 81 for a portrayal of the long spears of this period used by Mycenaean soldiers. Seymour suggests that they were sixteen feet long.

20. Yadin, *Art of Warfare*, vol. 1, 136.

21. Sandhu, *Military History of Ancient India*, 69.

22. Gabriel, *From Sumer to Rome*, 61.

23. Ibid.

24. Yadin, *Art of Warfare*, vol. 1, 45.

25. Peter Connolly, *Greece and Rome at War* (Englewood Cliffs, NJ: Prentice-Hall, 1981), 233.

26. O'Connell, *Of Arms and Men*, 38. For an excellent analysis of the *gladius*, see Steven Weingartner, "The Gladius," *Military Heritage* 2 (August 2000): 10–15.

27. I am indebted to Steven Weingartner for the information on the tactical use of the Sherden sword.

28. Richard A. Gabriel, *The Culture of War: Invention and Early Development* (Westport, CT: Greenwood Press, 1990), 9–91.

29. Singh, *Ancient Indian Warfare*, 93.

30. E. Stephen Gurdjian, "The Treatment of Penetrating Head Wounds of the Brain Sustained in Warfare: A Historical Review," *Journal of Neurosurgery* 39 (February 1974): 158.

31. This estimate provided by Richard Glantz, professional archer.

32. Yadin, *Art of Warfare*, vol. 1, 68.

33. Singh, *Ancient Indian Warfare*, 93.

34. Yadin, *Art of Warfare*, vol. 2, 348.

35. Fatigue estimates provided by Glantz.

36. Gabriel, *From Sumer to Rome*, 70–71.

37. Christopher Duffy, *The Military Experience in the Age of Reason* (New York: Atheneum, 1988), 207–208.

38. The definitive work on the military slinger is Manfred Korfmann, "The Sling as a Weapon," *Scientific American* 229, no. 4 (1973): 34–42.

39. Ibid.

40. G. R. Watson, *The Roman Soldier: Aspects of Greek and Roman Military Life* (Ithaca, NY: Cornell University Press, 1969), 60.

Ten

✳ ✳ ✳

ARMOR, HELMETS, AND SHIELDS

The most militarily significant impact of metal technology on war in the Bronze Age was its contribution to personal defensive systems, the armor, helmets, shields, neck collars, greaves, and other defensive equipment worn by the soldier to protect himself. The development of these protective systems had an enormous impact on warfare and tactics, and the development of new metal weapons during this period was stimulated mostly by the search for new ways to thwart and overcome the effectiveness of defensive armor. The inherent dynamic of weapon development operated then as now, but in reverse. In modern times we are prone to see the advent of some new offensive weapon which provokes a defense against it. In the Bronze Age the more significant military revolution was in defensive systems, which stimulated a search to overcome them.

The major protective devices of the ancient soldier were the helmet, neck collar, thorax body armor, and shield. The leather collar was probably another Mesopotamian invention. Between one and two inches thick, the collar was constructed of sewn leather layers, which sometimes had thin bronze or iron plates sewn between the layers to afford more resistance to penetration.[1] The leather collar could easily withstand a blow from a sword blade and was impervious to arrows. This characteristic made it a favorite of charioteers. The Assyrians used the same principle of sewing iron plates between leather layers to fashion boots that afforded good shin protection. By the time of Mycenaean Greece and Etruscan Rome, bronze greaves to protect the shins and forearms of the soldier were standard items of military equipment.

BODY ARMOR

The first recorded instance of body armor is found on the Stele of Vultures in ancient Sumer (circa 2500 B.C.E.), which shows Eannatum's soldiers wearing leather cloaks on which are sewn a number of spined metal disks.[2] The disks do not seem arranged in any particular order so as to protect the most vital areas of the body. We do not know if the disks were fashioned of copper or bronze. By 2100 B.C.E. the victory stele of Naram Sin appears to show metal scale armor, and although we cannot be certain, it is likely that metal scale armor had already been in use for a few hundred years. Certainly by 1700 B.C.E. the Hyksos armies possessed scale armor obtained either from the Aryans or the Mesopotamians. Once introduced to Egypt by the Hyksos invaders, metal scale armor became standard throughout the Near East. Like the leather collar, metal scale armor was a favorite with charioteers because of the excellent protection it afforded against all weapons, except the penetrating axe.

Scale armor was constructed of thin bronze plates sewn to a leather shirt or jerkin about one-quarter inch thick. The plates themselves were two millimeters thick and had slightly raised spines to allow them to overlap and hang correctly.[3] The plates were overlapped in the manner of shingles on a roof, an arrangement that ensured an overlap four millimeters thick for one-third of the body area covered by the armor. This type of armor became the standard protection of the Egyptian heavy spear infantry and charioteers of the New Kingdom. The rise of the iron army of Assyria saw the introduction of a similar, though much more effective, form of body armor called lamellar armor. Lamellar armor comprised a shirt constructed of laminated layers of leather or linen sewn or glued together. To the outer surface of this coat were attached fitted iron plates, each plate joined to the next at the edge with no overlap and held in place by stitching or gluing. This armor weighed about thirty to thirty-five pounds.[4]

By 600 B.C.E. the Greeks and Romans introduced the bell muscular cuirass made of cast bronze. Cast in two halves, front and back, the cuirass joined at the side with hinges and locks or belts. The cuirass bears no connection to earlier developments in armor in the Near East and represented an entirely new type of armor. The bell cuirass weighed about twenty-five pounds, was hot and uncomfortable, and slowed the soldier's movement, factors which worked against its wide use or adoption by other armies.[5] In all likelihood its development arose from the more primitive technology of wearing iron plates sewn to leather shirts. The use of bronze instead of iron at such a late date suggests as well that Etruscan and Greek metal applications may have lagged considerably behind those of the Near East. By the third century B.C.E. the bell cuirass had given way in Greece to the linen cuirass. Constructed of strips of linen glued and sewn together in laminated fashion, it was cheaper and more flexible than the bell cuirass. When outfitted with exterior metal plates, it weighed about fifteen pounds. Without plates it weighed eight pounds.[6] The thickness of both Greek and Roman varieties of this linen armor was around one-half inch.

Early Mycenaean and Minoan charioteers wore an arrangement of bronze armor that almost fully enclosed the soldier, the famous Dendra panoply. The bronze plates assembled to form front and back halves backed with linen or leather loosely fashioned together by leather thongs. The corslet was called a *torake* (literally, "thorax"), and the component parts were known as *opawota*. The complete kit came with lower arm guards called *quero* and leg greaves.[7] The charioteer also wore a boar's tusk helmet (*koreto*) with bronze cheek pieces. The kit was very heavy and was intended for use only by charioteers, who, armed with long spears, thrust at each other en passant. The design of the Dendra armor implies the tilt armor of the later Middle Ages and is clearly designed to deflect thrusts. This is, perhaps, what Nestor, a warrior of the old school, had in mind when he advised his warriors in the *Iliad* not to break ranks and fight alone, but "when a man in his own chariot comes within reach of an enemy chariot, he should attempt a spear thrust."[8]

The armor of the Chinese Shang Dynasty (1700–1100 B.C.E.) consisted of breastplates fashioned of bronze or leather. Heavy circular bronze neck protectors and bronze helmets were also worn. Some aristocrats were outfitted in two-piece armor kits that protected both chest and back.[9] A thousand years later, during the Spring and Autumn Era (771–464 B.C.E.), the heavy bronze and iron cuirass that had come into fashion were replaced by lighter, more flexible laminar armor made of overlapping rows of hard, lacquered, leather plates.[10] Chinese armor for lower ranks seems often to have been made of quilted cloth stuffed with cotton. It is interesting to speculate (no examples have survived) regarding the construction and effectiveness of this type of Chinese body armor. We find a similar type of armor among the Aztecs of South America circa 1500 C.E. The Aztec armor, *ichcahuipilli*, was constructed of unspun, brine-saturated cotton quilted between layers of cloth and made into a sleeveless jacket that reached to the knees. The jacket was two inches thick. The principle of using a thick fiber inside a sandwich of cloth to "trap" the projectile is the same principle used today in the construction of modern Kevlar body armor. The Aztec armor was lighter and cooler in the hot climate and afforded such good protection that the Spanish abandoned their metal cuirass for the cotton armor.[11] Cotton armor of this type would have been much cheaper to manufacture than metal armor.

In India, protective body armor was in use around 1600 B.C.E. The Vedic Epics use the word *varman* to describe what was probably a coat of mail,[12] probably a leather garment or coat reinforced with brass plates at critical points.[13] This arrangement was replaced by a series of shaped plates called *kavach* made of iron, apparently sewed to a leather coat. The armor was worn underneath the usual clothing garments.[14] There are references in Indian texts to the sewing of the armor, and it may have been that the corslet was made of linen, not leather.[15]

The third century B.C.E. saw the introduction of iron chain mail invented by the Celts, whose iron craft was much more advanced than the Romans and probably the best in Europe.[16] Chain mail was constructed of thousands of small iron circles linked together to form an iron mesh shirt. The shirt weighed about thirty-two pounds, but its close fit distributed the weight proportionally over the soldier's body. The mail shirt also permitted adequate mobility, unlike the cast bronze cuirass. Once the Romans adopted the Celtic chain mail armor for their troops, the mail shirt remained the basic armor of the Roman infantryman until the first century C.E. The weakness of chain mail was that the tip of a dagger, spear, sword, or arrowhead, if pointed enough, could slip within one of the small iron circles and, with continued thrust, expand the circle sufficiently to permit the penetration of the body.

By the first century C.E. the Roman army was equipped with laminated leather armor that provided sufficient protection against the tribal armies that they encountered

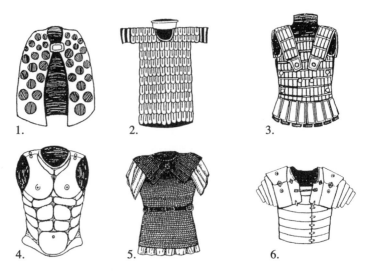

The development of body armor: (1) Sumer (2500 B.C.E.), (2) Egypt
(1700 B.C.E.), (3) Assyria (900 B.C.E.), (4) Greece (400 B.C.E.), (5)
Celtic chain mail (200 B.C.E.), and (6) Rome (100 C.E.). Courtesy of
Richard Gabriel.

most. Perhaps the ultimate in body armor appeared at the same time, the *lorica segmentata*. By this time Roman iron smiths had learned how to bleed off carbon from iron to less than 2 percent, with the result that Roman weapons and body armor were now made of high-grade steel. The *segmentata* was constructed of thin sheet steel plates riveted to leather plates held together by straps, buckles, and locks. It weighed about twenty pounds, considerably lighter than the thirty-pound mail shirt it replaced.[17]

HELMETS

The earliest evidence for the helmet is from Sumer at the Death Pits of Ur dating from 2500 B.C.E. Helmets of similar design appear on the Stele of Vultures. There are portraits of Egyptian soldiers wearing leather caps dating from 200 years earlier, but these caps are also portrayed being worn by nonmilitary personnel, and it is unclear if they were really military helmets. If so, they did not offer as much protection as the better-designed Sumerian helmet. The Sumerian helmet was a cap of hammered copper approximately two to three millimeters thick fitted over a leather or wool cap approximately four millimeters thick, providing a total protective thickness of one-quarter inch. It is unclear why the Sumerians did not use bronze for their helmets. Perhaps the ability to cast a sized bronze sphere with any consistency had not yet been developed, in which case, copper would have been far easier to mold to the shape of the head and obtain a good fit.

Once the helmet made its appearance, it became a standard item of military equipment at least until the seventeenth century C.E. The helmet is mentioned in the Vedic sagas in India dating to 1600 B.C.E., where the term *sipra* is used to describe it. It was presumably made of bronze or brass.[18] A thousand years later, the Indian helmet was fashioned of iron plates joined together. Common soldiers wore helmets made of hide or thick cloth reinforced with some hard substance, like animal hooves.[19] Achaean and

Mycenaean soldiers wore helmets (*koroto*) made from slivers of horn cut from boars' tusks and bound to a leather cap by thongs, to which horsehair plumes could be attached. The Homeric helmet was a cap, usually of leather but sometimes of bronze, that covered only the upper part of the head. It had a ridge of bronze over the temples and around the lower edge. The helmet was held firmly in place by a chin strap. Hector's helmet in the *Iliad* had three layers of leather with boars' teeth strung on the outside.[20] The Mitanni charioteers wore either a bronze helmet called a *gurpisu siparri* or the great bronze scale helmet (*gurpisu siparri kursimetu*), which was a leather cap onto which several layers of overlapping bronze plates had been sewn.[21] The common infantry soldier wore a leather helmet fashioned from goatskins cut into triangles and sewn together at the seams. It required seven goatskins to make three helmets.[22] The helmet of the Hittite guardsmen was very similar to the Mitanni helmet but had a chin strap to hold it securely on the head.[23] The Sea Peoples wore different types of helmets. The Sherden, for example, wore bronze helmets with horns sticking out from the sides, while the Peleset helmet was probably a circle of reeds, stiffened hair, horsehair, linen, or leather strips held in place by a fillet and chin strap.[24] Chinese helmets of the Shang Dynasty were bronze with a rounded crown, with sides and a back that came down low over the ears and the nape of the neck.[25]

The Assyrian helmet was constructed of iron and came in various shapes, depending on the combat role of the wearer. The Assyrians introduced the technique of shaping the helmet at an acute angle so the top came almost to a point, an effective design for reducing its area and increasing the helmet's ability to deflect blows.[26] The Assyrian helmets, as with all helmets since, required an inner cap of wool or leather to help absorb the energy of a blow and dissipate heat. The Assyrian helmet also had a chin strap. The chin strap was probably introduced by the Sea Peoples in their military service in Egypt during the New Kingdom, from where it was later adopted by the Assyrians.

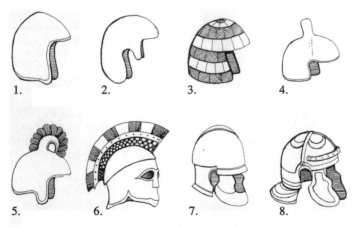

The development of the helmet: (1) Sumer (2500 B.C.E.), (2) Egypt (2300 B.C.E.), (3) Egypt (1700 B.C.E.), (4) Babylon (1500 B.C.E.), (5) Assyria (900 B.C.E.), (6) Greece (600 B.C.E.), (7) Macedonia (350 B.C.E.), and (8) Rome (100 C.E.). Courtesy of Richard Gabriel.

Greek helmets of the Classical and Imperial periods were constructed of bronze and had cheek and face plates. Face plates came to characterize later Roman helmets but were never a major feature of helmets in the Near East, probably because they made the head too hot. Roman helmets came in so many varieties as almost to defy description. Many were made of cast bronze, while others were made of low-grade iron. Their common features were strength, heavy weight, and a protective guard for the base of the neck and skull. The Romans were probably the first to mass-produce bronze helmets by casting them in state arms industries, a practice that led to continuous complaints from soldiers that they were of cheap quality and didn't fit.[27]

SHIELDS

The soldiers of the ancient world also carried shields, and like helmets, these came in a number of types. Most were made of laminated wood covered with cowhide, beaten bronze, and even sheet iron. Early Egyptian and Sumerian shields were fabricated of bull, oxen, and cowhide stretched over a wooden frame. These shields had to be oiled regularly with vegetable oil or animal fat to keep them from drying out, shrinking, and cracking. Other shields were made of woven reeds. Shields came in a variety of shapes: squares, rectangles, figure eights, keyhole shaped, and round. Since even the earliest shields afforded good protection against any type of deadly penetration by hand-wielded weapons, the most important considerations were weight, which affected the ability of the soldier to maneuver and protect himself in close combat, and size, which provided him with protection against hails of arrows fired by archers in concert. For the most part the ancient shield offered good protection against both close combat weapons and archery fire. There is, however, a description in the *Iliad* of a soldier being wounded by an arrow that passed through his shield, an occurrence that must certainly have been a rarity. Some shields were very large, reaching to seven or eight feet, and were bowed back at the top to provide protection from arrow counterfire while an archer fired from behind them. These shields stood on the ground by their own weight. Sometimes these large shields were attended by a shield bearer, who carried them into position and helped steady them or moved them forward during siege operations.

One of the reasons why training an infantry soldier in the ancient armies before the sixth century B.C.E. was difficult had to do with the handgrip with which the soldier held and wielded the shield in battle. Almost all the portrayals of shields that have come down to us from archaeology show a single handgrip in the center of the shield. These grips were probably a leather strap or a carved wooden handle. Held in this manner, the shield required considerable strength to raise and was difficult to press against an opponent with much force. Other shield grips, like those of the Achaeans and Mycenaeans and even of the early Greek city-states, were constructed of a collection of tethers that met at a ring in the center.[28] In only one case that I am able to discern was there a shield grip that had a different grip, and that was the grip portrayed on the shield of the Sherden warriors in the service of Egypt after the attack of the Sea Peoples around 1200 B.C.E.[29] This grip does not seem to have been imitated by other armies in the Near East but appeared in Greece in the sixth century B.C.E., where it was responsible for a military revolution.

The difficulty in using the old Greek tether shield grip was that it required a great deal of strength and training to use, factors which restricted military service in Greece to the nobility. The replacement of the tethers with a single loop through which the forearm could be passed and with another loop at the shield's rim that could be held by the hand in a strong grip reduced the strength and training required for its use.[30] This meant that the average citizen could now easily master the use of the shield. The mass production of the shields also made them cheaper. Both these developments made it easier to enroll the common citizenry for war. Very quickly, the practice of war shifted from the exclusive domain of the contest of noble champions to battles between highly disciplined groups of militia heavy infantry. Thus arose the famous Greek hoplite.[31]

The body armor, helmet, and shield of the ancient soldier afforded him good protection against the weapons of the day, indeed much better protection than was available to the modern soldier until recent times. The advent of gunpowder brought about the gun, which, 200 years after its first appearance, was finally powerful enough to pierce the plate armor of the Renaissance knight. The result was that armies abandoned the search for personal protection of the soldier, and body armor and the helmet began to disappear from the battlefield. This was a tragic mistake. The protective devices of the ancient soldier would have provided excellent protection against firearms well past the time of Napoleon. When the dispersion of battle formations, the inaccuracy of the firearms, and rates of fire are factored in, the ancient soldier would have been safer on the battlefield of the nineteenth century than he was on his own.

From the seventeenth to the nineteenth centuries c.e., no army wore helmets or body armor, even though this period saw the introduction of long-range artillery and exploding shells, both of which produced shrapnel at alarming rates. Infantrymen up to the early days of World War I went into battle with no protective headgear while a storm of steel crashed around them. The bronze shields of the ancient Greeks would easily have repulsed the gunfire of a Napoleonic rifle, and the severely angled helmet of the Assyrians would have made penetration difficult even by a Civil War musket. During World War I the French discovered that the Adrian helmet used by French firemen afforded excellent protection against head wounds. The French rushed this style of helmet into production to equip the rest of their troops with protective headgear. Body armor made a return to the battlefield during the Vietnam War and is now regularly used by most armies. It is difficult to avoid the impression that the military planners of the ancient world may have better understood the relationship between weaponry and personal protection than did many of those who came after them.

NOTES

1. Yigael Yadin, *The Art of War in Biblical Lands in the Light of Archaeological Study*, vol. 1, trans. M. Pearlman (New York: McGraw-Hill, 1963), 197.

2. Ibid., 135.

3. Ibid., 197.

4. The estimate as to weight was provided by Karl Netsch, professional blacksmith, and is based on the assumption that the iron armor was two millimeters thick.

5. Peter Connolly, *Greece and Rome at War* (Englewood Cliffs, NJ: Prentice-Hall, 1981), 58.

6. Ibid.

7. Nigel Stillman and Nigel Tallis, *Armies of the Ancient Near East: 3000 to 539 B.C.E.* (Sussex, UK: Flexiprint, 1984), 194.

8. Ibid., 195.

9. Richard A. Gabriel and Donald W. Boose, Jr., *The Great Battles of Antiquity: A Strategic and Tactical Guide to Great Battles That Shaped the Development of War* (Westport, CT: Greenwood Press, 1994), 179.

10. Ibid., 188.

11. Richard A. Gabriel, "Empires of the Americas," in *Empires at War*, vol. 3, *From the Medieval Realm to the Ottoman Empire* (Westport, CT: Greenwood Press, 2005), chap. 30.

12. Sarva Daman Singh, *Ancient Indian Warfare* (Delhi: Motilal Banarsidass, 1997), 97.

13. Gurcharn Singh Sandhu, *A Military History of Ancient India* (Delhi: Vision Books, 2000), 127.

14. Ibid.

15. Singh, *Ancient Indian Warfare*, 97.

16. Connolly, *Greece and Rome*, 230.

17. Ibid., 231.

18. Singh, *Ancient Indian Warfare*, 98.

19. Sandhu, *Military History of Ancient India*, 127.

20. Thomas D. Seymour, *Life in the Homeric Age* (New York: Biblo and Tannen, 1963), 662–664.

21. Seymour, *Life in the Homeric Age*, 93.

22. Ibid., 92.

23. Ibid., 114.

24. Ibid.

25. Gabriel, *Great Battles*, 179.

26. Richard A. Gabriel and Karen S. Metz, *From Sumer to Rome: The Military Capabilities of Ancient Armies* (Westport, CT: Greenwood Press, 1991), 54.

27. Ibid.

28. Richard A. Gabriel, *The Culture of War: Invention and Early Development* (Westport, CT: Greenwood Press, 1990), 87.

29. Stillman, *Armies of the Ancient Near East*, 107.

30. Connolly, *Greece and Rome*, 52–53.

31. Gabriel, *Culture of War*, 87.

Eleven

✳ ✳ ✳

CHARIOTRY

One of the most important advances in weaponry to appear in the age of metals was not made of metal at all. The chariot was composed almost entirely of laminated wood and leather. It introduced an important new dimension to ancient warfare—mobility—and added a new dimension to the traditional use of shock tactics. When equipped with an archer armed with the composite bow, the chariot provided ancient armies with their first mobile firing platform. In the hands of the Indians, Chinese, Hittites, and Assyrians, the chariot made possible the appearance of mounted infantry. Equally significant, the chariot was the first weapon of war that could participate in all phases of the battle with equal effectiveness. Its archer crews could engage the enemy at long range and, by switching to the javelin, spear, and axe, could close with the enemy and deliver shock to its infantry formations. Once engaged in close combat, the crews could themselves dismount or dismount the spear infantry carried with them, who could then participate in the fight. If the enemy formations cracked, the archer crews could remount and pursue the enemy with terrible effect, destroying the remnants of the enemy force.

Until the introduction of the chariot to the Near and Far East sometime around 1800 B.C.E., warfare had been a series of infantry battles in which mobility was completely absent.[1]

The chariot emerged early in the third millennium in Sumer, and to the Sumerians goes the credit for discovering the first *military* use of the wheel.[2] At about the same time in India the Indus Valley civilizations were also using the wheel, but not for military purposes. The Indians seem to have been the first to use the horse to draw wheeled carts, and a model made of copper of a Sumerian-style chariot being drawn by a horse has come down to us.[3] The similarity in the design of the solid wheels and the chariots found in Sumer and the Indus Valley at about the same time suggest strongly (but not certainly) that Indus traders may have established commercial ties with the Sumerians very early on. Whether the wheel reached India from Sumer in this way, or vice versa, is impossible to say with any certainty.[4]

EARLY CHARIOTS

Archaeological evidence suggests the existence of several types of chariots at this time. These early chariots, fully integrated into Sumerian battle tactics from an early date, were either of the two- or four-wheeled variety, were manned by a crew of two—one driver and one spearman—and were drawn by wild asses called onagers, which in Akkadian means "foreign ass from the mountains." The Sumerians also invented the "straddle car," a cabless platform pulled by a single onager on which the driver maintained his balance by straddling the car. It is difficult to imagine any military use for such a vehicle, and the straddle car may have been only a personal transport vehicle.[5]

The wheels of the Sumerian chariot were constructed of solid wood sections held together with pegs and may have had leather "tires" secured to the rims with copper nails.[6] The wheels turned in one piece with the axle attached by leather thongs or copper bolts to the vehicle's body.[7] The placement of the axle either in front or in the middle of the carrying platform made the Sumerian chariot heavy and unstable at speed. It is unlikely that these machines could make more than eight to ten miles per hour without becoming dangerously unstable and impossible to turn without risk of turning over.

The lack of a mouth bit for the onagers made controlling the animals in unison very difficult. The animals were yoked to each side of a center pole. Each animal pulled on the yoke on its own side. Under these circumstances it was difficult to get the animals to pull together. When four animals were used, the outside animal was linked to the collar of the inside animal and not directly to the pole. When the outside animal pulled, the collar tightened on the inside animal, making it difficult for the animal to breathe.[8] The onagers were controlled by reins attached to copper rings passing through their upper lips.[9] Their harness was a variant of that used on the broad-shouldered oxen. A breast band across the animals' throats transmitted their tractive power to the yoke so that the animals choked as they pulled. This arrangement did not change much throughout all antiquity. It was not until the invention of the true horse collar in the ninth century C.E. that the problems were solved, long after the chariot had ceased to be an important implement of war.[10]

Sumerian charioteers were armed with javelins and axes. The bow does not appear on Sumerian reliefs, and we may fairly conclude that it was not used as a chariot weapon. By 2300 B.C.E., however, the composite bow appeared in the hands of the armies of Sargon I of Akkad, who conquered Sumer. Sargon's armies also used the chariot, and it is not unreasonable that they might have been the first to use the composite bow from the chariot platform, giving rise to a new type of soldier, the chariot archer. No reliefs depicting Akkadian chariot archers have yet been found, and the matter must remain unsettled.

For all its shortcomings the Sumerian chariot revolutionized warfare and remained the prototype chariot in Sumer and India for almost 1,000 years. In the eighteenth century B.C.E. a new type of chariot that was lighter, had spoked wheels, and was drawn by two horses made its appearance. At the same time the mouth bit was invented, making it possible to better control the horses, increasing the vehicle's control at higher speeds.

The origins of this new type of chariot are obscure, but appeared more or less simultaneously among the Mitanni, the Hyksos, and in India. It is possible, as Sarva Daman Singh vigorously contends, that it was the Aryan invaders from central Asia who had overrun areas of the Near East (Mitanni, Hatti, Hanigalbat) and the Far East (India) who brought the new-style chariot with them.[11] Of great importance was the fact that the favorite weapon of the Aryans was the bow, with the consequence that it was likely the Aryan invaders who introduced the practice of mounting a bowman in the chariot.[12] Heretofore the chariot had carried spear and javelin men, unless, as speculated above, Sargon's armies had used bowmen in their chariots. In any event the mounted archer became the standard charioteer of antiquity after 1800 B.C.E.

The Hyksos invasion of around 1700 B.C.E. introduced the chariot to Egypt. By the fifteenth century the Egyptians had modified the heavier Hyksos machine into the finest and fastest in the world. Whereas the Hyksos, Mitanni, and Hittite machines of the day were heavier and sometimes carried a crew of three (driver, archer, and spearman), the Egyptian machine, fashioned entirely of wood and leather, was so light that two soldiers could carry it over rough terrain with little difficulty. The Egyptians were the first to move the axle to the far rear of the carrying platform, a development made possible by the reduction in weight. A heavy chariot of Mitanni weight and design with the axle moved to the rear would force the weight forward onto the collars of the horses, making it very difficult for them to breathe. A lighter machine could transfer its lesser weight with little effect. Moving the axle rearward made the Egyptian chariot faster, more stable at speed, and more maneuverable.[13]

An Egyptian chariot crew consisted of a driver and a chariot archer; the crew carried a quiver of arrows, axes, and a quiver of javelins strapped to the side of the machine. These weapons suggest that the chariot had acquired a varied tactical function under the Egyptians. The chariot crew could engage the enemy with arrows at long range, switching to aimed shots as the machine closed with enemy infantry formations. Once engaged at short range, the chariot crew switched to axes and javelins and engaged in close combat. After the enemy infantry formations were broken, the chariot crew could be used in lethal pursuit, hunting down and killing individual soldiers at close range with the bow.

Chariot design was driven by tactical requirements, which, in turn, were often influenced by the terrain in which the army had to fight. The Egyptian chariot and the Aryan Vedic chariot were designed to operate on flat open plains or desert. Both machines were light and flexible and designed for speed and maneuverability. Both models were designed as mobile firing platforms and were usually pulled by a pair of stallions, although later, the Indian chariot developed into a much larger and heavier vehicle.[14] The Hittite chariots encountered at Kadesh had heavier platforms, requiring six spoked wheels to support them. The rough terrain of Anatolia reduced the tactical emphasis on the speed and maneuverability of Hittite chariot units. Instead, emphasis was placed on a vehicle that could close quickly from ambush or surprise attack, delivering combat power to the point of contact. Thus the Hittite machine was heavier, larger, and

A typical Chinese chariot eighth century B.C.E., Zhou period. Reproduced by permission of the publisher from Alfred S. Bradford, *With Arrow, Sword, and Spear: A History of Warfare in the Ancient World* (Westport, CT: Praeger, 2001). © 2001 by Alfred S. Bradford.

usually carried three soldiers armed with spears, axes, and javelins instead of the composite bow. Hittite chariots gave rise to mounted infantry.[15] Assyrian chariot designers built even heavier machines capable of carrying four men; the machines required three- and four-horse teams to pull them. Like the Hittites, the Assyrians stressed the role of mounted infantry and used shield bearers to ward off arrow fire against the mounted spear infantry. The weight of the Assyrian chariot greatly limited its mobility, speed, and ability to operate in heavy terrain,[16] characteristics that probably were responsible for the need to supplement the chariot force with a new Assyrian invention: cavalry.[17]

Chinese and Mycenaean chariots were not designed primarily as fighting vehicles, but as transport to the battlefield for the nobility. Mycenaean chariots were low-riding, bare platforms with side rails and a step in the back that permitted the warrior to mount and dismount quickly.[18] These chariots may have, at one time, engaged in combat, with their charioteers armed with the long spear, striking at each other as their machines passed by. By Homer's time, however, they were no longer used in combat. Chinese fighting chariots were large, heavy vehicles with five-foot-high wheels and a wooden body mounted directly on the machine's axle. The three-man crew consisted of a driver, an archer, and a "striker" armed with a large halberd. Some models had bronze blades attached to the axles to cut down enemy foot soldiers. Chinese staff, command, and personal transport chariots were also very large vehicles pulled by teams of horses.

Combat vehicles are always compromises between speed, firepower, weight, and crew protection. Sometimes the designs are such compromises that they end up being worthless as fighting vehicles. The Persian chariot falls into this category. The Persian chariot was a tall, heavy vehicle with a very large platform, requiring thicker wheels with more spokes and heavier axles than any previous chariot. The vehicle was so heavy that it required four horses to pull it. For all this weight, however, the Persian chariot carried only a driver and a single archer or spearman.[19] The Persian charioteer carried the simple bow, further reducing firepower, and the weight of the machine made transport and movement over rough terrain difficult. Adding bronze scythes to the axles did little to improve the vehicle's combat lethality.

THE CHARIOT'S EFFECT ON WARFARE

The chariot added the new dimension of pursuit to the combat equation. Before the introduction of the chariot, victorious armies were rarely able to engage in pursuit with any significant degree of lethality. Exhausted from battle, soldiers had little energy to chase a fleeing enemy who, in any case, had a significant head start. As long as infantry formations arranged themselves in dense phalanxes, any attempt at pursuit in force required sacrificing the integrity of the phalanx as it advanced. Under these circumstances, pursuit became little more than a race between equally exhausted soldiers. The age-old habit of the defeated dropping its weapons and armor and scattering all over the countryside made a coordinated pursuit of a defeated army almost impossible.

The chariot changed all this. As the enemy formations broke apart, the chariots could ride through the fleeing mob at greater speed than a soldier could run. Over flat ground, a chariot could reach maximum speeds of almost twenty-five miles an hour, the speed of a galloping horse. At that speed, however, the platform would have been highly unstable, and the chariot archer would have been unsteady in his aim. Since the objective was to pick off individual targets rather than to plow through a massed formation, the "combat speed" of a chariot was between eight and twelve miles per hour, the speed of a cantering horse. At this speed the platform was stable, the driver had excellent control, and the archer had plenty of time to pick out and fire on specific targets. How effective were chariot archers under these conditions? Field experiments using mechanically pulled "chariots" weaving back and forth along a line of anatomically accurate targets placed at fifteen-yard intervals demonstrated that after a few practice attempts, a professional archer was able to hit the target 80 percent of the time with little effort.[20]

It is likely that a trained chariot archer working in coordination with an experienced driver trained to maneuver the chariot close to the target would have been able to hit the fleeing soldier in nine out of every ten attempts. If the fleeing soldier had thrown away his armor and shield, almost all of these aimed shots would have been lethal. Against soldiers still in their armor, the ancient charioteers probably became proficient at aiming for the back of the neck, the top of the central shoulders, and the lower lumbar region of the spine, all areas likely to be exposed on the back of a running man as his armor rode up or down on his back. Modern archers can easily hit a target the size of a half-dollar (four square inches) at ranges of fifteen yards. It seems fair to conclude that a trained chariot archer could easily have hit a running soldier in the neck or spine, almost always killing or crippling him. A blow from a stabbing spear or javelin wielded by a charioteer would have been equally lethal. For the first time in history the chariot provided ancient armies with the mechanical means for a genuinely lethal pursuit on the battlefield.

The chariot introduced a new dimension of lethality to ancient combat, a dimension that has been with us in one way or another ever since. Combining the bow with the chariot linked lethal firepower to enhanced mobility. When combined with two or three spearmen the chariot made possible the first use of mounted infantry. Under these circumstances, it is not surprising that the chariot corps became the elite striking force in most ancient armies. This tradition of elitism lingered through the centuries, even after the chariot itself had become only a minor factor in the conduct of warfare. In India the chariot gave way to the elephant as "the king of battle," and in China and Assyria it gave way to a completely new combat arm: horse cavalry. With the introduction of the internal combustion engine in the modern era the "chariot" has once more assumed the primacy of place in some armies. The elite striking arm of the modern Israeli army is the armored corps. Appropriately enough, the Israeli armored corps is equipped with a tank of their own design called the Merkava. In Hebrew, *merkava* means "chariot."

NOTES

1. For a good overview of chariot tactics, see Steven Weingartner, "Chariot Tactics," *Military Heritage* 3 (August 2002): 18–22, 79.

2. Yigael Yadin, *The Art of Warfare in Biblical Lands in the Light of Archaeological Study*, vol. 1, trans. M. Pearlman (New York: McGraw-Hill, 1963), 129–131.

3. Sarva Daman Singh, *Ancient Indian Warfare* (Delhi: Motilal Banarsidass, 1997), 24.

4. Ibid.

5. Richard A. Gabriel and Donald W. Boose, Jr., *The Great Battles of Antiquity: A Strategic and Tactical Guide to Great Battles That Shaped the Development of War* (Westport, CT: Greenwood Press, 1994), 52.

6. V. Gordon Childe, *New Light on the Most Ancient East* (London: Routledge and Paul, 1952), 239.

7. Ibid., 149–150. See also Sir Leonard Woolley, *Ur Excavations*, vol. 2, *The Royal Cemetery* (London: Oxford University Press, 1934), 64, 108.

8. Singh, *Ancient Indian Warfare*, 23; see also Henri Frankfort, *More Sculpture from the Diyala Region* (Chicago: University of Chicago Press, 1943), 13.

9. Andre Parrot, "The Excavations of Mari," *Syria* 16 (1935): 117–140.

10. V. G. Childe, *What Happened in History* (London: Hammondsworth, 1950), 83.

11. Singh, *Ancient Indian Warfare*, 25.

12. Gurcharn Singh Sandhu, *A Military History of Ancient India* (Delhi: Vision Books, 2000), 97.

13. Yadin, *Art of Warfare*, vol. 1, 87–89.

14. Sandhu, *Military History of Ancient India*, 99.

15. Richard A. Gabriel and Karen S. Metz, *From Sumer to Rome: The Military Capabilities of Ancient Armies* (Westport, CT: Greenwood Press, 1991), 77.

16. Richard A. Gabriel, *The Great Armies of Antiquity* (Westport, CT: Praeger, 2002), 132. See also Yadin, *Art of Warfare*, vol. 2, 297–300 and Georges Contenau, *Everyday Life in Babylon and Assyria*, trans. K. R. Maxwell-Hyslop and A. R. Maxwell-Hyslop (London: Edward Arnold, 1954), 145.

17. Yadin, *Art of Warfare*, vol. 2, 298–299.

18. See Thomas D. Seymour, *Life in the Homeric Age* (New York: Biblo and Tannen, 1963), 674–682 for a detailed analysis of the chariot in the Homeric age.

19. Gabriel, *Great Armies*, 163. See also Yaha Zoka, *The Imperial Iranian Army from Cyrus to Pahlavi* (Teheran: Ministry of Culture and Arts Press, 1971), 62.

20. Gabriel, *From Sumer to Rome*, 78.

Twelve

✷ ✷ ✷

CAVALRY

The chariot dominated the ancient battlefield from 1800 B.C.E. until the ninth century B.C.E., when it began to be replaced by horse cavalry. Several reasons account for the decline of the chariot as a battlefield weapon. First, chariots were very expensive to maintain. The cost of the chariot itself and the horses was not unreasonable,[1] but that was only a small part of the overall expense. Horses had to be fed, and in most countries of the Near East, Egypt excepted, there were no grasslands, and horses had to be fed on grain. It required the grain output of approximately nine acres of land to feed a single horse for a year. Other costs included stables, grooms, armor, and equipment. Second, training charioteers for war was a full-time occupation maintained at government expense. Since charioteers had no other function, maintaining large numbers of charioteers was a significant burden on the military budget. Armor for a charioteer was also very expensive. Third, chariots were fragile machines requiring large numbers of craftsmen to keep the vehicles in fighting trim. Fourth, the chariot was unable to traverse uneven terrain, greatly reducing its scope of tactical application. The chariot's dominance on the battlefields of India for almost 1,000 years came to an end once the Aryans began to push out beyond the Ganga plains and encountered thick forests and jungles, where the chariot was useless. It was then that the elephant began to replace the chariot as the primary battlefield "vehicle" in India.[2]

THE HORSE IN WARFARE

The horse had been known in Asia and the Near East for more than a millennium before anyone thought to use it as an instrument of war in a manner separate from the chariot. The horse was domesticated and ridden in India during the era of the Indus

Valley civilizations. The horse was introduced into the Near East much later, sometime around 1800 B.C.E., perhaps by the Mitanni, who may have acquired it from the steppe peoples of central Asia.[3] The Aryans rode horses in addition to using them to pull chariots; the horse was far more efficient than the chariot in carrying out the favorite Aryan pastime of cattle raiding.[4] The Hittites imported Mitanni horse trainers and used the horse to carry messengers in war,[5] and there are references in Assyrian records to Urartu and Ethiopian soldiers riding horses.[6] The Rig-Veda refers to Vedic horsemen fighting on horseback, but not as cavalry units.[7] Training horses for chariot teams required trainers who were riding other horses. Military men had been riding around on horses for a very long time before anyone thought of using soldiers on horses as implements of war.

It was the Assyrians who invented the new combat arm of horse cavalry. The first reference to a mounted warrior in the Near East is found in the sixth regnal year of Tukulti-Ninurta II (890–884 B.C.E.) of Assyria.[8] The new "cavalrymen" still fought in the manner of the old chariot system of driver and archer, operating in pairs, with one "charioteer" riding his horse while holding the reins of another, on which sat the chariot archer with his composite bow. The "charioteer" managed both horses, leaving the archer free to concentrate on shooting, just as if he were in a chariot.[9] The "charioteer" was armed with a spear, and both he and the archer wore the standard armor, helmet, and other equipment of the Assyrian chariot team. The cavalry team used the same horse harness and bit used for chariot horses. The Assyrians used these cavalry teams for almost fifty years before the individual horseman armed with either spear or bow made his appearance during the reign of Tiglath-Pileser III (745–727 B.C.E.), giving rise to the true horse cavalryman.

CAVALRY USES

The Assyrian cavalryman (*qurubuti sha pithalli*) of Tiglath-Pileser's time wore the standardized equipment of the Assyrian heavy units, comprising a pointed helmet of polished iron equipped with cheek pieces, a short corslet of lamellar armor, a short-sleeved linen tunic, a wrap-around kilt, and high boots with long socks. Assyrian cavalry were equipped with both a heavy thrusting spear (*azmaru*) three and one-half meters in length and a short, angular, composite bow (*qashtu akkadu*). When not in use, the bow was carried in a tubular quiver strapped to the horse's side. A short iron sword was suspended from a leather baldric over the cavalryman's right shoulder. The horse was sometimes protected by coats of textile armor. Neither the modern saddle nor the stirrup were invented in antiquity, and the Assyrians and others used the blanket, saddle girth, crupper, and breast strap to stabilize the rider.[10] Ancient cavalrymen learned to control their mounts with their legs and the heel pressure of their boots (the spur had not yet been invented). Assyrian cavalry were expert lancers and bowmen; as horse archers, they are mentioned in the Bible as the "hurricanes on horseback."[11]

The value of cavalry to ancient armies was that they could do everything a chariot could do and more. Cavalry could act as reconnaissance scouts and range farther afield and over rougher terrain than could the chariot. On the march, cavalry units could move farther and faster in a day than chariots and provide flank security through forested terrain where chariots could not go. Without the horseshoe, horses in antiquity often went lame, but far less so than when they operated in chariot teams. Cavalry horses were put out of action far less often than chariot horses, who were useless when the chariot broke down. A single cavalryman armed with a lance and bow provided more firepower than a chariot crew, which often needed a shield bearer and driver along with the archer or spearman. Cavalry could maneuver much more quickly than chariots on the battlefield, and their ability to assemble and reassemble for attack after attack made cavalry a far more flexible combat instrument than chariots. Still, the chariot remained a part of most ancient armies to the end of antiquity. The original identification of the chariot as the vehicle of kings and nobles, along with the high status the charioteer had acquired over centuries, enticed armies to keep the chariot around in small numbers for centuries after it had lost any real value as a weapon of war. Eventually, the chariot was reduced to a transport vehicle for officers and nobles.

Early experiments with mounted men were not limited to the horse. At the battle of Karkar (853 B.C.E.) the Assyrian king Shalmaneser III fought a battle against a coalition of forces led by Hadadezer of Damascus in which Hadadezer's Arab bedouin allies, led by Gindibu the Arab, provided 1,000 cavalry archers mounted on camels.[12] This was the first recorded instance of camel cavalry in an army of the Near East. The camel had been domesticated in Arabia as early as the third millennium B.C.E.,[13] where it had been used as a source of food. It was not until circa 1200 B.C.E. that the camel became a primary means of transport for the desert tribes. It was these bedouin tribes who invented the use of the camel in war. The first recorded instance of bedouin camel cavalry in war is recorded in the book of Exodus, when Amalekite cavalry archers attacked the Israelite column of march at Rephadim and were driven off by Joshua and his men.[14] Although never used extensively as an implement of war in either the ancient Near or Far East, camels were used later by the Persians and other armies as baggage animals.[15] The military tradition of the camel lived on in Arabia, however, and reemerged in the fifth century C.E., when camels were used to transport the heavy infantry of the early Moslem armies in their wars of conquest.[16]

CAVALRY LIMITATIONS

In no army of antiquity, with the exception of the army of Philip II of Macedon and, later, the army of Alexander, was cavalry used as the combat arm of decision. In Assyria, Persia, Carthage, Classical Greece, India, China, and Republican Rome the infantry remained the combat arm of decision. In India, cavalry never acquired an important status, first being subordinate to the chariot and then to the elephant corps of Indian armies. Mounted warriors did not make their appearance in China until at least the fifth century B.C.E.,[17] and it was another two centuries before cavalry was used routinely by Chinese armies.[18] It was not until the reign of Diocletian (284–305 C.E.) that the Romans finally adopted large cavalry forces, the heavily armored *cataphracti*, to meet the mobile threat of invasion from barbarian horsemen. By Constantine's time (306–337 C.E.), one in every three soldiers in the Roman army was a cavalryman, and cavalry became the Roman army's most important and powerful combat arm. Some armies, such as the Parthian army and the tribal armies employed by Alexander on his march to India, were composed entirely of cavalrymen, like the Mongol and Turkoman armies of a much later period. But these "one-armed" armies had no other combat arms, and as such, it is inappropriate to speak of them as having any other "arm" of decision.

Once introduced, why did cavalry not play a more important role in the tactics of the armies of antiquity? Several reasons, some cultural and others technical, suggest themselves. The lack of a firm saddle and stirrups made it almost impossible for a cav-alryman to wield his lance or spear effectively without being knocked from his horse by the force of impact. Nor could cavalry engage at the gallop for the same reason. The instability of the horseman on the animal's back made it difficult for him to wield his bow with any accuracy. The shock power and lethality of later medieval cavalry made possible by the invention of the high-backed saddle and the stirrup were absent in the cavalry units of antiquity. Xenophon, in trying to calm the fears of his infantry troops prior to an engagement with Persian cavalry, tells his men that "no one has ever died in battle through being bitten or kicked by a horse; it is men who do whatever gets done in battle. And we are on a much more solid foundation than cavalrymen, who are up in the air on horseback, and afraid not only of us but of falling off their horses; we, on the other hand, with our feet planted on the earth, can give much harder blows to those who attack us and are much more likely to hit what we aim at."[19]

The appearance of cavalry on the ancient battlefield forced infantry formations to find ways of dealing with cavalry, all of which resulted in the infantry being better able to defend itself. The Persian, Macedonian, Assyrian, and Classical Greek armies deployed very dense infantry formations that were invulnerable to cavalry as long as they retained their discipline and integrity. Even if struck in the flanks, these infantry formations usually could not be penetrated by cavalry nor subjected to much more than harassment by javelins. Commanders quickly learned to use their own cavalry to engage and occupy enemy cavalry to keep it away from the infantry. This often reduced cavalry engagements to sideshow skirmishes that had little influence on the outcome of the overall battle. The Roman army and Hannibal's Carthaginians solved the prob-lem of cavalry in a different way: by making their infantry units less dense and more maneuverable so that they could turn in any direction to face a cavalry attack or open their ranks to permit the onrushing horses to pass harmlessly through their ranks.

Cultural values also reduced the effectiveness of cavalry on the battlefield. Persian cavalry, for example, mostly comprised tribal armies, whose reliability varied greatly. Mercenary cavalry, too, was often unreliable, although some mercenaries, like the Germans who fought with Rome in the last days of the Empire, were quite reliable and ferocious. In an age where communication on the battlefield was almost nonexistent, commanders found cavalry difficult to control once launched. One side's cavalry often chased the other's cavalry from the field and spent the day pursuing them, returning to the battlefield too late to have any influence on the outcome. Finally, in countries like India and China, cultural values greatly retarded the development of cavalry. China continued to use the chariot almost up to the turn of the first millennium C.E., continu-ing its identification with kings and nobility. Indian commanders found the elephant much more useful in jungles and forests than the horse so that the elephant, not the horse, became the most important military animal in Indian armies until the end of the Gupta period in the fourth century C.E.

MACEDONIA'S EFFECTIVE CAVALRY

There was only one major army of the ancient period where cavalry played the major role as the combat arm of decision, and that was in the army of Alexander the Great, which had been designed by his father, Philip II of Macedon. While all of the technical limitations mentioned above were present in Philip's army, they never became major factors limiting combat effectiveness. There were two reasons for this. First, unlike the other states of Greece for which cavalry was an afterthought, in Macedonia, rival clans fighting on horseback was a basic form of military life. Macedonia during Philip's time most resembled the Homeric age, a society of powerful chieftains engaged in frequent conflicts with other chieftains and their armed warrior retinues. Philip's cavalry was accustomed to fighting on horseback and, most importantly, to fighting as disciplined units rather than as individuals. Second, Philip introduced a new tactical design in which the densely packed Macedonian phalanx was used not as a striking force, but as a platform of maneuver, with the cavalry trained as the primary striking force.[20] Philip's highly trained and disciplined cavalry became accustomed to operating in concert with infantry. It is from Philip and Alexander's success with cavalry in concert with infantry that the military maxim of never using cavalry without infantry support arose.

Macedonian cavalry was the centerpiece of the Alexandrian army. Except for the elite royal guard, which had 300 men, Alexander's cavalry, the Royal Companions, consisted of six squadrons (*ile*) of 200 men each. Armed with the fourteen-foot *sarissa*, which could be used as a lance, or with the shorter javelin, all cavalry wore armor and carried the curved *kopis* sword for use as a cavalry saber. Later, some units even carried the bow. Macedonian cavalry fought in an *emblon*, or a delta formation shaped much like an inverted ice cream cone, with the point consisting of a single horseman. This was different from traditional Greek cavalry, which attacked in a square formation with an eight-man front and an eight-man depth, or from the Thessalian cavalry, which attacked in a diamond formation. Different as well from both was the Macedonian habit of attacking at the gallop. Most ancient cavalry attacked at a walk or slow canter. Philip had adopted the *emblon* from the Scythians, who had invented it. This formation was ideal for rapid wheeling and withdrawal and made penetrating enemy cavalry formations easier.[21]

A Macedonian cavalry charge could be deadly, but this was not the case with cavalry in most other ancient armies. Usually, cavalry attacked at speeds which could not deliver shock against rival cavalry or infantry. Polibius tells us that as both sides approached each other, it was not uncommon for the horsemen to dismount and engage each other with sword or spear.[22] It was common for German, Gallic, and even Roman cavalry to dismount and fight on foot.[23] Sometimes cavalry formations charged directly at one another, only to slacken their speed once within javelin range in order to launch their weapons. They would then take to the rear once more and prepare to repeat the charge. Often, no contact was made between the rival formations. If one formation continued the charge into the other, it was not unusual for one to break and run, in which case the attackers spent the day in the pursuit of individual horsemen scattered over the countryside while the main battle raged behind them. Polibius tells us that at Cannae the rare event of two cavalry formations smashing into each other took place. Mounted on saddlecloths and without stirrups, encumbered with lance, sword, and shield, most horsemen were unable to remain mounted and tumbled to the ground, where they continued to fight on foot.[24] Caesar tells us, too, that ancient cavalrymen could achieve little against formed and disciplined infantry.[25] To become an effective combat arm, cavalry had to await the invention of the true saddle and stirrup, something which did not occur in the Near East or West until around the fifth century C.E.[26]

NOTES

1. Richard A. Gabriel, *The Military History of Ancient Israel* (Westport, CT: Praeger, 2003), 299–300.

2. Gurcharn Singh Sandhu, *A Military History of Ancient India* (Delhi: Vision Books, 2000), 100.

3. Ibid., 102.

4. Ibid.

5. O. R. Gurney, *The Hittites* (Baltimore: Penguin Books, 1952), 106.

6. Sarva Daman Singh, *Ancient Indian Warfare* (Delhi: Motilal Banarsidass, 1997), 55–56.

7. Ibid., 58.

8. Nigel Stillman and Nigel Tallis, *Armies of the Ancient Near East: 3000 to 539* B.C.E. (Sussex, UK: Flexiprint, 1984), 128.

9. Ibid.

10. Richard A. Gabriel, *The Culture of War: Invention and Early Development* (Westport, CT: Greenwood Press, 1990), 65.

11. Robert Laffont, *The Ancient Art of Warfare*, vol. 1, *Antiquity* (New York: Time-Life Books, 1968), 48.

12. Glenn M. Schwartz, "Pastoral Nomadism in Ancient Western Asia," in *Civilizations of the Ancient Near East*, ed. Jack M. Sasson (New York: Scribner, 1995), 256.

13. Ibid.

14. Gabriel, *Military History of Ancient Israel*, 81–84.

15. Sir Percy Sykes, *A History of Persia*, vol. 1 (London: Macmillan, 1985), 146.

16. Richard A. Gabriel, "Arab Armies," in *The Great Armies of Antiquity* (Westport, CT: Praeger, 2002), chap. 17.

17. Richard A. Gabriel and Donald W. Boose, Jr., *The Great Battles of Antiquity: A Strategic and Tactical Guide to Great Battles That Shaped the Development of War* (Westport, CT: Greenwood Press, 1994), 177.

18. Ibid., 199.

19. Xenophon, *The Persian Expedition*, trans. Rex Warner (Baltimore: Penguin Books, 1972), 152.

20. Richard A. Gabriel, "Philip of Macedon," in *Great Captains of Antiquity* (Westport, CT: Greenwood Press, 2001), chap. 4.

21. Gabriel, *Great Battles*, 238.

22. Polybius *Histories* 11. Chap. 5.

23. Singh, *Ancient Indian Warfare*, 70; also Ardant du Picq, *Battle Studies: Ancient and Modern Battle* (Harrisburg, PA: The Military Service Publishing Company, 1947), 78.

24. Singh, *Ancient Indian Warfare*, 70; Polyb. 11. Chap. 5..

25. du Picq, *Battle Studies*, 64.

26. Singh, *Ancient Indian Warfare*, 63; also see A. L. Basham, *The Wonder That Was India: A Survey of the Culture of the Indian Sub-continent Before the Coming of the Muslims* (New York: Grove Press, 1959), 374 for a picture of an ancient Indian copper vase that seems to show the first example of a stirrup. The stirrup is depicted as a looped rope and not as the proper leather, metal, and wood stirrup that appeared later. Still, the looped rope would have served well enough, and if so, then we may credit Indian armies with the invention of this important military device.

Thirteen

✷ ✷ ✷

LOGISTICS AND TRANSPORT

By the Iron Age the size of armies had grown enormously along with the scope of the battles and campaigns they fought. Ancient armies had to master the task of supporting these large armies in the field over greater distances and for longer periods of time. The logistical feats of ancient armies were often more difficult and were achieved more proficiently than those accomplished by the armies of the nineteenth century, when the railroad, mass production of supplies, standard packaging, and tinned and condensed food made the problem of supply considerably less difficult. Of all the achievements of the armies of antiquity, those in the area of logistics often remain the most unappreciated by modern military planners.

LOGISTICS

Vehicles

Ancient armies had to transport more than food and weapons, both of which could be carried by the soldier himself. The advances in military technology since 1800 B.C.E. had begun to make armies far more complex entities with a resulting increase in their logistical burdens. The development of the chariot required that ancient armies maintain repair depots and special mobile repair battalions to keep the vehicles combat ready.[1] Chariots were disassembled for transport, requiring oxcarts to transport the wheels while human porters carried the chariot bodies. More animals and humans had to be fed and watered as a result. The introduction of large cavalry squadrons to ancient armies after 850 B.C.E. brought into existence special logistics units whose task was to obtain and train the horses as cavalry mounts. Greater numbers of horses now had to be watered and fed on the march. The *musarkisus* was the Assyrian army's horse logistics branch. It obtained and processed 3,000 horses a month for military training and use,[2] a feat not repeated in the West until the time of Napoleon. The integration of chariots with cavalry forced ancient armies to learn how to sustain two types of military "vehicles" at the same time. The armies of India had to supply three types of combat vehicles—cavalry, chariots, and elephants. Elephants required large numbers of attendants to feed, wash, and tend them in addition to the mahouts (mounted "drivers") and combat archers and spearmen who rode the animal into battle. Unlike horses, elephants will not breed in captivity. Each animal had to be captured in the wild and trained, requiring corps of elephant hunters and trainers.

Siege Equipment

Other technological advances increased logistical burdens. Advances in siegecraft required armies to transport all kinds of siege equipment as they moved through hostile territory. Without siege equipment to reduce enemy cities an army risked leaving large garrisons across its line of supply and communication. Ropes, picks, levers, scaling ladders, shovels for tunneling, and covered battering rams all had to move with the army. The Persians moved huge siege towers on wheels pulled by teams of sixteen oxen along with their armies. Xenophon tells us that these towers weighed 13,920 pounds.[3] The use of artillery, introduced by the Greeks and brought to perfection by the Romans and Chinese, and siege machinery added another requirement: the transportation of catapults and shot. Indian siege machines were enormous and were transported by elephants. Although the siege machines of the ancient armies could be dismantled for transport, they required many more pack and baggage animals to carry the parts. Roman armies sometimes carried construction materials with them in anticipation of having to build a bridge. The need to repair tools and iron weapons brought into existence the military blacksmith with his traveling forge. Livy tells us that a Roman army of eight legions (approximately 40,000 men) required 1,600 smiths and craftsmen (*fabri*) to keep its equipment prepared for battle. Much of the new technology of war was too heavy or oddly shaped to be carried by pack animal, forcing ancient armies to use the wagon in ever greater numbers. Wagons, of course, also needed animals to pull them, often oxen, as well as repairmen and extra parts to keep the wagons operational. Wagons came to make up from 20 to 30 percent of the supply train relative to pack animals.[4]

Food and Water

The most important supplies were, of course, food and water for the soldiers and the pack animals. In hot climates like the Near East, India, and parts of China the nutritional and water requirements of man and beast were much higher than in moderate climates. The ancient soldier was issued about three pounds of wheat a day as his basic ration and required nine quarts of water a day. An ancient army of 65,000 men (about the size of Alexander's field army) required 195,000 pounds of grain a day to meet minimum nutritional requirements. To sustain the army's cavalry, baggage, and transport animals required 375,000 pounds of forage per day.[5] Horses and other pack animals require thirty to sixty quarts of water a day to stay healthy.[6] To meet the needs of an army of 40,000 soldiers required 21,000 gallons of water per day. An additional 158,000 gallons of water was needed for the animals.[7] Soldiers carried canteens, but these were for use between the springs and rivers that provided the major source of an army's water. Water supply in the Near and Far East is highly dependent on weather. In the summer, wells, streams, and even springs dry up so that logistics officers had to be aware of the locations of water sources and their rates of flow. Without sufficient water the army's animals would die within days, so providing water for them was as important as providing it for the troops. Campaigns in desert environments required armies to carry water with them. The Roman general Pompey, campaigning against the Albanians in the Caspian Sea region, ordered water for his troops to be carried in 10,000 water skins to permit his army to cross the waterless waste.[8]

Animals

The number of animals in the baggage trains of ancient armies was substantial. A Roman legion of 4,800 men had 1,400 mules,[9] or one animal for 3.4 men. This number of mules equaled the carrying capacity of 350 wagons.[10] By comparison, an American army of 10,000 men during the Mexican War (1844–1846) required 3,000 mules and 800 wagons.[11] General Sherman's army (1864) of 100,000 men had 32,600 pack mules and 5,180 wagons.[12] These numbers of pack animals to be fed and watered do *not* include cavalry and chariot horses, which also had to be cared for. The number of these animals was substantial. An Indian field army during the Mahabharata period (400 B.C.E.) had 6,561 chariot horses and 19,683 cavalry horses.[13] At Arbela, Darius III put 40,000 cavalry in the field,[14] and Alexander, at the battle of the Hydaspes (326 B.C.E.), deployed 13,000 Macedonian cavalry and 18,500 mercenary cavalry men recruited from central Asia.[15]

Fodder for the animals was the largest logistical requirement of any army of the ancient period. In the American Civil War, daily forage requirements were three times as great in weight as subsistence requirements for soldiers.[16] Fodder may be either rough fodder, grasses and hay cut from fields or grazed by the animals themselves, or hard or dry fodder, a grain, usually barley or oats.[17] Ten thousand animals required 247 acres of land per day to obtain sufficient fodder,[18] and an army would quickly consume its supply of fodder in a few days if it didn't move. Livy tells us that armies often waited "until there was an abundance of pasture in the fields" before undertaking a campaign.[19] One of the reasons why ancient armies broke off campaigns to go into winter quarters was that there was insufficient fodder to feed the army's animals.[20] Dry fodder (oats, barley) could be carried with the army in sufficient quantities to sustain the animals for a few days across desert or rocky terrain, but no army could carry sufficient grain to feed its troops and animals, so finding sufficient fodder was an important concern in planning the route of march. Table 13.1 summarizes the logistics requirements for a typical Iron Age army, in this case, the army of Alexander the Great.

Table 13.1
The Army's Grain, Forage, and Water Requirements for One Day

	Numbers	Ration	Weight (lbs.)
Personnel	65,000	3 lbs. grain 0.5 gal. (5 lbs.) water	195,000 325,000
Cavalry horses	6,100	20 lbs. grain and forage 8 gal. (80 lbs.) water	122,000 488,000
Baggage animals	1,300	20 lbs. grain and forage *average* 8 gal. (80 lbs.) water *average*	26,000 104,000
Animals carrying provisions	8,400	20 lbs. grain and forage *average* 8 gal. (80 lbs.) water *average*	168,000 672,000

Source: Donald W. Engels, *Alexander the Great and the Logistics of the Macedonian Army* (Berkeley: University of California Press, 1978), Table 7, 153.

Living off the Land

Even a well-supplied and logistically sophisticated army could not carry all the supplies it required to sustain itself in fighting condition for very long. In this sense, all armies had to live off the land. At the very minimum this meant finding sufficient daily supplies of water, fodder for the animals, and firewood for cooking, light, and warmth. Armies routinely augmented their carried food supplies with what they could obtain on the march. Living off the land meant supplying an army by foraging, requisitioning, and plundering. Foraging required sending out units of soldiers to find and bring back certain items, like fodder or firewood. Requisitioning involved obtaining supplies from friendly authorities or individuals, often by paying for them, other times simply taking them with a promise to pay. Plundering involved seizing provisions or property from the owners without compensation. Of the three logistical activities, foraging was by far the most difficult and dangerous work.

Foraging parties were always subject to attack, and sufficient security forces usually had to be sent with them to provide protection. Foragers always kept their weapons close by as they worked. Mowing and hauling hay for the animals, cutting firewood, or digging wells was hard work, precisely the kind of agricultural labor that many soldiers had joined the legions to avoid. The *Iliad* tells us that after the Greeks had established themselves before Troy, a great number of soldiers were kept busy pillaging the countryside and "turning the soil" (plowing and planting crops) to feed the army.[21] Foraging parties gathered only as much as the army's supply train could reasonably carry, usually not more than four or five days' provisions at a time.[22] Foraging took time and slowed an army's rate of advance.

Bases and Depots

As long as the army was moving within the borders of its own country or imperial realm, it could supply itself from stocks of food and supplies prepositioned at supply depots and forts along its route. Once in enemy territory, however, the problem of supply became more pressing. Almost all armies of antiquity used a system of operational bases, tactical bases, and depots to keep their armies supplied in enemy territory. The armies of Classical Greece, by contrast, usually fought no more than a few days' march from their homelands and supplied their armies by having each soldier and his attendants provide supplies for themselves. There was no military logistical system in Classical Greece, until Philip of Macedon introduced one for his army.

An operational base might be a port or a large city located in or close to enemy territory that could be used to collect large amounts of food and supplies. Livy described the Carthaginians' operational base at New Carthage as "a citadel, treasury, arsenal, and storehouse for everything."[23] When Thutmose III captured the coastal cities in northern Palestine, he did so to turn them into operational bases for his army for the war with the Syrians. The advantage of a port over an inland city was that larger amounts of supplies could be moved faster and more cheaply by ship than overland. Water transport during Roman times was forty times less expensive than overland transport.[24] It was for this reason that when Titus planned his attack on Jerusalem in 70 c.e., he assembled his army at Caesarea, a seaport, rather than at Joppa or another city closer to Jerusalem itself.

TRANSPORTATION

The tactical base served as the main resupply facility when the army was close to or in contact with the enemy. The army would move from its operational base and establish a tactical base, usually a fortified encampment, like the Roman marching camp. The forward tactical base advanced with the army, and previous tactical bases were converted into depots.[25] Supplies were then moved from the operational base to a series of depots positioned behind the army's line of march. Supplies were shuttled forward to the army over a series of intermediate supply storage depots by a series of rotating pack animal and wagon convoys that could be used repeatedly traveling only relatively short distances, perhaps twenty miles between depots.[26] If the army were forced to retreat, it could do so along its previous line of communication, finding supplies at each of the depots to replenish itself and maintain its integrity. This system made it possible for ancient armies to project force over long distances. This or some minor variation in the supply system of bases, depots, and pack convoys was found among all the armies of the Near East throughout antiquity and in India and China as well.[27]

Animal Transport

The main means of moving supplies in antiquity was the animal pack train composed of donkeys, mules, horses, oxen, camels, and elephants in some appropriate mix. These animals were used either as draft animals (load pullers) or pack animals (load bearers). It was Ramses II who revolutionized Egyptian logistics by introducing the ox-drawn cart to Egyptian logistics. For centuries the Egyptians had used donkeys and donkey-drawn carts. Ramses probably got the idea for ox-drawn carts from his experience with the Sea Peoples, who, like the Hittites, used the oxcart as a standard means of military transport. Although ox-drawn and mule-drawn wagons can move larger loads, pack animals can move both on and off prepared roads, go farther per day, and travel faster and for longer periods than wagons.[28] They are also less expensive and take up less space in camp. The oxcart slowed military movement to a crawl.[29] One reason was the use of an animal collar that pressed on the animals' windpipes, choking them and increasing their rate of physical exhaustion.[30] Ox-drawn wagons move much slower than mule-drawn wagons and are usually unable to make more than nine miles a day,[31] while a mule-drawn wagon can make nineteen miles a day.[32] Regardless of the animal, damaged hooves were a major source of lameness in pack animals. Logistics trains were further burdened by having to take along spare animals or finding some way to acquire them along the way. Ancient armies used "hipposandals," leather or cloth bags tied over the animals' hooves, to reduce damage to the animals' feet.[33]

With the introduction of cavalry and chariots the horse became an ever-present creature in ancient armies. Although some use was made of the horse as a draft animal (Assyrians, Romans, and Indians), they were used almost exclusively as cavalry mounts and not in the logistics train. Unlike mules or donkeys, horses are fragile creatures whose health fails quickly if forced to live on rough fodder or remain uncovered in the cold or wet. Nonetheless, when outfitted with panniers to carry cargo, they were comparatively efficient when compared to the oxcart. An oxcart could move a 1,000-pound load nine miles per day, while five horses could carry the same load thirty-two miles a day at twice the speed on half the forage.[34] The use of the horse as a prominent animal in a logistics train occurred first in the Persian army and was quickly adopted by Philip of Macedon.[35]

The donkey was the most common transporter of goods in the civilian and military economies of the ancient period. Properly equipped with pack saddles, panniers, or wooden frames, a donkey can carry a 220-pound load.[36] Mules are stronger and more sure-footed than donkeys and are cheaper to feed than the horse.[37] They were, however, more expensive than donkeys. A mule can easily carry 300 pounds. Although a relatively slow traveler, four to five miles per hour, the mule has incredible endurance and can march continuously for ten to twelve hours.[38] A mule can easily travel forty miles a day, and in the nineteenth century, U.S. Army mule trains could make 80–100 miles a day under forced march conditions.[39] The expense and low speed of the oxcart led Philip of Macedon to remove them from his army, an innovation that tripled the army's rate of movement and increased its ability to move over rough terrain.[40]

The camel was first domesticated around 1000 B.C.E. and quickly became a common logistics animal in the armies of the ancient Near East. The Romans did not use them in any numbers until the Imperial period. A camel can carry between 400 and 600 pounds,[41] usually in panniers. Camels are more difficult to control than mules and have softer feet, which makes them unsuitable for mountainous or rocky terrain. The ability of the animal to go long periods without water makes them ideal for desert campaigns. In India the elephant was considered the best animal with which to transport goods. It could carry very heavy loads and did double duty as a fighting animal.[42] Ox-drawn wagons were also used by the armies of later antiquity to carry heavy and bulky loads. The lack of brakes, a pivoting front axle, and axle bearings significantly reduced the wagon's efficiency on the march. Still, wagons were the basic form of transport for most tribal armies in the West and could be turned quickly to military advantage by forming them into a *laager* for defensive purposes.

Human Transport

Hired or conscripted human porters and the soldier's themselves were an important part of the carrying capacity of the logistics train. Alexander, the Romans, the Indians, and the Chinese made extensive use of porters, and Alexander and the Romans made maximum use of the carrying capacity of their own soldiers. Both the Greek and Roman soldier carried sixty to seventy pounds on his back; in an emergency the soldier could carry 100 pounds.[43] The ability of the soldier to carry his own load drastically reduced the overall logistical burden of the army. With soldiers carrying only one-third the load that would normally have been hauled by animals, an army of 50,000 men required 6,000 fewer pack animals and 240 fewer animals to haul feed for the others.[44] Sometimes supplies did not have to be carried. Armies often drove large cattle and sheep herds along with them to provide fresh meat for the troops. Livy tells us that at one point Hannibal had more than 2,000 head of cattle with his army of 30,000 men.[45]

Road Building

The speed and ease of the movement of supplies could be increased by improvements to the logistical infrastructure. By the time of the Persian Empire, states had begun to construct regular roads for logistical and military purposes. The Persian, Chinese, and Roman empires all built extensive road networks. In Persia these roads were mostly unpaved, packed dirt tracks sufficiently wide to permit the movement of wheeled siege towers towed by oxen harnessed eight abreast. A system of bridges made crossing streams and other terrain obstacles easier, greatly increasing rates of movement. The most famous of the Persian roads ran from Sardis on the Mediterranean to the Persian capital of Susa, a distance of 1,500 miles. A horse messenger could travel the distance in fifteen days. Without the road the journey would have taken three months.[46] The most amazing system of roads in the ancient world were the Roman roads. The Romans constructed 250,000 miles of roads, including 50,000 miles of paved roadways throughout the empire.[47] The effect on the movement of armies and supplies was dramatic. On dry, unpaved roads a Roman legion could move no more than eight miles a day.[48] In wet weather, movement was almost impossible at any speed. On paved roads, however, a legion could make twenty to twenty-five miles a day in all kinds of weather. The Roman road system revolutionized logistics and transport.

Bridge Building

The need to increase the armies' rates of movement while keeping them supplied led to the use of tactical engineering units that traveled with the armies. These units kept the supply trains moving by cutting roads, building bridges, and floating supplies across rivers. Assyrian engineers invented the world's first military pontoon bridges made from palm wood, planks, and reeds called *keleks*.[49] Persian engineers became skilled at the construction of bridges with vertical sides so that horses could cross steep ravines without the fear that often caused horses to bolt.[50] While armies such as Egypt and India had used small coastal vessels from time immemorial to supply their armies, the Persians were the first to introduce a large navy primarily to support ground operations.[51] Using the ship building and maritime skills of the peoples of their coastal provinces, the Persians commissioned special ships to transport horses, infantry, and supplies, including shallow-draft vessels for use on rivers. Herodotus tells us that Xerxes's expedition against the Greek states in 481 B.C.E. deployed 3,000 transport ships to supply the army.[52] The Roman army made extensive use of water transport by constructing a network of canals in Gaul and Germany to supply their armies.

THE BEGINNINGS OF NATIONAL CURRENCY

Another important means for supplying ancient armies was the sutler, or military contractor, which came into wide practice during the Persian Empire. Darius I was the first monarch to coin money on a national scale.[53] Backed by enormous Persian gold reserves, the 130-grain gold *daric* became the only gold currency of the early ancient world and could be spent anywhere. The use of currency led to the establishment of uniform weights and measures that allowed logistical planners to obtain military supplies in precise amounts. One result of this type of purchasing was the emergence of merchants whose business was the provision of supplies to the army, the first military contractors. A special kind of military-civilian supplier went along with the army on the march, setting up shop in the evening to sell everything from food to oil to the soldiers.[54]

The logistical apparatus of ancient armies was remarkable for what it could accomplish in an age without mechanical transport. It is worth remembering that no army of the modern period equaled or exceeded the rates of movement of the armies of the ancient period until the American Civil War, when the introduction of the railroad made faster troop movement possible.[55] Supported by a sound logistical train, ancient armies could easily conduct operations fifty to sixty miles beyond their last tactical base and remain well supplied.[56] It is only in the modern era of mechanical transport that armies have been able to better this performance.

NOTES

1. Yigael Yadin, *The Art of Warfare in Biblical Lands in the Light of Archaeological Study*, vol. 1, trans. M. Pearlman (New York: McGraw-Hill, 1963), 89.

2. Arther Ferrill, *The Origins of War: From the Stone Age to Alexander the Great* (New York: Thames and Hudson, 1985), 72.

3. Xenophon *Cyropaedia* 6.50–55; the weight is an extrapolation from Xenophon's statement that the number of talents carried by an ox was twenty-five. A talent never weighed less than fifty-eight pounds.

4. Jonathan P. Roth, *The Logistics of the Roman Army at War* (264 B.C.–A.D. 235) (Boston: Brill, 1999), 87.

5. Donald W. Engels, *Alexander the Great and the Logistics of the Macedonian Army* (Berkeley: University of California Press, 1978), Table 3, 145.

6. Roth, *Logistics*, 62–67.

7. Ibid., 119; see also Richard A. Gabriel and Karen S. Metz, *From Sumer to Rome: The Military Capabilities of Ancient Armies* (Westport, CT: Greenwood Press, 1991), 23.

8. As noted by Josephus *Jewish War* 1.395.

9. Roth, *Logistics*, 83.

10. Ibid.

11. Erna Risch, *Quartermaster Support of the Army: A History of the Corps, 1775–1939*, 2nd ed. (Washington, DC: Center of Military History, 1989), 291.

12. Duncan K. Major and Roger S. Fitch, *Supply of Sherman's Army during the Atlanta Campaign* (Ft. Leavenworth, KS: Army Service Schools Press, 1911), 10, 25.

13. U. P. Thapliyal, "Military Organization in the Ancient Period," in *Historical Perspectives of Warfare in India*, ed. S. N. Prasad (Delhi: Motilal Banarsidass, 2002), 77.

14. Richard A. Gabriel, *The Culture of War: Invention and Early Development* (Westport, CT: Greenwood Press, 1990), 73; see also Robert Laffont, *The Ancient Art of Warfare*, vol. 1, *Antiquity* (New York: Time-Life Books, 1968), 38–39.

15. Gurcharn Singh Sandhu, *A Military History of Ancient India* (Delhi: Vision Books, 2000), 186–187.

16. James A. Huston, *The Sinews of War: Army Logistics, 1775–1953* (Washington, DC: Office of the Chief of Military History, 1966), 219.

17. Roth, *Logistics*, 125.

18. Ibid., 128.

19. Livy *History of Rome* 27.12.7.

20. Ann Hyland, *Equus: The Horse in the Roman World* (New Haven, CT: Yale University Press, 1990), 92.

21. Thomas D. Seymour, *Life in the Homeric Age* (New York: Biblo and Tannen, 1963), 590.

22. Roth, *Logistics*, 133.

23. Livy *History of Rome* 26.43.8.

24. Keith Hopkins, "Taxes and Trade in the Roman Empire, 200 B.C.E. to C.E. 400," *Journal of Roman Studies* 70 (1980): 86, Table 2.

25. Roth, *Logistics*, 182.

26. Ibid., 187.

27. See Thapliyal, "Military Organization," 75–77 for an explanation of the Indian supply system.

28. Donald V. Sippel, "Some Observations on the Means and Costs of the Transport of Bulk Commodities in the Late Republic and Early Empire," *Ancient World* 16 (1987): 37.

29. Gabriel, *From Sumer to Rome*, 24.

30. *Animal Management* (London: British Army Veterinary Department, 1908), 299.

31. Bernard S. Bachrach, "Animals and Warfare in Early Medieval Europe," in *Armies and Politics in the Early Medieval West*, ed. Bernard S. Bachrach (Brookfield, VT: Variorum, 1993), 717.

32. Ibid.

33. K. D. White, *Roman Farming* (Ithaca, NY: Cornell University Press, 1970), 295.

34. Gabriel, *From Sumer to Rome*, 25.

35. Ibid.

36. James D. Anderson, *Roman Military Supply in North East England*, British Series 224 (Oxford: British Archaeological Reports, 1992), 15.

37. Hyland, *Equus*, 71–72.

38. White, *Roman Farming*, 132.

39. Emmett M. Essin, "Mules, Packs, and Packtrains," *Southwestern Historical Quarterly* 74, no. 1 (1970): 54.

40. Engels, *Alexander the Great*, Table 7, 153.

41. Ibid., 14.

42. Thapliyal, "Military Organization," 777.

43. Junkelmann, Marcus. *The Legions of Augustus: The Roman Soldier in an Archeological Experiment* [in German] (Mainz, Germany: Philipp von Zabern, 1986), 34.

44. Engels, *Alexander the Great*, Table 7, 153.

45. Livy *Histories* 11.16.7.

46. Laffont, *Ancient Art of Warfare*, 56.

47. Michael Grant, *History of Rome* (New York: Charles Scribner, 1978), 264.

48. "The Roman Empire and Military Airlift," *The Wall Street Journal*, 9 December 1987, A7.

49. H.W.F. Saggs, *The Might That Was Assyria* (London: Sidgwick and Jackson, 1984), 255.

50. Richard A. Gabriel, *Culture of War*, 76.

51. See Yaha Zoka, *The Imperial Iranian Army from Cyrus to Pahlavi* (Teheran: Ministry of Culture and Arts Press, 1970), 90–96 for the Persian navy.

52. Herodotus 7.89–97.

53. Sir Percy Sykes, *A History of Persia*, vol. 1 (London: Macmillan, 1985), 163–164.

54. Thapliyal, "Military Organization," 77.

55. Gabriel, *From Sumer to Rome*, 28.

56. Roth, *Logistics*, 198.

Fourteen

✶ ✶ ✶

STRATEGIC RANGE AND ENDURANCE

The ability of ancient armies to maintain larger armies in the field for greater periods resulted in a tremendous increase in their strategic range. Strategic range can be defined as the ability of a military force to project combat power over a given distance. The greater the distance to which military power can be operationally projected and sustained over time, the greater the degree of strategic range. The ability of Iron Age armies to project military power over great distances was not equalled in some cases until the armies of the nineteenth century.

The strategic range of an Early Bronze Age army was approximately 350 by 150 miles. The armies of Sumer and Akkad conducted military operations ranging from the Upper Tigris Valley to the city of Ur, or a range of about 250 by 125 miles.[1] Egyptian armies between 3000 and 1500 B.C.E. could project force from the Nile Valley to Syria, or a distance of 600 by 200 miles.[2] With the dawn of the Iron Age, strategic range increased greatly.

The Egyptian army of 1500–1250 B.C.E. had a strategic range of 1,250 by 200 miles, or more than twice the range of the Egyptian army of the Bronze Age. Chinese and Indian armies could project force over 1,000 miles. Assyria conducted military operations from Assur to Susa to Thebes, an area comprising 1,250 by 300 miles. This was five times the strategic range of the armies of Sumer and Akkad. The armies of Persia, Alexander, Rome, India, and China attained strategic ranges typical of modern mechanized armies. The Persian army, for example, conducted operations from the Iaxartes and Indus rivers to Thrace, Cyrene, and Thebes, a strategic range of 2,500 by 1,000 miles. Alexander's armies ranged from the Hellespont to the Caspian Sea to the Persian Gulf, a range of 2,600 by 1,000 miles.[3] Roman armies had the greatest strategic range of antiquity and controlled a land area from Germany to Morocco and from Scotland to Armenia and Babylon, a strategic range of 3,800 by 1,500 miles,[4] an accomplishment made possible by the excellent Roman system of military roads. The longest road in antiquity was a Roman road that ran from Hadrian's Wall in Scotland to Jerusalem, a distance of 2,520 miles, part of which was traversed via ships across the English Channel.[5]

The armies of the late Iron Age had, on average, a strategic range that was nine times greater than the range of the armies of the Bronze Age. Even in modern times, few of the world's armies can equal the strategic range of some of the great armies of antiquity.

What distinguishes modern warfare from ancient warfare is more than the level of destructive power and military capability attendant to each. The key defining quality of modern war is strategic endurance, the quality of integration of the social, economic, and political resources of the state in support of military operations. The Iron Age saw the emergence of armies whose combat capabilities had increased to levels never seen before in human history, giving birth to war on a modern scale. The increased size and complexity of these armies made it possible to fight battles involving numbers of men that were not usually exceeded in battles of the modern period until at least the battle of Waterloo and, in many cases, until the American Civil War.[6] For much of the early ancient period, armies could often force a strategic decision with a single battle. The fate of states and empires turned on a single victory or defeat. As the states of the Iron Age grew in social and organizational complexity, their ability to remain at war over prolonged periods greatly increased. Because armies could now draw on the total mobilized resources of their states to support military operations, a single battle no longer decided their fate. The strategic endurance of armies of the Iron Age often equaled the armies of World Wars I and II.

Persia, for example, could lose almost every battle against its Greek adversaries for 200 years with little effect on the empire as a whole. Even its eventual defeat at the hands of Alexander required a series of major battles to accomplish. Rome's military efforts in the Punic Wars and in later conflicts demonstrated that the new social organization of the state lent great military endurance to a nation with the moral and political will to use it. In 255 B.C.E. a Roman fleet of 248 ships was sunk in a storm off Cape Pachynus with a loss of over 100,000 men, a number equal to 15 percent of the able-bodied men of military age in all Italy.[7] Rome's response was to build another fleet and continue the war against Carthage. Polybius called the Carthaginian War the bloodiest and costliest in history. Roman losses alone approached 400,000 men, a number almost equal to the all the men lost by the United States in World War II. And still, Rome fought on.[8]

By the end of the ancient period, armies had learned how to fight wars on a modern scale, with accompanying casualty rates and material destruction. After the collapse of Rome in the West, the level of societal organization declined drastically, with the result that states could no longer conduct wars marked by high levels of strategic range and endurance. In the Near East, India, and China, however, the strategic capabilities of the ancient armies continued, lasting until 1453 C.E. in the case of Constantinople. By this time the armies of India and China had retreated to levels of war more characteristic of the West. In the West the use of relatively small professional armies drawn from society's marginals allowed the conduct of warfare without much risk to the survival of the states that fought them. It was not until Napoleonic times that Western states once again began to fight wars requiring the total integration of social, economic, and political resources to support its armies in the field, a capability that first emerged in the armies of the Iron Age.

NOTES

1. Robert Laffont, *The Ancient Art of Warfare*, vol. 1, *Antiquity* (New York: Time-Life Books, 1968), chart 3, 46.

2. Ibid.

3. Ibid.

4. These are my calculations using the same formula used by Laffont.

5. Victor W. von Hagen, *The Ancient Sun Kingdoms of the Americas: Aztec, Maya, Inca* (Cleveland, OH: World Publishing, 1961), 540. Later, the Incas constructed the famous Andean royal road to move their armies. The road ran for 3,250 miles.

6. Richard A. Gabriel and Karen S. Metz, *From Sumer to Rome: The Military Capabilities of Ancient Armies* (Westport, CT: Greenwood Press, 1991), Table 4.1, 85.

7. Robert L. O'Connell, "The Roman Killing Machine," *Quarterly Journal of Military History* 1 (Autumn 1988): 42.

8. During World War II, approximately 300,000 United States troops were killed in action and 700,000 were wounded, plus there were another 100,000 nonbattle deaths.

Fifteen

✳ ✳ ✳

TACTICS

Tactics is defined as the ability of combat units within an army to perform maneuvers and movements that increase their combat power, thereby increasing the combat power and effectiveness of the army as a whole. The maneuvers and movements of tactical units are of two kinds: (1) those undertaken before the battle begins (2) and those conducted while the battle is being fought. The first is called tactical mobility; the second is tactical flexibility and has to do with the commander's control of units engaged in battle. The armies of the Iron Age made great tactical advances that had a profound influence on the conduct of warfare. The increases in the tactical mobility of small units resulted from a number of small advances that, when taken together, had a great overall impact on their ability to fight.

TACTICAL MOBILITY

The Assyrian invention of the jackboot is an excellent example of such an advance. The knee-high leather boot with thick leather soles and hobnails for traction provided much better foot protection than the sandal or soft boot used by most armies. Worn over high woolen socks, the jackboot provided excellent protection against rain, snow, cold, and rocky terrain. This made it possible for Assyrian infantry units to move faster and with fewer injuries in all kinds of weather, contributing to the ability of the Assyrian army to develop an all-weather capability for ground combat. While most armies fought only during the campaign season of moderate weather, Assyrian units regularly fought in summer and winter, even carrying out siege operations during winter months.

Sargon II's campaign against the Urartu in 714 B.C.E. is a textbook example of improved tactical proficiency. Sargon undertook the campaign 600 miles from the Assyrian capital in the late fall. His army, complete with contingents of cavalry, infantry, and chariots, traversed mountains, streams, and rivers along the route of march, traveling through mountain passes blocked with snow.[1] Assyrian units also fought well in marshlands. Placed aboard light reed boats sealed with bitumen, these units became waterborne marines who used fire arrows and torches to burn out the enemy hiding amid the rushes and reeds of the swamp.[2] The ability to mount military operations in all kinds of weather and terrain became a vital military asset for all later Iron Age armies. Alexander, Hannibal, the Chinese, and the legions of Rome all developed the capacity to fight in rough terrain and harsh weather.

The regular use of tactical engineering units provided another increase in the tactical mobility of field units. Sargon's army traveled with hundreds of laborers and pick men to cut roads through forests; the Indian army employed teams of elephants to clear rocks and trees from the army's path. Assyrian engineers constructed the world's first portable military pontoon bridges from palm wood planks and reeds.[3] Inflated animal skins were used by Assyrian troops to float themselves and their equipment across rivers. The large cavalry contingents of the Persian army required engineers who could construct bridges with high sides so that the horses could cross over ravines and crevasses without bolting. Persian and Chinese engineers were capable of diverting the course of a river. Persian engineers diverted the course of a river to deprive the Egyptian fleet of sufficient water to maneuver, and in the Babylonian War, military engineers diverted the course of a stream running through the city so that infantry could enter under the walls by moving along the dry streambed. It was military engineers who constructed the Roman camp every night while on the march. The regular presence of combat engineering crews within field armies was a major innovation in warfare and greatly increased the tactical mobility of combat units.

TACTICAL FLEXIBILITY

The most difficult application of tactics, that is, tactical flexibility, occurs when the army is engaged in battle. It is a problem that has plagued commanders from the beginning of warfare and has only recently been solved by the use of modern communication technologies that permit instant communication between commanders and units. Tactical control of combat units in antiquity was achieved by the use of flags, horns, drums, and the signal mirror. None of these techniques were improved until the seventeenth century C.E., when the use of the field telescope permitted commanders to see what was happening on the battlefield at greater distances. Even so, the ability of a commander to communicate his instructions to units engaged in the fighting was still very limited. Alexander made use of a corps of staff riders, who rode to the combat units to pass instructions. Chinese armies, too, used this device, as did the Romans, who improved it by having a special signaler within each cohort. The Roman army stressed small-unit tactical proficiency more than any army in antiquity, training the soldier to respond quickly to commands given by his unit leader. The result was that no army matched the proficiency of Roman tactical units in the ability to communicate or rapidly change course once engaged.

THE EVOLUTION OF MILITARY TACTICS

The evolution of tactics over 1,500 years of military history is a fascinating tale of armies increasing their combat power by improving small-unit tactical capabilities. This evolution proceeded in stages, each stage building on solutions to problems confronted by the limitations of the previous stage. The beginnings of the evolutionary process were evident as early as the fifteenth century B.C.E., when Egyptian armies learned how to control large units of different combat capabilities, setting the stage for the emergence of a genuine combined arms capability. The earliest armies of antiquity (up to 1800 B.C.E.) were essentially infantry forces with little in the way of tactical capability. Sumerian, Akkadian, and Egyptian armies organized their infantry units by the types of weapons each carried—spear, bow, and sickle sword. This did little to increase tactical proficiency, and most battles were little more than raging melees. Once arrayed for battle, these dense infantry formations could hardly move in any direction, except forward, and then at a very slow pace. The rival infantry formations clashed head-on, slashing at one another until one side lost its nerve and fled. The victor's troops were equally exhausted, and no lethal pursuit was usually possible.[4]

All this changed with the Aryan invasions of the Middle and Far East, a development that brought the war chariot to the Near East and India at about the same time. The chariot introduced a radically new tactical capability to the battlefield: mobility. The chariot also added a new dimension to shock tactics against infantry and, when equipped with archers using the new composite bow, introduced the world's first mobile weapon platform. The chariot was the only weapon that could participate in all phases of the battle with equal effectiveness.[5] Once the enemy broke, the chariot could be used in pursuit, something that had been heretofore impossible. The chariot could also be used to inflict tactical surprise, something which had never been possible with packed infantry formations. The chariot permitted the development of another tactical innovation: the use of mobile reserves committed at different points and times to influence events on the battlefield. The Egyptians were the first to experience these new tactical capabilities when the Hyksos armies invaded Egypt around 1700 B.C.E., quickly defeated Pharaoh's infantry armies, and occupied the Nile delta for more than a century. Eventually, the Egyptians equipped their armies with Hyksos military equipment, copied their tactics, and drove the Hyksos from Egypt. For the next 500 years, the armies of Egypt dominated the Near East.

The combat power of the Assyrian army relied on its use of different types of units acting in tactical concert. The infantry remained the Assyrian arm of decision until the end of the empire. Its main tactical unit was a highly trained maneuver company that could be easily formed into units of 50 to 200 men, depending on tactical requirements of the moment. The infantry was supported by archer companies, whose use of the shoulder quiver increased their rate of fire by 40 percent.[6] The Assyrian chariot was a heavy, three-horse machine that carried three spearmen. The idea was to deliver shock against enemy formations from many directions at once, leaving the spearmen to dismount and fight as heavy infantry. Although the Hittites often used chariots to carry infantry into the attack, the Assyrians were the first to introduce the use of true mounted infantry, employing their chariots in much the same manner as modern armies use armored personnel carriers.

The Assyrians were the first army of the Near East and West to introduce a new combat arm: cavalry. Using the saddle girth, crupper, and breast strap to stabilize the rider—the stirrup had not yet been invented[7]—made it possible to place archers on horseback for the first time in the Near East; archers mounted on both horses and elephants had been known in India for two centuries prior to this. A stable horseman could effectively utilize the long spear, giving rise to the lancer. Cavalry was most tactically useful in reconnaissance and the pursuit and could be used as well to harass enemy horsemen. Because horses will not charge into a wall of infantrymen armed with spears pointing to the front, cavalry was not very effective as a means to deliver shock.

The Persians expanded the role of cavalry in their armies, eventually reaching a ratio of about 20 percent cavalry to 80 percent infantry.[8] Persian heavy cavalry was used primarily to draw the enemy into an infantry battle and to neutralize enemy cavalry by engagement. The main tactical weakness of the Persian army was its lack of heavy infantry in sufficient numbers, while its use of dense formations hindered the ability of its infantry to maneuver. Whenever the Persian army encountered Greek heavy infantry, the Persians were almost always defeated. The Greeks had discovered the secret of heavy infantry, and in the hands of Philip and Alexander the secret revolutionized small-unit tactics. The heavily armored infantry hoplite of Classical Greece fighting in a tightly packed phalanx had the single advantage of being almost invulnerable to cavalry attack. The densely packed Macedonian phalanx armed with the thirteen-foot *sarissa* pike was even more invulnerable. Against enemy spear infantry, the *sarissa* had nearly double the reach of the usual spear, making even a successful infantry attack against it very difficult.[9] Despite its weight and depth, the Macedonian phalanx was trained to change itself into a number of battle formations—square, rectangle, and circle—and tactical drills such as disciplined frontal, oblique, hinge, and even retrograde movements gave it more maneuverability once engaged than was ever possible with the hoplite phalanx that it replaced.

Alexander used these tactical capabilities to good advantage, using his heavy infantry formations to anchor the center of the line and to act as a platform of maneuver for his primary combat striking army, the heavy cavalry armed with the javelin.[10] Alexander coupled this tactical innovation with another: the oblique formation. Alexander often deployed his infantry formations in an oblique line, with one wing running back and away from the center. The heavy cavalry was deployed on the far right of the line, connected to the infantry line by a hinge of elite infantry. Using his forces in concert, Alexander would engage his enemy on the flank, forcing him to turn inward toward the attack. As the cavalry pressed the flank, the infantry advanced in hedgehog formation toward the enemy center. If the enemy flank broke, the cavalry could envelop, using the infantry as the anvil against which the cavalry could hammer the enemy. If the enemy flank held, the full weight of the heavy infantry could be directed against the enemy center. Alexander was the first commander in antiquity to use his cavalry as an arm of decision.

By the fourth century B.C.E. Indian tactical brilliance was in full bloom. If we are to believe the *Arthasastra*, an Indian army was capable of scores of tactical formations employed defensively and offensively.[11] Indian armies, besides being very large, were also the first armies to have four combat arms—infantry, cavalry, chariots, and elephants—and to employ all four arms in combination in sophisticated tactical arrays. As professional armies, the armies of India were very disciplined and well trained, perhaps to a level not seen in the West or Near East until Alexander and the Romans. Even the animals were superbly trained. In the battle of the Hydaspes River, Alexander's *sarissa* phalanx advanced against the Indian elephant line with their spears pointed at the animals' eyes. On command, the elephants retreated step by backward step, slowly to the rear, never losing their cohesion or organizational integrity. An army that could train its animals to perform this well was an army to be reckoned with on the battlefield. It is fair to say that the armies of India in the fourth century B.C.E. were both organizationally and tactically superior to any army found at the same time in the West or Near East.

By the second century B.C.E. the tactical proficiency of ancient armies had gone through several phases. The first was the primacy of infantry, brought to an end by the Egyptian use of the chariot acquired from the Hyksos and introducing the new element of mobility to the battlefield. The Assyrians changed the tactical role of the chariot to mounted infantry and introduced cavalry to provide mobility and flexibility. The great reliance on cavalry by the Persians led to the neglect of heavy infantry, heretofore the dominant arm among Greek and Chinese armies. At the same time the chariot fell into decline in India, cavalry, too, came to play a subordinate role to the war elephant. Alexander's use of infantry as a platform of maneuver signaled the leading role of cavalry, at least in the West. In each phase of tactical development the role of infantry as the main maneuver and killing arm of the armies of antiquity declined. How surprising, then, that during the final phase of tactical development in antiquity the infantry should regain its primacy on the battlefield.

Ancient Rome's Highly Developed Infantry

It fell to Rome to develop infantry to the highest degree in antiquity. The spine of the Roman army were its heavy infantry formations, which were more maneuverable than any infantry the ancient world had ever seen. Roman infantrymen were the first soldiers in the world to use the sword—the *gladius*—as a primary weapon, and the killing power of Roman infantry surpassed that of any other infantry to an almost exponential degree.[12] The secret of the Roman killing machine was that the Roman soldier was the first soldier to fight within a combat formation while at the same time remaining somewhat independent of its movement as a unit. Instead of fighting in a dense formation, Roman infantry fought in open formation, that is, in units—cohorts—of 600 men subdivided into maniples (literally, "handfuls"). The Roman innovation was to build in spaces between soldiers and units, greatly increasing tactical flexibility and mobility. The space between each soldier was approximately five square yards, sufficient to allow the soldier to wield his sword against individual opponents. Each maniple was separated from the next by twenty yards, a distance equal to the frontage of the maniple itself. The maniples in each line were staggered like a checkerboard—a quincunx—with each line of maniples covering the gaps in the line in front of it. This arrangement permitted each maniple or the whole line to turn in any direction to meet an attack.

Tactical flexibility was increased by the relationship between the lines of infantry. If the first line grew tired, it could break contact and retire through the spaces left in the second line, permitting the second line to step forward and continue the fight. Whole units or individual soldiers could retire and rest in this manner, guaranteeing that the enemy was always fighting rested soldiers. No army until the Roman army had learned how to break contact and conduct a tactical retreat in good order. The Romans were masters of the art of tactical withdrawal. Unlike earlier infantry formations, Roman maniples could operate totally independently of one another and could maneuver rapidly when left on their own.[13] This permitted Roman commanders to position their maniples to ambush the enemy and take him by surprise, something no other infantry army could do. The Roman infantry formations were the most tactically flexible and maneuverable of all infantry formations of the armies of the ancient world.

Roman infantry reigned supreme in the ancient world for 500 years until the fatal defeat at the battle of Adrianople (378 B.C.E.) at the hands of barbarian cavalry. Followed as it was by 200 years of barbarian invasions by tribal armies that stressed the role of the individual mounted warrior, the empire in the West collapsed. With it went the primacy of infantry, replaced by cavalry as the primary combat arm. During the Middle Ages the armored knight became the prototype of the warrior, and armies became little more than undisciplined coteries of knights engaging in individual combats. Compared to the time of the Romans, tactics and other military arts declined substantially, and battles of this period were little more than semiorganized brawls. At Laupen (1339 C.E.) the Swiss demonstrated that disciplined infantry could again stop a cavalry charge, and the battle of Crecy (1346 C.E.) showed that the armored horseman had become so heavy with armor as to be incapable of maneuvering.[14] Nonetheless, cavalry remained supreme on the battlefield for another 200 years before infantry could once again be employed with the skill of the ancients.

NOTES

1. Yigael Yadin, *The Art of Warfare in Biblical Lands in the Light of Archaeological Study*, vol. 1, trans. M. Pearlman (New York: McGraw-Hill, 1963), 303. See also Georges Contenau, *Everyday Life in Babylon and Assyria* (London: Edward Arnold, 1954), 149–159 for a good account of Sargon's campaign.

2. Yadin, *Art of Warfare*, 303.

3. Contenau, *Everyday Life*, 46.

4. The one exception to this rule was the Israelite army, which seems to have carried out lethal pursuits on foot in a number of battles. Joshua's battle at the Aylon Valley is one example.

5. Richard A. Gabriel, *The Culture of War: Invention and Early Development* (Westport, CT: Greenwood Press, 1990), 95.

6. The estimate of increased rates of fire for the shoulder quiver was provided by several professional archers and must be regarded as only a general indicator of the rate of fire that was actually accomplished.

7. Except in India, where the stirrup *may* have been invented. See Sarva Daman Singh, *Ancient Indian Warfare* (Delhi: Motilal Banarsidass, 1997), 63–64.

8. Yaha Zoka, *The Imperial Iranian Army from Cyrus to Pahlavi* (Teheran: Ministry of Culture and Arts Press, 1970), 19.

9. Macedonian *sarissa* infantry proved vulnerable to the Roman sword, however, when Roman infantry chopped off the metal heads of the spears, rendering the *sarissa* useless in close combat.

10. Richard A. Gabriel and Karen S. Metz, *From Sumer to Rome: The Military Capabilities of Ancient Armies* (Westport, CT: Greenwood Press, 1991), 33.

11. *Historical Perspectives of Warfare in India,* ed. S. N. Prasad (Delhi: Center for Studies in Civilizations, 2002), 55–62 for a description of Indian tactical formations during this period.

12. Robert L. O'Connell, "The Roman Killing Machine," *Quarterly Journal of Military History* 1 (Autumn 1988): 37–38.

13. Gabriel, *From Sumer to Rome,* 35.

14. The Swiss won at Laupen by the reinvention of the Macedonian phalanx, complete with long, *sarissa*-like pikes. The striking power of the Swiss phalanx was increased by the addition of halberdsmen, who attacked the mounted knights that had been brought to a standstill by the phalanx with double-bladed and hooked axes, and changing tactics plus improved fire weapons rendered plate armor superfluous, but much later than Crecy.

Sixteen

✷ ✷ ✷

MILITARY STAFFS

The emergence of large, complex armies brought into existence the specialized military staffs required to make them work. The invention of the military staff may be compared in importance with the rise of the general administrative mechanisms of the state that appeared at the same time. Egypt, for example, in 3400 B.C.E. was able to organize the human and material resources to construct and maintain a 700-mile-long irrigation system along the entire length of the Nile River within Egyptian borders.[1] Around 2500 B.C.E. the Sumerians constructed a 270-mile-long wall across southern Iraq to reduce the raids of desert bedouins—"those that did not know grain." We are so accustomed to various forms of social organization and bureaucracy in the modern age that we are prone to forget how important a social invention administrative mechanisms were. Without them it would have been impossible for states of the ancient period to evolve the high levels of social and economic complexity that they did, and it would have been impossible to produce the large and complex armies that these administrative mechanisms made possible. The great public works projects of the ancient world, the pyramids of Egypt, the irrigation systems of Sumer and Assyria, the great walls and roads of China, and the extensive fortifications of the Roman East and India were inherently dependent on sophisticated organizational institutions and practices, which were then applied to military use.

MILITARY STAFF DEVELOPMENT IN ANCIENT ARMIES

Sumer and Egypt

We know nothing about the military staff organization of ancient Sumer, except that the king was aided by professional staff officers to supply, house, and feed the army on a regular basis. The first identifiable military staffs emerged in Egypt during the period of the Old Kingdom (2686–2160 B.C.E.). The organizational structure of these staffs is unknown, but an analysis of titles provides evidence of a sophisticated staff organization. The principle of organization was function, and there are titles for quartermaster, various officer ranks, types of commanders, and specialist sections dealing with desert warfare and garrisons.[2] A much clearer staff structure is evident during the Middle Kingdom (2040–1786 B.C.E.), when titles for general officers in charge of logistics, recruits, frontier fortresses, and shock troops are found.[3] The command structure of the army is fully articulated in terms of titles by this time. Titles for military police, police patrols, and military judges are evident. For the first time, there is evidence of a military intelligence service, reflected in the title "master of the secrets of the king in the army."[4] The regular presence of scribes suggests that much of the administrative routine may have been committed to permanent record. By 1500 B.C.E. the Egyptian armies of the New Kingdom possessed special field intelligence units, translation sections, and the first use of the commander's conference for staff planning on the battlefield.[5]

Assyria

Our knowledge of military staffs in Assyria is limited largely to the description of the special staff of horse logistics officers who recruited, trained, and supplied the army with 3,000 horses a month.[6] During the imperial period Assyria was a military state, and it is likely that almost all aspects of life relevant to the military establishment were controlled by military staff officers, including the secret police, the civil bureaucracy, the intelligence services, logistics, and even the training of scribes to keep accounts and records. Given the high degree of social organization and integration generally characteristic of Assyria during this time, while we have only limited evidence of military staff organization, it is a safe conclusion that it existed and was organizationally sophisticated in most respects.

India

It was during the Mahabharata War (1000–900 B.C.E.) that something approaching a modern military staff structure appeared in India.[7] Indian military staffs provided for military training of soldiers (*dhanurveda*), logistics, military intelligence, fortifications, and direction over an army with four combat arms—chariots, cavalry, elephants, and infantry.[8] Several centuries later, during the reign of Chandragupta Maurya (321–297 B.C.E.), Indian military staffs became larger and capable of directing more complex armies. The first Indian text on politicomilitary organization, the *Arthasastra*, was written at this time by Kautilya, Chandragupta's Brahmin advisor. The *Arthasastra* is a combination of Machiavelli's *The Prince* and Plato's *Republic* and describes how to organize a state and an army and make both work efficiently.[9] It provides us with a good deal of our knowledge of the political and military organization of the Mauryan imperial state.

The Hittites, the Mitanni, and the Israelites

We know almost nothing about the military staffs of the Hittites and Mitanni since both were feudal societies whose armies comprised noble warrior retinues called to the service of the king. In this sense they were probably much like the later armies of medieval Europe: whatever staffs existed were personal retainers of the king with no functional authority beyond that of the king's retinue. The Israelite army under David and Solomon was very well organized and staffed with professional officers and administrative personnel, the last drawn heavily from the Canaanite population because of their previous experience and technical expertise.[10] The Israelites often lacked technical expertise and hired mercenaries and other technical personnel to administer to the army and the state. When Solomon wanted to construct the Temple in Jerusalem, he contracted the work out to king Hiram of Sidon, who provided the materials, workers, and design of the Temple itself, a classic example of a Canaanite temple.[11]

China

By the fourth century B.C.E. Chinese military staffs had grown large and complex in response to the need to direct and supply very large armies, often much larger than any seen in the West during the same period. The Confucian ideal of merit-based bureaucracies had already taken root in China, and while generals and higher nobility were still appointed by the emperor, many of the middle ranks on Chinese military staffs were selected for expertise and competence. An interesting innovation found on Chinese military staffs of this period was the Philosopher of War, the most famous of which was Master Sun of the state of Wu (Wu Sun Tzu), known to history as Sun Tzu (544–496 B.C.E.). Sun Tzu's treatise, *The Art of War*, was but one of dozens written by him and other intellectual *condottieri* who traveled from court to court, offering their advice on war. One of the most famous of these advisors was Sun Bin (380–326 B.C.E.), who wrote *Theories on the Art of War*.

It was during this period that the first written treatises on tactics and strategy appeared in the West.[12] There are extant cuneiform manuals for military doctors in Assyria that imply that the Assyrians may have also written and used military textbooks to train their officers. Xenophon's classic works on military affairs, the *Anabasis* and the *Cyropedia*, appeared at about this time as well.

Greece and Macedonia

The armies of the Homeric age, being clan warrior retinues, had neither need nor ability to develop military staffs. The same may be said for the barbarian armies— Germans, Goths, Gauls, and so on—that fought the Romans. Tribal social orders lacked clear organizational definition and did not develop the functionally lateral and hierarchical structure required by modern administrative organizations. The citizen armies of Classical Greece were part-time affairs, and there does not appear to have been any permanent staff organization, except for Sparta, itself a military society. The armies of Philip of Macedon and Alexander possessed primitive staffs that did not reach the level of sophistication of earlier armies in the Near East. Both these armies reveal special staff sections for logistics, artillery, intelligence, medical support, and, interestingly, military history. But the structures of both armies were essentially extensions of the personalities of their commanders and did not survive long enough to acquire any institutional foundations of their own.

Rome

The height of military staff development in the ancient world was achieved by the Romans. So effective was the Roman military staff system that more than any other army of the time, it could still serve as the model for modern armies. Each Roman senior officer had a small administrative staff responsible for paperwork. The Roman army, like modern armies, generated enormous amounts of permanent files. Each soldier had an administrative file that contained his full history, awards, physical examinations, training reports, leave status, retirement bank account records, and pay records. Legion and army level staff records show sections dealing with intelligence, supply, medical care, pay, engineers, artillery, sieges, training, and veterinary affairs.[13] There was almost nothing in the organization or function of the Roman military staff that would not be instantly recognizable to a modern staff officer.

The degree of organization and sophistication of the military staffs of the armies of the Late Iron Age was not achieved again until the armies of the American Civil War. Even the armies of Napoleon, as sophisticated as they were thought to have been at the time, did not equal the organizational skill of the Assyrian and Roman military staffs. In terms of operational proficiency, no military staff attained the level of the Roman army staff until the German General Staff in 1820. Like the military staffs before them, the most important officers of the German General Staff were logistics officers and engineers. In the conduct of war on a large scale, whether in ancient or modern times, some things remain unchanged.

NOTES

1. Richard A. Gabriel, *The Culture of War: Invention and Early Development* (Westport, CT: Greenwood Press, 1990), 48.

2. For more on the subject of Egyptian military titles, see Alan Richard Schulman, *Military Rank, Title, and Organization in the Egyptian New Kingdom* (Berlin: Bruno Hessling Verlag, 1964).

3. R. O. Faulkner, "Egyptian Military Organization," *Journal of Egyptian Archaeology* 39 (1953): 39.

4. Ibid.

5. Richard A. Gabriel, *Great Captains of Antiquity* (Westport, CT: Greenwood Press, 2001), 40.

6. Richard A. Gabriel, *The Great Armies of Antiquity* (Westport, CT: Praeger, 2002), 133.

7. Gurcharn Singh Sandhu, *A Military History of Ancient India* (Delhi: Vision Books, 2000), 129–149.

8. Ibid., 133.

9. Romila Thapar, *A History of India* (Middlesex, UK: Penguin Books, 1966), 24.

10. Richard A. Gabriel, *The Military History of Ancient Israel* (Westport, CT: Praeger, 2003), 288–289.

11. Ibid., 297.

12. Hans Delbrück, *History of the Art of War within the Framework of Political History*, vol. 1, *Antiquity* (Westport, CT: Greenwood Press, 1975), 159–163.

13. For more detail on the Roman military staff, see Peter Connolly, *Greece and Rome at War* (Englewood Cliffs, NJ: Prentice-Hall, 1981), 223; see also Trevor N. Dupuy, *The Evolution of Weapons and Warfare* (Indianapolis, IN: Bobbs-Merrill, 1980), 98–101.

Seventeen

✷ ✷ ✷

SIEGECRAFT AND ARTILLERY

THE FORTIFIED CITY

Siegecraft and artillery came into existence in order to deal with one of the most powerful defensive systems produced by the Iron Age: the fortified city. The first fortified city to appear in the Middle East was at Jericho, although it is by no means clear that the walls of this city were originally built for military reasons.[1] Fortified cities are found almost a millennium earlier, around 2000 B.C.E., in India, where they were constructed by the Indus Valley civilization.[2] These cities, located on hills and surrounded by brick walls, may have been originally constructed to protect against floods.[3] By the Bronze Age, there was unambiguous evidence of fortifications constructed for purely military purposes. The first undisputed example of a fortified city in antiquity was Urak in Iraq, dating from 2700 B.C.E. Its walls enclosed an urban population of 3,000–5,000 people.[4] Within 200 years, fortification of urban areas had become the norm.

The fortifications of the Bronze Age were remarkable. The fortress at Buhun built by the Egyptians in the Sudan around 2200 B.C.E. was 180 yards square and surrounded by a mud brick wall fifteen feet thick and thirty feet high. The wall had firing bastions every eighteen feet. Outside the wall was a second wall serving as a steep revetment, with its own set of firing enclosures every thirty feet. A moat twenty-six feet across and eighteen feet deep surrounded the outer wall, with yet another steep glacis on the inner slope. The gate complex was forty-five feet high and stretched from the inner wall across the moat, allowing archers to cover the parallel approaches with arrow fire.[5] Fortified cities in India had even more extensive walls, towers, and gates, often extending four miles in circumference.[6] As impressive as Bronze Age fortifications often were, they

The King's Gate: A section of the defensive walls of Boghazkoy. The Art Archive/Dagli Orti.

were dwarfed in size and complexity by the fortifications of the Iron Age. The Israelite fortress at Hazor had walls that ran 1,000 by 7,000 meters.[7] The city of Qatna had walls four miles long, and the Hittite capital of Boghazkoy was surrounded by walls six miles in length. The entire wall of Boghazkoy and its supporting strong points were made of solid rock and brick.[8] So important were fortifications to the ancient armies that the need to secure adequate stone and wood to construct them led both Egypt and Assyria to occupy Lebanon repeatedly in their attempts to secure these strategic materials.

Fortified cities put field armies at grave risk. Safe behind a city's walls, a defending army could provision itself for long periods, while attacking armies were forced to live off the land until hunger, thirst, and disease ravaged them. An army bent on conquest could not force a strategic decision as long as the defender refused to give battle. An army that chose to bypass fortified cities and garrisons placed itself at risk of attack from the rear and across its line of supply and communication. If an army was to achieve its strategic objectives, it had little choice but to find a way to subdue enemy fortifications. Alexander learned this lesson after the battle of Issus, when he attempted to subdue the fortified cities along the Phoenician coast. The ability to overcome fortifications was an art that no successful army in antiquity could afford to be without.

METHODS OF ATTACKING FORTIFIED CITIES

Yigael Yadin has observed that there are five ways for an attacking force to overcome a fortified city: an assault over the walls, penetration through the walls themselves, tunneling below the walls, gaining access to the city by trickery or ruse, and prolonged siege.[9] All other things equal, the advantage usually lay with the attacker whose army had the advantage of numbers. Most cities of antiquity, at least up to the middle Iron Age, were relatively small in population, about 240 people per urban acre enclosed by the walls.[10] Thus a city like Jerusalem in David's time (1050 B.C.E.) enclosed sixteen acres with a wall 1,540 yards long. Its population was about 4,000 people.[11] Approximately one-fourth of a city's population could be used in its defense,[12] or about 1,000 soldiers, each soldier defending one and a half meters of wall. An attacking army could easily deploy four or five soldiers against each meter of wall. Joshua's army at Jericho was sufficiently large to encircle the city with ranks of soldiers six men deep.[13] Moreover, the attacker could mount assaults at several places at once along the wall, forcing the defenders to shift forces from place to place, leaving other sections of the wall undefended. For reasons of simple mathematics, most assaults on fortified cities were successful.[14]

Siegecraft

Military engineers invented the techniques for overcoming the defenses of fortified cities. One of the earliest inventions was the battering ram, which dates from at least 2500 B.C.E.[15] By 2000 B.C.E. the battering ram was found in almost all armies of the ancient world. The Egyptians also invented the technique of securing a large metal blade to a heavy pole and using it to pry bricks and stones from the walls to create a breach. The Hittites used the technique of building an earthen ramp to a low spot in the wall and then rolling large covered battering rams up to the wall to attack it at its thinnest point. Assyrians and Persians constructed massive siege towers that were taller than the defensive walls, using archers to provide cover fire for the battering ram crews working below. Persian siege towers were set on wheels and moved with the army. The scaling ladder was one of the earliest siegecraft devices. Egyptian texts tell of soldiers strapping their shields on their backs to have both hands free to climb the ladders. The shields acted like a turtle's shell, protecting the soldiers from stones and arrows thrown down on them by the defenders. The Assyrians sometimes used a short scaling ladder to mount soldiers with axes and levers to dislodge stones mid-way up the wall, while tunnelers weakened it from below. Longer ladders were used by all armies to insert combat forces over the walls.

If an army was to preserve the offensive, it had to subdue fortifications quickly. The absolute masters of rapid assault on cities were the Assyrian armies of the seventh century B.C.E. The key to success was to coordinate several different types of assaults on the walls at the same time but at different points. Battering rams supported by siege towers were first brought into position at several points along the wall. Scaling ladders with lever crews were deployed at other points. Sappers and tunnelers worked to gain entry from beneath the wall by weakening and collapsing a section of the foundation. (This worked very well if the walls were casement walls. Casement walls are really two walls filled with rubble between them. By weakening the outer wall, the weight of the rubble itself pressing out against the weakened wall would cause the wall to collapse.) At the appropriate time, long scaling ladders were used to mount attacks over the walls at several points to force the defender to disperse his forces.[16]

The armies of Classical Greece were hopelessly primitive in the art of siegecraft, as were the tribal armies of Gaul and Germany. Carthaginian armies also lacked siege trains. After the battle of Cannae, Hannibal failed to attack Rome largely because he lacked the siege equipment to do so.[17] Greek armies relied primarily on blockade and starvation to subdue a city, methods far too slow to be used by an army trying to force a strategic decision. It was not until the late Classical period that the citizen armies of Greece made a few rudimentary attempts at using siege engines. In 440 B.C.E. Artmon used siege towers against Samos but failed to take the city.[18] In 424 B.C.E. the Boetians may have used a primitive flamethrower—a hollow wooden tube that held a cauldron of burning sulfur, charcoal, and pitch at one end—against the wooden walls of Delium.[19] In 397 B.C.E. Dionysisus successfully employed siege towers and rudimentary catapults in the attack on Motya.[20]

Greek armies did not begin to approach the siegecraft capabilities of the armies of the Near East until the reigns of Philip of Macedon and Alexander. Philip realized that the new Macedonian army would remain a force fit only for obtaining limited objectives if it was not provided with the capability for rapidly reducing cities. Alexander's victories would have been impossible without this capability. Philip introduced sophisticated siegecraft capabilities into his army, copying many of the techniques used by the Assyrians and passed to him by the Persians. Both Philip's and Alexander's armies made regular use of siege towers, battering rams, fire arrows, and the *testudo* (a device wheeled up to the wall of the fortified city that protected the attackers against the defenders).[21]

Alexander's campaigns against the Indian republics after the battle of the Hydaspes River (326 B.C.E.) provide a glimpse into the nature of Indian fortifications and Alexander's methods of reducing them. Curtius tells us that although most Indian towns had walls, probably erected to protect against bandits, most did not have proper fortifications and were easy targets. Others were more difficult because they took advantage of terrain characteristics, such as building on a hill or steep cliff.[22] Important towns, however, displayed impressive fortifications. Curtius described Massage as being defended by

> an army of 38,000 infantry . . . a city that was strongly fortified by both nature and art. For, on the east an impetuous mountain stream with steep banks on both sides barred approach to the city, while to the south and west nature, as if designing to form a rampart, had piled up gigantic rocks, at the base of which lay sloughs and yawning chasms hollowed in the course of ages to vast depths, while a ditch of mighty labor drawn from their extremity continued the line of defense. The city was surrounded by a wall 35 stadia [6.2 kilometers] in circumference which had a basis of stonework supporting a superstructure of unburnt, sun-dried bricks. The brickwork was bound into a solid fabric by means of stones.... Strong beams had been laid upon these supporting wooden floors which covered the walls and afforded passage among them.[23]

To overcome these defenses, Alexander had his troops demolish the houses outside the walls to make a platform. Depressions in the ground were filled in with stones and trees to make a level platform. On the leveled ground Alexander had his men construct several mobile wooden siege towers and placed his ballistae on their tops. The ballistae then hurled stones down on the defenders, shattering their walls.[24] Curtius says that the defenders were awed by the ballistae, implying that they might have been unknown in India at this time. The texts describing Indian siege techniques do not describe ballistae and focus mostly on defensive measures, such as firepots thrown from the walls or *satghanis*, a large wooden log with metal spikes that could be dropped from the walls to crush attackers below.[25] Another weapon, the *yantra*, may refer to a device for hurling stones and missiles at the enemy, but we have no information as to its design. We might reasonably conclude that both fortifications and the techniques for demolishing them were not as highly developed in India as they were in the Near East, at least during Alexander's time.

Military fortification seems to have come late to China, at least on any large scale. It is only with the dawn of the Warring States period (464–221 B.C.E.) that we begin to find the regular fortification of cities and towns for military purposes. Chinese military architecture, including the Great Wall, is credited with a major innovation in construction. By mixing mortar with rice milk instead of water Chinese engineers invented a new kind of mortar that was relatively impervious to rain and moisture. Its strength, when dry, also permitted the laying of bricks at very steep angles without having the structural load of the bricks pull the structure apart. The introduction of extensive fortifications led to developments in siegecraft, including the use of specialized equipment, such as chariots with large shields to protect workers, wheeled towers and rams, movable ladders, catapults, and powerful crossbows that could discharge several large bolts at once. On campaign it was customary for armies to construct fortified camps with walls of rammed earth.[26]

The Roman ability to reduce fortifications was probably the best in the ancient world, but it relied primarily on organization and application rather than on engineering innovation. Roman siege engines were mostly improved versions of the old Greek and Persian machines. The Romans used armored siege towers, some as high as twenty-four meters; massive iron battering rams far larger and heavier than any predecessor; large iron hooks to dislodge stones; covered platforms to protect miners and assault teams; and bridges, drawbridges, and elevators mounted on towers to swing assault teams over the walls.[27] Most important, Roman siegecraft depended on manpower, organization, discipline, and determination. Once the Romans were committed to a siege, the results were inevitable, no matter how long it took to succeed.

The Romans raised the art of circumvallation and countervallation to new heights. At Masada they constructed a stone wall around the entire mountain. Manned at regular intervals with soldiers, the purpose of the wall was to prevent anyone from escaping the besieged fortress. When there was a threat from a relieving army, circumvallation was supplemented by countervallation, where another wall was built so that the troops could defend against an attack from a relieving force. Caesar did this at the siege of Alesia in 52 B.C.E.[28] Constructing these walls took considerable time. In the case of Masada the Romans laid siege to the mountaintop fortress for three years. In the process they constructed a three-mile-long sloping earthen ramp to the top, along which they moved siege machinery and troops for the final assault.

It was Philip of Macedon who first organized a special group of engineers within his army to design and build catapults. Philip's and, later, Alexander's use of catapults allowed Greek science and engineering to contribute to the art of war. By the time of Demetrios I (305 B.C.E.), known to history as Poliorcetes ("the Besieger"), Greek inventiveness in military engineering was probably the best in the ancient world.[29] It fell to Alexander's engineers to develop a number of new ideas. Diades invented a hook mounted on a lever suspended from a high vertical frame that was used to knock down the upper parapets of a wall. Diades also invented the *telenon*, a large box that could hold a number of armed men. Suspended from a tall mast, the *telenon* could be raised and lowered on tackle like an elevator to hoist men over the walls. To this day, the military art of siege warfare is called "poliocretics," in honor of the Greek contributions to the art.

THE INVENTION OF ARTILLERY

The most important contribution of Greek military engineering of this period was the invention of artillery, the earliest of which took the form of catapults and torsion-fired missiles. The earliest example dates from the fourth century B.C.E. and was called a *gastraphetes*, literally, "belly shooter."[30] It was a primitive crossbow that fired a wooden bolt on a flat trajectory along a slot in the aiming rod. Later, weapons fired by torsion bars powered by horsehair and ox tendon could fire arrows, stones, and pots of burning pitch along a parabolic arc. Some of these machines were quite large and were mounted on wheels to improve tactical mobility. One of these machines, the *palintonon*, could fire an eight-pound stone over 300 yards, a range about equal to Napoleonic cannon. All these weapons were used by Philip in his sieges. It fell to Alexander, however, to use them in a completely new way—as covering artillery. Alexander's army carried smaller, prefabricated catapults weighing only eighty-five pounds. The larger machines were dismantled and carried along in wagons.

Roman advances in the design, mobility, and firepower of artillery produced the largest, longest-ranged, and most rapid-fire artillery pieces of the ancient world. The rate of fire of Roman field artillery was not surpassed until the invention of the breach-loading artillery gun firing fixed ammunition at the end of the American Civil War. Roman catapults were much larger than the old Greek models and were powered by torsion devices and springs made of sinew kept supple when stored in canisters of oil. Josephus recorded in his account of the Roman siege of Jerusalem that the largest Roman artillery pieces were the onagi, or "wild asses," so called because of their recoil kick. According to Josephus, an onager could hurl a 100-pound stone over 400 yards.[31] Vegetius tells us that each legion had ten onagi, one per cohort, organic to its organization.[32] Smaller versions of these machines, such as the scorpion and ballista, were sufficiently compact to be transported disassembled by horse or mule. These machines could fire a seven to ten pound stone over 300 yards.[33] Caesar required that each legion carry thirty of these smaller guns, giving the legion a mobile, organic artillery capability.

Smaller machines fired iron-tipped bolts. Designed much like the crossbow but mounted on small platforms or legs, these machines required a two-man crew to operate and were used as rapid-fire field guns against enemy formations. They could fire a twenty-six-inch bolt over a range of almost 300 yards.[34] Larger versions mounted on wheeled frames were called *carroballistae* and required a ten-man crew. These larger machines could fire three to four bolts a minute and were used to lay down a barrage of fire against enemy troop concentrations.[35] They were the world's first rapid-fire field artillery guns.

The development of siegecraft as a requirement of Iron Age armies represented a major innovation in warfare. Without the ability to reduce cities and fortified strong points, no army on the march in hostile territory could hope to force a strategic decision with any rapidity. Under these circumstances, the very idea of empire would have been unthinkable in much the same way as it was for the armies of Classical Greece, which had no siegecraft capability at all. The search for more effective ways to destroy fortifications produced the new combat arm of artillery. While Alexander was the first to use this new arm of war, it was the Romans who gave birth to the idea of using artillery as an antipersonnel weapon. Both siege engines and artillery represent the emergence of major new ideas in warfare, ideas that came to fruition with the introduction of gunpowder 1,000 years later.

NOTES

1. James Mellaart, *The Neolithic of the Near East* (New York: Charles Scribner, 1975), 50–58.

2. Gurcharn Singh Sandhu, *A Military History of Ancient India* (Delhi: Vision Books, 2000), 58.

3. Ibid., 26, 58.

4. *Encyclopaedia Britannica*, 15th ed., s.v. "Sumerian Civilization."

5. Leonard Cottrell, *The Warrior Pharaohs* (New York: Putnam, 1969), 45–48.

6. Sarva Daman Singh, *Ancient Indian Warfare* (Delhi: Motilal Banarsidass, 1997), 126–127.

7. *Encyclopaedia Britannica*, 15th ed., s.v. "Sumerian Civilization."

8. Ibid.

9. Yigael Yadin, *The Art of Warfare in Biblical Lands in the Light of Archaeological Study*, vol. 1, trans. M. Pearlman (New York: McGraw-Hill, 1963), 16.

10. Ibid., 18.

11. Richard A. Gabriel, *The Military History of Ancient Israel* (Westport, CT: Praeger, 2003), 241.

12. Yadin, *Art of Warfare*, vol. 1, 19–20.

13. Gabriel, *Military History of Ancient Israel*, 131.

14. Yadin, *Art of Warfare*, vol. 2, 313–328.

15. Yadin, *Art of Warfare*, vol. 1, 55, 147.

16. Yadin, *Art of Warfare*, vol. 2, 313–328.

17. Richard A. Gabriel and Donald W. Boose, Jr., *The Great Battles of Antiquity: A Strategic and Tactical Guide to Great Battles That Shaped the Development of War* (Westport, CT: Greenwood Press, 1994), 310–311.

18. Richard A. Gabriel, *The Culture of War: Invention and Early Development* (Westport, CT: Greenwood Press, 1990), 237–238.

19. Ibid.

20. Ibid.

21. A good account of Greek siege machinery can be found in J. K. Anderson, "Wars and Military Science: Greece," in *Civilization of the Ancient Mediterranean: Greece and Rome*, vol. 1, eds. Michael Grant and Rachel Kitzinger (New York: Charles Scribner, 1988), 679–689.

22. Sandhu, *Military History of Ancient India*, 233.

23. Ibid.

24. Ibid.

25. Ibid., 154.

26. Gabriel, *Great Battles*, 201.

27. Graham Webster, *The Roman Imperial Army of the First and Second Centuries* A.D., 2nd ed. (New York: Barnes and Noble Books, 1979), 240–243.

28. Gabriel, *Great Battles*, 367–369.

29. Trevor N. Dupuy, *The Evolution of Weapons and Warfare* (Indianapolis, IN: Bobbs-Merrill, 1980), 29.

30. Ibid.

31. Ibid., 30.

32. Ibid.

33. Ibid.

34. Josephus *Jewish War* 5.6,3.

35. Vegetius *On the Military* 2.25.

Eighteen

✸ ✸ ✸

DEATH AND WOUNDING

Infantrymen comprised the greatest number of soldiers in all armies of antiquity, with the consequence that most casualties were inflicted against infantry formations. With the exception of the Roman infantry, which was the first and only army in antiquity that fought in an open formation and could break contact with the enemy to its front, withdraw in good order through the other ranks, and be replaced by a fresh line of infantry, all other armies fought in some form of packed infantry phalanx. As long as the men within the phalanx held their ground and remained together, it was difficult for significant killing to occur. But within every army, there is a mob waiting to escape, and the motivation to flee is fear. Ardant du Picq, a French officer of the nineteenth century, describes the emotions of the soldier in battle thus:

> Nothing is changed in the heart of man. Discipline keeps enemies fact to face a little longer, but cannot supplant the instinct of self-preservation, and the sense of fear that goes with it. Fear!… The mass shudders; because you cannot suppress the flesh.[1]

FEAR

The real killer on the ancient battlefield was fear.[2] Men in combat have their instinctive response to flee the danger held in delicate check by either a thin string of intellect, the belief that they will somehow survive, or the ties of the herd, unit cohesion, that it makes it possible for men to endure in groups what they cannot endure alone.[3] The stress of battle increases the probability that someone within the ranks will lose his nerve and run. Often, the actions of a single soldier are sufficient to trigger the onset of panic in an entire unit. Once the integrity of the infantry phalanx began to erode, the ancient soldier was at a great risk of death.

Placed under sufficient pressure, the phalanx could suddenly shatter, its soldiers taking flight as the once cohesive fighting formation transformed itself into a mob of frightened, isolated individuals trying to escape. Men fled in all directions, often casting away their weapons, shields, and armor to speed their flight. For more than 2,000 years, soldiers could rely on their flight to save them as the victor's exhausted troops could pursue no more rapidly than the exhausted vanquished could run. The introduction of the chariot and mounted archer and the spear and archer cavalry of the Assyrians changed all that. Fleeing soldiers became vulnerable targets, easily overtaken by the horse. The pursuit, once a rare event on the battlefields of antiquity, now became the primary means of destroying a defeated army. Unless the commander of the victorious army halted the killing to take prisoners to be sold or used as slaves, often, an entire army would be mercilessly slain; not a single soldier would be left alive.

DEATH AND WOUND RATES FOR ANCIENT ARMIES

Table 18.1 presents strength and death ratios for fourteen battles that occurred between 2250 and 45 B.C.E.[4] and include battles involving the armies of Sumer, Persia, Classical Greece, Imperial Greece, Rome, and tribal engagements in both the Bronze and Iron ages. The data indicate that the percentage of dead (killed in action) suffered by a defeated army was, on average, 37.7 percent, or more than one-third its combat force. Death rates for victorious armies were only 5.5 percent of the field force. Even when an army enjoyed a considerable technical advantage, as the Romans did when fighting tribal armies, it was still necessary to kill at close range. The large disparity in the number of casualties suffered by defeated and victorious armies suggests that most of the killing occurred after one side's infantry formations lost cohesion and broke apart, leaving the soldiers to be hunted down and slain with comparative ease. Close-range killing is nasty business, and it must still have taken several hours of outright slaughter to destroy a vanquished army. At Cannae Hannibal's army encircled and pressed the legions in on themselves with such force that the legionnaires could not raise their weapons to defend themselves. Trapped in this manner, 78,000 Roman soldiers were slaughtered in the space of four hours.[5]

Kill Rates

Whenever a technically and tactically superior army fought an inferior one, the difference was immediately manifested in the kill rates. In the battles of Issus, Arbela, Granicus, Cynoscephalae, Pydna, and Aix-en-Provence (see Table 18.1) the technically superior army killed, on average, 42.6 percent of the inferior force, inflicting 5 percent more casualties than would normally have been expected had the armies been equal. Equally important was the fact that these increased kill rates were inflicted over a shorter period of time; that is, more soldiers were killed more quickly. This is reflected in the lower death rates suffered by the victorious armies. Alexander's armies suffered only a 0.5 percent average casualty rate in three battles against the Persians, and the Romans only 1.3 percent against the Macedonians and Teutones. Armies relatively equal in combat strength could expect to lose 5.5 percent of their forces killed in action. Tactically and technically superior armies suffered, on average, only 2.2 percent of

Table 18.1
Combat Death Rates of Ancient Armies

Date/B.C.	Battle	Adversaries		Number of troops		Number killed		Percent killed in action
		Victor	Defeated	Victor	Defeated	Victor	Defeated	
2250	—	King of Akkad	Ur	5,400	13,500	—	8,040	59.5
334	Granicus	Alexander	Memnon	36,000	40,000	125	10,000	25.0
333	Issus	Alexander	Darius III	36,000	150,000	200	50,000	33.0
331	Arbela	Alexander	Darius III	40,000	340,000	300	100,000	29.4
237	Mactaris	Hamilcar Barcas	Mercenaries	10,000	25,000	—	6,000	24.0
218	Trebia	Hannibal	Sempronius	50,000	40,000	few	20–30,000	50.0
216	Cannae	Hannibal	Varro	50,000	80,000	5,500	70,000	87.5
202	Zama	Scipio Africanus	Hannibal	50,000	50,000	2,000	20,000	40.0
197	Cynosephalae	Flamininus	Philip V	20,000	23,000	700	8,000	34.7
168	Pydna	Aemilius Paullus	Perseus	30,000	44,000	—	20,000	45.4
102	Aix	Marius	The Teutons	40,000	100,000	300	90,000	90.0
86	Chaeronea	Sulla	Archelaus	30,000	110,000	14	100,000	90.9
48	Pharsalus	Caesar	Pompey	22,000	45,000	300	15,000	33.0
45	Munda	Caesar	Pompey	48,000	80,000	1,000	33,000	41.2

their forces killed in action, a force multiplier of more than 100 percent. A defeated army could expect to lose 35.4 percent of its force to serious wounds. When the number of wounded is added to the number of soldiers killed, no less than 73 percent, seven out of every ten men who took the field, could expect to be killed or wounded before the battle was finished. The victors could expect to lose approximately one man in ten killed or wounded to enemy arms.[6]

Comparing Ancient Rates with Modern Times

How do these rates of death and wounding compare with the conventional wars of the modern era? Unlike armies of the modern era, ancient armies had relatively small logistical and administrative staffs, and even these were expected to fight when the time came. Modern armies have huge logistical and administrative staffs that do not usually take part in combat. Modern troop strength figures must first be adjusted for those who actually engaged in combat if the comparative death and wound rates are to have any meaning. Table 18.2 shows the adjusted engaged combat strength of four modern, conventional armies relative to the numbers and percentages of engaged strength killed and wounded in battle.[7] The data suggest that a conventional army in the modern period could expect to have 17.7 percent of its force killed in action and another 46.1 percent wounded in action. Almost six of every ten soldiers on the battlefield could expect to become casualties, not much of an improvement over the seven of every ten soldiers who became casualties on ancient battlefields. However, the data depicted in Table 18.2 are for *victorious* armies. Victorious armies in the ancient world suffered no more than 5.5 percent dead and 6 percent wounded, rates far below those for modern victorious armies. The analysis suggests that a soldier in a victorious army in modern times has about a three times greater chance of being killed than his ancient counterpart and a seven times greater chance of being wounded. The chances of a modern soldier being wounded in defeat are 6 percent greater than those of a similar soldier in ancient armies.

Relative to the intensity of combat, however, the modern soldier's chances of being killed or wounded are about the same as in ancient times. The U.S. Army estimates that the modern battlefield is about seven times as lethal as it was in World War II.[8] It is also instructive to note that in the same war the victorious Russian army suffered 5,000,000 dead and 9,000,000 wounded of the 20,000,000 soldiers it mobilized, a rate of death and wounding of approximately seven of every ten men, the same rate as for ancient armies.[9]

Table 18.2
Casualties as a Percentage of Engaged Strength

War	Engaged strength	Number killed in action	Percent killed in action	Number wounded	Percent wounded
Civil War	700,000	67,058	9.6	324,893	46.6
World War I	500,000	116,516	23.3	204,002	40.0
World War II	1,714,285	405,399	23.6	670,846	37.3
Korea	240,000	33,629	14.0	103,040	42.9

Wound Rates

Literary accounts of ancient battles usually do not provide information on the number of wounded. However, captured soldiers were booty who could be later sold as slaves. Roman and Assyrian armies were often followed by slave dealers, who bought up whole lots of captured soldiers on the spot. If we deduct the number of soldiers killed and taken prisoner from the strength of the total force, we are left with a rough approximation of the number of wounded.

Table 18.3 presents data on the number of soldiers killed, wounded, and taken prisoner for the six battles for which the information was available. On average, approximately 35.4 percent of a defeated army would be wounded.[10] We might surmise that most of these wounds would have been serious since those with only slight wounds would have been taken prisoner for later sale or use as slaves. Many of these severely wounded would simply have been abandoned on the battlefield to die.

There is no certain way to estimate the number of wounded for the victor's army. If the proportion held, the ratio of dead to dead in each army suggests a wound rate for the victorious army of 5.8 percent. It must be borne in mind that the manner in which wounds were inflicted differed greatly for each side. Most of the death and wounding suffered by the victorious army would have occurred after the enemy formations broke, a situation that presented maximum exposure for the defeated and almost no risk at all to the victors inflicting the wounds. If we remember that kill and wound rates were generally low while the armies were actually locked in battle, then a wound rate of 5.8 percent for the victor does not seem high. Donald Engels's analysis of Alexander's armies suggests that the Macedonians suffered roughly five wounded for every soldier killed in action.[11] Thus the average KIA rate suffered by the Macedonians at Issus, Granicus, and Arbela (refer to Table 18.3) of 0.5 percent produced a wound rate of no more than 2.5 percent. The Roman army medical system planned for a wounded casualty rate of between 2 and 10 percent, or an average of 5 percent. The legion medical hospital provided sixty-four wards with four to five men per ward. A Roman military hospital could accommodate 320 casualties, or about 5 percent of the battle strength of the legion.[12]

Table 18.3
Calculation of Wounded in Ancient Battles

Battle	Total force	Number killed	Number POW	Number wounded	Percent wounded
Granicus	40,000	10,000	20,000	10,000	25.0
Mactaris	25,000	6,000	2,000	17,000	68.0
Zama	50,000	20,000	20,000	10,000	20.0
Cynoscephalae	23,000	8,000	5,000	10,000	43.4
Pydna	44,000	20,000	5,000	19,000	43.2
Pharsalus	45,000	15,000	24,000	6,000	13.3

Table 18.4
Battle Wounds/Fatalities in the *Iliad*

Type of weapon	Number	Percent mortality
Spear	106	80
Sword	17	100
Arrow	12	42
Sling	12	66
	N - 147	114 or 77.6

The nature of close combat in ancient battles suggests that except in the pursuit, the chances of suffering a wound were greater than being killed. It is interesting to speculate as to the type and nature of wounds most commonly suffered by ancient soldiers. The *Iliad* provides the oldest account of battle wounds suffered during this period. H. Frolich's analysis—portrayed in Tables 18.4 and 18.5—although a century old, provides some basic data on battle wounds of the ancient Greek period.[13]

Of the 147 wounds recorded by Homer, 114 or 77.7 percent resulted in fatalities. This compares with a wound mortality rate of 20 percent during the Crimean War and 13.3 percent in the Civil War, considerably below the wound mortality rate of ancient armies. Not surprisingly, the areas of greatest lethality were the head and chest, areas that still account for most battle wound fatalities in the modern era. Frolich notes that of the thirty-one wounds to the head recorded by Homer, all were fatal. This compares to the Crimean War, where 73.9 percent of head wounds resulted in fatalities, and to the Civil War, in which 71.7 percent of head wounds caused death.

Frolich's analysis notes that arrows accounted for less than 10 percent of the wounds suffered by the soldiers of the *Iliad*. The mortality rate, 42 percent, is the lowest of all the weapons examined. Arrows from a composite bow would not penetrate body armor to sufficient depth, unless they struck a seam. Statistically, the most likely place for an arrow wound was in the extremities and the neck. Wounds to the arms and legs, which provided much greater target area, would have been much more common. Frolich notes that 16 percent of the total wounds in the *Iliad* were to the upper and lower extremities. These wounds would have caused fatal shock or bleeding only if the arrow struck an artery, a comparatively rare event.

Causes of Death

Blood loss and shock probably killed most men on the ancient battlefield. Until the time of the Roman military medical service, the art of tying off a major artery to stop bleeding was unknown. Even in World War II, in which ligature was widely practiced, 59 percent of the soldiers who underwent ligature and survived required the amputation of the limb. Amputation was not practiced until introduced by the Romans, and it is unlikely that it was much help. In the Civil War the overall mortality rate produced

Table 18.5
Wound Lethality in the *Iliad* by Area of Body

Area of wound	Number	Percent of wounds
Chest	67	50.8
Head	31	23.5
Neck	13	9.8
Arms	10	8.3

by surgical amputation was 40 percent, and in the early days of the war, it was as high as 83 percent.

The most lethal weapon of the ancient Greeks was the spear, responsible for 106 of the 147 wounds recorded by Homer. Later, of course, the Roman *gladius* became the most lethal weapon in antiquity. It was not easy to land a fatal blow with the spear. The most likely wounds caused by the spear were slashing cuts that, while not initially fatal, were debilitating enough to provide one's opponent with the opportunity to strike a fatal blow. As noted earlier, the sword was not a primary weapon of any of the ancient armies until Rome. The fact that only 15 percent of wounds described in the *Iliad* were taken by sword point suggests the propensity of the ancients to use this weapon only when their primary weapons were lost or broken.

Causes of Wounds

Probably the most common wound suffered by the ancient soldier was a broken bone. The fact that ancient Egyptian and Sumerian medical texts discuss the treatment of broken bones extensively indicates that military physicians were quite familiar with them. The first evidence for a splint applied to a broken bone appears on mummies in ancient Egypt. One reason that broken bones were common is precisely because they were so easy to inflict. With the exception of the skull, there is very little difference in the amount of force required to fracture any of the bones in the human body. Even the thicker bones of the upper leg require only marginally more force to fracture than do the thinner bones of the forearm. On average, 67.7 foot-pounds of impact energy will produce a fracture to any bone, except the skull.[14] Any of the ancient weapons could easily cause a fracture.

The data extracted from the *Iliad* and presented by Frolich provide the only glimpse into the wound profile suffered by the ancient soldier. The data have value insofar as they provide a primitive baseline of measurement since it is clear that the frequency and types of wounds must have varied considerably in light of the weapons, armor, and battle tactics employed by an army in a specific battle. Table 18.6 shows a "typical" distribution of casualties by battle, disease, and infection that a Roman legion of 6,000 men might expect to suffer when engaged.

In ancient armies the risk of death and wounding varied greatly, depending on the army in which the soldier served. An Egyptian soldier fighting against the Hyksos was

Table 18.6
Casualty Profile of a Roman Legion

Engaged strength		6,000 men
Killed in action		330 men
Wounded in action		360 men
Died from:	Shock bleeding	50 men (13.8)
	Tetanus	22 men (5.0)
	Gas Gangrene	15 men (4.0)
	Septicemia	5 men (1.2)
	Other causes	15 men (4.0)
Wounded recovery rate		70

almost totally vulnerable to their weapons. The same Egyptian soldier fighting against the Hyksos 200 years later would have stood a much better chance of avoiding death or injury. Any army at any time in history that lost its discipline and cohesion would have been defenseless to almost any type of attack by the pursuing force. Under these circumstances, the ancient soldier was at grave risk.

NOTES

1. Ardant du Picq, *Battle Studies: Ancient and Modern Battle* (Harrisburg, PA: The Military Service Publishing Company, 1947), 48.

2. For more on a history of fear and psychiatric collapse in battle, see Richard A. Gabriel, *No More Heroes: Madness and Psychiatry in War* (New York: Hill and Wang, 1987).

3. The subject of unit cohesion in war can be found in Richard A. Gabriel and Paul L. Savage, *Crisis in Command: Mismanagement in the Army* (New York: Hill and Wang, 1978).

4. Richard A. Gabriel and Karen S. Metz, *From Sumer to Rome: The Military Capabilities of Ancient Armies* (Westport, CT: Greenwood Press, 1991), 85.

5. Livy *War with Hannibal* 12.49–50.

6. Gabriel, *From Sumer to Rome*, 88.

7. Ibid., 89.

8. The changing levels of battle intensity from World War II to 1987 are explored in Gabriel, *No More Heroes*, chap. 1.

9. Richard A. Gabriel, *The Painful Field: The Psychiatric Dimension of Modern War* (Westport, CT: Greenwood Press, 1988), 72–74.

10. Gabriel, *From Sumer to Rome*, 87.

11. Donald W. Engels, *Alexander the Great and the Logistics of the Macedonian Army* (Berkeley: University of California Press, 1978), 151.

12. See Graham Webster, *The Roman Imperial Army of the First and Second Centuries* A.D., 2nd ed. (New York: Barnes and Noble Books, 1979), 260–265 for an account of Roman medical facilities.

13. H. Frolich, *Die Militarmedicin Homers* (Stuttgart, 1897), 56–60.

14. H. M. Frost, *Orthopaedic Biomechanics* (Springfield, IL: Charles C. Thomas, 1973), 198.

Nineteen

�֍ ✻ ✻

INFECTION AND DISEASE

INFECTION

The threat to the ancient soldier of dying from an infected wound in the period from the beginning of the Bronze Age until the first century C.E. was no greater than that faced by any soldier since then until at least the early days of World War I. The wounded soldier of ancient times was at risk of wound infection from three major microbiological threats: tetanus, gas gangrene, and septicemia. The most common of these infections was tetanus. Tetanus is caused by an anaerobic bacterium called *Clostridium tetani*, which enters the body through deep breaks in the skin and viscera typically accompanied by tissue damage and necrosis, a deep puncture wound of exactly the type caused by ancient weapons. As an anaerobic bacterium, tetanus thrives in wounds infected by other bacteria whose biological activity consumes most of the cellular oxygen within the wound. The tetanus bacterium produces a toxin that travels to the gray matter of the spinal cord and produces severe contractions of the skeletal muscles. These contractions typically cause arching of the back and great pain and can be so strong as to fracture the vertebrae of the spine. A description of these symptoms appears in the *Aphorisms* of Hippocrates, evidence that the Greeks were aware of the condition.[1]

Tetanus Infection

Tetanus is endemic to soil and is found mainly in the richly manured soil typical of the agricultural societies and battlefields of the ancient world. It is common where sanitation is poor and where human waste is present. Domestic animals also contribute to its presence. A soldier whose wound was contaminated with soil was at risk of infection. If the wound was not thoroughly cleansed with water, wine, or beer, a common medical practice of the military physicians of ancient times, or if the wound was sutured or bandaged too quickly, tetanus infection was almost a certainty. Military physicians of ancient Egypt, Assyria, Rome, and India knew to leave certain wounds unsutured or open for several days before bandaging, a procedure that was likely to result in fewer tetanus infections.[2] Military physicians in the British Army rediscovered this technique during World War I.

There was no means of preventing tetanus infection until the introduction of immunization in World War I, and it is likely that the rates of tetanus infection in ancient armies were equivalent to those found in armies of the modern era before World War I. Table 19.1 presents the rates of tetanus infection for five wars of the modern era. The average rate of infection was 5.6 percent, with a mortality rate of 80 percent.[3] A soldier's survival depended on the severity of the infection and the ability of the body's natural defenses to contain and defeat it. In neither ancient nor modern times was there any means for treating the infection once it began.

Gangrene Infection

Gas gangrene presented the wounded of ancient armies with another threat of infection. Gas gangrene is caused by six species of bacteria generically named *Clostridium perfingens*. Like tetanus, these bacteria are anaerobic and are found in common soil. A gangrenous wound produces a toxin that destroys muscle tissue by producing hydrogen gas bubbles within the muscle tissue itself. The wound becomes necrotic, and the infection spreads along the extremity affected. Gangrenous wounds are accompanied by a terrible stench from the dying tissue.[4]

Until the middle years of World War I, the average rate of incidence of gangrene infection among the wounded was 5 percent. With treatment the survival rate among British forces was 28 percent. We may safely assume, however, that in ancient armies, gangrenous wounds produced almost 100 percent mortality.[5] If caught in time, a soldier's life might have been saved by amputation of the infected limb, but amputation was an art not practiced by ancient military physicians. The traditional practice of repeatedly cleansing the open wound with beer, wine, or water for several days would have done much to reduce the initial onset of gangrene infection. Until the Boer War,

Table 19.1

Tetanus Rates for Combat Wounded in Wars of the Nineteenth Century

War	Rate of incidence
Peninsula War	12.5 out of 1,000
Crimean War	2 out of 1,000
Civil War	2 out of 1,000
Franco-Prussian War	3.5 out of 1,000
Early WWI (before antitoxin)	8 out of 1,000

British doctors routinely bandaged or sutured wounds as soon as they could treat the injured soldier. This permitted necrotic tissue to remain within the wound, increasing the onset of gangrene. By the middle years of World War I British physicians began leaving the wound open for several days and cleansing it several times a day before finally closing it with stitches or bandages. The rediscovery of this ancient method of treating wounds resulted in a drop in the gangrene mortality rate from 28 percent to only 1 percent.[6]

Septicemia Infection

Septicemia, or blood poisoning, was a third threat to the wounded soldier in ancient times. Blood poisoning occurs when the common body bacteria *Staphylococcus bacteri* enter the bloodstream. If a blood vessel is punctured or the accompanying wound is permitted to fester by secondary infection, the infection can spread to the sterile bloodstream. Wounds to major arteries and veins presented a major risk of blood poisoning. The rate of such wounds in antiquity was approximately 1.7 percent. Until very modern times, when antibiotics made it possible to combat a bloodstream infection, septicemia was usually fatal. Until late World War II, any soldier with a septicemic infection usually died.

If the data on wound mortality and infection are combined, it is possible to produce a statistical profile of the causes of death for wounded soldiers in ancient armies. Of 100 soldiers wounded in action, 13.8 percent would likely die of shock and bleeding within two to six hours of being wounded. Another 6 percent would likely contract tetanus infections, and 80 percent of them would die within three to six days. Another 5 percent would have their wounds become gangrenous, and 80 to 100 percent of these would die within a week. A septicemic infection from arterial or venous wounds would be contracted by 1.7 percent of the wounded, and 83 to 100 percent of them would die within six to ten days.[7] On average, one in every four wounded soldiers, 24.4 percent, would die of his wounds within seven to ten days. It is important to note that throughout history these same four causes remained the major causes of death among the wounded, as did the rates at which the wounded succumbed to them, at least until the closing years of World War I.

DISEASES

In ancient armies, as in all armies until the Russo-Japanese War of 1905, which saw the first systematic use of preventive military medicine by military physicians in modern times, more soldiers met their deaths as a result of disease than by the effects of enemy weapons.[8] Disease outbreaks in ancient armies were most likely to occur when large numbers of men were assembled for long periods out of garrison, where the usual, if primitive, sanitary facilities were not available. Aside from the Egyptian, Israelite, and Roman armies, which routinely took great care in the field to construct and segregate sanitation facilities from water and food supplies, most armies took no sanitary precautions at all. Greek armies, for example, provided no common sanitary facilities for their troops, who used whatever areas were handy when the need arose. This practice continued for military and civilian populations until modern times. It is often forgotten that in urban areas the chamber pot was the most common method of domestic sanitation and, until well into the 1870s, was emptied every morning by throwing its contents into the public streets. The word *privy* takes its meaning from the common practice of persons finding a private place behind a tree or hedge to relieve themselves. Much of the attraction of wooded public parks in urban areas was due to the privacy they provided for use as sanitary facilities.

Military operations also reduced the soldier's resistance to disease insofar as field rations often did not provide sufficient nutritional content, reducing the body's ability to fight off disease and infection. Armies on the march had less chance of being afflicted by an epidemic since they moved away from infection and unsanitary sites. The Mongol army, for example, seems only to have suffered from disease when it became an occupying force in urban areas or when it remained immobile for long periods during sieges. For all ancient armies the most likely place for a devastating outbreak of disease was during siege operations, in which large numbers of soldiers lived in crowded conditions amid sanitary and nutritional circumstances that were generally poor.

Most descriptions of diseases in the ancient world that have come down to us are insufficiently precise to permit their identification with certainty. Modern medical writers cannot agree if the great plague described by Thucydides that killed one-quarter of the Athenian army during the Peloponnesian War was in fact caused by typhus. And while the descriptions of the Antonine plague that decimated the population of Rome in the second century C.E. suggest an outbreak of smallpox, diagnosticians cannot be certain. Some diseases, such as cholera and bubonic plague, have relatively recent origins and can be safely omitted from the list of diseases that plagued ancient armies. Others, like dysentery, typhus, typhoid, and smallpox, can be asserted with some confidence to have afflicted ancient armies.

Dysentery

The most common disease of ancient armies was dysentery. Usually called "campaign fever," dysentery was probably the most common disease among soldiers throughout human history. The first description of dysentery occurs in an Egyptian medical text, the Ebers Papyrus, around 1550 B.C.E.[9] The text chronicles medical knowledge that was very old even at the time the Ebers text was written, and it is probably safe to assume that Egyptian armies suffered from dysentery from time immemorial. Dysentery is accurately described in Hippocrates's writings, and Roman medical texts outline procedures for preventing its occurrence. Dysentery afflicted the armies of the Middle Ages and accounted for more deaths during the Crusades than were caused by Saracen arrows.[10] It has been called the "most dangerous and pervasive disease in human history."[11]

Dysentery is a waterborne bacillus transmitted by ingesting contaminated food or water. Human and animal excrement are sources of transmission. During sieges, infected water supplies, the lack of adequate waste disposal, and failure to wash one's hands after toileting caused frequent outbreaks of the disease among ancient armies. If an army drank from a polluted well, the entire army could be debilitated. Some variants of the disease have a mortality rate of 50 percent; the usual mortality rate is 5 percent.[12] The disease can immobilize an entire army for two to three weeks, during which time the soldier is useless as a fighting man. Even marginal care of the sick requires additional manpower that is drained from the combat force. Some idea of the magnitude of the impact of dysentery on an army can be obtained from the fact that while 81,360 men of the Union Army (1860–1865 c.e.) died from dysentery, a mortality rate of about 5 percent, 1,627,000 soldiers, or twenty times as many soldiers, contracted the disease at one time or another.[13] The number of soldiers who contracted dysentery amounted to almost four-fifths of the entire Union Army of 2,100,000 men.

Typhoid Fever

Typhoid fever also afflicted ancient armies. It is caused by the bacterium *Salmonella typhi*, which lives in the human digestive tract and is transported by human feces. The disease is contracted by ingesting contaminated food and water, the same factors that can cause dysentery. Floods often cause outbreaks of typhoid fever by contaminating the water supply. It is likely that Egyptian, Assyrian, Indian, and Chinese armies, whose garrisons were often subject to river floods, were struck by the disease at various times. Typhoid can also be spread by the common housefly. Drawn to exposed feces, the fly transmits the disease to the human food supply. For this reason Roman engineering manuals specified that all latrines were to be dug to a depth of three meters and covered in order to keep sunlight away from the depository so that flies would not be drawn to it and later spread the disease.[14] The Romans used water to flush latrines, provided underground cesspools to catch the runoff, and supplied sponges for wiping oneself and sinks for washing one's hands. No army of ancient times took such extensive sanitary precautions as the Romans.

Water supplies were always a concern to ancient armies, especially when on the march. Mixing canteen water with wine was practiced by many armies in antiquity. While the alcohol might have had a marginal sterilizing effect on some bacteria, in general, the practice did little to prevent disease and seems to have been more a matter of taste. An army caught in the midst of a typhoid outbreak could be quickly rendered useless as a combat force. The disease's mortality rate was between 10 and 13 percent. The disease required four weeks of pain and delirium fever to run its course,[15] during which time the army was completely helpless. In the Napoleonic wars, 270 of every 1,000 men who succumbed to disease did so from typhoid.[16] In the Crimean War it was a more common cause of death than enemy fire. During the Boer War the British lost 13,000 men to typhoid, while an additional 64,000 were invalided home with the disease; by contrast, only 8,000 men were lost to hostile fire.[17] Ninety percent of American units shipped to Cuba during the Spanish American War suffered outbreaks of typhoid, and 20 percent of the entire American force contracted the disease.[18] In ancient times it is likely that the disease was endemic to southern Europe and the Near East, rather than epidemic.

Typhus

Typhus is among the most common and deadly of diseases associated with armies throughout history. It is caused by an organism midway between a bacterium and a virus that lives in the blood of various animals, including, but not limited to, rats. It is transmitted by several insect vectors, the most common of which is *Pediculus humanus*, the human body louse living in the clothes or hair of the individual. The disease follows the lice that move from one person to another. Typhus is a disease of crowded humanity, and it occurs most commonly in conditions where large numbers of people are required to live close to one another: in jails, on ships, and in armies.

The disease produces severe fever, chills, weakness, and aching joints, accompanied by severe headache. During the fourth or fifth day after the onset of the illness, skin lesions form on the extremities. Patients often become disoriented and deranged. The mortality rate of the disease is between 10 and 40 percent, but the disease has been known to kill entire armies.[19] The disease decimated the French army during Napoleon's Russian campaign. On the retreat from Moscow, Napoleon abandoned 30,000 soldiers suffering from typhus in the town of Vilna. Almost all died.[20] During World War I, no fewer than 2,500 cases a day were being admitted to Russian field hospitals on the eastern front, and during the Russian Civil War (1917–1921 C.E.) it is estimated that 25,000,000 Russians were struck by the disease and that between two and three million died.[21] Typhus is a disease of temperate zones, and it is probable that the armies of Greece, Rome, India, and China were familiar with it. The armies of Egypt and Babylon, operating in hotter and less humid climates and having a tendency to wear fewer clothes, may have suffered a smaller incidence of the disease. While medical writers do not agree, the preponderance of opinion is that the great plague that struck down the Athenian army during the Peloponnesian War was probably typhus.

Smallpox

Smallpox outbreaks were probably fairly common in the ancient world, although we cannot be certain.[22] Surviving texts suggest that smallpox was among the most feared diseases in ancient times because of its propensity to blind, cripple, and severely scar the victim. It is also likely that many accounts of outbreaks of leprosy were really epidemics of smallpox. Biblical accounts of leper colonies describe conditions commonly associated with smallpox. The Antonine plague that decimated Rome in the second century C.E. was probably smallpox brought by the legions returning from the eastern provinces.[23] Smallpox has several variants, some of which produce mortality rates upward of 90 percent. The more common *variola* strain often causes a mortality rate of between 20 and 40 percent.[24] The outbreaks among the armies of the ancient world must have caused great human suffering, so much so that epidemics were often characterized as a sign of punishment from the gods.

Disease was as much a scourge of ancient armies as it was of all armies up to World War I, when advances in the theory of contagion, knowledge of bacteriology, immunization, and antibiotics finally began to reduce death rates among armies due to disease. Armies on the march, in large garrisons, in winter quarters, or conducting sieges were ideal targets for outbreaks of contagious disease. Ancient armies were always subject to sudden and devastating epidemics that could kill thousands of soldiers and operationally cripple the army as a combat force. It is also important to realize that the outbreak of one disease did not preclude the simultaneous outbreak of another after the first onslaught had reduced a soldier's resistance to disease.

The retirement records of the Roman army allow a brief glimpse into the threat that disease in general played in the life of the ancient soldier. In a typical Roman legion of the first century C.E., 50 percent of the soldiers who began their service at age eighteen would still be alive at age forty-two to collect their military retirement benefits.[25] If the previous analysis is correct, about 6 percent of the soldiers would have died in battle, another 8–10 percent would have died as a result of wounds and infection, and approximately 35 percent would have died of some general health malady, including disease and exposure to epidemics.[26] Roman military medical and sanitary practice was the best in the world, not equaled until the late nineteenth century in the West, so that most of the armies that fought before the times of the legions, with the possible exceptions of the Egyptians and Indians, were far less skilled in preventing disease. It is likely, then, that the rate of death caused by disease would have been somewhat higher, perhaps from 40 to 45 percent, than in the Roman army. In any given case the death rate due to epidemics could easily double. It is not surprising that until the beginning of the twentieth century, armies lost far more men to disease than to enemy weapons.

NOTES

1. My sincere thanks to Professor Tom Lee of the biology department of Saint Anselm College for his many hours of consultation on the subject of disease. More technical information on the diseases and infections discussed herein can be found in *Professional Guide to Diseases* (Springhouse, PA: Intermed Communications, 1982). As regards disease in antiquity, Frederick F. Cartwright, *Disease and History* (New York: Barnes and Noble Books, 1991) and R. S. Bray, *Armies of Pestilence: The Effects of Pandemics on History* (New York: Lutterworth, 1996) are particularly valuable.

2. Richard A. Gabriel and Karen S. Metz, *From Sumer to Rome: The Military Capabilities of Ancient Armies* (Westport, CT: Greenwood Press, 1991), 97. For a detailed description of the medical techniques of military physicians in antiquity, see by the same authors *A History of Military Medicine*, vol. 1, *From Ancient Times to the Middle Ages* (Westport, CT: Greenwood Press, 1992).

3. *Professional Guide to Diseases*, 321–322.

4. Ibid., 323–325.

5. Peter A. Aldea and William Shaw, "The Evolution of the Surgical Management of Severe Lower Extremity Trauma," *Clinics in Plastic Surgery* 13, no. 4 (October 1986): 561.

6. Ibid.

7. Gabriel, *From Sumer to Rome*, 99.

8. Ibid.

9. Robert E. McGrew, *Encyclopedia of Medical History* (New York: McGraw-Hill, 1985), 104.

10. Gabriel, *From Sumer to Rome*, 100.

11. McGrew, *Encyclopedia*, 103.

12. Ibid., 104.

13. The figures presented here are extrapolated from those provided in *Historical Statistics of the United States: Colonial Times to 1970* (Washington, DC: Bureau of the Census, 1975), 1140.

14. Graham Webster, *The Roman Imperial Army of the First and Second Centuries* A.D., 2nd ed. (New York: Barnes and Noble Books, 1979), 259–260.

15. McGrew, *Encyclopedia*, 348.

16. Ibid., 349.

17. Ibid.

18. Ibid.

19. Ibid.

20. Ibid., 352.

21. Ibid.

22. Ibid., 313.

23. R. J. Doyle and Nancy C. Lee, "Microbes, Religion, and Warfare," *Canadian Journal of Microbiology* 32, no. 3 (March 1986): 195.

24. McGrew, *Encyclopedia*, 318.

25. Orville Oughtred, "How the Romans Delivered Medical Care Along Hadrian's Wall Fortifications," *Michigan Medicine* 17 (February 1980): 58.

26. Gabriel, *From Sumer to Rome*, 104.

Twenty

✴ ✴ ✴

INJURY

INJURIES TO THE ARMY ON THE MARCH

An army in the field suffers considerable manpower loss through injury. In World War I the manpower loss for Allied armies on the western front was almost 6,000 men a month from such injuries as accidents, falls, accidental wounds, frostbite, trench foot, and heat stroke. An army on the march can expect to lose a considerable percentage of its combat force to injuries in the act of moving to the battlefield. Moving an army of 40,000 men is no easy task, and the march took a heavy toll on the health and safety of the ancient soldier. Ancient armies moved in column for the same reasons eighteenth-century armies moved in column: There were no roads, and the column formation was the best device for maintaining organizational integrity of the army. An army of 40,000 men moving ten men abreast would take hours to pass a single point. Alexander's army of 65,000 men and 6,000 cavalry arranged in column ten abreast stretched for sixteen and a half miles, not counting baggage animals and pack trains.[1] In antiquity, armies moved in as compact a mass as possible; otherwise, they could hardly move at all.

Air Quality

The air breathed by the men in the center of the column was putrid. The dust choked their nostrils, eyes became irritated, and lungs became congested. In only a single day, nosebleeds, eye irritation, and respiratory problems would cause injury of such severity that men would begin to drop out of the formations to be left behind. In hot or cold climates the rate of injury increased. As Napoleon noted, the soldier's world on the march consisted entirely of his view of the knapsack on the back of the soldier in front of him.

Nutrition

Nutrition was a major problem. Modern armies estimate that an average soldier carrying a moderate load for eight hours of walking requires 3,402 calories and seventy grams of protein a day.[2] The stress and effort of combat field operations increases the amount of calories required to keep the soldier healthy and functioning. In desert or semiarid climates, climates with high temperature and low humidity, the soldier requires a minimum of nine quarts of water per day. These nutritional requirements are minimums and will keep the soldier functioning for the first few days. If nutritional requirements are kept at this level over a march of ten days, most of the soldiers will be unable to function at all, even if they suffer no additional health conditions or injuries. The military diet of the ancient soldier under these strenuous conditions was usually not nutritionally sufficient for sustained military operations.

Carrying Heavy Weight

Under these inadequate nutritional conditions, the ancient solider carried an average load of sixty pounds on his back. The more mobile an army became by reducing its reliance on its baggage train, the greater the load that had to be carried by the individual soldier. The Roman army was probably the lightest field force among the ancient armies, and its soldiers carried approximately fifty-five pounds on their backs.[3] Alexander's soldiers carried slightly more, about sixty pounds.[4] Under these conditions, it is not difficult to imagine a considerable part of the army falling by the side of the road from exhaustion.

Heat

An army on the march was vulnerable to heatstroke. Carrying sixty pounds amid conditions of high temperature and low humidity, aggravated by dust and putrid air, caused the soldier to succumb to heat exhaustion and dehydration. Sunburn was also a major problem; soldiers could protect themselves from sunburn by applying palm or olive oil, but there is no record of these supplies being used in this manner before the time of Rome. No doubt the wily veterans would have brought along their own supplies of ointment, just as sergeants in today's armies never seem to be without mosquito repellent or extra socks. Aelius Gallus, the Roman governor of Egypt in 24 B.C.E., led his army into Arabia. Almost the entire army died of heatstroke and thirst. Many of the survivors of the ordeal suffered permanent damage and had to be mustered out of service. The account of Gallus's disaster notes that the Romans were not unfamiliar with sunburn and heatstroke. The standard prescription was to drink a mixture of olive oil and wine. If not consumed, the mixture was to be rubbed on the skin. The account notes that someone had forgotten to make certain that the vital ointment was in the logistics train. Thousands of soldiers died as a result of this oversight.[5]

Loss Rates

A general idea of the loss rates that were experienced by armies in the field can be approximated from the results of a Navy/Marine experiment conducted at Twenty-Nine Palms desert training area in 1984.[6] Although the troops in the exercise were provided with the best nutrition, clothing, and shelter, more than sufficient water, frequent rest periods, and precise instructions on how to conserve body energy, even under these ideal conditions, 110 men had to be hospitalized for heat exhaustion over a fifteen-day period. Another fifty-three suffered debilitating headaches induced by heat, thirty-one were hospitalized for severe body cramps and nausea, forty-six suffered nosebleeds from the dust, and another forty-six were hospitalized for eye irritations, even though they had been issued protective goggles.[7] In all, 286 men were lost to heat-related illness alone, even though the exercise involved only foot and vehicle maneuvers and required no sustained marching.[8]

Other Injuries

Ancient armies suffered many of the injuries that plague modern armies, including accidents, falls, contusions, cuts, bruises, sprains, and broken bones, all of which can make a soldier a casualty. In the Twenty-Nine Palms study, 1,101 men suffered some injury serious enough to require attention at the battalion aid station or evacuation farther to the rear.[9] Among the most common injuries were blisters, lacerations, and abrasions; 228 men suffered these injuries. Another 169 suffered some general trauma serious enough to take them out of the field. Another 152 soldiers had irritations of the nose and throat. The generous category of "other" injuries listed 377 requiring medical treatment. Armies are accident-prone, and these accidents take a significant toll on combat manpower.[10] In the Twenty-Nine Palms experiment, no less than 17 percent of the total force required medical treatment or hospitalization for general injuries sustained on the exercise after only fifteen days. We might surmise that the large number of animals and wagons that accompanied ancient armies as well as the poor quality of military footwear probably resulted in a high rate of injuries to the feet and ankles.

Cold Climates

Ancient armies also fought in cold climates. The Assyrian incursions into Armenia and Kurdistan required fighting in snow, rain, and freezing temperatures. Roman armies fought in Germany, the Alps, eastern Europe, and the mountains of Spain, all of which have climates that challenged the survivability of modern soldiers in World War II. Xenophon recorded in the *Anabasis* that he almost lost his entire army in the mountains of Turkey when they slept unprotected and awoke to a snowstorm. Xenophon ordered his troops to build fires and cover themselves with a salve or lard, oil of almonds, and turpentine.[11] Sometimes cold weather wrought tremendous casualties. Alexander crossed the Hindu Kush with 100,000 men to arrive on the other side thirteen days later with only 64,000, a loss rate of 36 percent. Hannibal managed to cross the Alps, but at terrible cost. His army of 38,000 infantry and 8,000 cavalry lost 18,000 infantry and 2,000 cavalry by the time he reached Italy. Studies of cold casualties in World War II demonstrated that under modern conditions, only 15 percent of soldiers injured by cold could be returned to service, suggesting that most cold injuries then and now were serious indeed.[12] Modern studies show that soldiers born and raised in warm climates are more susceptible to cold injury than those born in cold climates.[13] When coupled with the fact that many ancient armies lacked sufficient cold weather clothing, gloves, and footwear, ancient armies probably suffered greatly when engaged in cold weather operations.

An ancient army on the march was a medical disaster. At the minimum an army of 10,000 could expect to lose 400 men to heatstroke or exhaustion. And 1,700 men would be lost to routine injuries on the way to the battlefield. As the army moved along, its general resistance to disease declined, and soldiers were subjected to chronic discomfort. Blisters from the leather thongs on sandals or from ill-fitting boots were endemic. In hostile climates, many soldiers died of extreme heat or cold. Others would be so afflicted that their health would be damaged permanently. Then, as now, warfare tended to be dangerous to the soldier's health.

TREATMENT

Except for the Roman and Indian armies, which had excellent military medical services, the soldier could expect only minimal treatment for injuries suffered on the march. In some armies, wives and camp followers (sometimes barbers and physicians) provided what little treatment was available. Soldiers who were injured or who could not keep pace were often left in towns or villages along the way; the sick were often simply abandoned on the side of the road. This practice continued even when the army was in hostile territory. Armies sometimes took along a few wagons to carry the sick and wounded, as Alexander did sometimes and as the Romans did routinely. Those abandoned would be retrieved when the army returned—if it ever did. The first task of the ancient soldier was to survive the march to the battlefield.

If this treatment of the sick and wounded seems harsh, it ought to be remembered that this same treatment was employed by armies until very modern times, when motorized transport made the ambulance corps a regular feature of the modern army. Until then, however, all armies throughout history abandoned their sick, injured, and wounded. During the American Civil War, for example, soldiers suffering from battle shock were turned out of their military encampments to wander in the countryside. The large numbers of deranged and benumbed soldiers roaming through the cities and towns of the North led to a public outcry that resulted in the establishment of the first military psychiatric hospital in the United States in 1863.

NOTES

1. Donald W. Engels, *Alexander the Great and the Logistics of the Macedonian Army* (Berkeley: University of California Press, 1978), 54.

2. Ibid., 123–126.

3. S.L.A. Marshall, *The Soldier's Load and the Mobility of a Nation* (Washington, DC: Combat Forces Press, 1950), 26–27.

4. Ibid.

5. S. Jarcho, "A Roman Experience with Heatstroke in 24 B.C..," *Bulletin of the New York Academy of Medicine* 43, no. 8 (August 1967): 767–768.

6. Morris Kerstein and Roger Hubbard, "Heat Related Problems in the Desert: The Environment Can Become the Enemy," *Military Medicine* 149 (December 1984): 650–656.

7. Ibid., 656.

8. Ibid., 659.

9. Ibid., 656.

10. Ibid.

11. Alan Steinman, "Adverse Effects of Heat and Cold on Military Operations," *Military Medicine* 152 (August 1987): 382–390.

12. P. Byron Vaughn, "Local Cold Injury: Menace to Military Operations," *Military Medicine* 145 (May 1980): 306.

13. Ibid., 307.

Twenty-one

�֍ ✶ ✶

MEDICAL CARE

The armies of the ancient world invented the first military medical services and were the first to stress the pragmatic aspects of medicine over the theoretical. The history of empirical medicine is at least 2,500 years older (Egypt and Sumer) than Classical Greece, and sophisticated surgery of the head can be found almost 8,000 years before it was attempted in the modern era. It seems apparent that the general level of medical care available to the Sumerian (2500 B.C.E.), Egyptian (1700 B.C.E.), and Assyrian soldier (900 B.C.E.) was superior to that which attended the hoplite warrior of Classical Greece. The apex of military medical care was reached under the Romans during the Imperial period and declined continually after that, only reaching the previous level of care during World War I. The ancient soldier often had a better chance of surviving a battlefield injury or wound than did his counterpart in the nineteenth century.[1]

Ancient physicians attending the wounded on the battlefield would not have encountered wounds that were remarkably different from those they routinely encountered in civilian practice. The cuts, bruises, fractures, and gaping flesh wounds produced by ancient weapons driven only by muscle power would have appeared commonplace. Fractures of the arms, legs, wrists, and skull, for example, were familiar to Egyptian doctors, who served a population that often suffered fractures of the extremities from slipping on rocks on the Nile riverbank. Archaeological evidence indicates that the most common fractures in ancient Egypt were of the wrist and arm.[2] It is no accident that the first evidence for the splint is found in ancient Egypt.[3] Skull, chest, pelvis, and lower leg fractures suffered by soldiers in siege operations were familiar to physicians who attended workers constructing the tombs, pyramids, and other public works.

Even gaping flesh wounds caused by a hacking sword had a more serious counterpart in civilian medical practice: crocodile bites.

While most armies of the ancient world had physicians attending the wounded, the regular presence of military physicians, that is, something akin to a military medical service, was more evident in some armies than others. The major difficulty in providing medical care to the wounded soldier in antiquity was not so much a lack of practical medical knowledge as the inability of armies to bring this knowledge to bear on the battlefield in an institutionalized and consistent manner. So, for example, despite a high level of empirical medical knowledge in both countries, the Greeks did little to establish a medical service for their armies, while the Romans established a military medical service that was truly modern by any standard and not surpassed until the Russo-Japanese War of 1905.

SUMER

It was the Sumerians who produced the world's oldest military medical texts and developed the first code of medical ethics more than 1,000 years before Hippocrates introduced a similar code in Greece.[4] The Sumerian text dates from the Third Dynasty of Ur (2158–2000 B.C.E.) and is almost 300 years older than the oldest surviving Egyptian medical text, the Kahun Papyrus written in 1850 B.C.E.[5] The Sumerian military doctor was the asu, and a surviving document tells us that Sumerian physicians were routinely posted to military garrisons.[6] Many of these physicians seem to have been full-time military personnel rather than conscripted for military service only in wartime. If so, this is the first evidence of a military medical corps in the armies of the ancient world. The Stele of Vultures (2500 B.C.E.) provides a glimpse into the role of physicians in the Sumerian army. The stele shows the wounded being assembled in a single place after the battle for examination and treatment. It also shows trenches being prepared to bury the dead.[7] Assembling the wounded and burying the dead remain two major functions of a military medical service to this day.

EGYPT

In Egypt the practice of medicine remained strongly under the control of the priesthood. Even so, there is evidence of the presence of empirical medical practitioners (swnw) in military service. Documents tell of the presence of physicians at outlying military posts, and Egyptian physicians were regularly employed on the great construction projects to care for the health and injuries of the workers. Egyptian medical literature refers constantly to the types of wounds received on the battlefield, with the result that Egyptian military physicians became highly pragmatic students of wounds and wound treatment. It was the Egyptians who first developed the splint and who were the first to use adhesive bandages; they were able to make bandages adhere to the skin by using resin from the acacia tree.[8] To counteract the shock and bleeding that was the most common cause of death on the battlefield, Egyptian physicians were the first to use the heated knife to cauterize wounds.[9] They were the first to use the extract of the poppy and distilled opium as painkillers and invented the use of wild honey as a treatment for infection[10] modern tests demonstrate that wild honey was the most effective bacteria-killing compound until the discovery of penicillin.[11] Egyptian military physicians were expert at surgical procedures for treating linear and depressed fractures of the skull, an injury that must have been common in an army whose primary weapon for centuries was the mace and which did not use the helmet for 2,300 years. Other Egyptian innovations include the roller bandage for immobilizing arm and shoulder fractures and the use of exotic mixed chemical compounds to treat various conditions. The Egyptians passed this practice to the Greeks. The root of the word chemistry, from the Greek chemi, meaning "black," is a reference to Egypt, known to the Greeks as the "Black Land," from which the Greeks first obtained their knowledge of chemical compounds.

Although Egyptian medicine remained strongly empirical, it remained under the control of the religious priesthood, which seems to have prevented the emergence of a military medical service that was as organizationally sophisticated as in Sumer. Unlike Sumer, the Egyptians never clearly placed the responsibility for providing medical care to the army in the person of the king. As a result, Egyptian military medical care never reached the degree of institutional regularity that it did elsewhere. And yet, Egyptian medical literature is replete with references to treating wounds and injuries of soldiers, references that hint strongly at a medical presence on the battlefield.

ASSYRIA

Assyria's military medical service was the most advanced in the ancient world, until the coming of the Romans. The heir to the 2,000-year-old Sumerian tradition of empirical medicine, the Assyrians possessed the most complete collection of empirical medical practice and remedies in the ancient world.[12] The military surgeon was a product of the secular military state and was a career medical professional. It was in Assyria that for the first time in history we find a surgeon whose profession was military medicine.[13] Assyrian military garrisons had full-time physicians, and they attended the army on the march and on the battlefield. Assyrian military medical doctors were also employed to oversee the health and treatment of populations that the Assyrians deported from their homelands.[14] It is likely that when the Assyrians deported the Israelite populations in the ninth and fifth centuries B.C.E., it was Assyrian military physicians who treated them on the march. The appearance of the professional military surgeon may be regarded as one of the more important innovations in military history. Unfortunately, the institution died with the destruction of the Assyrian state in the fifth century B.C.E. and did not reappear until the Romans created the most modern and effective military medical service in the ancient world.

GREECE

One reason why military medicine in Greece never reached the level found in earlier states of the ancient world was that the overall level of Greek institutional development never reached much beyond the tribe. The result was that Greece never developed a military medical service, and what medical aid there was on the battlefield depended on the few civilian physicians who could be hired, coaxed, or forced to attend the army at war. We find these physicians in the Iliad. Xenophon recorded the presence of eight surgeons accompanying the Army of Ten Thousand that met its fate at Cunaxa.[15] The presence of physicians with the army does not indicate the presence of a military medical corps. Rather, it demonstrates the nature of the citizen armies of the period. The medical profession in Greece remained a private, civilian enterprise that accompanied the army on an ad hoc basis. Even in Alexander's professional armies this was the case, although the presence of medical services can be seen as a much more integral part of the military force than had ever appeared before in Greece. Alexander also made special provisions for the use of wagons as ambulances.[16] The training and employment of physicians remained a private enterprise, and the army assumed no responsibility for it.

Mental Illness Treatments

The one significant Greek innovation in military medicine was its recognition and treatment of psychiatric casualties. The Greeks were aware of mental illness, were the first to practice a sophisticated psychiatry, and were the first to connect psychiatric syndromes to battle stress.[17] Greek literature is filled with accounts of soldiers driven mad by war; Ajax's slaying of sheep in the belief that they were enemy soldiers is but the most well known. It was Greek society that invented the mythos of military heroism, and it should come as no surprise that Greek physicians were acutely aware of the failure of nerve that often afflicts soldiers in battle.

ROME

The great advance of Roman military medicine was its incorporation of a professional medical service for delivering care to the troops in a regular and organized manner, something which the armies of the ancient world had not seen since the demise of Assyria. From the founding of Rome until the Imperial period in the first century c.e., Roman military medicine was largely indistinguishable from the Greek; that is, it employed civilian physicians on an ad hoc basis and relied primarily on the ability of the soldiers themselves to care for each other's wounds. With Augustus came the professional army, and with it came a professional military medical service. Roman military physicians were trained by the army itself, a development which no other army in the world undertook until 1865, and spent a career within the military.[18] The military produced its own medical manuals. Roman military surgeons, the immunes, were supported by surgical assistants, orderlies, and a corps of combat field medics whose task was to treat shock and wounds on the battlefield before evacuating the soldier to a legion aid station located close behind the battle line. This was the principle of proximity of treatment, and no army in the West practiced it again until World War I.

Each legion post had its full complement of medical personnel, who were responsible for maintaining the health of the legion. Their duties included overseeing the procurement, storage, and preparation of food; locating and securing safe water supplies; constructing latrines and sewers; and ensuring that the soldiers bathed regularly and practiced other sanitation habits, such as washing after toileting. They also trained medical personnel and staffed the legion hospital. Each legion fort had its own hospital that surpassed anything any army of the world used until the American

Civil War. The hospital was usually located in the quietest part of the camp to avoid disturbing the sick and wounded. Within its four wings were contained an entrance hall that could be pressed into service as a triage center, a well-lit surgical center, a kitchen, a heating plant, storage rooms, latrines, and baths. The wards were designed so that a corridor separated the rooms from the general hospital to minimize noise. The roof was constructed so as to provide adequate cooling and ventilation. The large central courtyard was a source of quiet, fresh air,

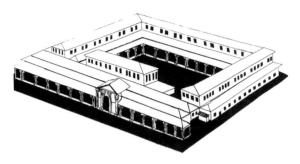

Reconstruction of the Roman military hospital at Vetera, Germany (second century C.E.). Courtesy of Richard Gabriel.

and light to be enjoyed by the recuperating patients. Each hospital was constructed to accommodate 6–8 percent of the legion's strength as casualties.[19]

Ancient Roman Medicine Was Effective

Roman medical practice was the most effective in the late ancient world and was not duplicated again by any army until World War I. The level of Roman surgical skill was not achieved again until the sixteenth century, the modern era. Roman operating rooms came complete with a beehive oven, in which water was heated to sterilize surgical instruments. Roman surgical instruments included disposable scalpels, hemostats, chest separators, forceps, probes, and needles. The Romans were the first to solve the old problem of arrow wounds by inventing the first surgical tool to extract arrows without causing further damage to the wound. They were the first in the West to perform amputation regularly and used henbane and opium to lessen the pain of surgery. Roman physicians invented the surgical clamp, which allowed them to tie off severed arteries without stopping the entire blood flow to the affected limb, reducing the prospect of gangrene. The surgical clamp disappeared from medical knowledge after the fourth century, until it was reinvented again by Ambroise Pare in the 1600s. Using ligature and another Roman innovation, the tourniquet, doctors could stop the massive blood loss that produced shock. Roman physicians were expert at wound cleansing, suturing, bandaging, and splinting broken bones and used prosthetic devices to replace missing arms and legs. Their plastic surgery was as good as that found in India, and the old Etruscan art of artificial dentistry was also practiced. The excellence of Roman military medical care is demonstrated by the fact that even though the Roman soldier was exposed to war, on average, he lived five years longer than his civilian counterpart.[20]

INDIA

The almost constant warfare between the Indian principalities of the Epic Age and the central role of the warrior caste in Indian society inevitably brought into existence a corps of physicians to care for wounded warriors. One of the oldest Indian texts, the Rig-Veda, contains accounts of battles, weapons, and wounds, complete with

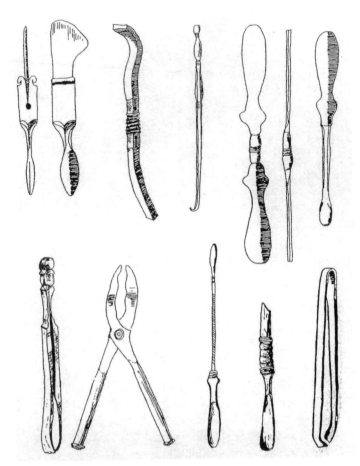

Roman surgical instruments (circa 200 C.E.). Courtesy of Richard Gabriel.

a list of medical treatments used to treat battle wounds.[21] Early Vedic texts testify to the presence of military doctors in war. The importance of warfare as a formative force in Indian medicine is reflected in the fact that a physician who specialized in surgery was called the shalyahara: The word shalya means "arrow," "sword," or "lance," while the word hara means "extractor" or "remover."[22] The concern for military medicine is evident in other texts. The king is urged to learn not only the methods of war, but also the diseases and injuries that can afflict his troops. A king was always to take proper care to see that drugs and medicines were stockpiled in advance and that sufficient surgeons were available to the army.[23] Military physicians were used to inspect campsites and to insure the cleanliness of food and water.[24] Other texts note that doctors were in attendance while the army was on the march.

The Arthashastra describes a military ambulance corps, whose wagons were drawn by horses and elephants. Instructions were given to insure that an adequate number of physicians were present and that drugs and bandages were in good supply. The text tells of women in the medical service who provided food and beverages to the wounded, perhaps the first evidence of a women's nurse corps. The medical tent was always to be placed near the commander's tent and was to fly a flag to mark its location to minimize delay in finding where the wounded could be treated.[25] The king was to accompany the physician on visits to the wounded to lift their spirits and praise their bravery.[26] Nowhere in the early ancient world do we find a military medical service so organized and integrated into the military structure as in Vedic India. One is left with the impression that a great deal of empirical clinical medicine in India was produced by military physicians in their efforts to treat the thousands of casualties that resulted from the incessant wars.

Indian physicians were required to memorize two basic medical texts: the 1,700-page Shusruta and the Charaka, which was twice as long. These texts show a remarkable medical knowledge. Indian physicians were expert in cleansing, suturing, and bandaging wounds, showing an awareness of infection and how to prevent it. No wound was to be stitched or bandaged "as long as the least bit of morbid matter or pus remains inside it."[27]

Surgical techniques available to Indian military physicians of this period included incising abscesses, lancing infected wounds, venesection, the use of probes to locate missiles that had penetrated the body, extracting missiles, suturing, bandaging, injections with syringes (the world's first), cautery, hemostasis, and even amputation.[28] In the Rig-Veda, there are descriptions of legs that were amputated and replaced by iron substitutes.[29] No physician had more treatment techniques at his disposal than Indian military physicians until World War I.

Nowhere in the early ancient world do we encounter a medical tradition that is more empirically and pragmatically oriented than the Indian tradition. It far surpasses anything that came before it and in most major aspects—empirical description of clinical traditions, treatment of infection, surgical skill, hemostasis, drugs, and amputation—surpassed any level of medical practice until the Romans. No military medical service, except the Romans, surpassed the skills of the military physicians of the armies of India.

NOTES

1. Richard A. Gabriel and Karen S. Metz, *From Sumer to Rome: The Military Capabilities of Ancient Armies* (Westport, CT: Greenwood Press, 1991), 113. For a detailed history of military medical care in the armies of the ancient world, see, by the same authors, *A History of Military Medicine*, vol. 1, *From Ancient Times to the Middle Ages* (Westport, CT: Greenwood Press, 1992).

2. Guido Majno, *The Healing Hand: Man and Wound in the Ancient World* (Cambridge, MA: Harvard University Press, 1975), 84. See also Fielding H. Garrison, *Notes on the History of Military Medicine* (London: W. B. Saunders, 1968), 59; see the section titled "Identity of Forms of Ancient and Primitive Medicine," 17–24.

3. Garrison, *History of Medicine*, 54.

4. For the text off Hammurabi's code governing the medical profession of Babylon, see Majno, *Healing Hand*, 43.

5. Martin Levy, "Some Objective Factors of Babylonian Medicine in Light of New Evidence," *Bulletin of the History of Medicine* 35 (January–February 1961): 65.

6. The text of the letter is available in Majno, *Healing Hand*, 66.

7. For a photograph of the Stele of Vultures depicting these events, see Yigael Yadin, *The Art of Warfare in Biblical Lands in the Light of Archaeological Study*, vol. 1, trans. M. Pearlman (New York: McGraw-Hill, 1963), 135.

8. Majno, *Healing Hand*, 94.

9. Ibid., 96.

10. Ibid., 111–115.

11. Ibid., 116–117.

12. Garrison, *History of Medicine*, 62.

13. Gabriel, *From Sumer to Rome*, 129.

14. P. B. Adamson, "The Military Surgeon: His Place in History," *Journal of the Royal Army Medical Corps* 128 (1982): 44.

15. Xenophon *Persian Expedition* 5.3.

16. Donald W. Engels, *Alexander the Great and the Logistics of the Macedonian Army* (Berkeley: University of California Press, 1978), 16–17.

17. For the development of psychiatry, including military psychiatry, in the ancient world, see Franz G. Alexander and Sheldon T. Selesnick, *The History of Psychiatry: An Evaluation of Psychiatric Thought and Practice from Prehistoric Times to the Present* (New York: Harper and Row, 1966), 49–76; see also Richard A. Gabriel, *No More Heroes: Madness and Psychiatry in War* (New York: Hill and Wang, 1987), 97–100.

18. Gabriel, *From Sumer to Rome*, 140.

19. Vivian Nutton, "Medicine and the Roman Army: A Further Reconsideration," *Medical History* 13 (1969): 263.

20. Orville Oughtred, "How the Romans Delivered Medical Care Along Hadrian's Wall Fortifications," *Michigan Medicine* (February 1980): 58.

21. A. M. Acharya, "Military Medicine in Ancient India," *Bulletin of the Indian Institute of Medicine* 6 (1963): 50–57.

22. Gabriel, History of Military Medicine, 131; see also U. P. Thapliyal, "Military Organization in the Ancient Period," in *Historical Perspectives of Warfare in India*, ed. S. N. Prasad (Delhi: Motilal Banarsidass, 2002), 92.

23. Acharya, "Military Medicine," 52.

24. Ibid.

25. Ibid., 56.

26. Ibid.

27. Majno, *Healing Hand*, 287.

28. Gabriel, *History of Military Medicine*, 138.

29. Thapliyal, "Military Organization," 92.

PART II

✦ ✦ ✦

Ancient Armies

Twenty-two

SUMER AND AKKAD (3500–2200 B.C.E.)

Modern Iraq is the site of ancient Sumer and Akkad, two city-states that produced the most sophisticated armies of the Early Bronze Age. The Greeks called the area Mesopotamia, literally, "the land between the two rivers," a reference to the Tigris and Euphrates valley. In the Bible the area is called Shumer, the original Sumerian word for the southern part of Iraq, the site of Sumer itself and its capital of Ur. It was in ancient Sumer that the first detailed records of military campaigns written on clay or carved in stone appeared. No society of the Early and Middle Bronze ages was more advanced in the design and application of military technology and technique than Sumer, a legacy it sustained for 2,000 years before bequeathing it to the rest of the Near East. The period of interest for the military historian seeking to understand the evolution of ancient armies is the period from 3000 to 2334 B.C.E., the date that Sargon the Great united all of Sumer into a single state and changed its governmental and military organization.

The almost constant warfare among the Sumerian city-states for 2,000 years spurred the development of military technology and technique far beyond any similar development found elsewhere in the Near East at that time. The first Sumerian war for which there is detailed evidence occurred between the states of Lagash and Umma in 2525 B.C.E. In this conflict Eannatum of Lagash defeated the king of Umma. The importance of this war to the military historian lies in a commemorative stele that Eannatum erected to celebrate his victory. This stele is called the "Stele of Vultures" for its portrayal of birds of prey and lions tearing at the flesh of the corpses as they lay on the desert plain. The stele represents the first important pictorial portrayal of war in the Sumerian period and portrays the king of Lagash leading an infantry phalanx of armored, helmeted warriors, armed with spears as they trample their enemies

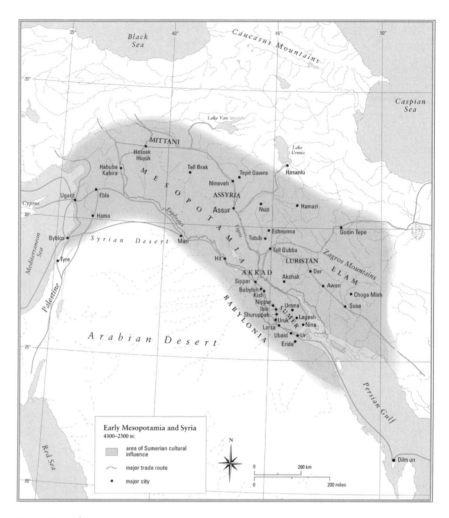

Sumerian influence.

underfoot. The king, with a socket axe in hand, rides in a chariot drawn by four onagers (wild asses). In a lower panel Eannatum holds a sickle sword.

ORGANIZATION OF SUMERIAN TROOPS

The stele indicates that Sumerian troops fought in phalanx formation, organized six files deep with an eight-man front, a formation similar to that used later in Archaic Greece. The Sumerians used both the decimal and sexagesimal system based on multiples of six (they were the first to divide an hour into sixty minutes), and most probably, the organization of the army was based on multiples of 6, 60, 120, and so on. Fighting in phalanx required discipline and training, permitting the conclusion that the soldiers portrayed on the stele were probably professionals. Another indication is the presence of titles associated with military command. Even in times of peace, temple estate employees were organized into groups commanded or supervised by *ugula* (commanders), and *nu.banda* (captains). The Sumerians seemed to have kept the same organization used for corvée labor for use in the military. The word for both laborers and soldiers was *erin*, which originally meant yoke or neck stock, perhaps implying the nature of such service. Other explicitly military titles were *shub.lugal*, or "king's retainer," and *aga.ush*, which literally means "follower." The *aga.ush* were really *erin* who regularly served as soldiers rather than as laborers in fulfilling their obligations as royal or temple tenants. Military units were of regular size and were designated by the rank of their commander with a numerical suffix indicating size. Thus *ugala.nam10* meant a unit of ten run by a commander. The Stele of Vultures seems to provide evidence of the world's first standing professional army.

OUTFITTING THE TROOPS: ARMOR, TRANSPORT, AND WEAPONS

The first evidence of soldiers wearing helmets is also provided on the stele. From the bodies of soldiers found in the Death Pits of Ur dating from 2500 B.C.E. we know that these helmets were made of copper and probably were worn with a leather cap underneath. Since bronze manufacturing technology was already known in Sumer at this time, the use of copper to make helmets remains a mystery. The appearance of the helmet marks the first defensive response to the killing power of an important offensive weapon: the mace. In Sumer the use of a well-crafted helmet indicates a major development in military technology which was so effective that it drove the mace from the battlefield.

The first representation of the military application of the wheel is depicted on the stele and shows Eannatum riding in a chariot. The Sumerian invention of the chariot has to be ranked among the major military innovations in history, although its true exploitation as a vehicle of war had to await the Mitanni. The Sumerian chariot was usually a four-wheeled vehicle, although there are examples of the two-wheeled variety in other records. It carried a crew of two and required four onagers to pull it. The Sumerian "chariot" is more accurately called a "battle car" since it lacked many of the refinements that later made it an effective fighting vehicle. Sumerians also used the "straddle car," a cabless platform pulled by onagers where the driver maintained his balance by straddling the car. One text indicates that the ruler of the state of Umma had an elite unit comprising sixty vehicles. This is the only evidence we have of the number of battle cars that could be mustered by one state. But even if each state could field only sixty such vehicles, a powerful ruler, such as Lugalzagesi, who controlled all southern Sumer, could field over 600 battle cars in a major engagement by drawing on his vassal states.

The Sumerians can also be credited with inventing the rein ring for use with the chariot in order to provide the driver some control over the onagers. At this early stage of its development, however, the chariot probably would not have been a major offensive weapon because of its size, weight, instability, and lack of maneuverability. The placement of the axle in the middle or front of the carrying platform made the vehicle heavy and unstable at speed. In all likelihood it was not produced for war in quantity, and its use was limited to high-ranking nobles in the king's household. Sumerian charioteers were armed with javelins and axes, and the absence of the bow in early Sumerian warfare suggests that the chariot was used to deliver shock to opposing infantry formations. In this role the chariot was used as transport for mounted heavy infantry. The Sumerian chariot remained the prototype for Near Eastern armies for almost 1,000 years. In the eighteenth century B.C.E., various Mesopotamian states introduced the horse-drawn chariot, a development that greatly increased the vehicle's military capability. At the same time the appearance of the bit improved maneuverability and control of the animal teams at higher speeds. Over time, the drivers, shield bearers, archers, and spearmen carried into battle by chariots became the elite fighting corps of the ancient world.

The lower palette of the Stele of Vultures shows the king holding a sickle sword, the weapon that became the primary infantry weapon of the Egyptian and biblical armies at a much later date. The version that appears on the stele was much shorter than the version that evolved later and appears very much like an agricultural sickle, which could well have been the prototype for the weapon. The sickle sword appears on two other independent renderings of the period, suggesting strongly that it was the Sumerians who invented this important weapon sometime around 2500 B.C.E.

The stele also shows Eannatum's soldiers wearing armored cloaks. Each soldier's cloak is secured around the neck and may have been made of wool cloth or, more probably, thin leather. At various places on the cloak were sewn metal disks with raised centers or spines, like the boss on a shield. It is not possible to determine if these disks were made from copper or bronze, but a spined plate of bronze was certainly within the capacity of Sumerian metal technology. Although somewhat primitive in application, the cloak on the stele is the first representation of body armor in history. Other surviving archaeological sources show portrayals of important military innovations appearing for the first time in ancient Sumer. The king of Ur, for example, appears on a carved conch plate armed with a socket axe. The development of the bronze socket axe remains one of Sumer's major military innovations. The use of the cast bronze axe socket that slipped over the end of the shaft and was affixed with rivets permitted a much stronger attachment of the blade to the shaft. It is likely that the need for a stronger axe arose in response to the development of body armor that made the cutting axe less effective. The portrayals of Sumerian axes by 2500 B.C.E. clearly show a change in design. The most significant change was a narrowing of the blade itself to reduce the impact area and to bring the blade to more of a point to concentrate the force of the blow. This development marks the appearance of the penetrating axe, whose narrow blade and strong socket made it capable of piercing bronze plate armor. The result was one of the most devastating weapons of the ancient world, a weapon that remained in use for 2,000 years.

SUMERIAN MILITARY ORGANIZATION

Sophisticated weaponry and tactics require some form of larger social organization and impetus to give them shape and direction if they are to be effective in war. We know very little about the military organization of Sumer in the third millennium B.C.E. We can judge from the Tablets of Shuruppak that the typical Sumerian city-state of this period comprised about 1,800 square miles in area, including its lands and fields. This area could sustain a population of between 30,000 and 35,000 people. The tablets record a force of between 600 and 700 soldiers serving as the king's bodyguard, the corps of a professional army, but a population of this size could easily support an army of regular and reserve forces of between 4,000 and 5,000 men at full mobilization. It is highly likely that some form of military conscription existed, at least during times of emergency.

Two hundred years after Eannatum's death, King Lugalzagasi of Umma succeeded in establishing his influence over all Sumer, although there is no evidence that he introduced any significant changes. Twenty-four years later, the empire of Lugalzagasi was destroyed by the armies of a Semitic prince from the northern city of Akkad, Sargon the Great (2325–? B.C.E.) All Sumer was now united under the control of the Akkadian king. Sargon bequeathed to the world the prototype of the military dictatorship. By force of arms Sargon conquered all the Sumerian city-states and the entire Tigris-Euphrates valley, bringing into being an empire that stretched from the Taurus Mountains to the Persian Gulf and, perhaps, even to the Mediterranean. In his fifty-year reign Sargon fought no fewer than thirty-four wars. One account suggests that his army numbered 5,400 men, soldiers called *gurush* in Akkadian. If that account is correct, Sargon's army would have been the largest standing army of the period.

That Sargon's army would have been composed of professionals seems obvious in light of the almost constant state of war that characterized his reign. As in Sumer, military units appear to have been organized on the sexagesimal system. Sargon's army comprised nine battalions of 600 men, each commanded by a *gir.nita*, or "colonel." Other ranks of officer included the *pa.pa/sha khattim*, literally, "he of two staffs of office," a title which indicated that this officer commanded two or more units of sixty. Below this rank were the *nu.banda* and *ugala*, ranks unchanged since Sumerian times. Even if they had begun as conscripts, within a short time Sargon's soldiers would have become battle-experienced veterans. Equipping an army of this size required a high degree of military organization to run the weapons and logistics functions, to say nothing of the routine administration that was characteristic of a literate people who kept prodigious records. We know nothing definitive about these arrangements.

An Akkadian innovation introduced by Sargon was the *niskum*, a class of soldiers probably equivalent to the old *aga-ush lugai*, or "royal soldiers." The *niskum* held plots of land by favor of the king and received allotments of fish and salt every three months. The idea was to create a corps of loyal military professionals along the later model of Republican Rome. Thutmose I of Egypt, too, introduced a similar system as a way of producing a caste of families who held their land as long as they continued to provide a son for the officer corps. The Akkadian system worked to provide significant numbers of loyal, trained soldiers who could be used in war or to suppress local revolts. Along with the professionals, militia, and these royal soldiers, the army of Sargon contained light troops or skirmishers called *nim* soldiers. *Nim* literally means "flies," a name which suggests the employment of these troops in spread formation accompanied by rapid movement.

During the Sargon period the Sumerians/Akkadians contributed yet another major innovation in weaponry: the composite bow. The introduction of this lethal and revolutionary weapon may have occurred during the reign of Naram Sin (2254–2218 B.C.E.), Sargon's grandson. Like his grandfather, Naram Sin fought continuous wars of conquest against foreign enemies. His victory over Lullubi is commemorated in a rock sculpture that shows Naram Sin armed with a composite bow. This sculpture marks the first appearance of the composite bow in history and strongly suggests that it was of Sumerian/Akkadian origin. The fact that the bow appears in the hand of the warrior king himself suggests that it was a major weapon of the time, even though there is no surviving evidence that the Sumerian army had previously used even the simple bow.

The composite bow was a major military innovation. While the simple bow could kill at ranges from 50 to 100 yards, it would not penetrate even simple leather armor at these ranges. The composite bow, with a pull of at least twice that of the simple bow, could easily penetrate leather armor and, perhaps, even the early prototypes of bronze armor that were emerging at this time. In the hands of even untrained peasant militia the composite bow could bring the enemy under a hail of arrows from twice the distance of the simple bow. So important was this weapon that it became a basic implement of war of all armies of the Near East for the next 1,500 years.

The use of battle cars seems to have declined considerably during the Akkadian period. Any number of reasons suggest themselves. Such vehicles were very expensive. In Sumer a powerful king could commandeer the cars of his vassals, which they maintained at their expense. But with the centralization of political authority under Sargon these vassals disappeared, making the cost of these cars a royal expense. The professionalization of the army resulted in an infantry-heavy force which under most circumstances would have required few battle cars beyond those needed to transport the king and his generals. Finally, the Akkadian kings fought wars far from home in the mountains of Elam and against the Guti farther north. These were lightly armed, highly mobile enemies fighting in mountains and heavily wooded glens. The chariot had come into being to fight wars between rival city-states on relatively even terrain. Their use in rough terrain at considerable distances from home probably revealed the battle car's obvious deficiencies under these conditions, leading to a decline in its military usefulness. They seem to have remained in use by couriers and messengers at least within the imperial borders, where they traveled regular routes known as chariot roads.

FURTHER READING

Charvát, Peter. *Mesopotamia Before History.* New York: Routledge, 2002.

Dupuy, Trevor N. *The Evolution of Weapons and Warfare.* Indianapolis, IN: Bobbs-Merrill, 1980.

Ferrill, Arther. *The Origins of War: From the Stone Age to Alexander the Great.* New York: Thames and Hudson, 1985.

Gabriel, Richard A., and Karen S. Metz. *From Sumer to Rome: The Military Capabilities of Ancient Armies.* Westport, CT: Greenwood Press, 1991.

Kramer, Samuel N. *The Sumerians: Their History, Culture, and Character.* Chicago: University of Chicago Press, 1963.

Littauer, M. A., and J. H. Crouwell. *Wheeled Vehicles and Ridden Animals in the Ancient Near East.* Leiden: Brill, 1979.

Mellaart, James. *The Neolithic of the Near East.* New York: Charles Scribner, 1975.

Nissen, Hans Jörg. *The Early History of the Ancient Near East, 9000 to 2000 B.C..* Chicago: University of Chicago Press, 1988.

Oakeshott, R. Ewart. *The Archaeology of Weapons.* New York: Praeger, 1963.

Oppenheim, A. Leo. *Ancient Mesopotamia: Portrait of a Dead Civilization.* Chicago: University of Chicago Press, 1977.

Pollock, Susan. *Ancient Mesopotamia: The Eden That Never Was.* Cambridge: Cambridge University Press, 1999.

Roux, Georges. *Ancient Iraq.* 3rd ed. New York: Penguin Books, 1992.

Saggs, H.W.F. *The Might That Was Assyria.* London: Sidgwick and Jackson, 1984.

Wenke, Robert J. *Patterns of Prehistory: Man's First Three Million Years.* New York: Oxford University Press, 1980.

Yadin, Yigael. *The Art of Warfare in Biblical Lands in the Light of Archaeological Study.* 2 vols. Translated by M. Pearlman. New York: McGraw-Hill, 1963.

Twenty-three

✳ ✳ ✳

EGYPT (1580–960 B.C.E.)

Egyptian society of 4000 B.C.E. was formed around province-like entities that the Greeks later called *nomos* and that were ruled by individual *nomarchs*, or chiefs. Over time, these *nomarchs* assembled in loose feudal arrangements into two clusters of kingdoms: Upper and Lower Egypt. In 3200 B.C.E. the king of Upper Egypt, known variously to history as Narmer, Menes, or, probably most correctly, Hor-Aha (the "Fighting Hawk"), unified the two kingdoms by force into a single Egyptian state. Thus began the reign of the pharaohs of the First Dynastic period, which lasted for 700 years.

The kings that followed from 3100 to 2686 B.C.E. expanded the Egyptian state. Successful campaigns were launched against the Nubians to the south and the Libyans to the west. Expeditions were undertaken in the Sinai, and trade was established with the states north of Lebanon and Jordan. During this period a state bureaucracy was brought into existence, writing was introduced as a tool of centralized administration, and political institutions were transformed from chiefdoms into a theocratic state led by a divine pharaoh supported by religious, administrative, and military castes.

THE OLD KINGDOM (2686–2160 B.C.E.)

Over the centuries, the pharaohs of the Old Kingdom were able to create a national identity, raise armies, fight wars on Egypt's borders, and generally pursue a national defense policy that kept Egypt free from foreign invasion and occupation. The structure of the army of the Old Kingdom is unknown, but it is clear that some distinctions were made between regular officer appointments and others. There appear a number of military titles, including those of specialists in desert travel and in frontier and desert warfare, garrison troops, frontier troops, quartermaster officers, and scribes, who seem to have functioned as senior noncommissioned officers. There are also titles that refer to "overseers of arsenals," "overseers of desert blockhouses and royal fortresses," and caravan leaders. The size of the combined army remains a mystery. Weni, a commander in the army of the Sixth Dynasty (2345 B.C.E.), recorded that his army was "many tens of thousands" strong. A string of twenty mud brick fortresses was built in approximately 2200 B.C.E. to guard the southern approaches to Egypt. Each required up to 3,000 men to garrison. This would suggest an army of at least 60,000 in the frontier force alone. With Egypt's population approaching 2,000,000 at this time, these force levels could easily have been achieved.

THE MIDDLE KINGDOM (2050–1786 B.C.E.)

The old problem of national authority versus local barons had occasionally resulted in periods of domestic unrest and instability, and such a period followed the demise of the Old Kingdom. As the national authorities gained more power over local barons, it was possible to raise larger armies and conduct a more aggressive defense policy. The Middle Kingdom saw the development of a new national defense strategy premised on the creation of buffer zones beyond the walls and forts to the south and east. This strategy was accompanied by the conduct of more frequent and larger military operations into hostile areas. No longer did Egypt react to military threats; now it attempted to preempt them.

Along the eastern border, Egyptian armies pressed the security zone farther out from the Wall of the Princes and established a major military garrison at Shechem in southern Palestine. From this forward base the Egyptians conducted "search and destroy" operations into Palestine proper. No attempts were made to permanently garrison strong points in the area of military operations. In the south, against Nubia, Egypt expanded its area of military control almost to the second Nile cataract, constructing no fewer than twenty-one permanent fortresses in the operations area. This was a classic defense in depth, and no attempt was made to colonize this new area. Instead, the area was turned into a military defense zone, designed to make it expensive for the enemy to penetrate to the Egyptian homeland.

This strategy worked well for almost three centuries. Egypt then entered another period of domestic turmoil, in which civil war broke out between local and national authorities. In Palestine, events took an ominous turn. A mysterious people, the Hyksos, burst on the Near East with sudden fury. Armed with chariots, horses, helmets, body armor, the composite bow, and the penetrating axe, none of which the Egyptian armies possessed, the Hyksos took advantage of Egyptian domestic instability. Sometime around 1750 B.C.E., the Hyksos armies struck with sudden and devastating military force, invaded Egypt, pressed the national army southward as far as Thebes, and occupied the fertile delta region, establishing their capital at Avaris (modern Tanis).

Sometime during this period, the Nubians overran the southern defenses and established themselves above the first cataract. Egypt was now occupied by foreigners to the north and south, while Egyptian national authorities occupied only slightly more than one-third of the country. The Hyksos invasion and occupation had an enormous impact on the Egyptian national psychology. The ejection of the Hyksos and the Nubians and the reestablishment of Egyptian national identity became the central goals of the Theban princes. Once it was finally achieved, the Egyptian national psychology was permanently accompanied by a fear of invasion. The result was a new national security policy built centrally around the aggressive use of military force to protect the state. Eventually, this policy produced the Egyptian empire.

THE NEW KINGDOM (1580–960 B.C.E.)

The struggle against the Hyksos required several generations to accomplish, and it began sometime in the 1580s B.C.E., when the first great warrior pharaoh, Kamos, conducted a series of wars against the enemy in the north. Kamos was killed in battle and was succeeded by his brother Ahmose I (1570–1545 B.C.E.), who ruled for twenty-one years and waged unrelenting war against the occupiers. Ahmose succeeded in driving the Hyksos from Egypt and pressed them back to their strongholds on the Palestine border. The new Egyptian army was at last a truly national instrument, designed to pursue national objectives. The pharaoh introduced the new military technology of the Hyksos to the Egyptian army.

At the end of his life Ahmose had restored the territorial integrity of Egypt from the Sinai to the Nubian border, established Thebes as the new capital, redesigned the army into a true instrument of national military power, and passed it all intact to his son Amenhotep I (1570–1546 B.C.E.). He also established the Eighteenth Dynasty of Egyptian kings. Over the next two centuries, this dynasty produced fifteen kings, eight of which were great warrior pharaohs. Throughout all Egyptian history, before or since, there has never been as long a line of talented rulers to oversee Egypt's security. The most resolute of them all was Thutmose III, the "Napoleon of Egypt."

A PROFESSIONAL MILITARY CASTE

The wars of liberation and expansion under the previous kings had wrought profound changes in Egyptian society. For the first time, there came into being a truly professional military caste. Military families were given grants of land to hold for as long as they provided a son for the officer corps. The army changed its structure and became a genuine national force based on conscription. The formula for conscription was one man in ten, allowing the Egyptians to raise a very large army. All the new weapons introduced by the Hyksos—chariots, helmets, armor, penetrating axe, composite bow, and sickle sword—were fully integrated into the new imperial army. Improvements were made in the design and construction of the chariot, making it stronger and lighter. Thutmose mounted his newly armed archers on chariots and produced the most important military revolution in ground warfare ever seen in Egypt.

The national army was centrally trained by professional and noncommissioned officers, and Pharaoh himself served as the commander in chief and led his troops in battle. The vizier served as the minister of war, and there was an Army Council that served as a general planning staff. The field army was organized into divisions, each of which was a complete, combined arms unit, including infantry, archers, and chariots. These divisions numbered between 5,000 and 6,000 men, each named after one of the principal gods of Egypt. Later, Ramses II organized Egypt and the empire into

Egyptian chariot from the New Kingdom (1400–1000 B.C.E.). Courtesy of Richard Gabriel.

thirty-four military districts to facilitate conscription, training, and supply of the army. The military administrative structure was improved, and there were professional schools to train and test officers and scribes in the military arts.

Chariotry

The two major combat arms of the Egyptian army were chariotry and infantry. The chariot corps was organized into squads of ten and platoons of fifty machines, each commanded by a "charioteer of the residence." The basic ratio of chariots to infantry seems to have been one chariot for every ten infantrymen, a ratio that provided each division with at least 500 machines as an organic force. Larger units of 50 and 150 machines could be rapidly assembled into chariot task forces, depending on the tactical needs of the moment. These units could be employed in concert with larger forces if required. The chariot corps was supported by quartermaster staffs, who recruited and trained horses, and by technical craftsmen, whose task was to repair the machines while the army was in the field. Egyptian divisions also had mobile chariot repair units to insure the operability of the machines when the army was on the march.

The Hyksos introduced the chariot to Egypt, and by the fifteenth century B.C.E. the Egyptians had modified the vehicle into the finest fighting vehicle in the ancient world. The Egyptian chariot was constructed of a light wooden frame covered by stretched fabric or hide to reduce weight. Two men could easily carry the vehicle over streams and rough terrain. The platform supporting the rider and archer was made of stretched leather thongs covered with hide and fashioned in the shape of a D. The cab was one meter wide, three-fourths meter high, and one-half meter deep. Two horses pulled the vehicle held by a central yoke pole and outer races guided by reins. The Egyptians were the first to move the axle to the far rear of the carrying platform, a development that increased the speed, stability, and maneuverability of the vehicle. Belly bars and leg straps helped steady the riders at high speed. Bow, arrow, and spear quivers as well as axes were attached to each side for easy access during battle. These weapons suggest that the chariot acquired new tactical functions under the Egyptians. It could now be used to engage the enemy with arrows at long range, while closing to deliver shock in massed formations, providing, of course, that the enemy infantry was not very cohesive. Horses will not charge a wall of spears. Once the enemy was engaged at short range, the axes and javelins were brought to bear. After the enemy force was shattered, the chariot could be used in lethal pursuit to kill, primarily with the bow. The Egyptian chariot combined the innovative dimensions of shock, lethality, and mobility, making the weapon the only one in ancient armies that could participate in all phases of the battle with great lethality.

The Infantry

Egyptian infantry was organized into fifty-man platoons, commanded by a "leader of fifty." A *sa*, or company, contained 250 men—five platoons, plus a commander, quartermaster, and scribe—and was identified by the type of weapon it carried. Units were further identified as comprising recruits, trained men, or elite shock troops. The next unit in the chain of command was the regiment, commanded by a "standard bearer," although we are not certain of the size of this unit. Above the regiment was the *pedjet*, or brigade, comprising 1,000 men commanded by a "captain of a troop." This rank was also given to a fortress commander and may have been a general officer rank. A typical Egyptian field division was organized into five *pedjets*, three heavy infantry brigades and two archer brigades. The addition of 500 chariots organic to the field division brought the Egyptian division to approximately 5,500 fighting men, with a supporting force of almost 1,000 men—technicians, carpenters, quartermasters, scribes, logisticians, intelligence officers, and so on—for a total of 6,500 men. The division was commanded by a royal prince or important retainer.

Egyptian infantry regiments were organized into axemen, archers, clubmen, and spearmen. The latter carried shields and six-foot-long spears. Their task was to protect against and disrupt hostile charges aimed at the chariot units. Infantry was the arm of decision in Egyptian tactical thinking and usually fought in formations five men deep, with a ten-man front in a fifty-man platoon. These units could quickly form marching columns ten men wide, providing a degree of flexibility in infantry employment. The roughest and most disciplined of the infantry were the *nakhtu-aa*, or the "strong-arm boys," tough, disciplined shock troops armed with the bull hide shield, the *dja*, or the short spear, the *kopesh*, literally, "goat's leg," or sickle sword, the cast bronze penetrating axe, and the *taagsu*, or dagger. The division contained special elite infantry units as well. The *kenyt-nesu*, or "King's Braves," appear to have been the Egyptian equivalent of elite special operations units of heavy infantry, used for overcoming difficult positions.

Egyptian archers and charioteers carried the same bow, an instrument of Hyksos design constructed of a central wooden core with thin strips of horn and leather laminated on it. The bow was 1.3 meters long and, when drawn to the ear, could send a reed shaft, fletched arrow with a bronze cast arrowhead through an ingot of copper three fingers thick. The bow was powered by a string of twisted gut. Both archers and spearmen wore textile armor and bronze helmets. Elite infantry and charioteers wore body armor fashioned of thin (two millimeter) bronze plates sewn in overlapping patterns on a leather jerkin.

Tactics

The tactics of the Egyptian army were well developed and supported by strong logistical functions. Ramses II introduced the oxcart as the basic form of logistical transport of the Egyptian army at the battle of Kadesh in 1275 B.C.E. The oxcart spread quickly to the other armies of the Near East and remained the basic military logistics vehicle until Philip II of Macedon replaced it with the horse 1,000 years later. Tactical expertise was increased by a professionally trained officer corps accustomed to maneuvering large units. By integrated use of field intelligence gathered through patrolling and special collection units, the Egyptians were adept at moving large armies over considerable distances across hostile terrain without being detected. Thutmose III moved an army of more than 20,000 men 300 miles and arrived outside the city of Megiddo without being detected. Egyptians used counterintelligence and deception to gain maximum surprise. They routinely used the commanders' conference, in which officers were urged to criticize operational plans and offer frank advice. The result of these practices was sound battle plans that permitted Thutmose III to conduct seventeen major campaigns and win them all.

On the battlefield Egyptian forces deployed chariot units to act as a screen for infantry and to cover their maneuvers during a movement to contact. Engaging the enemy with the long-range composite bow, the chariot archers began killing at a distance as they closed with the enemy. Archer units deployed ahead of the infantry, firing on the enemy as it moved to contact. Once the enemy was close, the archer units retired through the infantry ranks or to the flanks and continued to fire into the main body of enemy formations. If we can believe the Egyptian reliefs of the battle of Kadesh, the infantry continued to advance in close order with shields overlapping and spears presented at the walk until, as the lines closed, a general melee commenced. Chariot units engaged the enemy at any exposed point, often dismounting and fighting as infantry once in contact. If the enemy gave ground, chariots in reserve could be committed to exploit the weakness. The mobility of the chariot allowed the use of highly mobile reserves that could be committed at a propitious moment to turn a flank or exploit a breakthrough. If the enemy broke and a rout began, the chariot archers could engage in rapid pursuit with devastating effectiveness. If tactical surprise had been achieved, chariot units could engage an enemy not yet fully deployed for battle.

Each division was a self-contained combined arms force that could maneuver and fight as an independent tactical unit. This capability provided the Egyptians with a tactical flexibility that most armies of the day lacked. This maneuver capability was further enhanced by an experienced professional officer corps. A strongly articulated command structure throughout the army made it possible to use the entire army as an instrument of a single commander's will, something that provided the Egyptian force with a direction and cohesiveness not to be seen in any other army of the period until the Hittite armies two centuries later.

The Egyptian army lacked only cavalry formations, an innovation that was introduced 600 years later by the Assyrian army. The failure of the Egyptians to develop cavalry remains curious in light of their knowledge of the horse gained through the Hyksos occupation. It was once thought probable that the horse of that time was simply too small and weak to carry the weight of an armored soldier for very long. But as Steve Weingartner has pointed out, in fact, Egyptian horses of the period were *not* small, measuring fourteen hands at the withers. More likely, the reason may simply have been that no one thought of a tactical use for the horse in battle given the social and cultural predominance of the Egyptian nobility as charioteers.

With the exception of cavalry, however, the armies of the pharaohs of the Egyptian imperial era were in every respect modern armies capable of conducting military operations in a modern manner and on a modern scale, including the ability to mount seaborne operations and to use naval forces in conjunction with ground forces for transport and logistics. In its day the army of imperial Egypt was the largest, best equipped, and most successful fighting force in the world.

FURTHER READING

Breasted, James Henry. *Ancient Records of Egypt: Historical Documents from the Earliest Times to the Persian Conquest.* 5 vols. Chicago: University of Chicago Press, 1906.

Clayton, Peter A. *Chronicle of the Pharaohs: The Reign-by-Reign Record of the Rulers and Dynasties of Ancient Egypt.* New York: Thames and Hudson, 1994.

Cottrell, Leonard. *The Warrior Pharaohs.* New York: G. P. Putnam, 1969.

Ferrill, Arther. *The Origins of War: From the Stone Age to Alexander the Great.* New York: Thames and Hudson, 1985.

Gabriel, Richard A., and Donald W. Boose, Jr. *The Great Battles of Antiquity: A Strategic and Tactical Guide to Great Battles That Shaped the Development of War.* Westport, CT: Greenwood Press, 1994.

Gabriel, Richard A., and Karen S. Metz. *From Sumer to Rome: The Military Capabilities of Ancient Armies.* Westport, CT: Greenwood Press, 1991.

Gardiner, Sir Alan. *Egypt of the Pharaohs: An Introduction.* Oxford: Clarendon Press, 1961.

Grimal, Nicolas-Christophe. *A History of Ancient Egypt.* London: Blackwell, 1992.

Pritchard, James B. *Ancient Near Eastern Texts Relating to the Old Testament.* 2nd ed. Princeton, NJ: Princeton University Press, 1955.

Redford, Donald B. *Egypt, Canaan, and Israel in Ancient Times.* Princeton, NJ: Princeton University Press, 1992.

Shaw, Ian, ed. *The Oxford History of Ancient Egypt.* New York: Oxford University Press, 2003.

Weingartner, Steve. *Chariot Warfare.* Westport, CT: Praeger, forthcoming 2007.

Yadin, Yigael. *The Art of Warfare in Biblical Lands in the Light of Archaeological Study.* 2 vols. Translated by M. Pearlman. New York: McGraw-Hill, 1963.

Twenty-four

✦ ✦ ✦

THE MITANNI (1480–1335 B.C.E.)

The people known as the Mitanni appeared on the stage of history for only a short time, perhaps less than two centuries, before disappearing forever. The Mitanni occupied the area of the northern Euphrates steppe between the Euphrates and Tigris, an area the Assyrians called Hanigalbat, a name that became synonymous with the Mitanni. Its capital, Washukkanni, lay at the head of the Khabur River. The origins of the Mitanni are uncertain but seem closely related to the history of the Hurrians, about whom we know only slightly more. The Hurrians are first mentioned in the Amarna texts and again in the Bible (Genesis 36:20–30), where they are called "Horites." The Hurrian language is neither Semitic nor Indo-European but seems related to the Asianic group whose nearest relative is the language of the Urartu. It is likely, then, that the highlands of Armenia are the original homeland of the Hurrians.

THE MILITARY SIGNIFICANCE OF THE MITANNI

The Hurrians appear to have been a people given to migration or clan travel, and there is evidence that colonies of Hurrians had been extant in various parts of Mesopotamia for millennia. By 1800 B.C.E. the Hurrians comprised a majority in northern Iraq itself, and after 1600 B.C.E., the Hurrians became dominant in northern Syria. It was probably around this time that a warrior caste of Aryan (Indo-Iranian) dynasts came to impose themselves on the Hurrian people and become a new aristocracy in command of war and government. By 1550 B.C.E. Hittite texts report a major Hurrian-based kingdom, known now as the Mitanni, having come into being east of the Euphrates and having become a major competitor to Hittite and Egyptian influence in Syria. This powerful Mitanni kingdom was called Hanigalbat by the Assyrians and Naharin ("Two Rivers") by the Egyptians.

What did the Mitanni bring to the Hurrian society that permitted them to rise to such heights of international power and prestige? Two answers suggest themselves. First, they seem to have imposed themselves relatively peacefully and to have generally adopted the culture of the land into which they entered. Their main contribution seems to have been the introduction of a new form of political and social organization that was more effective at mobilizing and employing resources for war. The pattern was a familiar one among Indo-Aryans, namely a strong king drawn from a "great family" tied by blood to his vassals, who acted as a council of advisors. The Mitanni system was not unlike that found earlier among the Hittites, whose origins are also obscure and who superimposed a new caste on the then extant Hattian society.

Second, the Mitanni were the first to truly exploit the possibility of the horse as an instrument of war, most particularly, using the horse with the spoked-wheel chariot as a primary combat vehicle. The spoked-wheel war chariot made its first appearance among the Mitanni sometime soon after their arrival in the Hurrian land circa 1600 B.C.E. Almost simultaneously, the war chariot appeared in Kassite Babylonia among the Hittites, the Hyksos, and, a short time later, among the Egyptians. That the Mitanni claim to first use of this weapon may be valid can be deduced from the Hittite texts of this time that recount the story of Kikkuli of the Land of the Mitanni, who was hired by the Hittite king to instruct his army in the breeding and use of horses. While neither the horse nor the chariot as instruments of war can be attributed to the Mitanni with certainty, it is certainly true that the Mitanni were the inventors of the chariot system, an innovation that changed the face of battle among the armies of the Near East for the next 1,000 years.

Most of the information concerning the military organization of the Mitanni is derived from two sources. The first is the famous Nuzi archive in Syria, and the second is the rendering of Mitanni chariots and troops that appears on the sides of the war chariot of Thutmose IV of Egypt. The political structure of the Mitanni state was probably a Mitanni innovation superimposed on the old Hurrian social order and seems to have been imposed on Mitanni's vassal states as well, turning them into provinces whose governance and military administration were directed from the center. The administrative structure of the Mitanni province belies a concern for war as well as for government. Each province was divided into districts, called *halsu*, each of which possessed a fortified capital and armory. Other smaller towns, *alu*, throughout the district were also walled for defense. The province was administered for the king by a *halsuhlu* or *shakin mati*, a royal governor. The towns of the district were administered by a *hazannu*, or "mayor." The countryside was divided into large estates (*dimati*) worked by tenants (*ashshabu*) and owned by a *bel dimtu*, or "lord." The warrior ethos of the Mitanni is reflected in the fact that these estates comprised a few villages and a fortified manor house or keep for defense. The mayor or *hazannu* appears to have had military duties as well and was responsible for the security of his district. Whether or not he also served as a field commander is unknown. It is clear, however, that cities, towns, and estates were required to raise militia forces, while the larger cities and more strategic border towns were often garrisoned by professional troops of the royal army.

Mitanni Soldiers

The centerpiece of the Mitanni army was the *nakhushshu*, or the warrior caste of military professionals bound by an oath of loyalty to the king to serve at his request. This oath was called the *isharu*, literally, the "word of the man of arrows," or *ilku*. Soldiers were called *alik ilku*, or "those who perform the *ilku* duty." The elite corps of the professional army were the chariot warriors known as *maryannu*. The term itself means "young hero," which later became synonymous with "noble chariot warrior" and derives from the Indo-European word related to Sanskrit, *marya*, meaning "youth" or "hero." There seems to have been more than one grade of *maryannu* tied to military service, and a system of subvassals pledged to the main lord by oaths of military service were referred to as *maryannu* as well. The term seems to have been applied to both chariot and nonchariot warriors and professional and militia troops equally.

The organization of the army remains unclear. We are certain that the king possessed a bodyguard of chariotry known as *shepi sharri*, literally, "the feet of the king," consisting of ten chariots. This bodyguard probably had its roots in the coterie of the tribal chief's best warriors that accompanied him into battle. Much of the army comprised charioteers, known as *alik seri*, or "campaigners." There must also have been a central force of *maryannu* chariotry for we read of such units being sent to four towns to reinforce local garrisons. Infantry units, known as *shukuthlu*, comprised both spearmen and archers equipped with swords, daggers, leather armor, and helmets existed, but we know nothing of their organization or quality, except that the *ashshabu*, or "tenant farmers," were permitted to serve in their ranks.

Chariot units, or *emanti*, of five or ten vehicles were commanded by an officer called an *emanthuhlu*. These units could also be grouped into units based on multiples of six (the old Sumerian/Assyrian system) commanded by a "chief *emantuhlu*," who was also responsible for supplying rations to his men. One of these is also described as commanding a garrison, and it is possible that the *emantuhlu* applied to commanders of infantry units as well. Other texts refer to officers called *rab* with the decimal number of men under their command appearing next to the title. Thus *rab* (5), *rab* (10), *rab* (12), and so on refer to officers in command of units of these sizes. A confusing aspect of the Mitanni military organization is that it appears to have used no consistent numerical system as its base. There are textual references to 3,000 *alik ilki* (perhaps combined units of chariots and archers), 536 charioteers, 82 archers, 55 bowmen, and so on. There are references to "tablets of the left" and "brothers of the right," suggesting that the army had right and left wings.

Further compounding the organizational problem is the fact that estates, towns, and cities may have been required to raise levies of militia troops at the request of the king. If the feudal period of later Europe is any guide, such numbers became meaningless in a practical sense in that the strength and organization of these militia units for battle were rarely recorded. That the Mitanni army was well organized can be deduced from the fact that all armor, helmets, and other weapons were manufactured in royal arsenals as state industries and issued to the troops in a systematic manner.

When military equipment was worn out or broken, it was turned in to be replaced at royal expense.

Mitanni Chariotry and Infantry

The Mitanni chariot was constructed of light wood and hides. One text notes that twelve goatskins were required to cover a chariot frame and between nine and eleven sheepskins were needed to cover the floor, suggesting that the Mitanni chariot was somewhat larger and heavier than the Egyptian variety, but not as large as the Hittite chariot. Seals depict the Mitanni chariot with wheels of four, six, and eight spokes, suggesting again that at least some Mitanni machines were quite heavy. It was regular practice to oil the spokes to prevent the wheels from warping. A particularly interesting aspect of the Mitanni chariot was that some of them appear to have been armored with metal scales, called *sariam.*

One inventory mentions a unit of 100 chariots equipped with scale protection, and the depiction of the Mitanni chariots taken from the cab of Thutmose IV's war chariot shows them with armored cabs. A suit of Mitanni body armor consisting of 500 scales weighed approximately thirty-five pounds. Calculating the area of a Mitanni chariot cab to be almost twice the area required to outfit the human body in scale armor suggests that the armor added the considerable weight of seventy-five to eighty pounds to the chariot. It was Mitanni practice to armor their chariot horses as well. Horse armor consisted of a textile coat of felt or hair about three centimeters thick, called a *parashshamu*, extending from the withers of the horse to the loins. Equally common was covering this textile coat with a leather, copper, or a bronze scale overcoat. A coat of bronze horse armor would easily have weighed more than 100 pounds. Add to this that the Mitanni chariot warrior was usually equipped with a scale armor suit weighing approximately thirty-five pounds, and the load on the Mitanni chariot was considerable.

Both Mitanni charioteers and their horses wore heavy armor. Their armor and the weapons carried aboard—two composite bows, two quivers of arrows, a shield, and a lance—suggest that the tactical role of the Mitanni chariot was not to close and fight at close quarters, as the Hittites did. Both the bow and lance were to be used either from afar, as in a movement to contact, or en passant if closely engaged. Firepower and shock, then, were the two tactical roles afforded by a moderately heavy chariot carrying a well-armored charioteer. When fighting Egyptian chariots, the Mitanni machine afforded their charioteers an equal capability in firepower since both Egyptians and Mitanni were armed with the same composite bow. The Egyptian machine held the advantage in speed and mobility, but the terrain in Syria did not offer many opportunities for battle on flat plains. The heavier Mitanni vehicle, with its far better protected charioteer, offered a greater advantage in delivering shock as well as increasing the survivability of the archer when engaged en passant at close range or employed on uneven terrain, where the Egyptian advantage in speed and maneuverability could be neutralized by the ground itself.

The Nuzi archives refer to the Mitanni armor as "the armor of Hanigalbat." Scale and lamellar armor appears to have been a Hurrian invention of about the seventeenth century B.C.E. and to have been rapidly adopted by the Mitanni and everyone else in the Near East. Evidence for this lies in the fact that all the terms used for armor by the peoples of the Near East at this time are derived from the Hurrian term *sharyani*, or "coat of mail": This term appears in Akkadian as *sariam*, as *saryannni* in Hittite, as *shiryon* in Hebrew and Arabic, and as *tiryana* in Ugaritic and Egyptian. As described in the Nuzi texts, the armor of the Mitanni charioteer consisted of a mail coat with sleeves and a long skirt covered with individual bronze scale plates, called *kursimtu* after the Akkadian *kursindu*, meaning "snake," the analogy with the reptile's scales being obvious. The coat and skirt required almost 1,000 scales to assemble, with the sleeves of the coat alone requiring 200 plates. Two hundred smaller scales sewed over a leather cap served as a *gurpisu*, or "helmet." Sometimes these helmets had a crest of plaited leather. The most common helmet found among the Mitanni and throughout the Near East was the bronze helmet, or *gurpisu siparri*. Sometimes charioteers shaved their heads and wore a linen or leather cap beneath to tighten the fit. The most elaborate helmet was the *gurpisu siparri kursimetu*, the great bronze scale helmet, which offered greater protection than either the leather or sheet bronze models. The charioteer's neck was protected by a high, thick, bronze collar typical of the suits of armor of this period. A thick leather belt protected the charioteer's abdomen and helped him bear the weight of the armor. He carried a long dagger in the belt, a *patru*, for self-defense should he be forced from his machine.

In contrast to both Hittite and Egyptian practice, the Mitanni chariot driver was equally well equipped with scale armor and helmet, offering the same protection as for the charioteer. The drivers carried small shields, *aritu*, made of wood and covered sometimes with beaten bronze. Chariot shields seem to have had a double grip, one that could be held in the hand and another consisting of a pair of leather straps through which the driver could slip his arm, permitting him some protection while not interfering with his ability to drive the horses.

Chariot horses were prized and expensive military assets, and there was a system for acquiring, breeding, and training them. Horses began training to the chariot when they were a year old and began pulling chariots by their third year. By their fourth year they became proper chariot horses and usually served until they were nine or ten years old. Cavalry, of course, was unknown, but there is some evidence that messengers, *mar shipri*, may have traveled by horseback. The term horseman was *rakib susi*, suggesting at least that riding horses was not entirely unknown. There is, however, no evidence of horsemen having been put to military use.

We know little about the Mitanni infantry. That there were infantry units, *shukuthlu*, we can be fairly certain, and that there were infantry units of archers and spearmen is reasonably certain as well. Beyond that, we can only say that the infantry was equipped with swords or long dirks for protection and that they wore leather helmets. We have no idea as to how they were employed, but the primary role of the chariot in Mitanni tactical doctrine suggests that the Mitanni may have employed their infantry in a manner similar to that of the Hittites, that is, primarily as a platform of maneuver designed to engage the enemy and fix his position until he could be struck at a vulnerable point by the chariotry. As in other armies of the period, archer units provided covering fire for the infantry during its movement to contact and played only a supporting role once the infantry was engaged. Beyond these obvious and general comments, little else is known about Mitanni infantry tactical doctrine.

FURTHER READING

Alkim, U. Bahadir. *Anatolia*. London: Barrie and Rockliff, 1969.

Cambridge Ancient History. vol. 2, parts 2–3. New York: Cambridge University Press, 1970.

Gabriel, Richard A., and Donald W. Boose, Jr. *The Great Battles of Antiquity: A Strategic and Tactical Guide to Great Battles That Shaped the Development of War*. Westport, CT: Greenwood Press, 1994.

Redford, Donald B. *Akhenaten: The Heretic King*. Princeton, NJ: Princeton University Press, 1984.

Roux, Georges. *Ancient Iraq*. 3rd ed. New York: Penguin Books, 1992.

Saggs, H.W.F. *The Might That Was Assyria*. London: Sidgwick and Jackson, 1984.

Stillman, Nigel, and Nigel Tallis. *Armies of the Ancient Near East: 3000 to 539 B.C.E.* Sussex, UK: Flexiprint, 1984.

Twenty-five

✳ ✳ ✳

THE HITTITES (1450–1180 B.C.E.)

The Hittites occupied the Anatolian peninsula from approximately 1900 to 1000 B.C.E. The origins of this rugged people skilled in mountain warfare remain obscure, but the evidence suggests that their settlement in Anatolia began with the tribal migrations of peoples whose origins lay in the area that stretches from the lower Danube along the north shore of the Black Sea to the northern foothills of the Caucasus Mountains. The date of migration is uncertain but may have been as early as 2500 B.C.E. By 1900 B.C.E., there was clear evidence of the beginnings of a separate society that can be identified as Hittite. The Hittite society lasted until circa 1100 B.C.E., when, like the other states of Syria, Lebanon, and the upper Euphrates, it was overrun and destroyed by the invasion of the Sea Peoples.

Hittite society was a feudal order based on land ownership and fiefdoms governed nationally by a council of great families, called the *Pankus*. This same pattern of social development is found in early Sumer, Egypt, and Rome. Gradually, a governing aristocracy was formed, with its capital at Hattusas in northeast Anatolia. Social organization centered on the "fiefholder," who worked the land, and, as the need for defense and military power increased, on the "man of the weapon," who was given land and income in return for full-time military service to the high king. As in medieval Europe, there was constant tension between the central governing authority and powerful local vassals, who often could not be controlled. Hittite central authority waxed and waned from one period to the next. Only rarely was it possible for the Hittite kings to unify and control their country, and then only for relatively short periods. One result was that to the end of the empire, Hatti remained essentially a feudal society, whose army comprised a core of loyal troops of the king augmented by feudal armies contributed by vassals and foreign client states.

The imperial period of Hittite power is dated from 1450 to 1180 B.C.E. In 1346 B.C.E. a young and vigorous king named Suppiluliumas brought the domestic situation under control and moved militarily against the city-states of the Syrian zone. He succeeded in gaining control of most of the major city-states of the area before moving against the Mitanni. With the power of the Mitanni brought to heel, he installed his own governors there and created a new state to act as a buffer against the growing power of Assyria. Suppiluliumas was succeeded by his youngest son, Mursilis, who continued to strengthen Hittite control in the Syrian zone while bringing the new Mitanni buffer state further within his control. Hatti encroached farther south into the Syrian zone while the Egyptians were paralyzed by domestic turmoil.

Mursilis passed the Hittite throne to his son Muwatallis (1308–1285 B.C.E.), who suppressed revolts in Arzawa and the Gasgan lands, making certain that domestic events did not interfere with the emerging conflict with Egypt. He achieved a temporary diplomatic settlement to blunt renewed Assyrian pressure in the Mitanni region. Egypt was at last ready to attempt to counter Hittite influence in the Syrian zone and began by fomenting unrest in some of the city-states. Muwatallis moved quickly to reduce the threat with armed intervention against Kadesh, Carchemesh, and Allepo, bringing them to heel and installing Hittite rulers and garrisons. This was a clear challenge to Egypt, and armed conflict was inevitable. The basis of Hittite national security strategy remained unchanged for almost five centuries. The goal was to secure the homeland by suppressing domestic revolts and increasing the power of the national authorities to deal with the constant threats on the border.

In 1279 B.C.E. Ramses II, one of Egypt's great warrior pharoahs, came to the throne. Ramses understood that Egyptian influence in Lebanon and Palestine would never be secure as long as the Hittite threat hung over the Syrian zone. The passage of time would only work to the Hittite advantage as they strengthened their hold on the area. Egyptian strategic thinking held that a threat to Syria was a threat to Palestine, and a threat to Palestine was a threat to the Nile. The world's first "domino theory" was born. In the fifth year of his rule, 1275 B.C.E., Ramses II set out to destroy Hittite influence in Syria and to drive it back behind the Taurus Mountains. As the room for maneuver narrowed, the clash between the two great powers became certain. When it came, it came at the city of Kadesh on the Orontes River.

THE HITTITE MILITARY ORGANIZATION

The size of the armies that fought at Kadesh remains the subject of some dispute. The foremost experts on the Egyptian and Hittite armies of the period estimate the size of the Egyptian force at between 25,000 and 30,000 men comprised of four divisions of 6,000 each, plus some *nim* and allied Canaanite chariot contingents. The Hittite army appears to have been in the neighborhood of 17,000–20,000 men, which was probably the largest combat force ever deployed by the Hittites. The unusual size of the Hittite force is explainable by the fact that the Hittite king, Muwatallish, had been successful in uniting the various vassals of the country and in concluding a number of mutual assistance treaties with the city-states of Syria. Of the other great powers, only the

Mitanni deployed forces comparable in size to the Hittite armies, and they, too, relied heavily on allied contingents for maximum national efforts. The full military manpower pool of Hatti was available to the king, as were military contingents from allied states.

The Hittite army was organized around the decimal system common to armies of the area at that time. Infantry, chariots, and archers shared the same organizational structure, with squads of ten, companies of ten squads, and battalions of ten companies. Infantry deployed for battle in companies 10 men wide and 10 men deep, with battalions standing with 100-man fronts 10 men deep. The basic weapons of the Hittite infantry were the medium-length spear, the axe, and the sickle sword.

Hittite infantry was flexible in armament, equipment, and manner of deployment. Hittite infantry had been developed in the rough terrain of Anatolia, where the land itself placed a premium on ground troops used in various ways. Hittite commanders commonly changed the mix of infantry weaponry and even clothing and armor, depending on the nature of the terrain and the type of battle that the infantry was expected to fight. In mountain terrain the infantry carried the sickle sword, dagger, axe, and no spear, a mix of weapons suited primarily to close combat. Mountain infantry were issued metal helmets, good boots, leather or scale armor, and a specially designed shield in the shape of a figure eight. The narrow waist of the shield made it lighter while still affording good, full-length body protection. The narrow waist improved the ability of the soldier to see his adversary and provided greater room for him to wield his sword when in close-order battle. Later, the Hittites adopted the small round shield, a piece of equipment specifically designed for close combat.

The infantry's weapons and equipment were changed whenever the Hittite army was required to fight in open terrain. Under these conditions, the primary weapon was the long stabbing spear, and the fighting formation was the packed heavy phalanx. An army that tailored its units, weapons, and combat formations so readily required a high degree of discipline and training from its soldiers. The Hittite army was constructed around a core professional force loyal to the king and augmented by forces provided by the king's vassals. Hittite society provided for the "man of the weapon," who was given the income from land in exchange for military service. The Anatolian terrain placed a premium on stealth, rapid movement, movement at night, and quick deployment from the line of march to fighting formation to avoid ambush. These abilities are the characteristics of a professional army, not an army of conscripts. The Hittite army comprised almost professional-quality soldiers similar in experience and ability to the feudal military classes of Europe during the Middle Ages.

The Hittite arm of decision was its chariotry. The chariot's role was to close quickly with the enemy infantry, delivering maximum shock, then to dismount and fight as heavy infantry. The Hittite machine was heavier than the Egyptian chariot and had its axle positioned in the center of the carrying platform. This arrangement reduced speed and stability but made it possible for the machine to carry a crew of three. The crew was armed with the six-foot-long stabbing spear designed not to be thrown but to be used as a lance while mounted and as an infantry weapon when dismounted. The Hittites used their chariots as mounted heavy infantry, and they were the key to the success of the Hittite army fighting in open terrain.

One can understand the tactical role of Hittite chariotry by remembering that the Hittite art of war developed in the inhospitable terrain of the Anatolian plateau, which afforded few open plains where chariots could maneuver but offered numerous valleys and defiles from which a hidden army could suddenly strike at an unsuspecting enemy. Under these conditions of short distances to combat closure, even a heavy machine could move fast enough to inflict sudden and decisive shock. Whereas the open terrain of Egypt and Palestine encouraged an emphasis on speed of movement over expanses of open terrain, the Hittite experience emphasized tactical surprise. It was typical of Hittite strategy to attempt to catch the enemy on the march and ambush him with a sudden rush of infantry-carrying chariots and to be on him before he could deploy to meet the attack. This tactic was employed brilliantly at Kadesh and almost destroyed the Egyptian army.

FURTHER READING

Beal, Richard Henry. *The Organization of the Hittite Military*. Chicago: University of Chicago Press, 1992.

Breasted, James Henry. *The Battle of Kadesh: A Study in the Earliest Known Military Strategy*. Chicago: University of Chicago Press, 1903.

Bryce, Trevor. *The Kingdom of the Hittites*. New York: Oxford University Press, 1998.

———. *Life and Society in the Hittite World*. New York: Oxford University Press, 2002.

Burne, Alfred H. *The Battle of Kadesh*. Harrisburg, PA: Military Service Press, 1961.

Cottrell, Leonard. *The Warrior Pharaohs*. New York: G. P. Putnam, 1969.

Ferrill, Arther. *The Origins of War: From the Stone Age to Alexander the Great*. New York: Thames and Hudson, 1985.

Gabriel, Richard A., and Karen S. Metz. *From Sumer to Rome: The Military Capabilities of Ancient Armies*. Westport, CT: Greenwood Press, 1991.

Gardiner, Sir Alan. *The Kadesh Inscriptions of Ramses II*. Oxford: Griffith Institute, 1960.

Goedicke, Hans. "Considerations on the Battle of Kadesh." *Journal of Egyptian Archaeology* 52 (1966): 71–80.

Gurney, O. R. *The Hittites*. 2nd ed. New York: Penguin Books, 1990.

Macqueen, J. G. *The Hittites and Their Contemporaries in Asia Minor*. Boulder, CO: Westview Press, 1975.

Pritchard, James B. *Ancient Near Eastern Texts Relating to the Old Testament*. 2nd ed. Princeton, NJ: Princeton University Press, 1955.

Williamson, Joanne S. *Hittite Warrior*. Warsaw, ND: Bethlehem Books, 1999.

Yadin, Yigael. *The Art of Warfare in Biblical Lands in the Light of Archaeological Study*. 2 vols. Translated by M. Pearlman. New York: McGraw-Hill, 1963.

Yeivan, S. "Canaanite and Hittite Strategy in the Second Half of the Second Millennium B.C." *Journal of Near Eastern Studies* 9 (1950): 101–107.

Twenty-six

✳ ✳ ✳

THE CANAANITES (1500–900 B.C.E.)

The period between 1800 and 1550 B.C.E. is called the Middle Canaanite period, when climatic conditions improved and cultural development flourished, permitting the people of Canaan to rebuild their old fortified villages into powerful new urban centers. During this time the first written documents in Canaanite appear, and it is from this period that Canaan as a recognizable entity with its own culture can be said to have come into being. Egyptian documents from the time of Pharaoh Senusret II (1897–1878 B.C.E.) tell of an earlier time when there were a number of independent Canaanite kingdoms ruled by warrior princes who had learned how to fortify their towns, which then grew into city-states that the Egyptians were forced to deal with militarily. During this time Canaanite society was formed around tribes, each ruled by a warrior chieftain (*malek*), who held his position by virtue of being the fiercest warrior in the tribe. These chiefs maintained household guards (*henkhu*) as part of their personal retinues that probably constituted the main combat element in tribal wars.

CANAANITE MILITARY ORGANIZATION

The name "Canaan" is very old and in antiquity denoted that territory between Gaza in the south and the upper reaches of Lebanon north to Ugarit. To the east, the land of Canaan ran to the base of the central mountain massif of later Judah and Samaria, northward through the Jezreel valley to include the Beka up to Kadesh. In the Middle period Canaan was subject to the passage of a group of immigrant tribes originating somewhere in northern Syria that moved over the land bridge until they entered Egypt itself, settling in the delta near Avaris and defeating the Egyptians by force of arms. These were the Hyksos. While the origin of the Hyksos remains uncertain, there is no doubt that these sophisticated people introduced their military technology to Canaan, where it was adopted by the rival princes of the Canaanite city-states. The origin of this military technology, like the Hyksos themselves, is uncertain but may lie in the technology of the Hurrian-Mitanni of the Upper Euphrates.

The Hyksos, and later, Mitanni, military influence thus brought a number of new weapons to Canaan that revolutionized warfare. It was from the Hyksos that the Canaanites acquired the chariot and the horse as weapons of war. The composite bow, socket axe, and sickle sword also made their appearance in Canaan at this time. Within a century the long dirk or dagger that under the later influence of the Sea Peoples developed into the straight sword was in evidence. The coat of mail came into use at approximately the same time, probably worn only by the armed charioteer. Later, we find Canaanite infantry wearing body armor as well.

The new military sophistication of the Canaanites during this period was also reflected in a change in the nature of the military fortifications of Canaanite cities. Canaanite princes now constructed their cities atop a new kind of massive rampart, a slanted bank of packed earth called a glacis. The glacis joined an exterior ditch, a fosse, obstructing the most likely avenues of approach. This military architecture was a reaction to the widespread use of the twin technologies of the chariot and the battering ram in Canaanite warfare. The Mitanni influence was reflected in the new architecture and is evidenced by the fact that two powerful cities in northern Syria, Carchemish and Ebla, possessed the same fortifications. The influence of the Hurrian-Mitanni culture was also reflected in the transformation of Canaanite society during this period into one based on the Mitanni model. There now came into existence a feudal warrior caste in Canaan based on heredity and land possession. As in the land of the Mitanni, these warriors were called *maryannu*, and like their Mitanni cousins were an elite group of chariot warriors. This elite ruled over a half-free, Semitic-speaking class of peasants and farmers (*khupshu*) with no middle or merchant class in between.

With the creation of the Egyptian empire under the Eighteenth Dynasty, Egypt moved aggressively to strengthen its influence in Canaan, an initiative that met organized resistance from a coalition of Canaanite princes at Megiddo (1479 B.C.E.). In the wake of the Egyptian victory Egypt established garrisons in the major towns of the country, including Ullaza, Sharuhen, Gaza, and Joppa, the last two being major Egyptian administrative centers. Each Canaanite city of any size had an Egyptian "political officer" (*weputy*) and a small staff to oversee economic and political matters, including the collection of intelligence. Egyptian garrisons stationed in major towns were often established as "allies of the king" and could be used to support the Canaanite prince in his local quarrels.

The presence of foreign influence did not prohibit the Canaanite princes from fortifying their important cities and towns, and by the twelfth century B.C.E. the entire country was heavily fortified, and each city-state was ruled by an independent king. Although there was no Canaanite "high king" to direct it, the countrywide Canaanite fortification design was so well integrated as to suggest some degree of cooperation among the princes. The purpose of these fortifications was to protect the lucrative trade routes that crisscrossed the country, linking it to Syria and Egypt, and to protect

Canaan from the predations of migrating nomadic tribes. Taken together, the system of fortifications was designed to permit the Canaanite princes to mount a mobile defense in depth using chariot warriors.

By the beginning of the thirteenth century and well into the twelfth century B.C.E. the Canaanite armies reached the apex of their military effectiveness. Each city-state raised and trained its own armed forces, most of which were similar in weapons and organization. There was no unified "national" command for there was no "high king" that ruled over all Canaan, but in time of war the engaged city-states were capable of acting in concert and coordinating the movement and deployment of their forces. This had been true when Thutmose III had confronted the coalition of Canaanite princes at Megiddo. The king of the city-state usually took the field as commander in chief, but it was not unusual for military command to be delegated to trusted generals. Regular fully equipped troops, called *sabu nagib*, were distinguished from militia or irregulars. The term was applied to both infantry and chariotry, suggesting that regular infantry units existed. Field commanders were called *muru-u*, but we do not know the size of the units they commanded. It is likely, however, that the decimal system of unit sizing was employed as it was commonly elsewhere.

Chariotry

The primary striking arm of the Canaanite armies was the elite chariot corps manned by the social elite of feudal nobles serving as chariot warriors, called *maryannu*. Each *maryannu* was a professional soldier who maintained his chariot, horses, grooms, driver, runners, and equipment at his own expense. His wealth was derived from the holding of a fief, which, although originally conferred by the king, seems over time to have become hereditary. Among the general warrior caste of *maryannu* were an inner elite of "picked men," or *na'arun*, a term which appears in the Ugarit texts. Apparently, these elite units comprised infantry as well as chariotry. The chariot corps was commanded by the *akil markabti*, or "Chief of Chariotry." A smaller battle guard, called the "Maryanna of the King," also existed.

The Canaanite chariot, much like the Mitanni chariot, was heavier than the Egyptian vehicle but lighter than the Hittite machine. Canaan offered few smooth plains where the opportunity for wide-ranging maneuver and speed could afford dividends. The terrain of Canaan was like that of northern Syria (and the land of the Mitanni), characterized by rocky ground, hills and mountains, and forests and glens, conditions which put a premium on surprise, ambush, and shock. The Canaanite chariot was heavier than the Egyptian model, having a six-spoked wheel with the axle moved to the center of the platform to take the weight off the animals. This permitted a larger carrying platform, whose floor could be fashioned of wood for strength. One result was that the machine lost a good part of its maneuverability at speed, and the endurance of the animals was also compromised to some degree.

The Canaanite charioteer, like his Mitanni counterpart, was heavily protected by a mail coat of scale armor. His horse, too, wore a textile or bronze scale coat. The primary weapons of the Canaanite charioteer were the composite bow, a heavy spear, and a club, the latter to be used only in the direst emergency should the warrior find himself afoot. Depending on the tactical mission, the Canaanite chariot was capable of carrying a three-man crew, a fact suggested by the portrayal of the machine with javelin cases. The first recorded encounter by Israelite troops with Canaanite chariots is presented in Joshua 11:5,7–9, where, having defeated the Canaanites near the Waters of Merom (Hula Lake), Joshua "burnt their chariots with fire." In another passage, Joshua 17:16–18, the account speaks of the Canaanites possessing "chariots of iron." In fact, it was not until the Assyrians occupied Palestine that chariots had iron tire rims, which might account for the reference in the text. It is likely that the description of "iron chariots" is a redactor's invention for the light wooden frame of the chariots of Joshua's time would simply have collapsed under the weight of bronze or iron plates. Iron weapons at the time of Joshua (1250 b.c.e.) were still largely curiosities but later were introduced in some numbers by the Philistines.

The Infantry

Canaanite infantry, called *hupshu*, had both militia and regular units. Most of the infantry were semitrained militia (*khepetj*) or conscripted and corvée peasantry. These units were lightly armed with bows and spears. There was a long Canaanite tradition dating from tribal days that the infantry supplied their own equipment, but we are uncertain if this tradition persisted into biblical times. Canaanite regular infantry were probably well-trained professionals who were heavily armed. These units wore armored corslets, helmets, and carried a sickle sword and shield and the socket axe. Until the arrival of the Sea Peoples, the Canaanites used a shield of Hittite design. Shaped like a figure eight with a narrow waist, this shield allowed the soldier a greater field of view of his opponent in close combat and permitted a more flexible wielding of the sword. With the coming of the Sea Peoples the Canaanites adopted the round shield and outfitted their infantry with the spear. At the same time, however, the Canaanite sickle sword was replaced by the straight sword of the Sea Peoples. Scale armor for the regular infantry became commonplace at that time as well.

Elite units of heavy infantry, called *na'arun*, appear to have served as the palace guard of the Canaanite kings. The Ugaritic texts mention these units as an inner elite of the general *maryannu* warrior caste. The term itself means "picked men," that is, warriors chosen by their king for loyalty and bravery. At Kadesh Ramses II was rescued in the nick of time by a unit of these elite shock troops, who fell on the Hittite flank, breaking the Hittite encirclement. These *na'arun* were Canaanite mercenaries in the service of the Egyptians. A relief of the battle portrays the Canaanites attacking in phalanx formation line abreast in ten rows, ten men deep, armed with spears and shields, suggesting that they are elite heavy infantry.

The Canaanite kings supplemented their forces with hired freebooters called *apiru* (sometimes known as *habiru*). The *apiru* were a class of outcasts, debtors, outlaws, and restless nomads who formed themselves into wandering groups of raiders, often hiring themselves out to princes and kings for military duty. These wandering brigands were a serious threat and often had to be brought to heel by the Canaanite princes by force of arms. One of history's greatest generals, David, was an *apiru*. When forced to leave Saul's court for fear of being killed, David returned to his old mercenary occupation by raising a force of 600 "discontented men" and hiring his soldiers out to one of the Philistine kings. The size and military sophistication of these brigand groups could present a considerable threat to public order. A record from Alalakh tells of a band of *apiru* comprising 1,436 men, 80 of which were charioteers and 1,006 of which were *shananu*, probably some kind of archer. Another text records the capture of the town of Allul by a force of 2,000 *apiru*.

Canaanite tactics were similar to those of the Mitanni in that the army relied on its chariot units to strike the enemy from ambush, catching him while still in column of march or deploying for open battle. If surprise was not possible, Canaanite generals used the chariot to deliver shock against enemy infantry formations. This required that the chariots be accompanied by "chariot runners," or light infantry. The Canaanite charioteer engaged the enemy from close range, firing his bow again and again, relying on his heavy armor to protect him from enemy fire. In this tactical application, infantry phalanxes of spearmen supported by archers would act in support or, if on the defensive, hold their positions, providing the chariots with a platform of maneuver.

The primary role of the Canaaniate chariot, however, was as a strategic weapon. The Canaanite chariots were mobile, heavy vehicles that could range far from their bases to protect the Canaanite cities from being besieged. Protecting the city itself was at the center of Canaanite strategic thinking, and the chariots were the key element in achieving this goal. Chariots could be used to intercept armies long before they reached the city walls, forcing the enemy to fight on terrain not of its choosing. Chariots were ideal for ambushing enemy patrols, harassing an enemy's route of march, keeping interior lines open, and chasing down mercenary *apiru*. No infantry force could achieve such a mix of tactical and strategic flexibility. Chariots, of course, were expensive, and their crews required extensive training and permanent maintenance at royal expense. The expense was worth it, however, for the chariot allowed the Canaanite kings to erect a strategic defense in depth based on flexible mobile tactics.

The system of mobile defense worked well for more than two centuries, but Canaan's wealth and strategic position made it too tempting a target for the national predators who wished to control the land bridge. Over time, the encroachments, immigrations, settlements, and aggressions of the Egyptians, Aramaens, Sea Peoples, Israelites, and Philistines took their toll, with the result that by the time of King David the Canaanites had been deprived of three-fourths of their land area and 90 percent of their grain-growing land. All that remained of these proud warrior people settled along the central Phoenician coastal strip and its immediate hinterlands. Within a century they had reconstituted their city-states, from which they embarked on a campaign of trade and settlement throughout the western Mediterranean. They became known to history as the Phoenicians.

FURTHER READING

Dever, William G. "The Peoples of Palestine in the Middle Bronze I Period." *Harvard Theological Review* 64 (1971): 197–226.

Drews, Robert. "The Chariots of Iron of Joshua and Judges." *Journal for the Study of the Old Testament* 45 (1989): 15–23.

Gabriel, Richard A. *Gods of Our Fathers: The Memory of Egypt in Judaism and Christianity.* Westport, CT: Greenwood Press, 2002.

———. *The Military History of Ancient Israel.* Westport, CT: Praeger, 2003.

Gale, Sir Richard. *Great Battles of Bible History*. New York: John Day, 1970.

Grant, Michael. *The History of Ancient Israel*. New York: Charles Scribner, 1984.

Herzog, Chaim, and Mordechai Gichon. *Battles of the Bible*. Jerusalem: Steimatzky's Agency, 1978.

Hobbs, T. R. *A Time for War: A Study of Warfare in the Old Testament*. Wilmington, DE: Michael Glazier, 1989.

Isserlin, B.S.J. "The Israelite Conquest of Canaan: A Comparative Review of the Arguments." *Palestine Exploration Quarterly* 115 (1983): 85–94.

Liver, Jacob, ed. *The Military History of the Land of Israel in Biblical Times* [in Hebrew]. Jerusalem: Israel Defense Force, 1964.

Malamat, Abraham. "The Egyptian Decline in Canaan and the Sea Peoples." In *World History of the Jewish People*, vol. 3. Philadelphia: Jewish Publications, 1979.

Osterley, W.O.E., and Theodore Robinson. *A History of Israel*. 2 vols. Oxford: Clarendon Press, 1948.

Redford, Donald B. *Egypt, Canaan, and Israel in Ancient Times*. Princeton, NJ: Princeton University Press, 1992.

Rohl, David M. *Pharaohs and Kings: A Biblical Quest*. New York: Crown, 1995.

Strange, John. "The Transition from the Bronze Age to the Iron Age in the Eastern Mediterranean and the Emergence of the Israelite State." *Scandinavian Journal of the Old Testament* 6 (1987): 1–19.

Wright, George Ernest, and Floyd Vivan Filson, eds. *The Westminster Historical Atlas to the Bible*. Philadelphia: Westminster Press, 1945.

Yadin, Yigael. *The Art of Warfare in Biblical Lands in the Light of Archaeological Study*. 2 vols. Translated by M. Pearlman. New York: McGraw-Hill, 1963.

Twenty-seven

✳ ✳ ✳

THE PHILISTINES (1200–900 B.C.E.)

The penetration of Canaan by the Israelites (circa 1200 B.C.E.) was already under-way when another nation began its assault on Canaan: the Philistines. The Philistines came from the west by land and sea. They were the Peleset of the Sea Peoples, and their attempt to conquer Egypt was recorded by Ramses III (1192–1160 B.C.E.) on the great reliefs of Medinet Habu. The Philistines, from which we get the name "Palestine," were of Aegean stock and related to both the Minoan and Mycenaean peoples of the Mediterranean islands and mainland Greece and thus to the later Classical Greeks. The Sea Peoples swept down the shores of the southeastern Mediterranean in swift ships accompanied by overland movement of their entire tribes and with fire and iron swords attempted to capture new lands for settlement. Pharaoh Merneptah (1213–1203 B.C.E.) fought a battle with them in Canaan, and even before the great battle with Ramses III, which halted their advance against Egypt, there is evidence to suggest that Philistine ele-ments had already settled in places along the coast of Canaan.

After their defeat by Ramses III, the Philistines settled in significant numbers in the land of Canaan. The Egyptians employed Philistine warriors as mercenaries in what might have been an attempt to check both Canaanite and Israelite influence on the land bridge. The Philistines settled along the southern coastal plain of Canaan, a fertile strip forty miles long and fifteen miles wide. They inhabited the fortified cities of Ashkelon, Ashdod, and Gaza on the coast and Gath and Ekron farther inland. As Egyptian power weakened, Philistine influence in Canaan increased, and in a short time they became free of Egyptian influence and began to push out from their coastal enclaves toward the interior central mountains. This brought them into conflict with the Israelites.

The political structure of the Philistines resembled, at least in its broad outlines, that of their Greek relatives. Each city was independent and ruled by a prince, whose claim to power rested, as in ancient Mycenae, on his royal blood and prowess as a warrior. There was no high king to rule other kings. When the Philistine cities had to act in concert to counter a military threat, they met in a council of princes, called the sarney. Whenever the Philistine city-states took the field in concert, they acted under a unified military command. The armies of the Philistines comprised mostly a well-armed, professional, feudal military caste. The Philistine settlement of Canaan was successful, and in a relatively short time they assimilated into Canaanite culture so thoroughly that their own language was lost and replaced by a Canaanite dialect. Their gods of Aegean origin had their names changed, and the Philistine army adopted the full panoply of Canaanite weapons and techniques of war. With the settlement of the Philistines in Canaan and their introduction of iron weapons the iron age of military technology can be said to have begun.

THE PHILISTINES INTRODUCE IRON WEAPONS

The first portrayal of Philistine weapons comes down to us from Ramses III's memorial reliefs at Medinet Habu of his defeat of the Sea Peoples. The Peleset are easily recognizable by their combat dress and weapons. Their soldiers wear a distinctive helmet with a band of what were originally thought to be feathers on the crown. More recent evidence suggests that these were not feathers but a circlet of reeds, stiffened horsehair, or even leather strips. The leather helmet was secured by a chin strap. Body armor was a corslet of bronze or leather shaped in an inverted V, probably indicative of overlapping plates of either material. Shoulder guards to protect the clavicles are in evidence. A short kilt, like that worn by the Hittites, is shown, an item of equipment that may well have been acquired by the Peleset during their wanderings in Asia Minor.

The long, straight, iron sword was the main weapon of the Philistine soldier, although some Peleset soldiers are portrayed with the short spear, similar to the Greek dory of a much later period. The Peleset shield was round, probably fashioned of wood covered with leather or bronze, with an iron rim to ward off sword blows, and was equipped with a boss. We know nothing of the shield's handgrip, but if it was of Aegean origin, it is likely that the shield was held by a collection of tethers that met in the center of the shield. With this grip the shield was difficult to maneuver, required great strength to use effectively, and required a high degree of training. The round shield was smaller and much lighter than the old full-bodied shield or figure eight shield, permitting the sword-bearing infantryman much greater speed and mobility on the battlefield. The appearance of the straight sword and light javelin at this time reduced the spear-bearing infantry to a secondary role, permitting the light infantryman to move about the battlefield with increased effectiveness. The light round shield and the leather body corslet provided his main protection.

The Philistine way of war originally placed its greatest reliance on infantry, as befits an Aegean people, where the war chariot was rarely used in combat. Once settled in Canaan, however, the Philistines seem to have quickly adopted the primary weapon of Canaanite armies, the war chariot, and transformed some of their warrior caste from heavy infantry into chariot warriors, even though the use of Philistine infantry in later battles remained substantial. The first mention of Philistine chariots in the Bible occurs during the time of Saul at the battle of Michmash, more than a century after the Philistines arrived in Canaan, plenty of time to have become acquainted with the Canaanite chariot. To a much greater degree than Canaanite armies, the Philistines appear to have maintained a large number of heavy infantry of professional quality, in contrast to the light infantry of the Israelites. At both Michmash (a Philistine defeat) and Mount Gilboa (a Philistine victory), infantry troops were employed in large numbers, with the chariots in support. The maintenance of large infantry units made good sense in light of the fact that the main antagonists of the Philistines were Israelites, whose armies comprised almost exclusively light infantry that specialized in surprise and night attack. The areas of Israelite-Philistine conflict, at least in the early days, were confined mostly to the mountains of the central massif, terrain highly unfavorable to chariots. Under these conditions, the primary tactical emphasis of the Philistines was on infantry, with chariots used in support.

Conflict between the Israelites and Philistines grew increasingly frequent as the Philistines pushed out from their main coastal bases and sought to establish trade routes and trading stations that cut across the central mountains into Jordan. The Philistines established a number of trading stations deep in Israelite territory, with small military garrisons to protect them. These stations were seen by the Israelites as a prelude to invasion. From the Philistine perspective Israelite patrols and occasional forays into the coastal lowlands were seen as a burgeoning threat. Circa 1050 B.C.E. the Philistines forced the Israelites into a contest of arms, with the result that the Israelites suffered a defeat at the battle of Aphek. A short time later, the Israelites were defeated once more by the Philistines. The result of these defeats was the expansion of Philistine influence and control as far north as the Jezreel Valley and the occupation of the central mountain spine of the country, the main area of Israelite settlement, for more than twenty years. These circumstances set off a tremendous cry among the Israelites for a national leader who could defeat their enemies and lift the Philistine yoke. The result was the rise of Saul, the first king of Israel.

Saul had little success in reducing Philistine influence, and it fell to David to defeat them in a series of battles that led eventually to the Philistines becoming vassals of the Israelite king and even providing military units to serve in David's wars against the Syrians. The Philistines served in this same capacity under Solomon until they completely assimilated into Israelite society. Whatever remnants were left were deported by the Assyrians during their invasions of Israel in the sixth century B.C.E.

FURTHER READING

Bonfante, G. "Who Were the Philistines?" *American Journal of Archaeology* 50 (1946): 251–262.

Dever, William G. "The Peoples of Palestine in the Middle Bronze I Period." *Harvard Theological Review* 64 (1971): 197–226.

Freedman, D. N. "The Age of David and Solomon." In *World History of the Jewish People*, vol. 3. Philadelphia: Jewish Publications, 1979.

Gabriel, Richard A. *Gods of Our Fathers: The Memory of Egypt in Judaism and Christianity.* Westport, CT: Greenwood Press, 2002.

————. *The Military History of Ancient Israel.* Westport, CT: Praeger, 2003.

Gale, Sir Richard. *Great Battles of Bible History.* New York: John Day, 1970.

Grant, Michael. *The History of Ancient Israel.* New York: Charles Scribner, 1984.

Herzog, Chaim, and Mordechai Gichon. *Battles of the Bible.* Jerusalem: Steimatzky's Agency, 1978.

Isserlin, B.S.J. *The Israelites.* New York: Thames and Hudson, 1998.

Liver, Jacob, ed. *The Military History of the Land of Israel in Biblical Times* [in Hebrew]. Jerusalem: Israel Defense Force, 1964.

Malamat, Abraham. "The Egyptian Decline in Canaan and the Sea Peoples." In *World History of the Jewish People*, vol. 3. Philadelphia: Jewish Publications, 1979.

Mazar, Benjamin. "The Era of David and Solomon." In *World History of the Jewish People*, vol. 4. Philadelphia: Jewish Publications, 1979.

————. "The Philistines and Their Wars with Israel." In *World History of the Jewish People*, vol. 3. Philadelphia: Jewish Publications, 1979.

Redford, Donald B. *Egypt, Canaan, and Israel in Ancient Times.* Princeton, NJ: Princeton University Press, 1992.

Rohl, David M. *Pharaohs and Kings: A Biblical Quest.* New York: Crown, 1995.

Strange, John. "The Transition from the Bronze Age to the Iron Age in the Eastern Mediterranean and the Emergence of the Israelite State." *Scandinavian Journal of the Old Testament* (1987): 1–19.

Tidwell, N. L. "The Philistine Incursions in the Valley of Rephaim." In *Studies in the Historical Books of the Old Testament*, edited by J. A. Emerton. Leiden: Brill, 1979.

Wainwright, G. A. "Some Sea Peoples." *Journal of Egyptian Archaeology* 47 (1961): 71–90.

Yadin, Yigael. *The Art of Warfare in Biblical Lands in the Light of Archaeological Study.* 2 vols. Translated by M. Pearlman. New York: McGraw-Hill, 1963.

Twenty-eight

✳ ✳ ✳

THE ISRAELITES (1100–921 B.C.E.)

The military history of the Israelites during the biblical period begins with the Exodus (1275–1225 B.C.E.), followed by the invasion of Canaan by the tribes of Israel under Joshua (1225–1200 B.C.E.), followed by the period of the Judges (1200–1050 B.C.E.), the period of Saul (1025–1005 B.C.E.), and David (1005–961 B.C.E.), and ends with Solomon (961–921 B.C.E.). The period from Solomon to 587 B.C.E., the period of the Hebrew kings, is verifiable through sources outside the Old Testament. In each of these periods the army and politicomilitary structure of the Israelites changed significantly in terms of organization, weapons, and tactics.

THE ISRAELITES' FIRST MILITARY FORMATIONS

The first Israelite military formation, including its means for command and control, is described in the Bible as the Israelites prepare to depart from Sinai and travel to the land of Canaan. The book of Numbers describes the arrangement of the Israelite camp and how it is to assemble for and conduct the march. Within the camp, each tribe was allocated a fixed area that corresponded to a fixed position in the line of march. Tents were pitched around the tent of the tribal commander, whose standard was displayed to mark his position. The Ark was positioned in the center of the camp under the watchful eyes of the Levite guard. Command and control over the tribal host in camp and on the march was accomplished by signals blown on two silver trumpets. A single blast from both trumpets was the command for tribal leaders to gather at the central tent for instructions. A special signal, called the Alarm, signified the movement of each wing.

It is likely that a special trumpet call was used to turn the formation from line of march toward any direction to meet a surprise attack, with the noncombatants falling behind the newly assembled battle line for protection. The Israelite organization portrayed in Numbers offers a graphic example of how it was possible to manage the migration of an entire people over long distances while providing for their defense on the march.

The campaigns of Joshua offer additional insight into the nature of the Israelite armies. Israelite armies of this period were composed of tribal levies of militia configured as light infantry armed with sickle swords, spears, bows, slings, and daggers. There was no permanent core of professional officers, and units fought under the command of their own tribal leaders, with Joshua in overall command. The lack of an institutionalized military command structure paralleled the absence of a centralized political structure. At this point the Israelites had no king over all the tribes. The leader at any given time was the first among equals of the tribal leaders involved in the battle. An army of light infantry under Joshua made perfect sense. Light infantry did not require prohibitively expensive armor and helmets, and the terrain in which the Israelites were fighting favored light infantry. Joshua was fighting mostly in the hills and mountains of the central massif, where light infantry could be decisive.

Chariots were useless in the uneven terrain, and even heavy infantry was at a considerable disadvantage that made fighting in phalanx very difficult. The Israelites had not yet reached a level of military sophistication that permitted the use of the chariot. Saul's later inability to field chariots at Mount Gilboa cost him his life, and it was not until the end of King David's reign that there is tentative evidence that the Israelite armies possessed even a single squadron of chariots. It fell to Solomon to change the nature of the Israelite army completely by introducing large chariot units for the first time.

The size of Israelite armies remains a matter of some speculation. Deborah, drawing on only four of the twelve tribes in confederation, put 10,000 men in the field against Sisera, according to biblical accounts. To relieve the siege of Jabesh-gilead, Saul called on the entire nation to provide manpower. The population of the Israelite tribes at this time was about 100,000–150,000 people. Calculating 25 percent of the entire population as being of military age, the Israelites could field about 25,000–30,000 men at maximum effort. Under most circumstances, however, Saul would have been fortunate to be able to deploy half that number for any given battle. Under David and Solomon, the establishment of a centralized political structure led to the introduction of a centralized mechanism for conscription, which could more efficiently call up larger levies for national defense.

The presence of standing enemy forces just beyond the Israelite borders emphasized the need for a similar standing force within Israel itself. Saul selected 3,000 warriors to serve as the core of a permanent standing army. Some of these men were mercenaries. David himself came to Saul's court not from the Israelite levy, but as a trained soldier. The Israelite army remained a light infantry force under Saul, although it is not beyond possibility that the professionals were equipped with the protection and arms of heavy infantry. There were no chariot units, however. Saul's army was divided into two divisions, with the smaller one of 1,000 men placed under the command of his son Jonathan. One of Saul's important innovations was the introduction of the fortified camp for prolonged campaigns. These were well-organized, semipermanent base camps divided into special zones for training, ordinance manufacture, and quartermaster. Each of these zones was overseen by details of specialists. Saul's reforms shaped the character of the Israelite armies until King David made other changes. Although Saul's reforms made it possible to place larger Israelite armies in the field, they were still underarmed and ill equipped when compared to Philistine armies. The lack of chariot units, if only for reconnaissance and scouting, was a major disability.

KING DAVID

King David's reign was marked by a number of important changes in the Israelite army as he shaped it into an instrument for the acquisition and maintenance of an empire. David's reforms began with establishing firm control over the national tribal levy by requiring military service of every able-bodied male. For tactical purposes the levy was organized into divisions of thousands subdivided into units of hundreds and subunits of fifty and ten, the latter being the smallest unit to have a permanent commander. David's conscript army was exclusively a light infantry force, just as it had been under Joshua and Saul. While light infantry provided for great flexibility, there remained the problem of how to obtain a proper mix of weapons and other capabilities in sufficient quantities to achieve the overall tactical objective. This was accomplished in the army of David the same way Joshua had done it, by relying on tribal units who possessed specific military specialties. In 1 Chronicles the Bible records some of the special military proficiencies of the tribes. The Benjaminites, for example, were armed with bows and "could use both the right hand and left hand in hurling stones and shooting arrows out of a bow." Gadites were proficient at "shield and buckler ... and were as swift as the roes upon the mountains." The sons of Judah "bore shield and spear," as did the Naphtali. The Zebulunites may well have been the Israelite equivalent of rangers for "they were expert in war, with all instruments of war ... and could keep rank." A bit less clear was the skill of the tribe of Issachar, which was explained as "understanding of the times, to know what Israel ought to do," a description that might suggest scouting and intelligence gathering.

The tribal chiefs were responsible for the training of their levies in the use of weapons particular to their clan as well as for the maintenance of weapons. Most importantly, they were responsible for providing the tribe's manpower quota to the central army. Alongside this tribal levy was another force comprising twelve monthly, nontribal and nonterritorial divisions, each of which came on active duty for one month a year. Officered by a permanent professional cadre, this provided the king with a large, permanently available cadre of soldiers on one-month service duty every year. This force was expected to take the field immediately in case of emergency and purchase sufficient time for the national levy to be mobilized. A similar system is employed by the Israeli Defense Force today.

The spine of the Davidic army were two corps of professional regular soldiers. The first of these were the "mighty men," or *gibborim*, two regiments each built on a group of special soldiers personally loyal to David, called the "Thirty." The first "Thirty" group was the band of loyal followers that had fought with David during his exile. This was a group of hardened combat veterans, whose tales of courage were the subject of Israelite poems and ballads. The second "Thirty" was a group of David's followers who formed around him after he had been anointed king of Judah. These were trusted advisors and combat veterans who were highly skilled in unconventional warfare and tactical innovation. From the groups of Thirty David selected his personal bodyguard and many of his high-ranking civil and military dignitaries. The Thirty were very similar to Alexander's *hetairoi* and Charlemagne's *schara*. The second corps of regulars in David's army comprised mercenaries, including Philistine troops. These hardy professionals were tough combat soldiers whose armament was heavier than most Israelite troops and who could be relied on to fight well, a not insignificant contribution to morale among soldiers who were mostly conscripts.

Among David's many victories, some came against enemies that deployed chariots against his army in large numbers. The ability to stop charging chariots with infantry alone arrayed on open ground appears to have been one of the Israelite army's talents. The key to stopping a chariot charge was to engage the machines far forward of the heavy infantry phalanx with light troops, using slings, arrows, and javelins to harass and slow the momentum of the charge until it was no longer sufficient to penetrate the massed heavy infantry phalanx, which then engaged it with spears. Once slowed or stopped, the light infantry, either units in reserve or those recovered from the initial engagement, swarmed over the chariots in close combat, where their swords had the advantage over the chari- oteers' bows. Whereas in Canaanite and Philistine armies the chariot was used as the primary element to deliver shock, in the infantry armies of the Israelites this role fell to the heavily armored spearman, most often regulars or mercenaries, arrayed in phalanx.

The Israelite infantry soldier at the time of David was called a "valiant man" (*ish hayil*) or a "selected man" (*ish bachur*), or an elite troop. Israelite infantry equipment was a mix of Canaanite and Philistine equipment and included a round shield (*magen*), a short thrusting spear (*romah*), an iron straight sword (*hereb*), and a bronze helmet (*koba*). Regular troops like the *gibborim* probably wore scale or lamellar armor, called a *shiryon*, like Canaanite soldiers. The tribal militia would be even more lightly armed, mostly with javelins, daggers, and slings.

Governing an empire requires trained administrative personnel, and David's court reflected the increased complexity of the Israelite national defense establishment, one that was far larger and more sophisticated than under Saul. David's court had a com- mandant of the tribal levy, a commander of mercenary troops, chiefs and high priests of the religious establishment, a superintendent of corvée labor, various high-ranking military staff officers and advisors, a chancellor, and an official scribe, who we might imply from the Egyptian model was chief historian and, perhaps, chief of intelligence as well. The whole arrangement bears a striking similarity to the structure of the Egyptian court, although the superintendent of corvée labor was probably derived from Canaanite practice.

KING SOLOMON

David had created an empire, and now it was Solomon's task to maintain it. With David's death the national strategy of the Israelites passed over to the defense. An army configured for conquest is not always well suited for defense. David's defense establish- ment lacked two important elements: a well-planned system of fortifications and a pow- erful strategic striking arm, a chariot corps. Solomon immediately turned his attention to these deficiencies. Under Solomon, Israel acquired a chariot corps, transforming the

Israelite army from a light infantry force into an army whose chariots were its arm of decision. The tribal levy remained, but more and more, the regular standing army comprised professional chariot crews and specialized regular infantry, the "runners," who accompanied the chariots into battle, providing them with strong infantry support in close combat. The regular militia levy probably continued to function as light infantry. The Old Testament gives the size of Solomon's chariot corps at "a thousand and four hundred chariots and twelve thousand horsemen [charioteers]."

Information regarding the type of chariots employed by Solomon's army is completely lacking, but it seems reasonable that Israelite chariots would be of Egyptian, Syrian, or Canaanite design since they were the most commonplace machines of the day. It is unclear, however, why 1,400 chariots would require a force of "twelve thousand horsemen." One possibility whose logic is militarily compelling is that the Israelites maintained double crews for each vehicle. This would still leave sufficient manpower to provide a mix of chariot types. Some Israelite chariots may have followed the Egyptian example, being light, fast, and maneuverable machines armed with a driver and an archer. Others, following the Syrian and Canaanite examples, might have been heavy machines carrying a crew of three, driver, archer, and lancer/spearman, and used to deliver shock and mounted infantry.

Solomon equipped Israel with a system of fortifications from which the nation could be defended with a mobile strategic defense in depth, the same strategic design employed by the Canaanites two centuries earlier. Major fortifications were built or improved at Hazor, Megiddo, Tamar, Gezer, Baalath, Lower Beth-Horon, and Tadmor (Palmyra). Each of these "chariot cities" controlled a key road or pass, possessed a good water supply, and offered suitable ground on which to employ chariots. At Megiddo and Hazor, Solomon replaced the old casement walls with walls of massive stone, this in reaction to the growing use of effective battering rams by armies of the period. Solomon positioned his chariot forces and regular infantry units in some of these "chariot cities," from which they could react to an enemy threat. These cities could also be used as bases from which offensive punitive expeditions could be mounted and from which regular combat or reconnaissance patrols could be staged. The guiding strategic concept was to engage the enemy on ground of one's own choosing and to do so before the enemy reached the cities. Like the Canaanites before them, Israelite commanders would permit themselves to be besieged only as a last resort.

The general strategic reserve of Solomon's army was kept in Jerusalem, including the strategic reserve of the chariot corps. To position the reserve in this manner implies that there must have been a network of well-guarded and packed earth roads leading from Jerusalem to all major defensive positions; otherwise, Israelite commanders would have been unable to react in sufficient time. This network of roads would have required road stations, watering points, repair shops, and storage depots along its way and must have run fairly close to existing settlements. Such a system would have had to be maintained on a regular basis, as would the entire military system of defense, and brought into existence a governmental structure centered around Solomon's court that was far more complex and articulated as a response to the growing administrative and military burdens that needed to be dealt with.

Solomon rationalized the military logistics system. The country was divided into twelve administrative districts, which were only generally identical with the tribal districts. The size of each district varied considerably and was determined with a view to making all districts equal in productivity and wealth so that the burden of military supply would not fall too heavily on any one district. Each district was to supply the food and materials required by the court and military garrisons for one month, thus rotating the burden from district to district, while at the same time assuring a continuous and adequate supply of needed materials. Solomon's reforms and innovations bequeathed Israel a truly modern state in terms of its military, economy, political institutions, and infrastructure. With Solomon the Israelites ceased to be a tribal society and become a national entity for the first time in their history.

FURTHER READING

Bright, John. "The Organization and Administration of the Israelite Empire." In *Magnalia Dei: The Mighty Acts of God*, edited by Frank Moore Cross, Werner E. Lemke, and Patrick D. Miller, Jr. New York: Doubleday, 1976.

Cohen, Rudolph. "The Fortresses King Solomon Built to Protect His Southern Border." *Biblical Archaeological Review* 11 (1985): 56–70.

Freedman, D. N. "The Age of David and Solomon." In *World History of the Jewish People*, vol. 3. Philadelphia: Jewish Publications, 1979.

Gabriel, Richard A. *The Military History of Ancient Israel*. Westport, CT: Praeger, 2003.

Gale, Sir Richard. *Great Battles of Bible History*. New York: John Day, 1970.

Gichon, Mordechai. "The Defense of the Solomonic Kingdom." *Palestine Exploration Quarterly* 4 (1963): 113–126.

Grant, Michael. *The History of Ancient Israel*. New York: Charles Scribner, 1984.

Herzog, Chaim, and Mordechai Gichon. *Battles of the Bible*. Jerusalem: Steimatzky's Agency, 1978.

Hobbs, T. R. *A Time for War: A Study of Warfare in the Old Testament*. Wilmington, DE: Michael Glazier, 1989.

Liver, Jacob, ed. *The Military History of the Land of Israel in Biblical Times* [in Hebrew]. Jerusalem: Israel Defense Force, 1964.

Mazar, Benjamin. "The Aramean Empire and Its Relations with Israel." *Biblical Archaeologist* 25 (1962): 98–120.

———. "The Era of David and Solomon." In *World History of the Jewish People*, vol. 4. Philadelphia: Jewish Publication, 1979.

———, ed. *World History of the Jewish People*. 4 vols. Philadelphia: Jewish Publications, 1979.

Osterley, W.O.E., and Theodore Robinson. *A History of Israel*. 2 vols. Oxford: Clarendon Press, 1948.

Redford, Donald B. *Egypt, Canaan, and Israel in Ancient Times*. Princeton, NJ: Princeton University Press, 1992.

Wright, George Ernest, and Floyd Vivan Filson, eds. *Westminster Historical Atlas to the Bible*. Philadelphia: Westminster Press, 1945.

Yadin, Yigael. *The Art of Warfare in Biblical Lands in the Light of Archaeological Study*. 2 vols. Translated by M. Pearlman. New York: McGraw-Hill, 1963.

Twenty-nine

�֎ ✤ ✤

ASSYRIA (890–612 B.C.E.)

In the twelfth century B.C.E. Hittite power collapsed, and Assyria began a 300-year rise to power under the direction of successive powerful kings that resulted in the establishment of the Assyrian empire in the ninth century B.C.E. Assyria emerged as the most powerful and successful military empire the world had seen to that time. Between 890 and 640 B.C.E., the height of Assyrian power, the Assyrians fought 108 major and minor wars and conducted punitive expeditions and other significant military operations against neighboring states. During the reign of Sargon II (721–705 B.C.E.) the Assyrians carried out no fewer than ten major wars of conquest or suppression in sixteen years. The result was the establishment of an empire that ran from the Persian Gulf to the Mediterranean Sea, from Armenia and northern Persia to the Arabian desert, and farther west to include parts of the Egyptian delta. It was the largest military empire in the world, and it was sustained by the largest, best-equipped, best-trained, and most effective military organization that the world had ever witnessed.

The imperial period witnessed the reigns of six important monarchs, beginning with Assurnasirpal II (883–859 B.C.E.), who was followed by his son Shalmaneser III (858–824 B.C.E.). There then was a period of eighty years in which the archaeological records reveal little about monarchical rule until Tiglath-Pileser III (745–727 B.C.E.) came to power. Six years after his death, the greatest Assyrian ruler and military conqueror, Sargon II (721–705 B.C.E.), ascended the throne. History has accorded this most brutal of Assyrian kings the title of Sargon the Great. He was succeeded by his son Sennacherib (704–681 B.C.E.) and, thirty years later, by his grandson Ashurbanipal (668–630 B.C.E.). Under three of these monarchs, Assurnasirpal II, Tiglath-Pileser III, and

Sargon II, significant reforms of the Assyrian army were carried out that allowed the development of a powerful and modern military machine.

ASSYRIA'S MILITARY ESTABLISHMENT

The establishment and maintenance of an empire the size of Assyria's required a military establishment of great size. No accurate figures exist as to the total size of the army, but at the very least the Assyrian army would have had to comprise between 150,000 and 200,000 men. A large part of this force, probably as much as one-third, was composed of auxiliary troops used to garrison the provinces. An Assyrian combat field army numbered 50,000 men, with various mixes of infantry, chariots, and cavalry. When arrayed for battle, an Assyrian field army took up an area 2,500 yards across and 100 yards deep. Under Sargon II, the professional praetorian corps of the army was expanded to several thousand, and an inner elite, known as "the companions" or "troops of the feet," formed the spine of the army. Provincial governors were required to raise and support local forces for use in time of war. These local forces were substantial and in at least one instance comprised 1,500 cavalry and 20,000 archers. Auxiliary units were thoroughly integrated into the field fighting force but still retained the major function of garrison duty to ensure control of captured populations.

It was the Assyrians who invented the new combat arm of horse cavalry. The first reference to a mounted warrior in the Near East is found during the reign of Tukulti-Ninurta II (890–884 B.C.E.) These "cavalrymen" were actually cavalry teams, in which the "charioteer" managed both horses, riding his own while holding the reins of the other, leaving the archer free to aim and shoot his composite bow. In 853 B.C.E., at the battle of Karkar, Shalmaneser III fielded a force of 35,000 men comprising 20,000 infantry, 1,200 chariots, and 12,000 cavalry. The individual cavalryman armed with either spear or bow made his appearance during the reign of Tiglath-Pileser III (745–727 B.C.E.), when cavalry units were integrated into the force structure, and eventually replaced the chariot corps as the elite striking arm. By Sargon's time the army had been reorganized into a thoroughly integrated fighting force of infantry, chariots, cavalry, siege machinery, and specialized units of scouts, engineers, intelligence officers, and sappers. Sargon also equipped the army entirely with weapons of iron, thereby producing the first iron army of the period. The Assyrian army was also equipped with iron armor and helmets.

The combat forces of the field army were organized in units of ten formed around national and regional formations, each of which specialized in the weapons and tactics at which it excelled. The ten-man squad under the command of a noncommissioned officer was the smallest fighting unit. The normal tactical unit was the company, which could be tailored into units of 50–200 men. The company was commanded by a *kirsu*, or "captain." In battle, infantry units of spearmen deployed in phalanxes with a ten-man front and files twenty men deep. These units were highly trained and disciplined in maneuver. Their gradual but persistent movement toward and through enemy ranks, killing as they went, represented a main shock force of the Assyrian army.

The Infantry

Assyrian infantry was divided into three types: spearmen, archers, and slingmen. The spearmen deployed in phalanxes to anchor the main line in the center of the battlefield.

Each phalanx comprised 200 men, ten ranks across and twenty files deep, commanded by a captain. Assyrian spearmen were heavy infantry armed with a long, double-bladed spear and a straight sword for hand-to-hand combat. The sword was secured to a thick belt that ran around a knee-length coat of iron mail armor. The spearmen carried small iron shields and wore conical iron helmets with wool or fabric liners, which helped to absorb the energy of a blow and dissipate heat. An important Assyrian innovation was the introduction of knee-high leather boots reinforced with iron plates to protect the shins. The combination of weapons and personal protective equipment slowed the movement of the heavy infantry considerably, and the Assyrians continually experimented with various types of lighter shields to reduce the load carried by the soldier in battle.

Units of archers comprised the second type of Assyrian infantry. The Assyrian composite bow seems to have been of a more advanced type than that usually found in the Near East, and bas-reliefs show that it had to be bent with the knee, often requiring two men to string it. Assyrian arrows were iron tipped and had great penetrating power. Some arrows had an iron tang proceeding backward from the shank to which oil-soaked wool was attached. The wool would be set afire and the arrow used as an incendiary device against buildings and wooden gates. The archer wore a long coat of mail armor, the weight of which considerably reduced his mobility. Before Tiglath-Pileser, a shield bearer carrying a small round shield was employed to protect the archer from counterfire. Later, a larger, man-sized shield of braided reeds with a slightly bow-backed top was introduced to provide protection from missiles fired from defensive walls. The Assyrian archer also carried a sword for close combat. The Assyrians increased the rate of fire of their archers by introducing an innovation in the arrow quiver. Carried on the back and secured by a shoulder strap, the quiver had a short rod protruding from the bottom front opening slightly above the shoulder. This innovation allowed the archer to reach back and pull down on the rod, tipping the quiver forward and bringing the arrows within easy and ready reach. Modern archery experts estimate that this type of quiver increased the rate of fire by as much as 40 percent.

The third type of infantry used by the Assyrians were the slingmen. The sling was probably introduced to the Assyrians by mercenaries or conquered peoples, and the Assyrians were slow to adopt it. While some bas-reliefs show slingmen deployed alongside archers in battle on open terrain, the slingmen saw their primary use in siege warfare. Slingers could direct high-angled parabolic fire against the defenders on the wall.

Chariotry

The Assyrian chariot corps constituted the primary striking arm of the army and gradually underwent major design changes over the imperial period. Originally, the Assyrian chariot was used in much the same way as the Egyptian and Mitanni chariot, as a mobile platform for archers. But the Assyrian chariot was always a heavier machine with a stiff and heavy front end, a characteristic that made it less maneuverable at high speed. Originally, the crew had consisted of a driver and an archer, with the driver armed with a spear and an axe. The archer wore body armor but had little other protection. The mission of the chariot was to attack massed infantry formations, deliver shock from ambush, and then, as the Assyrian infantry clashed at close range, to aid in the pursuit.

As enemy armies became more developed, there was a need to protect the chariot crew in close combat. The result was the development of an even heavier chariot carrying a crew of three, with the third man acting as a shield bearer to protect the archer and driver. By the time of Ashurbanipal the Assyrian chariot had evolved into a four-man vehicle with a driver, archer, and two shield bearers. The weight of the machine now required three and then four horses to pull it, and the wheels became thicker, requiring eight spokes for strength. All crewmen carried a spear, sword, shield, and axe, a development that turned the chariot crews into mounted infantry. After administering the initial blow to the enemy from ambush by mounted charge, the chariot crew dismounted and fought as heavy infantry. The Assyrians maintained a large corps of chariots, but as early as 85 B.C.E., Shalmaneser III had already begun to develop a new combat arm, the cavalry, which eventually eclipsed the chariot corps as the arm of decision.

The major advantage of the chariot in battles on open terrain was its ability to deliver troops close to the massed infantry formations. Its major disadvantages were that in rough terrain its mobility was severely limited, or even lost altogether, and against a cohesive infantry phalanx, its ability to deliver a shocking blow was marginal. As the Assyrian empire grew, the army was required more and more to traverse difficult terrain and to conduct operations in areas where the terrain was not favorable to the chariot. The need to fight in other than open terrain required another combat arm that could maneuver and deliver firepower. The solution was cavalry. It was the steppe peoples who lived in the northern areas above the Tigris valley to whom armies probably owed the development of the horse as a fighting vehicle. The presence of Assyrians in Armenia and in the Zagros Mountains most likely brought them into contact with the horse-riding steppe peoples, from whom they obtained the stronger breeds of horses.

The Importance of the Cavalry and Horses

The introduction of horses and their growing importance to the Assyrian army required that they be obtained in adequate numbers. Since Assyria itself offered few of the conditions necessary to breed these animals in sufficient numbers, the Assyrians developed a remarkable logistical and supply organization to insure an adequate supply of horses for the army. The horse recruitment officers, called *musarkisus*, were high-level government officials appointed directly by the king. The fact that they reported directly to the king and not the provincial governors under whom they served testifies to the importance of their function as horse quartermasters. Usually, two horse recruitment officers were assigned to each province. Assisted by a staff of scribes and other officers, they insured that adequate numbers of horses were assembled and trained for military use.

The *musarkisus* obtained horses on a year-round basis and were responsible for sustaining them in a national system of corrals and stables. Surviving documents indicate that in the city of Nineveh these officers were able to secure 3,000 horse a month, arriving on schedules of 100 animals a day. One report notes that of the 2,911 horses received for a single month, 1,840 were used as yoke horses in the chariot corps, 27 were put to stud, and 787 were riding horses assigned for cavalry use. The horse recruitment officers were responsible for securing adequate supplies of mules and camels for use in the logistics train. This efficient logistical apparatus was unknown in any other army of the world at that time.

Originally, the Assyrian cavalryman was an ordinary foot soldier equipped with armor, lance, sword, shield, and heavy boots. This great weight severely limited his mobility. Over time, the armored coat was reduced to waist length and the shield made smaller. The Assyrians used a blanket, saddle girth, crupper, and breast straps to stabilize the rider. Later, Assyrian cavalrymen learned to control their mounts with their legs and the heel pressure of their boots. This made it possible to place archers on horseback and gave birth to the first use of mounted archers in the Near East. Writers of the Old Testament called these Assyrian cavalry archers "hurricanes on horseback."

There is some debate as to the proportionate strength and role of the cavalry in the Assyrian army. Some analysts suggest that the chariot corps remained the primary fighting arm until the end of the empire, and perhaps so. As early as the eighth century B.C.E., Shalmaneser III put ten times more cavalrymen in the field at Karkar than chariots. An Assyrian chariot required at least three horses, and sometimes four, to deploy in battle. It may well have been that the supply system could not provide the numbers of horses required to sustain both large chariot and cavalry forces. Reports suggest that for every horse sent to the cavalry, three had to be sent to the chariot corps. A field chariot force of 4,000 machines would require 12,000 horses at the very minimum and 16,000 thousand at the maximum, not counting the ready reserve or the horses supplied to the forces on garrison duty throughout the empire. Add to this the number required of a small cavalry force of 6,000, and the number of horses that had to be acquired and trained for the army's immediate use in time of war was almost 20,000—for a single field army.

Assyrian Army Tactics

The Assyrian army was the first army of the Near East to develop an all-weather capability for ground combat. They fought in winter as well as in summer and conducted siege operations during the winter months. The fact that the army was almost continually at war somewhere in the empire for more than 200 years provided adequate opportunity for developing field technique by trial and error. And it developed these techniques to a high art indeed. When moving through wooded terrain, for example, the infantry proceeded line abreast in separate ranks. Smaller units were sent ahead as point, while others provided flank security. If engaged in battle within heavily forested areas, the spear-bearing infantry was used as the primary striking or defensive force as circumstances warranted. In hilly terrain with light woods the mounted archers and spearmen of the cavalry became the primary striking force. While the cavalry usually moved in column, the infantry provided flank security in line formation. As the army deployed in mountainous terrain, the Assyrians developed the practice of spreading scouts and snipers over wide areas to provide adequate security for the main body. The Assyrians also experimented with mixed units, combining infantry, archers, and slingers in a single unit. So adaptable were the Assyrian ground forces that they also fought well in marshlands. Placed aboard light reed boats, they became waterborne marines.

In open terrain Assyrian tactics were straightforward and relied on shock, firepower, and discipline. Once the army had been formed for battle, archer and slinger units began firing their missiles from a distance to inflict casualties on enemy infantry formations. Archers were specialists at killing chariot horses and directed their fire at the chariot units. Then Assyrian chariots attacked from as many different directions as the terrain would permit, their archers firing as the machines closed with the enemy infantry. As the chariots closed with the mass of infantry, their crews dismounted and fought in close combat. As the enemy mass began to waiver, the phalanxes of Assyrian spearmen, supported by direct fire from archer units, began in disciplined and slow march to close with the enemy. The cavalry, which to this point had been used to pin the enemy flanks, now took up positions to prevent the retreat of the broken enemy, sometimes acting as an anvil against which the infantry and chariot units could drive the fleeing remnants. Once the enemy army broke ranks, the spearmen, archers, charioteers, and cavalry singled out individual targets, rode them down, and killed them.

The Assyrian military machine was the most sophisticated, largest, and best-organized military force in the ancient world for its day and far exceeded the military capabilities of previous armies of antiquity. In the hands of a dedicated and ruthless ruler the Assyrian army became a finely tuned instrument of national policy, dedicated to the protection of the Assyrian empire and the survival of the Assyrian state. The centerpiece of Assyrian national policy was the use and threat of force against all actual and potential adversaries.

FURTHER READING

Contenau, Georges. *Everyday Life in Babylon and Assyria.* Translated by K. R. Maxwell-Hyslop and A. R. Maxwell-Hyslop. London: Edward Arnold, 1954.

Ferrill, Arther. *The Origins of War: From the Stone Age to Alexander the Great.* New York: Thames and Hudson, 1985.

Gabriel, Richard A., and Donald W. Boose, Jr. *The Great Battles of Antiquity: A Strategic and Tactical Guide to Great Battles That Shaped the Development of War.* Westport, CT: Greenwood Press, 1994.

Gabriel, Richard A., and Karen S. Metz. *From Sumer to Rome: The Military Capabilities of Ancient Armies.* Westport, CT: Greenwood Press, 1991.

Luckenbill, Daniel David. *Ancient Records of Assyria and Babylonia.* London: Histories and Mysteries of Man, 1989.

Nissen, Hans Jörg. *The Early History of the Ancient Near East, 9000–2000 B.C.* Chicago: University of Chicago Press, 1988.

Olmstead, A. T. *History of Assyria.* Chicago: University of Chicago Press, 1951.

Postgate, J. N. *Taxation and Conscription in the Assyrian Empire.* Rome: Biblical Institute Press, 1974.

Roux, Georges. *Ancient Iraq.* 3rd ed. New York: Penguin Books, 1992.

Saggs, H.W.F. *The Might That Was Assyria.* London: Sidgwick and Jackson, 1984.

Wiseman, D. J. "The Assyrians." In *Warfare in the Ancient World,* edited by Sir John Hackett. New York: Facts on File, 1989.

Yadin, Yigael. *The Art of Warfare in Biblical Lands in the Light of Archaeological Study.* 2 vols. Translated by M. Pearlman. New York: McGraw-Hill, 1963.

Thirty

✳ ✳ ✳

CHINA (1750–256 B.C.E.)

Chinese civilization began some 4,000 years ago in the broad valley of the Yellow River with the establishment of a series of Neolithic cultures that developed over a millennium into a civilization marked by an aristocratic political order and administrative state capable of mobilizing and directing large labor forces in public building and warfare. The three dynasties of this early Chinese civilization were the Xia (2200–1750 B.C.E.), Shang (150–1100 B.C.E.), and Zhou (1100–256 B.C.E.) All three existed in overlapping periods, with their power centers located in different regions within the vast expanse that is China. Each in turn achieved some degree of control over all of civilized China. No writing has survived from the Xia period so that much of what we know of it is shrouded in myth and not useful to the historian. The Warring States period (464–221 B.C.E.) saw the seven surviving states war against each other until one, the Qin, finally achieved dominance and established the first Chinese empire. By 206 B.C.E. the Qin had been overwhelmed by the Han Empire (206–220 B.C.E.), which rivaled Rome in wealth, power, and territorial expanse.

THE SHANG DYNASTY

The Shang civilization left a rich legacy. The Shang state consisted of 200 clans, one of which came to constitute a ruling aristocracy from which a high king was selected through a complex system of rotating kingship from among ten subclans. War was a dominant element in Shang culture. The very structure of Shang civilization was based on warfare, with the basic social unit, the clan (zi), also serving as a military unit.

The zi comprised about 100 families, which lived in a walled compound and provided a military unit equal in size to one man from each family. The zi chief was also the military commander of the unit. The royal capital or large manor houses of powerful barons were larger and more complex versions of the zi and its fortified compound or town. These compounds were protected by rammed-earth walls and a standing military force supplemented by citizen soldiers drawn from the zi. In time of war these professionals and large numbers of citizen soldiers were mobilized from the clans and subclans.

The regular military establishment consisted of the standing army (*lu*), which was officered by nobles with titles of "garrison commandant," "frontier commandant," "archery commandant," and "horse attendant." The army itself was commanded at the highest levels by the king, royal princes, or an especially talented chief of a powerful zi. At the height of Shang power the royal standing army possessed about 1,000 men but could be expanded rapidly by conscription from the zi. Surviving records indicate that Shang armies could be as small as 3,000–5,000 men for local campaigns or border skirmishes or as many as tens of thousands for major conflicts.

Mounted warriors did not appear in China until at least the fifth century B.C.E., and horses were used exclusively to pull chariots and supply vehicles. The Shang chariot was a two-wheeled contrivance pulled by two horses. It had five-foot-high wheels and a low-sided wicker or wood body mounted directly on the vehicle's axle. Each chariot was manned by a driver armed with a whip, an archer who rode on the driver's left, and a "striker" who stood on the driver's right and wielded a dagger axe, a wooden haft with a dagger-like blade mounted crosswise near the tip. There is some question as to whether Shang armies fought extensively from chariots or whether the chariot was used primary as a command platform or to convey the warrior nobility to the battlefield. There is also some fragmentary evidence that Shang armies may have included war elephants as well. If so, the elephant was not used for long due to its vulnerability to missile weapons and because Shang warriors soon hunted the wild elephant to extinction.

Shang military organization below army level is largely conjectural, but the generally accepted view is that five infantry soldiers or five chariot crews comprised a *wu*, or "unit of five," perhaps the equivalent of the squad or, in the case of five chariots, the equivalent of a modern tank platoon. Groups of three to five chariot platoons formed a company, each chariot accompanied by a number of foot soldiers. Infantry and archers were organized into companies of 100 men, and in later times, each five-chariot platoon was employed with a 100-man infantry company in direct support, much like a modern company-size task force or combat company. One chariot company plus the associated three to five infantry companies formed the operational equivalent of the battalion.

The basic weapon of the foot soldier was the *ge*, or dagger axe, a wooden shaft three to four feet long with a bronze, knife-like blade attached at a right angle near one end. A soldier could wield a *ge* with one or two hands and could swing it down and inward, hooking and cutting the enemy. The "striker" on the chariot crew carried the *mao*, or spear, which differed from the dagger axe in having a leaf-shaped bronze blade that formed an extension of the shaft itself. While the dagger axe was a hooking, slashing weapon, the *mao* was a stabbing weapon and could also be thrown. Battle axes, or *fu*, with broad, ornate, bronze blades, were also used by Shang infantry and seem to have been the weapon of choice for beheading prisoners and sacrificial victims.

Archers were armed with composite recurved bows that averaged five feet in length. The bow was fabricated of laminations of cattle sinew and horn or strips of bamboo glued together and bound with wrapped silk. Shang arrows had fletched wooden shafts about two and one-half feet long and were tipped with stone, bone, shell, horn, and bronze points. Shang armies did not use the sword, but charioteers and some foot soldiers, presumably officers, guards, and other elite soldiers, carried hatchets or ornate bronze knives with seven-inch blades sharpened on the lower edge and slightly curved downward, like a Gurkha *kukri*. The knife in its sheath was tucked into the warrior's belt or suspended from it along with a small sharpening stone.

Officers and aristocrats wore silk gowns, helmets, heavy circular bronze neck pro-tectors, and armored breastplates made of bronze or lamellar leather. Some warriors wore two-piece armor that protected the chest and back. The Shang bronze helmet had a rounded crown, and the sides and back came down low over the ears and the nape of the neck. Common soldiers wore a knee-length gown made of hemp cloth gath-ered at the waist with a belt or length of rope. Their protection in battle was limited to shields made of wicker or painted leather stretched over a square or oval wooden frame. Charioteers also carried shields on occasion.

By the thirteenth century B.C.E. Shang armies had pushed west to the Yellow and Wei river valleys into the lands of the Zhou. The Zhou were a people who shared aspects of both the Shang high civilization and the barbarian cultures. Their military equipment and capability rivaled those of the Shang. Around 1100 B.C.E., the Shang king, weakened by successive military expeditions in the southeast, succumbed to a Zhou assault.

THE ZHOU DYNASTY AND THE WARRING STATES ERAS

The early Zhou kings exerted control over China through a system of decentralized domains ruled by royal relatives, loyal supporters, and native leaders who had submit-ted to the Zhou conquest. This system of "vassal states," led by rulers bound by oaths of loyalty to the Zhou king, was superficially similar to medieval European feudalism. The parceling out of fiefs to their vassals left the Zhou kings with insufficient lands with which to support a large standing royal army, a situation that made the king mili-tarily dependent on his vassals for troops and with insufficient troops of his own to dis-cipline his vassals should the need arise. Over time, the system broke down, a process accelerated by the spread of military technology, the disintegration of the old clan sys-tem, and the weakening of the bonds of kinship and loyalty that had originally bound the vassals to their king. By the eighth century B.C.E. the Zhou were under increased military pressure from the border tribes and had difficulty getting vassals to provide sufficient military manpower to meet the recurrent threats. In 771 B.C.E. a combined army of rebellious vassals and western barbarian tribesmen launched an attack on the Zhou capital and killed the king. The rule of the Zhou came to an end.

While the Zhou kings could field armies from the lands under their direct control, they had to depend on levies from the vassal states for large expeditions. Each vassal provided from one to three armies, depending on the size and wealth of his domain. A single army might be as large as 3,000 chariots and 30,000 infantry divided into three divisions. Accounts of military engagements of the time suggest that the chariot force was still the heart of the Zhou army. The Zhou apparently retained the Shang military organization of three-man chariot crews, five chariot platoons, and five platoon companies.

Zhou military equipment and weaponry was generally similar to that used by the Shang, although some improvements in military technology were evident. While the chariot was still the primary shock and mobility weapon, the two-horse Shang chariot gave way to the four-horse chariot with larger, stronger wheels. The *ge* (dagger axe) developed into a longer, two-handed weapon with an oval shaft so that it would not twist in the soldier's hand. In some cases the dagger blade was lengthened so that the weapon could be used more effectively to slash and cut. Although not yet widely used, swords began to make their appearance in the Zhou armies, initially as lengthened versions of the Shang knife. The characteristic armor of the early Zhou period was made of rhinoceros or buffalo hide, either solid layers formed over a wooden mold or leather plates laced together. Hide or leather was also formed into helmets shaped much like those used in the Shang era.

By the middle of the fifth century B.C.E., major changes had taken place in every aspect of Chinese life. Only seven major states now remained of the scores of lineage-based states that existed at the beginning of the Spring and Autumn period (771–464 B.C.E.). These were the so-called *Zhongguo*, or "central states," from which the Chinese name for China is derived. These major states were Shu, Qin, Chu, Hann, Wei, Zhao, and Yan. The political, economic, and military structure of China had been transformed. Everything was now on a larger scale. The potential rivals were now exponentially larger than their predecessors. The populations of China's cities had grown into the hundreds of thousands. These multitudes could be housed, fed, and called to military service because of advances in administrative technique. Vast amounts of land were now under cultivation due to improvements in irrigation and agriculture. The bloody wars had destroyed many of the old lineages. The state's capacity to control its people was enhanced by the division of the populace into households, neighborhoods, and districts. Each unit in this structure had collective responsibility for the behavior of its members, for surveillance, collection of taxes, and the mobilization of men for military service or public works. Each household was required to provide one soldier for war, each neighborhood a five-man squad.

The people of this period were wall builders, constructing walled cities, fortresses, and walls along the state borders and barbarian frontiers to the north. These projects helped develop the skills of command and control that could also be utilized by commanders in war. Now large armies could be mobilized, moved, and brought to battle on a scale heretofore impossible in China. Major military innovations were brought into being, including the introduction of ironworking, the sword, the crossbow, and horse cavalry. Many of these important new technologies were not invented by the Chinese themselves but were adopted from the barbarian peoples with which Chinese armies often fought border wars. During this period, wars were no longer fought by hot-headed aristocrats pursuing individual glory but by mass armies led by professional officers. Codes of vengeance evolved into codes of law for the administration of the state and the maintenance of the armies.

The standing professional army of these warring states could be mobilized quickly and expanded greatly by the mobilization of the peasantry already organized into squads, platoons, companies, and battalions to perform public labor. The Warring State rulers maintained the old organizational form of the previous period, but with the advent of professional soldiers, military advisors, and large numbers of soldiers, the organizational schema took on a more realistic application. The ideal formation for an army on the march was a division of five elements: advance guard army, left and right flank armies, commander in chief with his staff accompanying the center army, and rearguard army. The model was still five divisions (*shi*) per army, each comprising five battalions (*lu*), each of 500-man companies (*zi*) made up of five twenty-five-man platoons (*liang*), each of five five-man squads (*wu*).

The Chinese armies of this period were largely infantry armies, although chariot units were employed regularly as well. During the Warring States era the Chinese began to use mounted warriors, adopting the cavalry warhorse and riding trousers (more suitable for horse-mounted warriors than for the traditional Chinese silk gowns) from the steppe barbarians. By the mid-fourth century B.C.E., cavalry formations were already in limited use, but the widespread use of this new combat arm did not occur in China until at least the third century B.C.E. Ironworking for military purposes had begun to appear as well, and some iron weapons found their way into Chinese armies, although bronze remained the preferred material for weapons. The major technological innovations of the Warring States era were the sword and crossbow. Although Chinese infantry had used elongated knives for centuries, the true sword, with a blade substantially longer than the hilt, did not appear in China until the Spring and Autumn era. As infantry became more important on the battlefield, the need for an effective close-order combat weapon became evident. By the time of the battle of Guiling (353 B.C.E.) the well-balanced bronze sword with a blade optimized for cutting and slashing (not stabbing) was the most popular infantry weapon. The double-curved compound bow remained in service during that time. Sometime around 500 B.C.E., the crossbow had been adopted from the barbarians. A century later, it had become an exceptionally deadly weapon, accurate and powerful enough to penetrate armor. In the hands of a trained shooter the crossbow introduced a deadly new dimension to Chinese warfare.

The traditional long weapons, the dagger axe and spear, were still in use but were supplemented by another innovation in weaponry: a combination of spear and dagger axe known as the *ji*. The *ji* was a two-pronged spear, a dagger axe with a knife at the end of it, that could be used for piercing, slashing, or hooking an adversary. The term *ji* is most closely translated as "halberd" since the weapon shared many of the same characteristics of the Western weapon of that name. In Warring States armies, even the ordinary soldier now was equipped with armor made of molded leather or lacquered leather strips laced together. Chariot crews wore long, cumbersome armor tunics, while the infantry, who had to be more able to maneuver, wore short leather tunics or cuirasses of hard leather plates. Molded leather or bronze helmets were now available to the common soldier.

The introduction of extensive fortifications, walled cities, long walls along borders, and other obstacles led to developments in siegecraft, including specialized equipment, such as chariots with large shields, wheeled towers and battering rams, movable ladders, catapults, and powerful crossbows that could fire multiple bolts and function as field artillery. On campaign it was now common practice for armies to construct fortified base camps from which to conduct operations. These camps were like miniature Chinese cities, with rammed-earth walls and intersecting streets with interlocking fields of archery and crossbow fire. The commander's tent and headquarters was at the center of the camp. During the Guiling campaign, both armies constructed such camps.

FURTHER READING

Balmforth, Edmund Elliott. "A Chinese Military Strategist of the Warring States: Sun Bin." PhD diss., Rutgers University, 1979.

Chang, Kwang-chih. *Shang Civilization*. New Haven, CT: Yale University Press, 1980.

Creel, Herrlee Glessner. "The Origins of Statecraft in China." In *The Western Chou Empire*, vol. 1. Chicago: University of Chicago Press, 1970.

Eikenberry, Karl W. "Sun Bin and His Art of War." *Military Review* (March 1991): 51–57.

Kierman, Frank A., Jr. and John K. Fairbank, eds. *Chinese Ways in Warfare*. Cambridge, MA: Harvard University Press, 1974.

Lewis, Mark Edward. *Sanctioned Violence in Early China*. Albany: State University of New York Press, 1990.

Peers, C. J., and Angus McBride. *Ancient Chinese Armies 1500–200 b.c.e.* London: Osprey, 1990.

Sunzi. *Sun-Tzu: The Art of Warfare*. Translated by Roger T. Ames. New York: Ballantine Books, 1993.

Walker, Richard Louis. *The Multi-State System of Ancient China*. Hamden, CT: Shoe String Press, 1954.

Wu Jing Qi Shu. *The Seven Military Classics of Ancient China*. Translated by Ralph D. Sawyer. Boulder, CO: Westview Press, 1993.

Zuoqiu, Ming. *The Tso Chuan: Selections from China's Oldest Narrative History*. Translated by Burton Watson. New York: Columbia University Press, 1989.

Thirty-one

✳ ✳ ✳

INDIA (1200–120 B.C.E.)

Sometime in the early part of the second millennium, perhaps around 1600 B.C.E., a people that history came to call Indo-Europeans or Aryans began to migrate westward, southward, and eastward from the great land of steppes that stretches from Poland to central Asia. Probably under the pressure of desiccation of the land or overpopulation, they invaded Anatolia and imposed themselves as a warrior aristocracy on the natives and became the Hittites; they imposed themselves on the native Hurrians and became the Mitanni. Over several more centuries, they moved farther southeast, invading Iran and, eventually, India.

ARYAN MILITARY DEVELOPMENT

For the next 500 years the Aryans spread throughout the Indian subcontinent, gradually displacing the original population and becoming the dominant culture. This period of war and conquest (1200–700 B.C.E.) was the time of the Rig-Veda, the great collection of epic and heroic myths and tales chronicling the battles and settlement of the Aryans. The most famous of their epic poems is the *Mahabharata*. Comprised of 90,000 verses, the *Mahabharata* is the longest poem in the world and falls into the same category as the great Irish, Icelandic, and Greek sagas telling the tale of a warrior people. The Aryans, or Vedics, imposed their culture, societal structure, martial values, and military technique on the original Indian population, completely transforming it into a martial culture.

The social order that the Aryan-Vedics imposed on the indigenous tribal population was tribal and ruled by a warrior aristocracy. The Vedic king was a warrior chief, whose skill at war and bloodline provided legitimacy for his claim to rule. The tribal kingdom, or *rashtra*, comprised tribes (*jana*), tribal units (*vish*), and villages (*grama*). The nucleus of the tribe was the family (*kula*), with the eldest male as its head (*kulapa*). The warrior king was called the raja, a term closely related to the Latin *rex*. The king was assisted in governing by a council of elders (*sabha*) and other advisors, like the *purohita*, or chief priest and astrologer; the *senani*, or military commander, although it was the king who personally led the army into battle; and the charioteer, often the king's oldest military comrade, who drove his chariot in battle. Vedic society was divided into four groups: the military aristocracy, originally *rajanya*, but more commonly *kshatriya*; the priests or *brahmins*; the more prosperous land owners and traders, the *vaishyas*; and the agricultural cultivators or *shudras*. The Vedic tribal social order lasted until circa 700 B.C.E., when it gave way to larger, more stable societies of regional scope, while preserving its essential social and governing institutions within the new monarchies and republics. By 600 B.C.E., northern India was divided into sixteen such states, all constantly at war with one another.

Our understanding of warfare in Vedic times is clouded by a lack of information. We are forced to deduce much of what we know from descriptions on a few reliefs and the lines of the *Mahabharata*, which, because it was written down long after the events portrayed in it, is not a reliable source. This aside, some approximation of the tribal warfare conducted by Aryan chiefs against the indigenous peoples and each other can be assembled. The Aryans were horse and chariot people. The chariot provided a great military advantage against a people barely out of the stone age, and the newcomers must have quickly established their dominance on the plains of the Indus, driving the original peoples into the jungles and forests. The Aryan chariot was a light, two-man vehicle drawn by a two-horse team, probably (like the early Hurrian model of the same period) with its axle forward of the rear wheel. The chariot was used only by the warrior aristocracy, while the common members of the tribe—warfare was a tribal activity involving all social classes—fought on foot. The chariot warriors probably wore armor, perhaps leather or scale plate, but there is no evidence of the helmet until much later. The chariot warrior carried a lance, spear, or javelin. The simple bamboo bow was used extensively in this period by foot soldiers and was probably adopted from the local model. The chariot warrior, when he used a bow, most likely used the composite bow fashioned of animal horn.

Swords, axes, and slings were used as well by infantry. The Aryans were a Bronze Age culture and were adept at fashioning weapons of bronze. We know little of Aryan tactical doctrine during this period, but on the plains, at least, it could not have been very much different from that of the Mitanni, essentially clashes of chariot-borne warriors in individual combat as the rest of the scuffle raged around them, every man fighting for himself, with no coordination with other combatants. At least this is the impression one receives from the epic literature of the time.

The chariot had originally been the spine of the Aryan armies. Over time, however, the chariot gave way to the war elephant and the ridden warhorse as the primary mounts of the warrior aristocracy. By the sixth century B.C.E., armies contained cavalry contingents in the thousands. The chariot seems to have disappeared as a true implement of war probably circa 650 B.C.E., although some Indian state armies retained the chariot in small numbers until the third century B.C.E. As in the Near East, the chariot gave way to cavalry in India because of its greater ability to traverse and maneuver over difficult terrain. But there was another reason for replacing the chariot: One role of the chariot, especially against tribal or otherwise primitive armies, was to deliver shock, and nothing could deliver shock like an elephant.

ELEPHANTS IN MILITARY USE

It was probably not until the sixth century B.C.E. that the elephant was tamed and probably another fifty years before it made its appearance on the Indian battlefield. The first mention of the elephant as an instrument of war appears in the account of one Sung Yun, a Chinese traveler who visited the kingdom of the Hunas in the early sixth century B.C.E. His report speaks of fighting elephants with swords fastened to their trunks that produced great carnage, but there is no other mention of this practice elsewhere. The report of another Chinese traveler, Hiuen Tsan, of about the same time makes mention of "war elephants covered with a coat of mail [probably scale armor], and his tusks are pointed with sharp barbs [metal tips]. On him rides the commander in chief who has a soldier on each side to manage the elephant." By the end of the sixth century B.C.E. the elephant had replaced the chariot as a major combat arm in Indian armies.

The Indian elephant was much larger than the African forest cousin used by the Seleucid Greeks and Carthaginian armies three centuries later. The Indian elephant was ten to eleven feet high at the shoulders and carried tusks averaging more than six feet in length. They were trained and cared for with great reverence by their mahouts, or handlers, who rode them into battle. Their great bulk made them an excellent instrument for shock, and they were often employed in the van of the army, using their great strength to break enemy ranks and smash palisades, gates, and other defenses. They could even be employed next to one another in a line like a living bridge, over which troops could walk to cross a stream or river. Elephants were often equipped with leather, textile, or scale armor to protect against arrows and pikes. They were usually employed with a basic combat load of the mahout and three other soldiers equipped with composite bows, javelins, and a long spear to ward off any attackers.

Like modern tanks, elephants in the Indian tactical scheme of things were rarely deployed alone and were usually accompanied by a small infantry contingent whose task it was to protect the animal from attack by infantry. The animals were trained diligently for war. Porus's elephants at the battle of the Hydaspes retained their discipline in the face of massed infantry advancing with long pikes pointed at the animals' eyes. Calmly, the animals retreated one step at a time, retaining formation and composure as they went. In other cases, however, they simply broke and ran, stampeding over everything in their way. No matter how great the number of instances where the animal panicked or otherwise proved useless, Indian commanders continued to place great faith in the war elephant, often to their regret. Centuries later, the Muslim rulers of India placed the same heavy reliance on them, only to be equally disappointed.

By the beginning of the fifth century B.C.E. the regional monarchies and republics had become the dominant form of sociopolitical life in northern India. Far larger, richer, and more populated than any of the old tribal fiefdoms of the Vedic age, these states battled each other for predominance for more than 100 years. Four northern states—Magadha,

Kashi, Kosala, and Vrijis—struggled with one another until around 550 B.C.E., when Bimbisara succeeded in bringing two of them to heel. His son Ajatashatru took over from his father in 493 B.C.E. and conquered the Vrijis state. Ajatashatru died in 461 B.C.E. and was followed by five kings, all of whom gained the throne by parricide. In 413 B.C.E. a usurper, Mahapadma Nanda, came to the Magadha throne and established a short-lived dynasty. In the space of fifty years the Nandas proved themselves powerful and capable kings who expanded Magadha control and introduced the first attempt at an Indian empire in the north. In 321 B.C.E. the Nandas were overthrown by another usurper, Chandragupta Maurya, who established the first and last genuine Indian empire of any significant size.

THE MAURYAN EMPIRE

Chandragupta governed a true monarchical imperial state. The king ruled with the help of a small body of elder statesmen, the *mantri-parisad*, that functioned as advisors. These included the great councilor, or *mantrin*; the *purohita*, or chief priest; the treasurer, or *sannidhatr*; the chief tax collector, *samahartr*; the minister of military affairs, *sandhivigrahika*; the *senapati*, or chief military advisor or general; and the chief secretary, or *mahaksapatalika*. Below this council, the state was governed on a day-to-day basis through powerful individuals, called superintendents, who oversaw various government departments. The military system itself was controlled by high-ranking civilian superintendents who oversaw the operations of state armories, where all military equipment and weapons were manufactured, as well as supply depots, cavalry, elephants, chariot corps, and infantry, including provisions, training, and general combat readiness. According to Megasthenes, the Seleucid ambassador to Ashoka's court, the imperial army was run by a committee of thirty of these superintendents, while each branch or department—infantry, cavalry, elephants, chariots, navy, commissariat, and so on—was run by a committee of five men. It is likely that these committees reported directly to the chief military man, the *senapati*, who then reported to the king.

There were six types of troops in the Mauryan imperial army: the *ksatriya*, or troops of the hereditary warrior class who formed the spine of the professional army; mercenaries and freebooters hired as individuals seeking military adventure; troops provided by corporations or guilds; troops supplied by subordinate allies; deserters from the enemy; and wild forest and hill tribesmen used in the same manner as the French and British used Native American tribes in their wars in North America. The troops of the corporations are little understood and may have been units maintained by guilds to guard their caravan routes and trade stations. Such units were later found in the armies of medieval Europe. The imperial armies were not conscript armies. In Vedic times, war fighting was the responsibility of all members of the tribe. By the time of the Mauryas, whatever sort of conscription had once existed earlier had disappeared, and the imperial armies comprised professional warrior aristocrats and other professionals fed, equipped, trained, paid, and otherwise maintained at great cost to the state.

The Mauryan army was quite large. Classical sources (Pliny) state that the size of the army of the last Nanda king was 200,000 infantry, 20,000 cavalry, 2,000 chariots, and 3,000 elephants when it was overwhelmed by Chandragupta's force of 600,000 infantry, 30,000 cavalry, and 9,000 elephants. When Alexander confronted Porus on the banks of the Hydaspes, he faced an army of 30,000 foot, 4,000 cavalry, 300 chariots, and 200 war elephants, an army of considerable size to be deployed by a minor king of a minor state in the Jhelum region. Less than a year later, Alexander confronted the army of the Malavas state, another minor regional entity, and faced an army of 80,000 well-equipped infantry, 10,000 cavalry, and 800 chariots. Even accounting for the exaggeration common in ancient accounts, it is by no means unlikely that these armies were this large. The population of India during this period was somewhere between 120,000,000 and 180,000,000 people. Even excluding the lower social orders, the Mauryan empire possessed an enormous manpower pool. Moreover, India was rich in gold and metals and the skills to produce weapons in great quantities in state armories. The Ganges plain and other areas farther north were excellent for breeding mounts for the cavalry. Whatever the true size of the imperial armies, they are all recorded as smaller than those said to have existed during the later medieval and Muslim periods of Indian history.

The tactical organization of the Mauryan army may have been influenced somewhat by the Chinese innovation of combining several combat arms within a single tactical unit and training it to fight together, employing their arms in concert. Indian armies of this period had within them a basic unit called the *patti*, a mixed platoon comprising one elephant carrying three archers or spearman and a mahout, three horse cavalry-men armed with javelins, round buckler, and spear, and five infantry soldiers armed with shield and broadsword or bow. This twelve-man unit when assembled in three units formed a *senamukha*, or "company." Three of these formed together comprised a *gulma*, or "battalion." Units were added in multiples of three, forming an *aksauhini*, or "army," comprised of 21,870 *patti*. Sources also speak of military units formed around multiples of ten, and there were no doubt units of single arms that could be employed individually or in concert with other arms. The *Arthasastra* mentions a unit called the *samavyuha*, or "battle array," that was about the size of a Roman legion (5,000 men). This unit comprised five subunits joined together, each subunit containing 45 chariots, 45 elephants, 225 cavalry, and 675 infantrymen each. It goes without saying that managing such units in battle required a high degree of tactical sophistication.

The military equipment of the Mauryan imperial army was essentially the same as it had been for the previous 500 years. The Indian bow was made of bamboo and was between five and six feet long and fired a long cane arrow with a metal or bone tip. Nearchus, the Cretan chronicler who accompanied Alexander into India, noted that the bowman had to rest the bow on the ground and steady it with his left foot in order to draw it full length. The arrow fired from the bamboo bow could penetrate any armor. At the Hydaspes the battle took place over muddy ground, which prevented the archers from steadying their bows in this manner, rendering them useless. The composite bow, or *sarnga*, was also used but probably far less so and not by cavalry. When Alexander's Asian cavalry archers at the Hydaspes attacked the Indian cavalry with bow and arrow, the Indian cavalry took heavy losses and had no means of returning fire. It is unlikely that the Indian cavalry ever became proficient with the bow, relying completely on the lance and javelin, the weapons of light cavalry. If the Mauryan army possessed heavy cavalry, they appear to have done so in small numbers.

Infantrymen carried a long, narrow shield made of raw ox hide stretched over a wooden or wicker frame that protected almost the entire body, unlike the small round buckler carried by the cavalry. Armed with spear, bow, and javelin, the infantry tended mostly to be of the light variety. Heavy infantry carried the *nistrimsa*, or long, two-handed slashing sword, while others were armed with iron maces, dagger axes, battle axes, and clubs. A special long lance, the *tomara*, was carried by infantry mounted on the backs of elephants and was used to counter any enemy infantry that had fought its way through the elephant's infantry screen to attack the animal itself. What evidence we have suggests that from Vedic times until the coming of the Greeks, only slight use was made of body armor, and most of that was of the leather or textile variety. With Alexander's invasion, however, the use of metal and lamellar armor became more widespread, as did the use of scale plate armor for horses and elephants. The helmet did not come into wide use until well after the Common Era, and for most of the ancient period the Indian soldier relied mostly on the thick folds of his turban to protect his head.

By the Mauryan period the Indians possessed most of the ancient world's siege and artillery equipment, including catapults, ballistas, battering rams, and other siege engines. A distinguishing characteristic of Indian siege and artillery practice was a heavy reliance on incendiary devices, such as fire arrows, pitch pots, and fireballs. There was even a manual instructing how to equip birds and monkeys with the ability to carry fire inside buildings and onto rooftops. This was not surprising in a country whose military fortifications and buildings were made mostly of wood. Fire was such a constant threat to Indian towns that thousands of water containers and buckets were required to be kept full and placed outside dwellings at all times to extinguish fires. All citizens were required by law to assist in fighting fires, and it was required that people sleep in the room nearest the street exit to escape fire more easily and to be quickly available to help in fighting them. So serious was the concern for fire that the punishment for arson was death by burning alive.

The *Arthasastra* declares that a good army can march two *yojanas* a day and that a bad army can only manage one. This is a rate of march for an effective army of about ten miles a day, considerably below what the armies of the Near East could manage during the same period. It is likely that the Mauryan army followed the old Vedic practice of agreeing with the enemy as to the location of a battlefield in advance. Under these conditions, tactical surprise was likely to have been a rare event. Much of the advice offered by the *Arthasastra*, at least from the tactical perspective, seems to be of the same variety as that proffered by Sun-Tsu, more a set of maxims designed to make the commander think than a set of rules to be applied in certain circumstances. That is why, to the Western mind, such maxims often appear obvious. Hints of a tactical system appear, however, in the suggestion that whether the attack is from the center, right, or left, it should always be led by the strongest troops. The weakest troops are to be kept in reserve. But the reserve is very important. The king should always station himself with the reserve to exploit any enemy failure, and a king should "never fight without a reserve."

FURTHER READING

Basham, A. L. *The Wonder That Was India: A Study of the History and Culture of the Indian Sub-continent Before the Coming of the Muslims.* New York: Grove Press, 1959.

Bhatia, H. S. *Vedic and Aryan India*. Delhi: Deep and Deep, 2001.

Bradford, Alfred S. *With Arrow, Sword, and Spear: A History of Warfare in the Ancient World*. Westport, CT: Praeger, 2001.

The Cambridge History of India. Delhi: Cambridge University Press, 1968.

Dikshitar, V. R. Ramachandra. *War in Ancient India*. Delhi: Motilal Banarsidass, 1987.

Jackson, A. V. Williams. *History of India*. London: Grolier Society, 1906.

Prasad, S. N., ed. *Historical Perspectives of Warfare in India*. Delhi: Motilal Banarsidass, 2002.

Sandhu, Gurcharn Singh. *A Military History of Ancient India*. Delhi: Vision Books, 2000.

Singh, Sarva Daman. *Ancient Indian Warfare*. Delhi: Motilal Banarsidass, 1997.

Smith, Vincent Arthur. *The Oxford History of India*. 3rd ed. Oxford: Clarendon Press, 1958.

Thapar, Romila. *A History of India*. Middlesex, UK: Penguin Books, 1966.

Thirty-two

✸ ✸ ✸

CLASSICAL GREECE (600–338 B.C.E.)

Greek military development began in the archaic age from 1500 to 1200 B.C.E. During this time a warlike people, the Achaeans, occupied the territory of mainland Greece. So far as we know, in most respects the armies, technologies, and conduct of war in Greece were far less sophisticated than in other armies of the same period. Greek warfare developed along a separate path from that of the more ancient eastern states. The links with the past that remained into the Classical period were links to Achaean Greece, and the Greek idea of war that emerged in the Classical period emulated those forms and methods passed to it through the Homeric sagas. More important than the pragmatics of war, these sagas bequeathed a notion of war that linked its practice to the development of the human spirit expressed in moral terms.

Warfare among the ancient Greeks consisted of localized battles between loose assemblies of individual combatants who fought for plunder, glory, and fame. Armies were small, usually less than 1,000 men. There is no evidence of the development of tactics or the ability to coordinate even small groups of soldiers to achieve battlefield objectives. Nor is there evidence of the development of the various combat arms—infantry, cavalry, chariots, archers, siege trains—or of the art of coordinating these forces with one another. Logistics was also unknown. Wars tended to be one-day affairs involving unorganized scuffles between groups of warriors fighting as individuals.

Yet this period is important to the development of warfare in later Classical Greece for it was precisely this military legacy that was transmitted to and affected the conduct of war in the Classical period. The transition, however, was difficult. Between 1200 and 1000 B.C.E. Achaean Greece was subject to a number of invasions by mysterious peoples of unknown origin, who completely destroyed its civilization. For 400 years, until the eighth century B.C.E., Greece was plunged into a dark age about which we know almost nothing. This dark age, nonetheless, had a profound effect on future Greek military development. The invasions severed whatever contact the Greeks had with other, more advanced armies of the period, cutting the continuous line of military development that had begun in the East 3,000 years earlier. Anything the Greeks *might* have learned from the Egyptians, Assyrians, or Hittites was lost. The result was that the already rudimentary Greek practice of war under the Acheans was frozen as if in amber and remained largely unaffected by military developments elsewhere. It was this ancient Greek tradition of war that was eventually passed to Classical Greece as the culture reemerged in the eighth century B.C.E.

The conduct of war in the early Classical period was much the same as it had been in the earlier Achaean period. The emphasis on individual combat worked against the development of coordinated group formations and tactics. Sometime in the sixth century B.C.E., just as Greece was developing the city-state as its basic form of sociopolitical organization, there appeared a military innovation that made possible the transition of war from individual combat to combat by men in organized groups. This new technology was the Argive shield, and it made possible the emergence of the famous Greek hoplite, the heavily armed infantry soldier.

Ancient Greek civilizations.

THE GREEK ARMY

The old shield used in individual combat was held by a collection of tethers that met at a ring in the center. The ability to maneuver this shield required great strength and a high degree of training. Even when the grip was mastered, the shield could not be used to press against an opponent with much force. The great military innovation of the sixth century B.C.E. was the replacement of the group of tethers in the center of the shield with a single loop through which the forearm could be passed and another loop at the shield's rim that could be held in a strong handgrip. This new grip meant that the average citizen could now easily master what had previously been among the most complex implements of war, a development that made it easier to enroll the citizenry of the city-states in the practice of war. The conduct of war quickly shifted from the contest of noble champions to battles between disciplined groups of heavy infantry. The heavy infantry phalanx emerged as the basic war fighting formation of the Greek citizen armies.

The armies of the city-states were small. Thucydides noted that at the beginning of the Peloponnesian War in 431 B.C.E. Athens had a population of 100,000 free men and 140,000 slaves and aliens. The Athenian army of this time comprised 13,000 hoplites, 16,000 older garrison soldiers, 1,200 mounted men, and 1,600 archers. This force of almost 30,000 men represented a supreme military effort. Thucydides noted that eleven years later, when the military situation had stabilized and Athens returned to normal military manpower standards, Athens could muster only 1,300 hoplites, 1,000 horsemen, and 1,400 recruits. Battles of the Greek Classical period usually involved no more than 20,000 men on both sides and often less than 10,000 men.

As military service was expected of all citizens, all young men underwent military training. In Athens, boys were trained in games, running, wrestling, bow, and javelin at private camps (*palestra*). At age eighteen, healthy males were taken into the militia for training. On completion of this training, the young soldier was sent for a year's tour of duty at a garrison. After the second year, the soldier remained a member of the active reserve until age forty-nine and was subject to immediate call to service. After that, until age sixty, the soldier became a *presytatoi* (literally, "an older soldier") and served as a territorial, guarding camps and forts.

Equipment

Regardless of the method of recruitment or degree of military training, all Greek armies of the period carried the same equipment. The primary striking arm of the Greek armies was the hoplite heavy infantryman. The basic weapon of the hoplite was the *dory*, a wooden-shaft spear five to seven feet long with a metal point at each end. The hoplite also carried a sword with a blade approximately eighteen inches long and two inches wide. Used mainly as a cutting weapon, the sword was used only if the spear was broken or lost. The primary defensive weapon of the hoplite was the Argive shield. Greek soldiers wore leather or bronze helmets, a neck guard of leather, and leather or bronze greaves that covered their shins to the ankle. Armor was also worn on the forearms. In the eighth century B.C.E., armor was originally a body cuirass made of bronze, but by the sixth century B.C.E. it was replaced by a linen cuirass made of layers of stiffly glued fabric. Hoplites sometimes wore a semicircular bronze plate hung from

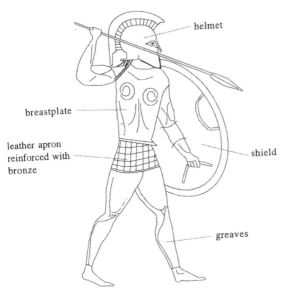

helmet

breastplate

leather apron
reinforced with
bronze

shield

greaves

The panoply. Reproduced by permission of the publisher from Alfred S. Bradford, *With Arrow, Sword, and Spear: A History of Warfare in the Ancient World* (Westport, CT: Praeger, 2001), Figure 20. © 2001 by Alfred S. Bradford.

the belt to protect the abdomen. Others attached leather skirts to their shields to provide similar protection. The complete military kit was called a *panoply* and weighed eighty-five to ninety pounds.

Organization

All Greek armies organized themselves for battle in essentially the same manner. The basic combat formation was the infantry phalanx. Since ancient times, the standard depth of the phalanx was eight men deep (the archaic *lochos*). After the fifth century B.C.E., as a reaction to the Theban practice of using deeper ranks, most city-states adopted thicker ranks as well. In some cases the depth of the phalanx reached twenty-five men. The smallest unit of the phalanx was the *enomotia*, comprising three files of twelve men. This unit could be employed with a six-man front with six men deep. Two *enomotia* comprised a *pentekostyes* of seventy-two men, while two *pentekostyes* comprised a *lochos*, the basic unit of the phalanx, commanded by a company commander. Four such *lochi* comprised a *mora* of 576 men, commanded by a regimental commander. Every phalanx had an elite *mora* comprising its best warriors. This unit usually anchored the right wing of the battle line. These formations were probably originally Spartan inventions, and it appears to have been Sparta that was the first to train the subunits of the phalanx to maneuver as units. It was Spartan practice to place all officers in the front rank so that they were the first to meet the enemy and set the standard for bravery.

The Cavalry

The hoplite infantry was drawn mainly from the middle and upper classes. Cavalry remained the province of the nobility, if only for the reason that it alone could bear the cost of horse and equipment. Auxiliary light infantry was drawn from the lower classes but was haphazardly organized and of little use. While the Greeks used some light infantry and cavalry prior to the Persian Wars, it was their experience with the excellent cavalry and light infantry of the Persians that finally prompted the Greeks to pay some attention to these combat arms. In the fourth century B.C.E. Iphicrates reorganized the light infantry into an important combat arm, the *peltast*.

This new mercenary soldier carried a light, crescent-shaped shield made of wicker and covered with hide (the *pelta*). The shield had a strap so it could be slung over the back, allowing the *peltast* maximum mobility on the run. The *peltast* wore no armor, relying instead on speed to get out of harm's way. Armed with two javelins, these soldiers acted as skirmishers for the phalanx. Deployed in front of the phalanx, they could rush the enemy formation, hurl their javelins into the packed ranks, and then retreat. *Peltasts* could also be used to protect the flanks of the phalanx against cavalry attack or, in the offensive, to attack the exposed flanks of the enemy phalanx. With this new force Iphicrates destroyed an entire Spartan regiment of hoplites during the Corinthian War (394–386 B.C.E.).

The phalanx. Reproduced by permission of the publisher from Alfred S. Bradford, *With Arrow, Sword, and Spear: A History of Warfare in the Ancient World* (Westport, CT: Praeger, 2001), Figure 21. © 2001 by Alfred S. Bradford.

Greek cavalry in the Classical period never reached the level it did under the Assyrians or Persians and did not become an important combat arm of Greek armies until Philip and Alexander made it one. This may have been due to the rugged geography of the land and its pattern of farming, both of which limited the use of cavalry in large numbers. The short distances between the city-states also worked against the need for mobility over long distances, as did the fact that horses were very expensive. The individual horse-borne soldier of the eighth through sixth centuries B.C.E. had almost been driven from the battlefield by the emergence of the hoplite phalanx. Cavalry after this period still comprised the nobility but was used largely as flank security, as skirmishers, and, in rare cases, for pursuit.

The Greek cavalryman rode small, unshod horses without a saddle. He sat on a blanket held by a single strap around the animal's belly. Control was managed by means of bit and reins. Armed with a javelin and a sword, the cavalryman of Classical Greece was not a formidable threat to the phalanx. Any cavalry charge was inherently unstable as the control of the animals at full gallop became uncertain. Using the javelin as a lance risked unseating the horseman himself, who had no saddle from which to gain purchase. After the Persian Wars, the Athenians created a cavalry force of 1,000 men, but these famous "Knights of Athens" were used mostly in traditional roles and oftentimes fought dismounted. Even during the Peloponnesian Wars, cavalry was never a significant or decisive combat arm.

Slingers

Slingers had been around since Neolithic times in Greece, as in almost all areas of the Mediterranean, but did not come into major military use in Greece until the period following the Persian Wars, when small specialty units of slinger infantry appeared. Greek slingers easily outranged the bow and fired stone, clay, bronze, or lead shot. These missiles, averaging between twenty and fifty grams in weight, could be flung up to 600 feet and inflicted terrible wounds. Lead and bronze shot was often cast in the shape of a plumb, a shape that concentrated the penetrating force at the head of the projectile, while the narrow tail allowed the wound to close around the penetrating shot, causing almost certain death from infection. Slinger units were invariably small and used as skirmishers or against unarmored light infantry. Their effect on the massed phalanx of heavily armored infantry was usually negligible, however.

LOGISTICS

The logistics system of the armies of Classical Greece was rudimentary by the standards of any Bronze Age army, and by Iron Age standards it was even more primitive. The short distances between the city-states worked against the development of logistics. In most cases the battlefield was less than a three-day march away, and battles were short-lived events. There appeared no real need for a logistics capability. During the Peloponnesian War, when armies were required to move longer distances and sustain themselves in the field for longer periods, the lack of a logistical apparatus often proved crucial. The Greek failure to develop logistics during this period had two effects: (1) it prevented the development of the strategic forced march, at which the Egyptians and, later, the Romans excelled, as a vehicle of power projection and (2) the lack of logistical capability prevented any single city-state from aspiring to control all of Greece. It was no accident that the man who did aspire to such control, Philip of Macedon, was also the commander who first introduced a sophisticated logistical apparatus to Greek warfare.

Oxcarts were the standard transport of the baggage train, as they had been since the Bronze Age. Special units of pioneers cleared the way with axes, sickles, and other tools. With most food carried by the soldier, the baggage trains carried other items, including harnesses, straps for weapons, files for sharpening weapons, shafts for extra spears, and wood for making field repairs on the wagons themselves. These baggage trains were slow, inflexible, and easily subject to attack. But the tactics of the period did not require mobility or flexibility, and the achievement of tactical surprise with a phalanx was almost an impossibility.

As with all other elements of Greek military skill in the Classical period, sophistication in siegecraft and fortification remained primitive. Greek armies had no siege trains and relied on blockade and starvation to subdue a city. The absence of siege towers and archers to neutralize the defense atop the walls made a successful assault on a city very difficult indeed. The Athenian experience in Sicily introduced the Greeks to Carthaginian siege machinery and techniques, but little was done to implement this aspect of war, until Alexander raised siegecraft to high levels in his campaigns against the Persians. It was Philip of Macedon who first created a special corps of engineers to study the application of siege machinery to warfare.

Greek tactics never reached the degree of sophistication found in the armies of other countries of the same period. The phalanx formation dominated Greek warfare for more than 300 years without any significant change. The phalanx battle consisted of opposing masses of infantry aligned in simple rectangles several hundred feet long and thirty feet thick. Opposing formations marched toward one another until their front ranks clashed. Once engaged, only the first two ranks could wield their weapons as the second soldier in each file stepped into the gap separating the first rank of combatants. As the front ranks clashed, those in the rear ranks pressed forward with their shields in a compact mass in an attempt to force the enemy formation to flex or break. While these tactics required a courageous soldier who could stand the stress of close combat, they did not require a high degree of military skill.

It is commonly assumed that battles involving this type of close combat were horrifically bloody; in fact, they were rarely so. Only the first two ranks could actually engage in any kind of dangerous behavior toward one another, and in most battles one side usually gave way within minutes of the initial clash so that the rear ranks rarely encountered any actual fighting. The real purpose of the massed formation behind the front ranks was to enforce both a physical and moral pressure on the cutting edge of the battle formation to prevent panic. Modern studies have also shown that the press of the ranks, the large shield, sufficient armor, and the use of the spear for overhand thrusting actually made it very difficult to land a killing blow. It has also been estimated by researchers that the phalanx could actually remain engaged in combat for no more than thirty minutes before exhaustion took its toll on the fighting men. Men in the front ranks would be quite fortunate to be able to remain in contact for half that time without collapsing.

The need to retain the organizational integrity of the phalanx even after the other side broke as well as the phalanx's inability to move rapidly over uneven terrain meant that a lethal pursuit was impossible. Once a unit broke contact, the killing usually stopped, and the vanquished were allowed to escape. The rudimentary nature of Greek cavalry prevented its use as a major killing arm in the pursuit. Unless an army found itself trapped by a successful double envelopment (rare indeed) or its retreat limited by the terrain, once panic set in, most of the killing stopped.

The pressure of the mass within the phalanx forced the soldier to move to his right as the battle went on. Protected on the left by his shield, every soldier moved closer to the shield of the man on his right to secure greater protection from his comrade's shield. As the spaces between the men closed, the soldier could still employ his spear in an overhand thrust in the small angle between his shield and that of the man next to him, although visibility in locating targets must have been a problem. This same situation, however, made the use of the sword very difficult, a fact that contributed to the Greek failure to develop this weapon to anywhere near its maximum potential. As the pressure to the right increased, the whole phalanx began to rotate in a counter-clockwise direction. The guiding tactical principle was to have the right wing break to the left as the enemy formation rotated to its right and achieve a single envelopment, forcing the enemy in on itself from the flank. The tendency toward rotation, however, reduced the exposure of any clear points of attack for either cavalry or light infantry.

Although the Greeks had no military academies in which to train their officers in the practice of war, they were the first in the West to produce systematic military treatises on tactics and strategy. Xenophon's *Anabasis* was the first surviving work to analyze systematically the nature and conduct of war. His *Cyropaedia* is a study of the strategic relationship between war and politics and emphasizes the role of the policy maker. The first comprehensive work in Western literature on military theory stressing purely pragmatic applications to the battlefield was written in 357 B.C.E. by Stymphalian Aenaes. The Greeks wrote in a language that all could understand, so what they wrote received wide distribution. The effect was to introduce Greek military thought into the mainstream of Western civilization.

Despite the rudimentary nature of warfare in the Classical period, its impact on the development of war in later periods of the West was important. The Greeks may have lagged behind in the application of most military skills, but they were the first to develop the combat arm of heavy infantry in the West and to use it in a way that armies of the later period, most notably the Romans, would emulate. The most important contribution of the Classical Greek period to the military development of later armies was its unique view of the role of war in human development to the West. It is correct to say that the Greeks introduced a new morality of war derived from the Homeric tradition. It was not a morality that attempted to limit death or casualties, but one that placed the practice of war at the center of human activity as a means of ennobling the human spirit. The Greek ideal of war entered the mainstream of Western civilization and remained the main intellectual force that shaped professional perceptions of war over the next two millennia.

FURTHER READING

Adock, F. E. *The Greek and Macedonian Art of Warfare*. Berkeley: University of California Press, 1957.

Anderson, J. K. *Military Theory and Practice in the Age of Xenophon*. Berkeley: University of California Press, 1970.

Cawkwell, George. *Philip of Macedon*. Boston: Faber and Faber, 1978.

Chadwick, John. *The Macedonian World*. New York: Cambridge University Press, 1976.

Connolly, Peter. *The Greek Armies*. Morristown, NJ: Silver Burdett, 1985.

Delbrück, Hans. *History of the Art of War within the Framework of Political History*. Vol. 1, *Antiquity*. Westport, CT: Greenwood Press, 1975.

Engels, Donald W. *Alexander the Great and the Logistics of the Macedonian Army*. Berkeley: University of California Press, 1978.

Gabriel, Richard A. *Great Captains of Antiquity*. Westport, CT: Greenwood Press, 2001.

Gabriel, Richard A., and Karen S. Metz. *From Sumer to Rome: The Military Capabilities of Ancient Armies*. Westport, CT: Greenwood Press, 1991.

Green, Peter. *Alexander of Macedon, 356–323 B.C.: A Historical Biography*. Berkeley: University of California Press, 1991.

Hanson, Victor Davis. *The Western Way of War: Infantry Battle in Classical Greece*. New York: Knopf, 1989.

———. *Hoplites: The Classic Greek Battle Experience*. New York: Routledge, 1991.

Kagan, Donald. *The Peloponnesian War*. New York: Viking, 2003.

Lazenby, J. F. *The Spartan Army*. Warminster, UK: Aris and Phillips, 1985.

Pritchett, W. Kendrick. *The Greek State at War*. 4 vols. Berkeley: University of California Press, 1971–1991.

Snodgrass, Anthony M. *Arms and Armor of the Greeks*. Baltimore: Johns Hopkins University Press, 1999.

Warry, John Gibson. *Warfare in the Classical World: An Illustrated Encyclopedia of Weapons, Warriors, and Warfare in the Ancient Civilizations of Greece and Rome*. New York: St. Martins Press, 1980.

Xenophon. *The Persian Expedition*. Translated by Rex Warner. Baltimore: Penguin Books, 1972.

Thirty-three

✳ ✳ ✳

PERSIA (546–323 B.C.E.)

At its zenith the Persian Empire stretched from the Aegean Sea in the West to the Indus River in the East, a distance of 2,500 miles. From north to south the empire encompassed the territory from the grasslands surrounding the Aral Sea to the deserts of Libya and reached as far west as Thrace and Macedonia. The Persians introduced armies the size of which the world had never seen, rivaling those of the Napoleonic era in tactical flexibility and logistical support. Persia invented the science of naval warfare and applied it with consummate skill, invented the javelin, and developed the new combat arm of cavalry to its full military potential. Credit is usually given to the Medean king, Cyaxares (625–585 B.C.E.), for forging the first army out of the rival tribes of the Zagros Mountains in Iran. The Persians were only one tribe in this larger coalition. In 546 B.C.E. Cyrus II (Cyrus the Great) acceded to the throne of Persia and, in a series of short wars, conquered the Medes in 549 B.C.E., forming the core of the Persian Empire. With his hold on the Persian throne secure, Cyrus set about expanding Persian rule. In 529 B.C.E. Cyrus met a soldier's death while battling the armies of the Massagetae. To his heir, Cambyses, he bequeathed an empire complete except for the inclusion of Egypt. Cambyses defeated the Egyptians at the battle of Pelusium in 525 B.C.E., and Persia then controlled all the territory from the Mediterranean to the Persian Gulf. Its territories stretched along the Mediterranean coast from Egypt to the Black Sea.

THE PERSIAN ARMY

The centerpiece of the Persian army was a force of 10,000 men called "the Immortals," a name derived from the fact that the force was never permitted to go below 10,000 men.

A dead, wounded, or ill soldier was immediately replaced in the ranks so that the force was always maintained at full strength. Augmenting the Immortals was the king's body-guard of 2,000 foot soldiers and 6,000 cavalry. These Persian forces comprised a substantial part of the national standing army, although the Persians themselves always remained a minority in the vast tribal empire as well as in the army itself. Core units were stationed in each of the *satraps* (provinces), where they maintained royal garrisons. These units were under the direct command of Persian officers appointed by the king. These forces were augmented by local forces drawn from the different nationalities of the empire.

Cyrus introduced universal military training among the Persians. The Greek historian Strabo records that Persian youths underwent at least ten years of military training before being enlisted in the regular army. Training was vigorous and included physical conditioning, instruction in the bow and javelin, and horsemanship. In the early wars against the Medes the Persians had no cavalry units of their own and had to rely on those provided by other tribes. Cyrus recognized the importance of cavalry and set about making horsemanship the central element in the Persian army.

All Persian males were required to serve in the military under a form of universal conscription. These soldiers formed the bulk of the regular army. Each *satrap* was required to maintain a force of specified size, armed and organized along its own traditional national lines. In times of war these forces were levied and were expected to serve for the duration of the conflict. With this system the Persian king could raise an army of 300,000 men. Armies of this great size introduced a new dimension to warfare. Darius's army in the Scythian campaign numbered 200,000 men, and the force deployed by Xerxes against the Greeks comprised 300,000 men and 60,000 horsemen. In 331 B.C.E., shortly before Alexander destroyed the empire at the battle of Arbela, Darius III fielded a force comprising 300,000 men, 40,000 cavalry, 250 chariots, and 50 elephants.

The Persian army was well organized with a clear chain of command. The smallest unit was a six-man section led by a corporal. Two of these units formed a squad of ten men and two corporals, led by a sergeant. Two squads formed a platoon of twenty-four men, commanded by a lieutenant, and four platoons comprised a company, led by a captain. Ten companies comprised a 1,000-man regiment, commanded by a colonel. The regiment was the main fighting unit of the Persian army. Ten regiments constituted a brigade of 10,000 men, comprising a *myriad*, and commanded by a general, the largest combat unit in the army.

The levied national forces that augmented this well-organized regular force were by no means equally as well organized or trained. For the most part, national forces received only limited training, wore different uniforms, carried different weapons, spoke a variety of languages, and fought in very different ways. Most often, they were commanded by their own chiefs and were often unreliable. It was the Persian practice to occupy the center of the line with their own reliable infantry and position their cavalry at the rear and on the flanks, forming a kind of tactical container within which national units were deployed to insure that the tribal contingents did not break and run when in battle.

The Persian Cavalry, Infantry, Chariotry, and Naphtha Throwers

The Persian army comprised infantry, cavalry, charioteers, archers, engineers, and naphtha throwers. In its early days Cyrus's army had few cavalry, and the normal mix of infantry to cavalry was 90 percent to 10 percent. After Cyrus, the ratio changed to 80 percent infantry to 20 percent cavalry, with the Persians and Medes comprising the bulk of the heavy cavalry as the elite striking arm. Cyrus realized the importance of cavalry to an army that had to move quickly over long distances and fight in many different types of terrain. He personally forged the Persian cavalry into the world's largest mounted army. The greatest number of Persian cavalry were light cavalry armed with the simple bow (noncomposite) and comprised mostly of irregular nationality troops officered by Persians. The tactical role of this light infantry was to harass the enemy and draw it into battle.

The elite of the Persian army was the heavy cavalry, made up almost exclusively of Persian regular units. In its early days the cavalry was armed with the standard weapons of the Persian infantryman: the bow, battle-axe, and oval shield. Later, heavy cavalry was equipped with the short stabbing and throwing javelin. Long lances made of wood or entirely of metal, oval shields, and spears were also used. The javelin, properly so called, was invented by the Persians and later adopted by Alexander for use by his Greek cavalry. It was a short spear about a yard long made of date palm wood, thick reed, or the wood of the jujube tree. It was tipped with bronze or iron. The Persian javelin could be thrown like a spear, used as a stabbing weapon, or even thrown end over end. Each heavy cavalryman carried two javelins as a basic combat load. Cavalrymen wore body armor made of a heavy leather coat covered with overlapping disks of bronze, iron, and sometimes gold. Armor was often colored in order to distinguish one unit from another. Leather greaves protected the cavalryman's legs. Personal protection was augmented by a small oval shield made of leather with a metal rim. Two holes were pierced in the upper shield near the top rim to permit the soldier to see through the shield when engaged in battle.

Persian infantry were of the light and heavy varieties. Light infantry were armed with the bow and sling, weapons that made them excellent at harassment and mobility but weak in killing power. The fact that light infantry carried no short-range weapons or protections made it impossible for them to close with the enemy with any lethal effect. Cyrus corrected this deficiency by requiring the infantry to carry spears and swords and training the soldiers in close-order battle. Heavy infantry carried the long spear, short sword, and battle-axe, weapons designed for maximum lethality at close range. The heavy infantry wore black hoods over their heads and faces when engaged in close combat. When arrayed for battle, the front rank of the phalanx carried a tall wicker shield and a single spear, while the ranks behind them carried two spears and no shields, presumably one for throwing before contact and the other for close-order fighting. Elite Persian infantry was trained to advance in mass and in silence, a rather striking departure from the normal practice of yelling to strike terror in the hearts of the enemy.

The Persian chariot corps was small compared to those employed by Egypt and Assyria and under Cyrus reached a peak strength of only 300 machines. Initially, the Persians attempted to improve the chariot by making it heavier and higher with a larger platform. They also thickened the wheels, used heavier axles, and increased the number of wheel spokes. The result was that four horses were required to pull the vehicle. Since the chariot required a driver and mounted only a single archer or spearman, it required considerable man- and animal power for very little firepower in return. The Persian use of the simple bow further reduced the lethality of the chariot-borne archer, and the weight of the machine made transport and movement over rough terrain difficult.

Cyrus tried to increase the lethality and shock power of the chariots by introducing the scythed chariot. Metal scythes attached to each of the chariot's main axles extended outward two yards in length away from the sides of the machine. The idea was to drive the chariots through massed infantry and cavalry formations, letting the scythes do the work of killing as they went. While these chariots worked well enough against light infantry or undisciplined tribal armies, they were useless against a disciplined infantry or cavalry unit. As long as the infantry phalanx held its ground in packed formation, the horses would not charge through the wall of spears and shields.

The Persians introduced the use of wheeled mobile siege towers constructed of wood. These towers were three stories high (about twenty-four feet) and were pulled along by sixteen oxen linked by four shafts. Xenophon recorded that the weight of a tower was 13,920 pounds, or seven tons, when fully manned with men and equipment. Each story of the tower was manned with twenty archers, who, because of their vantage point above the battlefield, could rain down a hail of arrows on the enemy. The battle commander could also use the tower as a command and control center, its height providing him with an excellent view of the entire battlefield.

The Persian army used special squads of naphtha throwers in its siege tactics. Like "Greek fire," we are unsure as to exactly what naphtha was or where it came from; it was similar in nature to oil, but of a thinner consistency, and it burned hot, thus allowing the Persian army to ignites structures during a siege. Cotton soaked in naphtha was attached to arrows and fired against wooden fortifications. The most famous use of this technique was against the Greeks when Xerxes used it to burn the wooden walls of Athens and the roof of the Acropolis. Persian engineers were excellent and, like the combat engineers of today, often traveled ahead of the main body of the army, preparing roads, building bridges, digging ditches, and constructing marine jetties for use by the navy. Like the Assyrians before them, Persian engineers mastered the technique of using inflated animal skins and pontoon boats as floats for bridges. The Persians became expert at constructing bridges with covered sides and tops to prevent their horses from looking over the sides and bolting in fear. In the Babylonian War, military engineers diverted the course of the river running through the city to allow a Persian infantry force to gain entrance to the city by moving along the dry riverbed.

Persian Army Supplies and Logistics

Supplying an army of 300,000 men and 60,000 horses was no easy task, but the Persians managed it again and again. On the march it was Persian practice to divide the commissariat in two. In advance of the army, squads of supply officers ranged ahead in search of campsites, water sources, and grazing fields. To the rear was a second commissariat that transported and managed expendable military supplies: arrows, bows, armor, naphtha, and other items. The Persians had a number of advantages in supplying their armies in the field. Most military sorties enjoyed the advantage of internal lines of communication that led to the empire's rim. Each *satrap* was required to maintain specified quantities of military supplies on hand to make supply along these internal lines relatively easy. Taxes paid to the king were paid in gold and silver and in kind, the latter usually in the form of militarily usable supplies. By creating a uniform monetary system based on gold coinage and stabilizing tax rates and collections on the basis of each *satrap*'s ability to pay, the Persian empire became the first state of antiquity to operate on an annual budget, which permitted it to plan expenditures for military purposes in advance. Among the most effective instruments for provisioning the army was the use of hard currency. Darius I was the first Persian monarch to coin money, using as a standard the *daric* coin weighing 130 grains of gold. It became the only gold currency of the ancient world and could be spent anywhere. Supplying the military became big business, in which regular suppliers established themselves as providers of military stores. The passage of a military force through an area was often welcomed by cities and towns as an economic boom.

Logistics was also made easier by the existence of a number of all-weather government roads, although it must be remembered that these were not paved roads, but earth-packed tracks and trails. These roads were wide and solid enough to permit the passage of wooden mobile siege towers that weighed almost seven tons. Movement of military supplies was also accomplished by large corps of oxen, horses, mules, and camels. Not to be overlooked was the ability of the soldier to carry his own supplies and equipment. Because the Persian light infantry was so lightly armed, its soldiers could easily be pressed into service carrying other supplies. Horse cavalry, of course, could also carry 100 pounds slung over the saddle.

THE PERSIAN NAVY

The Persian navy could move large bodies of troops, animals, and supplies to support military operations on rivers and in coastal provinces. During Xerxes's expedition against the Greek states in 481 B.C.E. Herodotus tells us that the Persians deployed 3,000 transport ships, not counting fighting ships of the line. The Persians were not accomplished sailors but knew how to take full advantage of the shipbuilding and other maritime skills of their coastal provinces along the Mediterranean. They closely supervised the design of special ships and commissioned specially designed long transports powered by fifty oarsmen to transport horses and troops. Smaller thirty-oar ships were used as supply vessels, and shallow-draft boats were used on rivers. Taken in historical perspective, the Persian armies were larger and more effective than any army the world had seen to that point. With the exception of the Roman army, no military force would equal the Persian army's ability to support its forces in the field over such long distances, until the armies of the Mongols 2,000 years later.

It is somewhat paradoxical that a people of the mountains and plains of Iran should have deployed the world's first large standing naval force. The Persians seem to have been the first to use naval vessels on a grand scale primarily in support of ground operations in order to prosecute their grand strategy of empire. It is unclear if the Phoenicians or the Greeks invented the first ship designed only to fight other ships. By the time of Cyrus, however, the first fighting ship, the trireme, had made its appearance in the Mediterranean. Cyrus was quick to appreciate the importance of these new implements of war and is regarded as the father of the Persian navy. Darius I seems to have been the first to commission the construction of ships for specific military tasks—ships of the line, transports, horse carriers, and supply ships—and shortly thereafter, the Persians had fully integrated the use of naval warfare and tactics into their grand strategy designed to counter Greek power in the Aegean and Mediterranean.

As a ship of the line, the trireme represented the ultimate combat ship of its time. It was essentially a decked galley about 120 feet long and 15 feet wide and was powered by 170 oarsmen and could carry thirty combat marines, often archers, on its top deck. Steering was accomplished by a large oar on each side of the stern. The front of the ship mounted a ten-foot, iron-tipped spike placed at the waterline. In attempting to sink an enemy vessel, the ship aimed the spike to ram into the opponent's broadside. A trireme could reach full speed in about thirty seconds from a dead stop and had a maximum speed of eleven knots. It is important to note that the trireme was specifically designed for naval combat and was too crowded for normal seafaring. It did not, for example, have sufficient room to carry its own supplies, not even sufficient water and food for its crew, and the crew normally disembarked for the shore each evening to eat and sleep.

PERSIAN MILITARY WEAKNESS

The main weakness of the Persian military machine lay in the fact that its army was always a hodgepodge of tribes and nationalities of varying degrees of military effectiveness. The well-trained and well-disciplined Persian national force was always in a minority within the army itself. The Persian army was not a tactically integrated fighting force in the sense that all units of the army were trained in the same weapons and tactics. The sophistication of the Persian army in deploying infantry, cavalry, and chariot units disguised its weakness in possessing few heavy infantry units. For the most part, armies formed up in opposing lines, with the light infantry and archers acting as skirmishers in the front trying to inflict as much damage with their missiles and javelins as possible. As the two lines clashed, the Persians would attempt to strike the flanks and rear with their cavalry and chariots to scatter the enemy using their usually large numerical advantage to attack from several directions at once. Once enemy infantry began to scatter, cavalry could ride it down and finish it off with lance and javelin. The success of this simple tactical design depended on the inability of the enemy infantry to withstand the Persian assault. Usually, the Persian advantage in numbers carried the day.

Where this deficiency did matter, of course, was in Persia's wars with the Greek city-states. In every major engagement with Greek armies the Persians were defeated or badly mauled, despite their advantage in manpower. The ability of Greek hoplite armies to field tactically integrated and disciplined forces of heavy infantry exploited the main weaknesses of the Persian army to their maximum. The Persian weaknesses, disguised by centuries of military success against equally flawed enemies, brought the great empire to its knees before the skill and dedication of Greek heavy infantry and cavalry under the brilliant command of Alexander the Great.

FURTHER READING

Adcock, F. E. *The Greek and Macedonian Art of War*. Berkeley: University of California Press, 1957.

Arrian. *The Anabasis of Alexander*. Translated. London: Penguin Books, 1976.

Burn, A. R. *Persia and the Greeks: The Defense of the West*. New York: St. Martin's Press, 1962.

Connolly, Peter. *Greece and Rome at War*. Englewood Cliffs, NJ: Prentice-Hall, 1981.

Delbrück, Hans. *History of the Art of War within the Framework of Political History*. Vol. 1, *Antiquity*. Westport, CT: Greenwood Press, 1975.

De Souza, Philip. *The Greek and Persian Wars: 499–386* B.C.E. New York: Routledge, 2003.

Frye, Richard N. *The Golden Age of Persia: The Arabs in the East*. London: Phoenix Press, 2000.

Fuller, J.F.C. *The Generalship of Alexander the Great*. New York: Da Capo Press, 1989.

Gabriel, Richard A., and Karen S. Metz, *From Sumer to Rome: The Military Capabilities of Ancient Armies*. Westport, CT: Greenwood Press, 1991.

Hackett, Sir John, ed. *Warfare in the Ancient World*. New York: Facts on File, 1989.

Laffont, Robert. *The Ancient Art of Warfare*. 2 vols. New York: Time-Life Books, 1968.

Lowe, W. D. *Herodotus: The Wars of Greece and Persia*. Wauconda, IL: Bolchazy-Carducci, 1990.

Olmstead, A. T. *History of the Persian Empire*. Chicago: University of Chicago Press, 1948.

Rawlinson, George. *The Great Monarchies of the Ancient World: Babylonia, Media, and Persia*. London: Gorgias Press, 2002.

Sekunda, Nick. *The Persian Army: 560–330* B.C.E. London: Osprey, 2002.

Sykes, Sir Percy. *A History of Persia*. 2 vols. London: Macmillan, 1958.

Wiesehöfer, Josef. *Ancient Persia: From 550* B.C. *to 650* A.D. Teheran: Center for Arab Studies, 2001.

Zoka, Yaha. *The Imperial Iranian Army from Cyrus to Pahlavi*. Teheran: Ministry of Culture and Arts Press, 1971.

Thirty-four

✳ ✳ ✳

IMPERIAL GREECE (356–323 B.C.E.)

In the spring of 334 B.C.E. Alexander the Great led his army of 40,000 troops to Sestus on the Dardenelles, the same place where Xerxes had crossed to invade Greece 146 years earlier. Prior to the crossing, Alexander stopped at Illium (Troy) to lay a wreath at the tomb of his mother's ancestor, Achilles. At the grave Alexander removed Achilles's shield and took it with him. He left Parmenion to supervise the crossing to Abydus, while Alexander himself crossed over in a single ship. With that crossing the invasion of Persia began.

THE ATTACK ON PERSIA

An attack by Greece on the Persian superpower appeared at first glance to be the act of a madman. The Persian Empire was enormous and encompassed many natural barriers and vast stretches of desert, mountains, and other hostile terrain. While the Greeks could easily get to Ionia, it was still 1,500 miles from the Ionian coast to the Persian capital at Susa. The empire itself comprised almost 2,000,000 square miles and had 50,000,000 inhabitants. Persia possessed vast economic wealth. Its gold reserves were enormous, and these financial resources could be used to raise large armies. The Persians had a large and excellent navy to control and defend the Mediterranean coast; the navy operated a considerable fleet of boats on the inland waterways that could transport and resupply Persian armies in the field with great efficiency. Persia had huge manpower reserves, and the Persian army was potentially enormous. It could easily deploy a field force of over 100,000 men, and if the tribal levies were brought to bear, the total Persian forces that could be put into the field outnumbered Alexander's army by more than fifteen to one.

But Alexander's strategic eye saw clearly that the quality of Persian political leadership was the major weakness of the Persian state. The size and heterogeneity of the empire required strong leadership at the center to make it function as an integrated whole and to direct the marshalling of military resources against an invader. And the political center of the empire was rotten. The days of Cyrus the Great and Darius I were long gone. The political system had decayed as a result of repetitive coups and the promotion of sycophants to positions of authority. The famed Persian civil administrative service was no more than a shell of its former self. The *satrap* system of imperial provincial rule had decayed to the extent that most citizens viewed the *satrapies* as little better than foreign oligarchies imposed on them from Susa and were ripe for revolt. Whatever the military and economic resources of the Persian state, Alexander knew that if he could paralyze the state's political will, Persian advantages in manpower and resources would be neutralized.

Alexander's Conquest

Alexander's plan of conquest can be divided into five phases. First, he had to secure his home base of support in order to prevent revolution in his rear and to insure that the mainland Greek states continued to be a source of resupply and manpower reinforcement. Second, he had to successfully conduct the invasion of Ionia and expand the bridgehead to sufficient depth to provide room for maneuver. Third, the Persian navy had to be neutralized so that it could not be used to sever his supply line or, worse, to conduct a counterinvasion of Greece while his forces were deployed in Persia. Fourth, Alexander had to find the Persian army, draw it into battle, and destroy it. Then the Persian capital could be taken and the political leadership dismantled and replaced. Fifth, if he was serious about creating a social order based on Greek notions of justice, Alexander's strategy required him to find a way to consolidate the empire and administer it while incorporating Greek and Persian cultures into a new national identity. If he failed in the latter, history would recall him as only a great general. To be truly remembered as the descendant of Hercules, Alexander would have to do much more than destroy the Persian army.

The army that Alexander took with him into Ionia in 334 B.C.E. was, in its essentials, the army that Philip had crafted and then bequeathed to Alexander on his death. Diodorus tells us that the army with which Alexander crossed the Hellespont comprised 32,000 infantry and 5,100 cavalry. The size and composition of Alexander's forces changed frequently over the course of his twelve-year campaign, at one point, in 326 B.C.E., reaching 120,000 men. These troops comprised the various tribal armies that were available to Alexander as he continued his march of conquest across Persia. Even when the army grew in size, the core of the force remained Macedonian and relatively small.

Alexander went much further than Philip in developing the logistical and siegecraft capabilities of his army. The siege train consisted of towers, rams, penthouses, elevators, hoists, pontoon boats and bridges, miners, and sappers. Alexander needed this equipment to subdue enemy cities quickly. But he also required speed and mobility for his army. His solution was to carry with him only the metal or other specialized parts that the siege machinery required. The rest could be built on the spot by a unit of engineers under the command of Diades, a Thessalian, "the man who took Tyre with Alexander." Even his artillery was highly mobile. We are relatively certain that Alexander had the *euthytona*, a huge javelin thrower similar to a large crossbow, and the *palintona*, a form of catapult that could throw stone shot of more than 100 pounds in weight. It is also likely that lighter-weight machines of similar type were used. Alexander's artillery also carried with it only the critical metal parts that could not be duplicated on the march. The rest of the machines were assembled when needed from local materials.

Other aspects of Alexander's army were different from Philip's army. Expecting to fight in unknown terrain, Alexander brought along a surveying section that collected data about routes, campsites, wells, and distances marched. We might expect as well that this information was condensed and presented in some form resembling military maps. Architects also went along, and they came in handy when Alexander founded and laid out the plans for no fewer than seventy cities. One architect, Deinocrates, laid out the plans for the city of Alexandria. Alexander had a secretariat consisting of a geographer (one of his great ideas was to produce the first accurate geography of Asia), naval experts, scientists, and one Eumenes of Cardia, charged with keeping a daily official journal of the expedition. Even an official historian, Callisthenes, a nephew of Aristotle, went along. No previous army had ever possessed such a sophisticated staff structure.

THE ORGANIZATION OF ALEXANDER'S ARMY

The death of officers on campaigns in antiquity was a special problem for any commander and no less so than for Alexander. Experienced officers, especially those that were politically loyal and accustomed to knowing the intentions of their commander in battle, were hard to come by. To deal with this problem, Alexander created the Corps of Royal Pages, a group of sons of leading Macedonian nobles who attended to the needs of the commander in camp and in the field. These young royals could be gradually trained in the arts of war and their loyalty continually assessed. It was this corps that served as a general replacement pool for officers killed on campaign. It must be said, however, that the corps probably originally comprised the sons of the Macedonian nobility who were held as hostages to insure the loyalty of their powerful fathers left behind in Greece.

The army of Alexander at the time of the invasion of Persia consisted essentially of the traditional Macedonian army augmented by additional forces provided by the League of Corinth. The centerpiece of the Macedonian army was the famed infantry phalanx armed with the long *sarissa*. Philip had given the name of *Pezhetairoi*, or "Foot Companions," to his infantry to raise their status to that of the Royal Cavalry in recognition of their importance in his new army. The soldier also carried a sword and shield but relied mostly on the grouping of *sarissae* to act as a spiked hedgehog capable of holding the center of the line. In fact, there was no such thing as the phalanx per se, it being a collective term for the entire infantry contingent of the Macedonian army. The phalanx comprised several *taxeis*, a complete and fully maneuverable unit of 1,536 men commanded by a brigade commander. This unit could deploy in any number of length and depth combinations, the most common being a ninety-six-man front with a sixteen-man depth. Each *taxeis* was further tactically divided into subunits under separate command. There is some evidence that at times a unit of 256 men, called the *syntagma,* may have been created ad hoc between the usual 128-man *lochos* and the higher *pentacosiarchy* of 512 men. The original Macedonian army had 24,000 phalangites. The Macedonian phalanx comprised a number of *taxeis* arrayed together in common formation.

Additional infantry organic to the Macedonian segment of the army were the *Hypaspists,* or elite infantry. These units were organized in 1,000-man brigades called *chiliarchies,* and Alexander had a total of 3,000 of these troops. The debate continues over how the *Hypaspists* were armed, either with the *sarissa* or the more traditional *dory* spear of shorter length. Their value, however, rested not in their armament, but in their training. They were handpicked troops noted for their endurance, speed at the run, and intelligence to absorb complex plans of maneuver. The *Hypaspists* were normally positioned on either side of the massed phalanx and acted as a hinge connecting the infantry to the cavalry on the wings. If the command was given to move the line into the oblique, the *Hypaspists* were the critical unit that lengthened or contracted to keep the infantry in contact with the cavalry. At times they were required to move obliquely to the front, forcing them to run in unit formation to keep up with the charging cavalry. They were the key to Alexander's ability to alter formations, to maneuver, and to coordinate his infantry and cavalry in combined attack. Their organization was structurally similar, if not identical, to that of the subunits of the phalanx. The *Hypaspists* could also be equipped with their own mounts.

The centerpiece of the Alexandrian army was the famed Macedonian cavalry, divided into *ile,* or "squadrons." Except for the elite royal guard *ile,* which had 300 men, Alexander's cavalry, the Royal Companions, consisted of six squadrons of 200 men each. Armed with the fourteen-foot *sarissa* that could be used as a lance, or the shorter javelin, all cavalry wore armor and carried the curved *kopis* to use as a cavalry saber. Later, some units even carried the bow. The Macedonian cavalry fought in an *emblos,* or delta formation, shaped much like an inverted ice cream cone with a single horseman at its point. This was different from traditional Greek cavalry, which attacked in a square formation with an eight-man front and eight men deep, and the Thessalian cavalry, which attacked in diamond formation. Philip had initially encountered the *emblos* formation among the Scythians, who invented it and adopted it for his own troops. This formation was ideal for rapid wheeling and withdrawal and made penetrating other cavalry formations easier. Different as well was the Macedonian habit of attacking at the gallop. Traditionally, Greek cavalry attacked at a walk or slow canter.

Alexander's army had an elite guard called the *Agema* comprised of one *ile* of 300 horse and a *chiliarchy* of 1,000 *Hypaspists.* This unit was originally the royal guard under Philip, who used them as a last-ditch reserve and as a specialty striking force. Since Alexander had little use for reserves, the *Agema* was turned into a special striking unit that accompanied their chief whenever he charged directly into the battle at some propitious moment. The Macedonian component of the army also had about 6,000 various light infantry troops of various skill. This force encompassed Cretan archers, slingers, Agrianian javelin throwers, and Thracian swordsmen. They were used as light troops had always been used: as skirmishers, flank guards, and to hold uneven terrain. These units comprised both subject and mercenary troops.

The tactical dynamics of Alexander's army were radically different from the traditional armies of Classical Greece and even significantly different from the army of Philip. Its strength lay in its flexibility. It could respond swiftly to any number of commands to shorten or elongate its line, withdraw in step backward, move to a forward or rear oblique, and otherwise act in integrated unison with all combat arms. It could perform whatever maneuver was required by the battle plan of its commander, a characteristic which expanded its combat repertoire far beyond that of any previous army.

Alexander's arm of decision was the cavalry, which could descend on the enemy with incredible speed and force. In another sense, however, the infantry was the arm of decision. Although Alexandrian infantry was primarily designed to act as a platform of maneuver, to anchor the infantry line while the cavalry probed and found the weak point, once the cavalry had done its job and punched a hole in the enemy line, it was the infantry that closed and accomplished most of the killing. In other circumstances the force of the cavalry blow shattered the enemy infantry, forcing it into a rout. In these cases the cavalry conducted a lethal pursuit. In the final analysis it was the ability to orchestrate the various combat arms according to the circumstances of a particular battle that gave the army of Alexander its effectiveness. It was a finely tooled instrument that could only achieve maximum results when wielded by the hands of a master strategist and tactician.

FURTHER READING

Arrian. *The Campaigns of Alexander the Great.* New York: Penguin Classics, 1976.

Bose, Partha Sarathi. *Alexander the Great's Art of Strategy: The Timeless Leadership Lessons of History's Greatest Empire Builder.* New York: Gotham Books, 2003.

Bosworth, A. B. *Conquest and Empire: The Reign of Alexander the Great.* New York: Cambridge University Press, 1988.

Brunt, P. A. "Alexander's Macedonian Cavalry." *Journal of Hellenistic Studies* 83 (1963): 27–46.

Delbrück, Hans. *History of the Art of War within the Framework of Political History.* Vol. 1, *Antiquity.* Westport, CT: Greenwood Press, 1975.

Devine, A. M. "Grand Tactics at the Battle of Issus." *Ancient World* 12 (1985): 39–59.

———. "The Strategies of Alexander and Darius III in the Issus Campaign." *Ancient World* 12 (1985): 25–38.

———. "The Battle of Gaugamela: A Tactical and Source Critical Study." *Ancient World* 13 (1986): 87–116.

———. "The Battle of the Hydaspes: A Tactical and Source Critical Study." *Ancient World* 16 (1987): 91–113.

Fuller, J.F.C. *The Generalship of Alexander the Great.* New York: Da Capo Press, 1989.

Gabriel, Richard A., and Karen S. Metz, *From Sumer to Rome: The Military Capabilities of Ancient Armies.* Westport, CT: Greenwood Press, 1991.

Grant, Michael. *From Alexander to Cleopatra: The Hellinistic World.* New York: Charles Scribner, 1982.

Green, Peter. *Alexander of Macedon, 356–323 B.C.: A Historical Biography.* Berkeley: University of California Press, 1991.

Griffith, G. T. "Alexander's Generalship at Gaugamela." *Journal of Hellenistic Studies* 67 (1947): 77–89.

Heckel, Waldemar. *The Wars of Alexander the Great: 336–323 B.C.* New York: Routledge, 2003.

Plutarch. *The Life of Alexander the Great.* Translated by John Dryden. New York: Modern Library, 2004.

Warry, John Gibson. *Alexander, 334–323 B.C.: Conquest of the Persian Empire.* Westport, CT: Praeger, 2005.

Xenophon. *The Persian Expedition.* Translated by Rex Warner. Baltimore: Penguin Books, 1972.

Thirty-five

✳ ✳ ✳

THE SUCCESSORS (323–168 B.C.E.)

The fundamental weakness of the empire forged by Alexander the Great was its lack of an institutional base that could manage the transition of power after Alexander's death. The empire was at its end what it was at the beginning: the product of one man's dream. While there is little doubt that Alexander planned to create formal governmental institutions that would manage the empire after his death, his demise occurred before any of these plans could be put into effect. When Alexander died, his empire died with him, and the future of the realm was settled in traditional Greek fashion: by a series of wars among would-be successors for control of the spoils.

THE WARS OF ALEXANDER'S SUCCESSORS

The result was the Wars of the Successors from 323 to 280 B.C.E., where Alexander's generals and their heirs fought one another to carve out spheres of influence within which to establish their own dynasties. The political entities that finally emerged were mostly defined by the territories occupied by the various contending armies at the end of the wars. When it was over, three major imperial realms came into existence. The Antigonids ruled mainland Greece and Macedonia, the Ptolemies ruled Egypt, and the Seleucids controlled most of southwest Asia, an empire that ran from the Aegean to the Hindu Kush. The Successor empires represented the imposition of Greek military oligarchies on various conglomerations of native populations conditioned to docility by centuries of foreign occupation by one power or another. Greek rule was perpetuated by establishing military garrisons at key points throughout the respective realms and by settling these garrisons with Greeks, sometimes by forcible resettlement. The three empires continually viewed one another with suspicion and often fought over one issue or another.

The period from 280 to 197 B.C.E. was a transitional period in the political and military history of Greece and the eastern Mediterranean. When it began, Alexander's Successors (the *Diadochi*) held the entire area in a firm military and political grip. Greek values remained the dominant cultural form of the area, and Greek arms dominated the practice of military science. When this period ended, however, the three Successor empires were in ruins, Greek culture was held prisoner to Roman *gravitas*, and Greek influence on military history was swept from the historical scene, never to emerge as a major force again. Simultaneously, the Macedonian military system, which had remained unchallenged for more than a century and a half, also met its death at the hands of a new military system: the legions of Rome. It is difficult to find any other period in ancient history that was more momentous for the development of warfare in the West.

Macedonian Armies

The general structure of the Macedonian armies under the Antigonids during the period of the Successors remained essentially as it had been during the Alexandrian period, a force comprising the central phalanx organized into *taxeis* of infantry coupled with *ile*, or "squadrons," of cavalry. While the general structure of the army remained, the manner in which the Macedonians tactically employed their armies was significantly different from the manner in which Alexander had used them. The major difference between the Macedonian model and the armies of Alexander was that the role of infantry in tactical application changed substantially. Alexander used the infantry phalanx as a platform of maneuver to pin the enemy in place until he exploited the development of the battle with his cavalry. The Alexandrian cavalry was typically the arm of decision. Under the Macedonians, the roles were reversed, with infantry used as the primary striking and killing force, while the cavalry was relegated to a secondary role. It is difficult to find a battle of the later Successor period where cavalry played a decisive role.

A number of factors contributed to this reversal of tactical roles. First, unlike the Seleucid empire, the Macedonians quickly lost interest in affairs in Asia, where the enemy armies consisted mainly of cavalry. The Macedonians fought mostly against the former city-states of Greece that had relinquished the old hoplite phalanx and adopted the weapons (*sarissa*) and formations of the Macedonian phalanx. Great improvements in siegecraft made the city-state more vulnerable than ever before, and the social system that supported the old hoplite system collapsed. More and more, the armies of the smaller city-states comprised mercenaries and professionals who adopted the phalanx as the more effective form of ground warfare. As a consequence, Macedonian armies fought mostly infantry battles against fellow Greeks armed with similar weapons and arrayed in similar battle formations. The result was a renewed emphasis on infantry as the primary arm of decision. A second reason for the reemphasis on infantry lay in the fact that the Macedonians generally perceived these conflicts more as police actions than as genuine wars. A similar development occurred in the other Successor empires. The role of the imperial armies was more domestic suppression than combat against foreign enemies. Under these conditions, trained infantry were considerably cheaper and more effective than expensive cavalry.

The Macedonian emphasis on infantry had changed the combat power of the phalanx. It became a cumbersome thing that had lost almost all the flexibility it once possessed under Alexander. Under the Antigonids, the phalanx grew considerably heavier, and it is likely that the *syntagma*, a unit of about 1,800 men, replaced the *taxeis* as the basic component of the phalanx. Smaller organizational units would have made the phalanx somewhat more manageable. Alexander deployed his phalanx in various depths, depending on the demands of the tactical situation. At its heaviest the Alexandrian phalanx was sixteen men deep. The Macedonian phalanx ranged in depth from sixteen to thirty-two men and, in some instances, even denser than that. This increase in depth adequately demonstrates the change in tactical concept for the use of infantry. When used as a platform of maneuver, it was the stability and training of the phalanx that was most important. But when used as a decisive arm, the bulk and momentum of the phalanx became most important. The increased density of the phalanx reflected its changing combat role under the Macedonians.

The weaponry of the Macedonian phalanx also changed. Alexander's infantry carried the *sarissa*, and while there is some debate as to its length, it is generally held that the Alexandrian spear was no longer than twelve to fourteen feet. It was sufficiently light to be wielded at the balance with one hand. The length and weight of the Alexandrian *sarissa* made it possible for the phalanx to shift formations to meet an attack from any direction. The Macedonian *sarissa* had grown in length and required two hands and considerable strength just to hold it out straight. The length of the infantry spear when coupled with the denser phalanx deprived the phalanx of any tactical flexibility. It could move in only a single direction, forward, and the propensity of the longer spears to tangle when moved about made it next to impossible for the phalanx to shift its formation to meet an attack from the flank or rear.

Only the first five rows of the phalanx could actually engage the enemy, and it is possible that the two front rows carried shorter spears. The rest of the ranks in the phalanx held their spears upward at a forward angle to provide some protection against arrow and missile fire. No matter how many ranks were arrayed in depth, all but the first five remained essentially reserves. To increase the bulk of the phalanx even further, the Macedonians reduced the gap between individual soldiers to only one and one-half feet. To protect the soldiers within the phalanx, the technique of "locking shields"—used by Alexander at the Hydaspes—became a standard maneuver. With both hands holding the spear and with the shield held by a shoulder strap, the men of the phalanx pressed against the men to their right in an effort to permit their neighbors' shields to overlap their right sides. In this formation it was impossible for the phalanx to maneuver in any direction except straight ahead. The press of the mass of humanity within the phalanx decreased the speed of movement to a crawl.

This cumbersome body of men could hold its ground and slowly advance forward only as long as the ground was level. Even the slightest unevenness in terrain tended to throw the ranks of the phalanx out of alignment. There was an additional tendency for the wings of the phalanx to move outward from the center as it moved and to create gaps between the individual *syntagmae* within it. This was a dangerous condition. A first-rate commander could easily use his cavalry to exploit these gaps, as Alexander had at Issus and Gaugamela. As the Romans demonstrated at Pydna, it was also possible to insert an infantry maniple into the gaps and to hack at the phalanx from within. But the experience of the Macedonians was largely against armies that used phalanxes and had equally poor cavalry, and while the risk of creating gaps was recognized, few of the opposing forces in the Macedonian military experience were capable of exploiting this vulnerability.

The inability of the phalanx to maneuver made it extremely vulnerable to flank or rear attack. The Macedonian phalanx fought four major battles against the Romans— Cynoscephalae, Pydna, Magnesia, and Corinth—and in every instance the phalanx crumbled to flank or rear attack. The paradox of the Macedonian phalanx during the time of the Successors was that the decline in cavalry resulted in the rise of an infantry formation that was even more in need of flank protection at precisely the time when the new cavalry doctrines could not provide this vital combat function.

The Macedonian solution to the problem of flank vulnerability was to create two modified forms of the phalanx, the articulated phalanx and the double phalanx. The articulated phalanx may have been introduced by Pyrrhus in his wars against the Romans (281–275 B.C.E.). The idea was to make the phalanx more flexible by compensating for its tendency to spread out and create gaps between its component battalions. Companies of *sarissa*-carrying phalangites were interspersed with companies of lighter-armed and more loosely organized units. These units acted as flexible joints connecting the various battalions to the main body when the phalanx began to spread. The idea may have been derived from Alexander's use of the *hydaspists* that acted as connecting joints between his cavalry and the main body of the phalanx.

Yet another way of protecting the flanks and rear of the phalanx was to use the double phalanx. The main phalanx was protected by a reserve line, sometimes a double line, of phalangites deployed behind or to the rear oblique of the main body. This formation was probably first used in 222 B.C.E. at the battle of Sellasia. While the articulated phalanx and the double phalanx represented workable solutions against another infantry phalanx, they were poor compromises to solving the problem of cavalry attack against the phalanx. In the end the problem of the phalanx's vulnerability was never satisfactorily solved.

It might be added that the quality of the phalanx infantryman under the Macedonians had fallen considerably when compared with the soldiers who had fought under Alexander. The truly national army of Alexander comprising men with long terms of service that produced discipline and cohesion ceased to exist under Alexander's Successors. Even in Macedonia, the most nationally conscious of all the Successor states, the system was impossible to maintain. It cost too much and took manpower from the land and economy, just as it had during the period of the early city-states. Now, however, there was no treasury of conquest to finance the military system.

The national army motivated by patriotic fervor and long professional experience disappeared under the Macedonian Successors. It was replaced by a small national force comprising mostly mercenaries, who served full time in return for the promise of a farm on retirement. These mercenaries were also used as garrison forces throughout the empire and could be called to service in times of trouble. The Macedonian army, in essence, went back to what it had been before Philip and Alexander reformed it, a levy of peasant farmers called to the colors for urgent situations. In less urgent situations, mercenaries were used and the national troops saved for dire emergencies.

The decline in the quality of the Macedonian army was paralleled by a decline in quantity. In 334 B.C.E. Alexander could raise 24,000 phalangites from Macedonia and 4,000 cavalry to take with him on campaign. By the time of the battle of Cynoscephalae (197 B.C.E.) Philip V could only raise 16,000 phalangites, 2,000 cavalry, and 2,000 mercenary *peltasts* from Macedon itself. Even this number required enrolling sixteen-year-olds and recalling retired veterans to national service. Philip attempted to reconstitute the manpower base of Macedonia by requiring families to produce children, forbidding the traditional practice of infanticide, and even resettling large numbers of Thracians in Macedonia proper. Twenty years later (171 B.C.E.), when Persus raised an army to resist the Romans, he could field 21,000 phalangites, 3,000 cavalry, and 5,000 *peltasts*. This was the largest army ever led by a Macedonian king since Alexander's time.

The problems of quantity and quality of manpower worked to reenforce the Macedonian emphasis on infantry over cavalry. In the same manner that Napoleon adopted the column formation as a solution to controlling troops of poor quality with little training, so, too, the phalanx had the singular advantage of not requiring much training. As in the old hoplite phalanx, very little skill was required of the phalanx soldier, except that he hold his ground and move along with his comrades. While the phalangite also carried the sword to use in desperate situations, the degree of training in using this weapon was universally poor. In a fight with the Roman legionnaire, who used the sword as his primary weapon, the Macedonian soldier was a poor match.

The transformation of infantry in the Successor armies was paralleled by a transformation in the quality, numbers, and tactical use of cavalry. The same forces that worked to emphasize the importance of infantry worked to reduce the importance of cavalry on the battlefield. The Wars of the Successors destroyed any national spirit that remained after Alexander's death, and the expense of cavalry led the Successors, especially the Macedonians, to recruit cavalry from the populace in much the same way as mercenaries were recruited. The monarch retained around his person a squadron or two of elite cavalry, but in terms of numbers and the ability to recruit and train cavalry, the cavalry forces of the Successors were but a pale copy of what they had been during Alexander's time.

The tactical employment of cavalry changed as well, most strongly so in Macedonia. Wars in Macedonia were between phalanxes of heavy infantry, and the one thing cavalry could not do was successfully charge a disciplined line of spear infantry. The Macedonians reverted to the traditional uses of cavalry that were common during the hoplite era. Cavalry actions were now largely confined to the wings of the army with cavalry attacking cavalry, usually with no significant influence on the outcome of the battle. As it had been for centuries before, the defeat of the enemy's cavalry again became an end in itself with little regard for how it affected the overall tempo or direction of battle. It became almost a tactical stereotype to open the battle with a cavalry attack rather than to wait until events unfolded and use the cavalry to exploit or create exploitable situations. This regression to cavalry tactics of the type found in the pre-Alexandrian era precluded the effective use of cavalry on the battlefield, and cavalry ceased to be the decisive arm it had been in the hands of Alexander. Cavalry doctrine remained static for more than two centuries, until the Parthians redesigned it entirely with the use of both the horse archers that defeated the Romans at Carrhae and the heavy *cataphracti*,

One of Pyrrhus's elephants. Reproduced by permission of the publisher from Alfred S. Bradford, *With Arrow, Sword, and Spear: A History of Warfare in the Ancient World* (Westport, CT: Praeger, 2001), Figure 38. © 2001 by Alfred S. Bradford.

armored knights that could break even the most disciplined body of infantry.

THE ELEPHANT'S USE IN WESTERN WARFARE

The Successors were, however, responsible for one significant innovation in the art of Western warfare: the use of the elephant. The time between Alexander's death and the battle of Pydna (168 B.C.E.) was the only time in Western military history when the elephant played an important role in warfare. Alexander had first come in contact with the elephant at the battle of the Hydaspes and employed them in a small way in his own army. It fell to the Successors, particularly the Seleucids and Ptolemies, to acquire elephants in large numbers, and in a short time, every major power from Macedonia to Carthage had integrated them into their respective armies.

The most common use of the elephant was to screen the deployment and maneuver of cavalry and, on rare occasion, to lead attacks against infantry. Rarely were they used against fortified positions, and then almost always with failure. In concert with light infantry, elephants could be used to protect the flanks of the phalanx and, indeed, a new and important combat role for light troops was to distract and destroy enemy elephants. Given the expense and difficulty associated with acquiring, training, and employing elephants, these animals seem to have been among the most expensive and least effective instruments of ancient warfare, at least in the West. The last serious use of elephants by Western armies was at the battle of Magnesia (190 B.C.E.), and they failed to prevent the defeat of the Seleucids at the hands of Roman infantry.

FURTHER READING

Adcock, F. E. *The Greek and Macedonian Art of War.* Berkeley: University of California Press, 1957.

Berthold, Richard M. "The Army and Alexander the Great's Successors." *Strategy and Tactics* 152 (June 1992): 45–47.

Cambridge Ancient History. 14 vols. New York: Cambridge University Press, 1970.

Delbrück, Hans. *History of the Art of War within the Framework of Political History.* Vol. 1, *Antiquity.* Westport, CT: Greenwood Press, 1975.

Jouquet, Pierre. *Alexander the Great and the Hellenistic World: Macedonian Imperialism and the Hellenization of the East.* 2 vols. London: Ares, 1978.

Seaton, Stuart. *The Successors.* London: Charnwood, 1987.

Tarn, William W. *Hellenistic Military and Naval Developments.* London: Ares, 1975.

———. *Hellenistic Civilization.* New York: Dutton, 1989.

Thirty-six

✳ ✳ ✳

REPUBLICAN ROME (500–28 B.C.E.)

The traditional Roman military formation from the time of the Republic's founding (circa 500 B.C.E.) was modeled on the Greek hoplite phalanx. The weaponry of the Roman citizen soldier was also Greek: the short spear, round shield, helmet, armor, greaves, and sword. In the usual case of set-piece battles on level ground against armies using similar formations, the phalanx worked well enough. In uneven terrain, however, the phalanx could not maneuver. In the wars against the Samnites (340–290 B.C.E.) fought in the rugged Apennine hills, valleys, and glens the phalanx proved unworkable and very brittle to surprise attack. The wars with the wild Gauls demonstrated how easy it was for the highly mobile formations of the Gallic armies to envelop the open flanks of the phalanx and crush it from all sides once the cavalry was driven from the field. Given that Roman cavalry was never very good, driving it from the field prior to surrounding the phalanx was not usually difficult.

REPUBLICAN ROMAN ARMY ORGANIZATION

During and after the Samnite wars the phalanx legion was gradually replaced by the manipular legion. It was during this war that the Romans replaced their heavy Argive-type shields with the larger and lighter wooden scutum shield. The Romans also adopted the *pilum* from the Samnites. Both pieces of equipment remained standard Roman issue until the end of the Imperial period. The manipular legion was the basic fighting formation of the Roman army throughout the Punic Wars. However, Scipio Africanus found that the new legion was too fragile against the massed attacks of

Hannibal's heavy Spanish infantry. Scipio strengthened the maniples, increasing their numbers to 600 men. These new cohorts gradually replaced the maniples, and around 100 B.C.E., the Romans adopted the cohortal legion as their basic fighting formation.

The Roman army was also reorganized on the basis of age. The youngest, most agile, and least trained men (*velites*) served as light infantry. Armed with darts and small javelins, they acted as skirmishers. The front line of the legion was occupied by a second class of men, the *hastati*, who were somewhat older and more experienced. Armed with the sword, two *pila*, and the scutum shield, they formed the first line of heavy infantry. The center line comprised the best and most experienced veterans (*principes*). Averaging thirty years old, these were the battle-hardened veterans. The third line comprised older men (*triarii*) and constituted the last line of resistance. Armed with the long spear, they lent stability to the formation and in times of retreat remained in place and covered the passage of the other ranks through their lines.

The basic tactical unit of the new Roman army was the maniple (literally, "handfuls of men"), somewhat equivalent to the modern infantry company, with a strength of 120 men. Each maniple was divided vertically into two centuries equivalent to platoons of sixty to eighty men each. Originally, the centuries had comprised 100 men, but the number proved too large to be controlled effectively by a single centurion. The number was reduced to eighty, although the name "century," meaning "one hundred," was retained.

The key to the flexibility of the legion lay in the relationship between the maniples within each line and between the lines of heavy infantry. Each maniple deployed as a small, independent phalanx with a twenty-man front and a six-man depth. The spacing between each soldier allowed independent movement and fighting room within an area of five square yards. Each maniple was laterally separated from the next by twenty yards, a distance equal to the frontage of the maniple itself. In line the maniples were staggered, with the second and third lines covering the gaps in the lines to their front. Each line of infantry was separated from the next by an interval of 100 yards. The result was the quincunx, or checkerboard formation, that permitted maximum flexibility for each maniple and for each soldier within it.

ROMAN MILITARY TACTICS

Flexibility was increased by the relationship between the lines of infantry. If, after the first line engaged, it was unable to break the enemy formation or grew tired, it could retire in good order through the gaps left in the second line. The second line then moved to the front and continued to press the attack, while the first rank rested and regrouped. This maneuver could be repeated several times, with the effect that the Roman front line always comprised rested fighting men. This was an important advantage. Modern studies demonstrate that men engaged in phalanx close combat could sustain the effort no more than thirty minutes before collapsing from exhaustion. The *triarii* remained in place in the last rank, resting on one knee with their spears angled upward. The *triarii* represented the organic reserve of the legion, to be employed at the commander's will.

The ability to pass through the lines of infantry in planned fashion offered another advantage. In most armies of the period, defeat of the front ranks often turned a battle into a rout. No army until the Romans had learned how to break contact and conduct a tactical retreat in good order. The manipular formation solved the problem. On command, the first line of infantry formed into close-order maniples, turned, and withdrew to the rear through the gaps left in the other two lines. The second rank followed. The *triarri* covered the retreat with their spears, and the *velite* light infantry deployed to the front to engage the enemy while the main body withdrew in good order. The ability to conduct an ordered retreat represented a major revolution in infantry tactics.

Tactical flexibility was further enhanced by the ability of each maniple to fight and maneuver independently. This flexibility allowed Roman commanders to make maximum use of the element of surprise. It was not unusual for a commander to position a few maniples in hidden positions, often at the flanks, or even to attempt to insert them to the rear of the enemy position. Once the main forces were engaged, these maniples could be brought into action, surprising the enemy with an attack from an entirely unexpected direction. Often, the sight of a few maniples marching on the main force from an unexpected direction was sufficient to cause the enemy to break. This capability provided the legions of Rome with a new tactical dimension of ground warfare.

The Roman soldier was the first soldier in history to fight within a combat formation while at the same time remaining somewhat independent of its movements as a unit. He was also the first soldier to rely primarily on the sword instead of the spear. The Roman sword of this period was a short slashing sword of Italian origin (*antennae* sword). During the Punic Wars the legions gradually adopted the famous *gladius*, a short sword incorporating many of the features of the Spanish *falcata*. The *gladius* was twenty inches long and approximately three inches wide and was made of Spanish steel. It was stronger in composition than any existing sword, and because it would not bend or break, it provided a psychological advantage to the Roman soldier. To use it well required a high level of training and skill. The Roman army introduced military training programs in the use of the *gladius*, and in 100 B.C.E. the army began to be trained in the same methods used in the Roman gladiatorial schools.

The *gladius* was primarily a stabbing weapon, and Roman soldiers were trained not to use it as a slashing weapon, the common method of sword use in most armies of the day. The shield parry, followed by a sharp underthrust to the chest, became the killing trademark of the Roman infantry. In the hands of the disciplined Roman soldier the *gladius* became the most destructive weapon of all time prior to the invention of the firearm. If the phalanx formations of past armies armed with the spear can be described as resembling spiked pincushions, then the Roman legion, with its reliance on the *gladius*, resembled a buzz saw.

A Roman legion had the strength of approximately 5,000 men and usually deployed with an allied counterpart of the same size and generally the same organization. The allied legion usually had a heavier cavalry section of approximately 600 horses, the Roman legion commonly possessing only 300 horses. The combined legions had 9,000–10,000 men. Two Roman legions and two allied legions under the same command comprised a consular army of 20,000 men deployed across a combat front of one and one-half miles.

The legion commander had a staff of professional officers who handled administrative, supply, medical, veterinary, and training matters. Combat command rested in the hands of six senior tribunes, two for each infantry line. Below them were the combat unit commanders of the maniples, sixty centurions, two for each maniple. The real combat leadership was provided by the centurions. Promotion of centurions through the ranks was based on demonstrated bravery and competence. The most noble soldiers of Rome were the First Centurions (*primus pilum*, literally, "the first spear") of the legions, and right to the end, they remained the best combat commanders the nation could field.

ROMAN ARMY WEAKNESSES

The Roman legion had two significant weaknesses. The first was the lack of a professional senior officer corps. Roman senior officers were civilians, often state officials or politicians, appointed to command the legions during time of war. Worse, this counselor system required that the same army have *two* appointed senior commanders who rotated command each day. Despite the best military organization in the ancient world, the practice of divided command often made it difficult for the legions to maintain good command direction. Changing senior commanders on a daily basis made it impossible for the army to become the instrument of a single commander's will. Hannibal frequently chose the time of battle to coincide with the daily command of a specific adversary.

The second weakness of the Roman armies was the poor quality of its cavalry. Like the Greeks, the Romans regarded service in the cavalry as little better than tending animals. The best soldiers from the best families refused to serve in the cavalry, and it was the most poorly trained of the combat arms. Roman cavalry often retained the old habit of using their mounts to arrive at the battlefield only to dismount and join the fray as infantry. Roman cavalry seemed ill suited to maintain the direction of the charge and showed a tendency to break up into small clusters of loose formations and wander all over the battlefield. They used no special armament, preferring instead to carry the weapons of the infantry. The Romans eventually gave up trying to develop cavalry and simply hired it from allied units.

At first Roman units usually did not provide for a fortified field camp on the march. During the wars against Pyrrhus and the Gauls the Romans were often caught in morning or evening surprise attacks while encamped. The solution was to construct the famous Roman fortified camp every evening. A fortified encampment not only prevented surprise attacks but provided the Roman commander with the tactical option of attacking from the base camp or using it as a defensive redoubt. The Romans were slow to learn the need for security on the march, and in the early battles against Hannibal they were often surprised while still in column of march. Hannibal's penchant for appearing from nowhere eventually led the Romans to stress the value of tactical intelligence. Under the empire, Roman tactical intelligence capabilities reach the state of a high art.

ROMAN INFANTRY AND FIGHTING

The Roman arm of decision was its heavy infantry, and Roman tactics centered on using the infantry for "simple bludgeon work." The idea was to commit the infantry to the center of the line and let it hack away until the center of the enemy formation broke. Given adequate room to stab with their swords, and if organizational integrity was maintained, the Roman infantry would eventually hack its way through any infantry formation in the world. Against the open formations of the Gauls, however, it was often man-on-man. But where the Gaul and other tribal soldiers fought as individuals, the Roman soldier could depend on the man to his left or right for help if he was not otherwise engaged. Against the Macedonian phalanx formation with its long spears, the Romans simply hacked off the spear points and moved inside the spear shafts to close with the enemy. Once inside the phalanx, the individual spearman was helpless, and the Roman buzz saw did its deadly work.

The Roman soldier was trained to stab and not to slash with his sword. The legionnaire was also trained to engage the man not directly in front of him, but the opponent to his immediate right. Using the sword as a slashing weapon required the soldier to raise it above his head and away from his body, exposing the entire right side of his body as a target. The shield, held in the left hand, became useless as a protective device. Under these circumstances, training the Roman soldier to strike to his right allowed him to cut down the enemy soldier as he was raising his shield against the opponent directly to his front. More than 1,700 years later, in 1746, at the battle of Culloden Moor in Scotland, the British army rediscovered this technique after being hacked to pieces in two successive battles by the warriors of the highland Scottish clans. Instead of the sword, the British infantry employed the fluted bayonet.

Stabbing to the right provided yet another tactical advantage in close combat. Having struck a target to his right, the Roman infantryman stepped back to pull out the sword. As he did, he moved slightly to his right to get new footing for the next assault. As a result, the Roman line tended to move to the right and slightly to the rear. This forced the enemy line to move to the left and forward, having to step over the bodies of the dead and wounded. The dynamics of the two lines resulted in the Roman soldier always being prepared to meet the next opponent, who had to stumble over the corpses while watching his footing.

A typical Roman battle opened with light infantry skirmishing in front with darts, javelins, and slings. As the lines closed, the skirmishers fell back through the gaps in the checkerboard and were usually never used again. When both lines were within range, about twenty-five yards, the front rank threw its *pila* and rushed to close the gap quickly, smashing into the enemy front. The Roman lines would fight, retire, and reenter the battle until the enemy center broke and the slaughter could begin. The flanks were anchored by the cavalry. The combat strength of the legion lay in its tactical flexibility and the determination, courage, and training of its heavy infantry.

FURTHER READING

Arnold, Thomas. *The Second Punic War*. London: Macmillan, 1886.

Boardman, John. *The Oxford Illustrated History of Rome*. London: Oxford University Press, 2001.

Cornell, Tim. *The Beginnings of Rome: Italy and Rome from the Bronze Age to the Punic Wars*. New York: Routledge, 1995.

Delbrück, Hans. *History of the Art of War within the Framework of Political History*. Vol. 1, *Antiquity*. Westport, CT: Greenwood Press, 1975.

Dodge, Theodore A. *Hannibal: A History of the Art of War Among the Carthaginians and the Romans Down to the Battle of Pydna, 168 B.C., with a Detailed Account of the Second Punic War.* 2 vols. Boston: Houghton Mifflin, 1891.

Fuller, J.F.C. *A Military History of the Western World.* 3 vols. New York: Funk and Wagnalls, 1954.

Gabba, Emilio. *Republican Rome, the Army, and the Allies.* Berkeley: University of California Press, 1976.

Grant, Michael. *The Army of the Caesars.* New York: Charles Scribner, 1974.

Harris, William V. *War and Imperialism in Republican Rome: 327–70 B.C.* New York: Oxford University Press, 1979.

Holland, Tom. *Rubicon: The Last Years of the Roman Republic.* New York: Doubleday, 2003.

Liddell Hart, Sir Basil Henry. *A Greater Than Napoleon: Scipio Africanus.* London: Blackwood and Sons, 1926.

Livy. *The History of Rome.* Translated by Henry Bettenson. London: G. Bell and Sons, 1919.

O'Connell, Robert. "The Roman Killing Machine." *Quarterly Journal of Military History* 8 (1988): 30–41.

Polybius. *The Histories.* Translated by W. R. Paton. London: William Heinemann, 1922.

Santosuosso, Antonio. *Soldiers, Citizens, and the Symbols of War: From Classical Greece to Republican Rome, 500–167 B.C.* Boulder, CO: Westview Press, 1997.

Starr, Chester G. *The Roman Imperial Navy: 31 B.C.–A.D. 324.* New York: Barnes and Noble Books, 1960.

Vegetius Renatus, Flavius. *The Military Institutions of the Romans.* Harrisburg, PA: Military Service Press, 1944.

Watson, George Ronald. *The Roman Soldier.* Ithaca, NY: Cornell University Press, 1969.

Webster, Graham. *The Roman Army: An Illustrated Study.* Chester, UK: Grosvenor Museum, 1956.

Williams, J.H.C. *Beyond the Rubicon: Romans and Gauls in Republican Italy.* New York: Oxford University Press, 2001.

Wise, Terence. *The Armies of the Carthaginian Wars, 265–146 B.C.* London: Osprey, 1988.

Thirty-seven

✳ ✳ ✳

CARTHAGE (814–146 B.C.E.)

Carthage was founded thirty-eight years before the first Olympiad (about 814 B.C.E.) as one of a number of colonies established in Sicily, Spain, and North Africa by the Phoenician city-state of Tyre in an effort to expand its influence into the western Mediterranean. Tyre was a Canaanite city whose name in Greek was *Phoenicia*, meaning "land of the purple," a reference to the city's production of purple dye from the murex snail found in its coastal waters. The purple cloth manufactured in this area was so expensive that it was only affordable by kings, a fact that came to identify "being of the purple" with royalty in the ancient world. The Romans called the people of Carthage *Poeni* or *Puni*, hence the name "Punic Wars."

By the fourth century B.C.E. Carthage had evolved an oligarchic republican regime based on an annually elected dual magistracy, that of the *shofets*, or judges; the *Gerousia*, or Grand Council, with an inner permanent committee of thirty Elders; a high court of 104 judges selected for life by a college of pentarchs; and a popular Assembly comprising all citizens who met the minimum property qualifications. All offices were reserved for the aristocracy so that the basis of political privilege in Carthage was wealth, not heredity. Carthage was a commercial society where war and the military took second place to profit, where military adventures were subjected to the test of cost-benefit analysis, and where generals were distrusted and kept on a short leash.

CARTHAGE'S MILITARY COMPOSITION

The population of Carthage in the third century B.C.E. probably did not exceed 400,000, counting all classes, a number far too small to provide for her commercial and military manpower needs, even with the addition of levies from the other colonies. Carthage's population was mostly composed of merchants, tradesmen, and artisans, whose absence from economic activity was costly to Carthage's revenue. It was cheaper to hire soldiers than to conscript them, and by the fourth century B.C.E. the citizen levy had been abandoned and replaced with mercenaries. Carthaginian recruitment agents became a common sight throughout the Near East, Italy, Greece, Gaul, and Africa, where they hired soldiers and complete military units from princes and kings. The last date for which we have evidence of Carthaginian units participating in war outside Africa is 311 B.C.E. It was around this time that Carthage created a new unit called the Sacred Band, comprising elite citizen soldiers. This unit, Polybius tells us, was 3,000 strong and was armed like Greek heavy infantry, by which we suppose he meant the infantry of Alexander and not Classical Greece. The Carthaginian Sacred Band could not by law be employed outside the *chora* of Carthage itself, suggesting that it may have been some sort of praetorian or civic guard.

The mercenary system presented Carthage with a number of problems. First, mercenary armies were expensive. But Carthage was very rich, and as long as her armies protected her trade and metal monopolies throughout the western Mediterranean, the cost was manageable. Second, mercenary armies must be kept busy or they become ill disciplined and even mutinous. This difficulty was solved by having the army almost constantly occupied somewhere outside of Carthage itself. For more than a century Hanno occupied them with the conquest of North Africa's hinterlands, which Carthage exploited for raw materials and agriculture. Third, mercenary soldiers were one thing, mercenary commanders quite another. Command of the armies was always in the hands of Carthaginian field generals. At first this presented some problems as a commercial people usually do not produce great military commanders. After the fourth century B.C.E., however, Carthage had begun to establish a handful of powerful families whose sons were experienced military commanders. This new military caste was established by Mago (hence the military dynasty known as the Magonids) and soon produced others. Carthaginian commanders were some of the best in the Western world. Finally, powerful generals in command of mercenary troops can become a serious threat to civilian political authority. The Carthaginians hit on a novel solution to deal with this problem.

After 300 B.C.E., military commanders were no longer permitted to hold public office of any kind. A complete separation of military from civic authority was introduced. Generals and admirals were now appointed only for specific periods of time or for specific conflicts by the Grand Council. Nor was it uncommon for a member of this court or even a senator to accompany the general in the field and report on his performance and political loyalty. Generals could be removed at any time by the council. To make certain that the council's edicts were taken seriously, any Carthaginian commander who failed in the field or who otherwise failed to carry out his orders with diligence could be publicly crucified in the city's main square. The system worked admirably, and Carthaginian commanders never presented a risk of praetorianism to the civil authority. The success of the Carthaginian military system is evident in two respects. First, right to the end, Carthage was able to place large forces in the field sufficient for the missions set for their commanders. Second, the quality of Carthaginian commanders was generally excellent, by far tactically superior to Roman commanders, with the notable exception of Publius Scipio.

As to the size of the armies, a few examples will suffice. The walls around Carthage were also used as barracks and stalls for animals and supplies. In the two-and-one-half-mile-long wall that protected Carthage from an attack, there were stables sufficient for 300 elephants, 4,000 cavalry horses, and barracks for 20,000 infantry and 4,000 cavalry. A force of this size represented the central core of the Carthaginian army to be expanded in time of crisis. One advantage of a mercenary army is that their commanders could hire troops as they went from the very country within which they were conducting operations. While Carthage's military system could produce adequate manpower to deal with most military situations, what it could not do was fight a war with an adversary whose manpower reserves *and* disciplined stubbornness could draw Carthage into a war of attrition.

HANNIBAL'S ARMY

Our knowledge of the Carthaginian armies is limited. The destruction of Carthage at the hands of the Roman army at the conclusion of the Third Punic War was so complete that no Carthaginian records survived. What we know of the Carthaginian armies comes from the accounts provided by their enemies, mostly Roman sources like Livy and Polybius. This aside, it seems that the army of the great Carthaginian general Hannibal (247–c. 182 B.C.E.) in his war against the Romans was probably typical and can offer insights into Carthaginian armies in general. Hannibal's army was composed of the usual odd mixture of soldiers from many lands and cultures. The foot soldiers were mostly heavy infantry and came largely from Libya, Spain, and Gaul. The most loyal and talented of Hannibal's infantry were the citizens of Libya-Phoenicia, the only group subject by law to military service. Originally armed with the traditional weapons of the Greek hoplite, these units fought in the old phalanx formation. As the war wore on, they were equipped with captured Roman weapons and gradually adopted Roman tactics.

Hannibal's Spanish infantry were recruited from the Iberian tribes and were both heavy and light infantry. The heavy infantry carried the thrown javelin (akin to the Roman *pilum*) but relied mostly on the Spanish sword, the *falcata*. Made of fine Spanish steel and stronger and wider than the Roman *antennae* sword of the period, its main features were adopted by the Romans and incorporated into the famed Roman *gladius* during the war with Hannibal. Spanish heavy infantry used the scale, lamellar, or chain mail of the day, the latter an innovation of the Celts and standard issue in the Roman armies of the period. Spanish heavy infantry were strong and courageous fighters and were every bit a match for Roman infantry. Spanish light infantry were armed with the standard kit of darts, javelins, light wooden shields, and slings. Some of the light infantry in Hannibal's army comprised Balaeric slingers, who carried two slings, one for long distance and one for short. The long-range sling could fire a stone the size of a tennis ball almost 300 yards. These slingers were the finest in the ancient world, and for almost 600 years they were hired by one army after another as mercenaries.

Hannibal recruited large cohorts of Celtic infantry from the Gallic tribes north of the Po River. Organized into clans, these tribal warriors lived for war, glory, and plunder. They used the sword as a basic weapon, wore no armor, and sometimes fought stark naked as they charged in wild groups into the enemy formations. They were incapable of any field discipline or maneuver. Hannibal often used them as shock troops to strike the enemy center before committing his cavalry. This, of course, produced heavy casualties, but they were generally expendable in any case. Their poor-quality weapons were gradually replaced from captured Roman stocks. Completing the Carthaginian mixture of forces were various African tribes carrying all sorts of tribal hunting and agricultural implements.

Hannibal's cavalry was no less a mixed bag. There was a small number of elite heavy cavalry, probably comprising professional warriors drawn from Carthage itself. Additional contingents came from the upper classes of Libya-Phoenicia. The Spanish contributed the greatest numbers of heavy cavalry armed with a buckler shield, a long and short lance, a short sword, mail armor, a helmet, and greaves. Spanish cavalry sometimes carried an extra infantryman aboard, who dismounted into the enemy formations. The best and most reliable cavalry were the Numidian light cavalry. Sometimes enemies of Carthage, sometimes serving out of common interests, but mostly paid mercenaries, these units came from Numidia, the area of present-day Morocco. They rode bareback and carried short javelins, lances, and swords. Normally armed with a shield, they sometimes wore a leopard skin over their arm in place of the shield. They were specialists in maneuver warfare, often attacking, retreating, maneuvering, and attacking again at a different place on the battlefield.

Hannibal's Elephants

Hannibal also took along thirty-seven elephants when he crossed the Alps to invade Italy. As an instrument of war, the elephant has a long and generally unimpressive history. The Carthaginians encountered the elephant in their war with Greece and took to capturing and training the smaller African elephant for their own armies. The elephant frightened those armies, who had never seen them. Unless a horse had been trained around them, elephants easily spooked the cavalry mounts of the enemy. Under the control of their handlers (mahouts), a charge of rampaging elephants against an infantry formation could have tremendous shock effect. Elephants were used in Persia and India as platforms for archers and javelin throwers. They were also used to anchor the center or ends of infantry lines, and their height was sufficient to use them as a screen behind which to shift cavalry units.

Like all implements of war, however, the elephant came with built-in disadvantages. Experienced light infantry skirmishers could meet the elephants in advance of the infantry line and strike them with darts, swords, and javelins, wounding them into a rage. Once enraged, the elephants became uncontrollable and had a tendency to turn back in the direction from which they had come, running over the very formations that had launched them. Out-of-control elephants rumbled around the battlefield, disrupting everyone's plans. To prevent this, the mahouts carried a large iron spike and a hammer. If an elephant could not be brought under control by normal means, the mahout drove the spike into the elephant's brain, killing it instantly. Another defensive tactic was to move behind the elephant and cut its hamstring tendon. In light of all this it is interesting to ponder why Hannibal took elephants along on such a difficult march. Most probably Hannibal used them as instruments of propaganda to impress the Gauls and convince them to join him in his campaign against the Romans.

CARTHAGINIAN TACTICS

The Carthaginian armies of Hannibal's campaigns were such a mixture of groups, weapons, and even languages that they could not be disciplined to a standard set of tactics. It is testimony to the brilliance of Carthaginian commanders that for more than a century they were able to field these kinds of armies and still be very effective in battle. Carthaginian field commanders were known for their personal bravery and courage, traits which endeared them to tribal and clan units. They could also be ruthless in disciplining their troops with beatings and death sentences if they did not perform well. This is hardly surprising among an officer corps acquainted with seeing their comrades who failed in battle crucified in the public square of Carthage. Truly, the soldiers of the Carthaginian armies often had more to fear from their commanders than from the enemy.

The nature of the Carthaginian armies made any standard tactical system impossible. The tactical brilliance of Hannibal and previous Carthaginian commanders lay in their ability to employ various types of units creatively in a given battle to obtain maximum collective effect. At the same time the battlefield tapestry still had to be woven into some sort of tactical whole if victory was to be achieved. This was no easy task. Hannibal placed most reliance on cavalry as his arm of decision, with infantry used as a platform for maneuver or as shock troops. This development is hardly surprising. In the first place, close contact with the Greeks in the eastern Mediterranean made the Carthaginians thoroughly familiar with Alexander's military system, one that also used cavalry as the arm of decision and infantry as a platform of maneuver. Second, Numidia bordered on Libya-Phoenicia, and Carthage had to defend Libya and its valued grain crop against the lightening raids of Numidian cavalry. The size of the border made fixed fortifications expensive and impractical against the nomadic Numidians. Carthage developed its own indigenous cavalry force to deal with the problem. One consequence was the development of a tactical doctrine that stressed the use of the horse over infantry, exactly the reverse of the Romans.

The mix of Carthaginian armies made it impossible for Carthaginian commanders to develop a standard tactical system. The trick was to use the various types of units in a manner that maximized the effectiveness of each while sustaining an overall tactical plan specific to each battle situation. It is possible, however, to discern some "tactical constants" or general rules that appear to have governed Carthaginian battle tactics. The first was always to maximize shock and surprise by engaging the enemy while he was still deployed in column of march. Another was to engage only after the enemy was made to work hard to transit some obstacle, like a river, stream, or forest. A third rule was to use the terrain and tempt the enemy to fight uphill. Hannibal often anchored his lines of infantry with heavy formations of phalanx infantry that could swing against the pivot points of an extended infantry line, forcing the enemy into a smaller and smaller area. Cavalry tactics centered around the use of horsemen to drive the enemy cavalry from the field as a prelude to it returning and staging a shock attack against the rear or flanks of the enemy infantry. If none of these advantages could be obtained, Carthaginian generals avoided battle. If they could not fight on their terms, they would not fight at all, and they conserved their manpower for another day.

FURTHER READING

Arnold, Thomas. *The Second Punic War*. London: Macmillan, 1886.

Bagnall, Nigel. *The Punic Wars 264–146 B.C.* New York: Routledge, 2003.

Cottrell, Leonard. *Hannibal: Enemy of Rome*. New York: Holt, Rinehart, and Winston, 1961.

De Beer, Gavin. *Hannibal: Challenging Rome's Supremacy*. New York: Viking Press, 1969.

Delbrück, Hans. *History of the Art of War within the Framework of Political History*. Vol. 1, *Antiquity*. Westport, CT: Greenwood Press, 1975.

Dodge, Theodore A. *Hannibal: A History of the Art of War Among the Carthaginians and the Romans Down to the Battle of Pydna, 168 B.C., with a Detailed Account of the Second Punic War*. 2 vols. Boston: Houghton Mifflin, 1891.

Lamb, Harold. *Hannibal: One Man against Rome*. Garden City, NY: Doubleday, 1958.

Lancel, Serge. *Hannibal*. Translated by Antonia Nevill. Malden, MA: Blackwell, 1998.

Liddell Hart, Sir Basil Henry. *A Greater Than Napoleon: Scipio Africanus*. London: Blackwood and Sons, 1926.

Livy. *The History of Rome*. Translated by Henry Bettenson. London: G. Bell and Sons, 1919.

Polybius. *The Histories*. Translated by W. R. Paton. London: William Heinemann, 1922.

Prevas, John. *Hannibal Crosses the Alps: The Invasion of Italy*. New York: Da Capo Press, 2001.

Vegetius Renatus, Flavius. *The Military Institutions of the Romans*. Harrisburg, PA: Military Service Press, 1944.

Warmington, B. H. *Carthage*. New York: Praeger, 1960.

Wise, Terence. *The Armies of the Carthaginian Wars, 265–146 B.C.* London: Osprey, 1988.

———. *Hannibal's War with Rome: The Armies and Campaigns*. London: Osprey, 1999.

Thirty-eight

✷ ✷ ✷

THE BARBARIANS: GAULS, GERMANS, AND GOTHS (58 B.C.E.–445 C.E.)

THE GAULS

Gaul was a region that today includes France, part of Belgium, western Germany, and northern Italy. The Gauls were a Celtic people, and their Gallic society was governed by an aristocracy of nobles surrounded by groups of retainers who acted as a warrior class not unlike the warrior retinues of the European Middle Ages. The rest of the social order comprised various types of free landholders and tenant farmers, a large portion of which had been reduced almost to serf status. The Druidic priesthood constituted another social caste and, while influential, was unable to act as an organizer for Gallic society outside of its religious functions. Unlike the Germans, however, Gallic society was not primarily a warrior society. The Gauls practiced extensive agriculture, constructed roads, forts, and bridges, and used currency rather than the more primitive barter as a form of economic interchange. Shifting alliances among the rival nobilities precluded any significant degree of national integration. One consequence was the lack of a national army or genuine level of military sophistication that could be marshaled to defend Gaul against the Roman invasion.

The Gallic Armies

Among most of the tribes of Gaul the primary fighting arm was cavalry. Caesar called these horse-borne nobles *equites*, commonly translated as "knights," and they typically constituted the tribal command structure for war. The Gallic armies had spent centuries in intertribal warfare with the consequence that they had made few improvements in their weapons, tactics, or style of war. Cavalry was generally poor in quality and accustomed to fighting as individuals rather than in coordinated groups. When combined with infantry, significant coordination in battle was rarely achieved.

In a social order divided feudally between warrior knights and tenant farmers, serfs and freeholders, it was hardly surprising that Gallic infantry amounted to little more than an untrained, temporarily assembled mob of armed rabble incapable of any significant degree of tactical sophistication, discipline, or direction on the battlefield. The typical infantryman was armed with the long slashing sword. Little use was made of spearmen or archers, although Caesar occasionally encountered javeliners and slingers. The infantry and cavalry carried wooden or wattle shields, and Caesar recorded that some Gallic troops fought stripped to the waist. The nobility wore bronze cuirasses, chain mail, and highly decorated helmets, more as signs of military status and rank than as genuine defensive implements.

The Helvetii and the Nervii tribes were exceptions to the generally poor condition of Gallic infantry. The Helvetii had refined their art of war through centuries of running battles on their borders with the Germans. They were first-rate infantrymen who fought in disciplined formations under good commanders. They seem as well to have acquired some of the Germanic skill at cavalry. In all Caesar's battles in Gaul it was only the Helvetii and Nervii who dared challenge the legions of Rome to infantry combat in open field, and they consistently gave a good account of themselves.

The conduct of warfare by the Gauls left much to be desired. Long centuries of tribal civil wars made any military coalition a fragile entity. The Romans were masters at playing one tribe off another to prevent a concentration of superior military force mounting against them. By engaging the Gallic armies piecemeal, an isolated victory against one contingent was often sufficient to fragment the entire coalition, whose members simply returned home. The Gauls were incapable of sustained military operations if they required sustaining a tribal political coalition for any length of time.

The Gauls lacked any significant military organization as well. When the tribe went to war, the whole tribe went, including the women and children. There was no logistical system, and after a few days in the field, when supplies ran low or the countryside proved incapable of supplying the army and its following, the army often melted away as various contingents returned to their villages. In the field the Gallic army anchored itself around a ring of wagons—a wagon *laager*—within which the women, children, and supplies of the tribe were concentrated for protection. The integration of a tribal army with its larger social structure proved a terrible disadvantage in defeat. A local defeat often turned into a rout that gathered around the wagon *laager*, exposing the women and children to capture and massacre. On a number of occasions Caesar surrounded, captured, and enslaved entire tribes. In other instances he massacred entire peoples trapped in this manner.

The Gauls had no discernible tactical system of combat engagement. Led by their mounted nobles, an unorganized mob of undisciplined infantry would launch a frontal attack, hoping to overwhelm the adversary with sheer numbers. These attacks were not conducted by units, but by masses of individuals fighting as individuals. During the first few encounters with the Gauls these frontal attacks unnerved the Romans and caused some cohorts to break under the assault. The physical stature of the Gaul was significantly more impressive than that of the average Roman. One authority suggests that the average Gaul may have been as much as seven inches taller than the average Roman. These huge people attacked the Roman infantry with their long swords held above their heads. On smashing into the Roman formations, the broadsword was brought crashing down on the heads of the Roman infantry to great effect. The Roman shield, made entirely of wood, frequently proved unable to absorb the force of the sword blow and broke apart.

After a few engagements, the Romans learned to cope with the challenges of Gallic infantry. First, the shield was reinforced with a metal rim capable of withstanding the force of the sword stroke. Second, the front line of the Roman infantry was trained to raise their shields above their heads and to permit the enemy swordsmen to bring their swords down directly onto the shields. As the blow struck, the Roman infantry-man absorbed the blow by gradually bending to one knee. The enemy infantryman was defenseless, with his sword on top of the Roman shield and the force of the blow expended. At that point the Roman soldier sprang upward and forward from his crouched position, driving his *gladius* into the unarmored body of his adversary. The long sword of the Gaul proved to be no match for the Roman short sword, especially so since the Roman infantryman was a trained professional fighting against a part-time tribal warrior. The problem in dealing with Gallic infantry was usually numbers. Wave after wave of howling swordsmen crashed into the ranks of the legion. If the legion had possessed good-quality cavalry, it could have made short work of the Gallic infantry by attacking and enveloping the flanks.

It is difficult not to read Caesar's *Commentaries* without reaching the conclusion that much of Caesar's brilliance had to do with exploiting the obvious weaknesses of his enemy to good effect. At the operational level Caesar was always fighting an enemy that could not bring its numerical superiority to bear on the battlefield either because it could not achieve political unity or because it lacked a significant logistical capability that made it capable of sustained operations. In fighting the Gauls the Roman army was years ahead of its adversary in the development of organizational skills that made possible an armed force with maneuver, supply, and tactical capabilities that the enemy could not hope to match. As a consequence, the wars between the legions of Rome and the tribal armies of Gaul were never really a serious contest.

THE GERMANS

The Germanic armies that the Romans encountered in their efforts to subdue the territory between the Rhine and Elbe were products of a social order far less developed than that of the Gauls. The social order of the Germanic tribe was essentially premodern in that it was not strongly articulated and lacked a varied specification of social roles. The bonded male warrior group became the dominant form of military organization. Every German male was first and foremost a warrior, and the entire society was formed around the conduct of war. Prowess in war was the road to social advancement, and behavior on the battlefield was the primary determinant of social rank and status.

Tacitus's description of the Germans as "fierce looking with blue eyes, reddish hair, and big frames" recalls earlier Roman descriptions of the Gauls, and it is likely that, like the Gauls, the average German was much taller than the average Roman. The Germans had not yet reached a level of political development where state institutions had come into existence. The German peoples were divided into tribes (*volkerschaften*); twenty-three different tribes lived between the Rhine and the Elbe. An average tribe numbered about 25,000 people living on a land area of approximately 2,000 square miles. Some of the larger tribes comprised 35,000–40,000 people and occupied a comparatively larger land area. The tribes were divided into extended family clans called "Hundreds" (*Hundertschaften*) comprised of 400–1,000 people living in a single village and controlling an area of twenty square miles. Agriculture was not extensively practiced by the Germans, and what cultivation was undertaken was done by women, the men contributing to the food supply by hunting and fishing. Land was held in common, as were some cattle herds, and their utilization was determined by the head of the community, the *altermann* or *hunno*.

The Germanic Armies

Within each tribe were a small number of richer noble families who met in assembly with the clan *hunni* to address major issues, including war and peace. In wartime, however, it was common for the council to select a war chief, usually from the most powerful warrior noble families, to command the tribal army. An average German tribe could put 5,000–7,000 warriors in the field under the command of the war chief. The actual fighting units, however, were centered around the clans, and a Germanic army of 5,000 warriors would have at least twenty and as many as fifty subordinate unit leaders, the clan chiefs.

In assessing the fighting quality of German tribal armies it must be kept in mind that Germanic tribes were warrior societies in which all other social roles were defined by or influenced by the warrior ethos. Thus Germanic men did not farm because it was beneath them (women's work), but they did hunt because hunting improved their combat skills. The relationship between man and wife and family was also conditioned by the warrior ethos. It was the woman who brought weapons to her husband as a gift of her dowry. Germanic women acted as the tribe's "military medical corps," and it was to these *wilde weiber* (literally, "wild women") that the wounded turned for medical aid. Women accompanied their men into battle, urging them on to greater efforts by reminding them of the cost of enslavement to themselves and children. The German soldier was a professional warrior whose very social existence was defined by war.

In times of war, each clan provided its own coterie of warriors under the leadership of the village *hunno*. The cohesion of the family and clan was extended to the warrior group with the result that German combat units were highly cohesive, strongly disciplined, self-motivated, well led, and well trained in the skills of individual close combat. They could be relied on to make murderous charges on command and to fight well in dispersed small groups. While blood ties usually assured that clan units remained loyal to the larger tribal military command, in fact, there was probably only the most rudimentary command and control exercised by the war chief over the behavior of the clan units. Once the tribal levy had been assembled and a general battle plan decided on, implementation was left to local units with little in the way of any ability to direct the battle.

German weaponry was the result of many years of intertribal wars, the lack of contact with any other culture from which new weapons could be acquired, and, as Tacitus and others tell us, the German difficulty in working with iron. Tacitus does not tell us why the Germans were poor iron smiths, but it is clear that they were far behind the Celts and Gauls, who were making chain mail armor superior to the Romans' in the second century B.C.E. Roman sources note as well that only a few of the German warriors, probably their nobles or the best warriors, wore body armor or metal helmets. The basic protection from wounds was afforded by a large shield of wood or braided reeds covered with leather. Some troops wore a covering of leather or hide on their heads as well.

The basic weapon of the German was the *framea*, the seven- to ten-foot spear of the type used by the Greek hoplite tipped with a short, sharp blade. The spear was used in close combat or could be thrown. It seems likely as well that German units carried somewhat longer spears, which might have been used by the front rank of a charging infantry formation to break through the enemy. Once inside the enemy formation, the *framea* was used as the primary killing weapon. The sword was not commonly used by German combat units. The German warrior also carried an assortment of short, wooden javelins with fire-hardened tips that, as Tacitus tells us, they could hurl long distances. Other missiles, most probably stones and sharpened sticks, were also salvoed at the enemy. Although some German tribes developed into excellent cavalrymen, for the most part German cavalry was limited in numbers and used rather poorly. Battle accounts note that German cavalry moved at such a slow pace in the attack that the infantry had little difficulty in keeping up. The primary strength of the German tribal levy was infantry.

The Germanic infantry fought in a formation that the Romans called *cuneus*, or "wedge." Vegetius described the *cuneus* as "a mass of men on foot, in close formation, narrower in front, wider in the rear, that moves forward and breaks the ranks of the enemy." This formation, also called the Boar's Head formation by the Romans, was not a wedge with a pointed front, but more resembled a trapezoid, with a shorter line in front, followed by a thick formation of closely packed troops with a rear rank somewhat longer than the front rank. The formation was designed to deliver shock and to carry it through to a penetration of the enemy ranks.

The use of the wedge against the Roman open phalanx explains other Germanic battlefield habits. If the object of the wedge was penetration, then there was no need to armor the men in the center of the wedge. Those German warriors who had body armor and helmets probably fought in the front rank and in the outside files of the wedge. Fourteen centuries later, it became the Swiss practice to armor only the front and outside ranks, while the men in the center of the Swiss pike phalanx had only leather armor or none at all. If the wedge did its job and broke the enemy formation, the fight was reduced to either a pursuit or a scramble of individual combats. Under these conditions, the troops least encumbered by armor and other weighty equipment had the advantage.

The German strength lay in the highly disciplined and cohesive nature of its clan combat groups *(kampgruppen)*. These groups could move quickly through the forest and swamps and could fall with terrible ferocity on an enemy not yet deployed for battle. They could break contact and withdraw just as rapidly for group discipline was central to the clan fighting unit. The Germans were particularly competent in scattered combat, surprise attacks, ambushes, feigned withdrawals, rapid reassembly, and most other aspects of guerrilla war.

THE GOTHS

The Goths probably originated in Scandinavia and then migrated to the upper Vistula River area, gradually moving southward toward the middle Danube and then east toward the upper rim of the Black Sea. By the third century c.e. the Romans distinguished two Gothic kingdoms in this area. North of the Danube, in the former Roman province of Dacia, lived the Visigoths, called, alternatively, the West Goths or the "Wise Goths." North and east of them, in southern Russia, north of the Black Sea, were the Ostrogoths or East Goths. The Goths lived a semiagricultural existence centered around the village in which hunting, cattle raising, and a pastoral style of life predominated. The Gothic society did not differ very much from the social order found among the Germans in the first century. The social order revolved around the clan—the *hunno*, or hundred, headed by the *alderman*—which conducted most of the important political and social functions of the village. Tribal leadership was conducted by an oligarchy of nobles. During wartime a tribal assembly—presumably comprising *hunni* and nobles—selected a war chief who conducted the campaign. It is also probable that during periods of war the Goths organized their military commands into units of 10, 100, and even 1,000 men, the latter under a *comites* (later, count) or, perhaps, a *dux* (duke), but this is by no means certain.

The Gothic Armies

The size of the Gothic armies of the third and fourth centuries was not as large as some ancient commentators would have us believe. While it seems probable that by the fourth century the Goths were among the most numerous and powerful of the Germanic tribes, it is unlikely that they could muster more than 12,000–15,000 warriors under arms, another 45,000 noncombatant men, women, and children, and, perhaps, 10,000 slaves, or a body of people 70,000 strong.

The fighting power of Gothic combat units was quite good. Unlike the earlier Germanic tribes, the Goths had been serving in Roman units for more than a century and were as well armed as the Roman soldier. This opportunity permitted the Goths to develop a powerful and highly skilled class of warrior nobles under the leadership of a war chief. As a consequence, the combat leadership of the Gothic army was experienced and tough. Of all the Germanic tribes, the Goths were the first to place their main military reliance on the horse. Gothic heavy cavalry relied on experienced horsemen armed with the lance and sword. However, horses and military equipment were expensive, and it is unlikely that Gothic cavalry was a large combat force. It seems logical as well that some Gothic cavalry had served in Roman cavalry squadrons and were thoroughly familiar with Roman cavalry doctrine. Gothic cavalry used the saddle, but there is no evidence of the stirrup.

Most of the Gothic army was infantry. Unlike the infantry of their earlier Germanic ancestors, who had fought as light infantry with javelin and spear, Gothic infantry were well-armed, heavy infantry. The infantry carried the shield and sometimes a pike. Their major arms were the short sword (*scramasax*) or the long cutting sword, the *spatha*. Some infantry carried the *fransica*, a single-bladed battle-axe that could be wielded or thrown and could easily split Roman armor, shields, and helmets. As best as can be determined, the Gothic infantry did not fight with body armor, although it is likely that some Roman shirt mail must have made its way into the Gothic army. The Goths fought in the fluid wedge formation, designed more for its ability to be led by the *hunno* (village chief) than for its military effectiveness.

The army of the Goths moved with and around its wagon forts, or *laager*. These wagons carried the army's food supply for the soldiers and their families and whatever logistical items were required for campaigning. The wagons were drawn into a circle to form a wagon fort, behind which a camp could be constructed. The wagon fort served as a base from which to launch raids or as a defensive position from which the entire army could fight. In dire circumstances the Gothic army could fall back on the *laager* in retreat to regroup its forces or to offer a last point of resistance. The way in which the *laager* was used by the Goths strongly parallels the functions that the Roman field camp served for the Roman army.

FURTHER READING

"Battle of the Teutoburg Forest." *Archaeology* 12 (September–October 1992): 26–32.

Burns, Thomas S. "The Battle of Adrianople: A Reconsideration." *Historia* 22 (1973): 336–345.

Caesar, Julius. *The Battle for Gaul*. Translated by Anne Wiseman and Peter Wiseman. Boston: D. R. Godine, 1980.

———. *Commentaries on the Gallic War*. Translated. New York: Penguin Books, 1982.

Carcellinus, Ammianus. *Roman History of Ammianus Carcellinus*. Translated. Rolfe. 1939.

Creasy, Edward Shepard. *Fifteen Decisive Battles of the World*. New York: Dorsett, 1987.

Delbrück, Hans. *History of the Art of War within the Framework of Political History*. Vol. 2, *The Barbarian Invasions*. Westport, CT: Greenwood Press, 1980.

Dio. *Roman History*. 18–25.

Dupuy, R. Ernest, and Trevor N. Dupuy. *The Encyclopedia of Military History from 3500 B.C. to the Present*. New York: Harper and Row, 1986.

Ferrill, Arther. *The Fall of the Roman Empire: The Military Explanation*. New York: Thames and Hudson, 1986.

Fuller, J.F.C. *A Military History of the Western World*. 3 vols. New York: Funk and Wagnalls, 1954.

Gothic History of Jordanes. Princeton, NJ: Princeton University Press, 1915.

Grant, Michael. *Armies of the Caesars*. New York: Barnes and Noble Books, 1997.

Holder, P. A. *Studies in the Auxilia of the Roman Army from Augustus to Trajan*. Oxford: B.A.R., 1980.

O'Connell, Robert. "The Roman Killing Machine." *Quarterly Journal of Military History* Vol. 1 (1988): 30–41.

Oman, Sir Charles William Chadwick. *A History of the Art of War in the Middle Ages*. 2 vols. London: Greenhill Books, 1998.

Shuckburgh, E. S. *Augustus Caesar*. New York: Barnes and Noble Books, 1995.

Tacitus, *The Annals*.

Tacitus, *Germania*.

Tacitus, *The Histories*.

Thirty-nine

✳ ✳ ✳

IMPERIAL ROME (9–450 C.E.)

The military strategy set in place by Augustus, the first emperor of Rome (63 B.C.E.–14 C.E.), and followed by his successors for more than a century was premised on the ability of the legions of Rome to prevent, preempt, and defeat the empire's enemies before they could penetrate the frontiers and run rampant in the interior of the empire. This had to be accompanied by a military establishment that did not exceed twenty-five legions, or approximately 300,000 men, and a similar number of auxiliary troops raised from the provinces and Rome's allies. The spine of the Roman defense was its infantry legions posted along the rim of the empire in permanent camps, ready to pounce on any enemy who ventured too close. The legions could be launched on preemptive and punitive expeditions when required by events.

ARMIES AND TACTICS: THE FIRST AND SECOND CENTURIES

By the time of the emperor Trajan (who ruled from 98 to 117 C.E.) Roman military policy had succeeded for more than a century in keeping the borders secure. His adopted son, the emperor Hadrian (117–138 C.E.), adjusted the empire's borders to coincide with extant military capabilities. The legions were positioned along natural barriers. In Germany the lines of defense ran along the Rhine River and farther east along the Danube River. The area between the upper Rhine and upper Danube was fortified by constructing a ten-foot-high, 200-mile-long wooden palisade complete with guard towers and forts along which the legions were deployed. Behind the border posts

Hadrian's Wall: Roman wall built by Emperor Hadrian marking the northern border of the Roman Empire and guarding against barbarian invasion. The Art Archive/ Jarrold Publishing.

Hadrian constructed a connecting network of military roads that allowed the legions to move rapidly along the border to reinforce any outpost under assault. As under Augustus, there was no central strategic reserve. As long as Rome was not required to fight on two fronts at once, Roman strategy worked well.

The army of Hadrian's time comprised about 157,000 Roman legionnaires organized into twenty legions augmented by 227,000 auxiliary troops, the *auxillia*, which had first been introduced by Augustus. By the middle of the second century c.e. there were 257 cohorts of auxiliary troops, of which 130 were mixed cohorts. These mixed cohorts had approximately a four-to-one ratio of infantry to cavalry, with the cavalry comprising 120 horses. In addition, there were forty milliary units (units of 1,000 strong), of which twenty-two were mixed. This new type of unit was first introduced by the Flavians in the East. There were eighty-two ordinary cavalry regiments and eight milliary cavalry regiments. The total Roman army of this period was approximately 384,000 men, of which 71,000 were mounted.

As the mix and types of military units gradually changed during this period, so, too, did the equipment. The Roman helmet was now made in arms factories in Gaul to take advantage of Celtic skill in iron making. A new helmet, called the Port type and originating in the Alpine area, was introduced. Its most distinguishing feature was its extended neck guard, which gave substantially better protection down to the shoulders. Body armor also underwent radical changes. The chain mail that the legionnaire had worn for more than two centuries gave way to a new type of body armor, the *lorica segmenta*. This was a Celtic innovation and consisted of connected steel bands held around the body by straps and hooks. The new armor weighed only twenty pounds, compared to more than thirty pounds for the chain mail.

The traditional oval Roman scutum shield, which had been in use for more than four centuries, was replaced by a shorter, rectangular shield of the same name. Constructed like half a cylinder with straight sides, the new shield was made of laminated wood and was covered with leather. Unlike the old shield, the new model was reinforced around the edges with metal and had an iron boss and a protected handgrip. The shield weighed about twelve pounds. The straight sides of the shield probably allowed a tighter inter-locking of shields with less exposed space between each, a considerable advantage when facing either infantry or cavalry whose primary weapon was the stabbing spear.

The traditional *pilum* remained but went through several design changes, some-times becoming heavier and then lighter. One heavier model had a plumb weight at the base of the striking point to give it greater force in penetrating the enemy shield. The traditional function of the *pilum* was to disable the enemy's shield. As the Roman legions came to face cavalry and spear-carrying infantry more often, the *pilum* gradually gave way to the spear, a more effective instrument against both types of adversaries.

The Roman sword underwent changes that made it shorter and straighter in design. The *gladius* remained essentially the same weapon, but what was changing was the nature and armament of the adversary, which, in turn, forced a change in infantry tactics. More and more, the legions fought in closed lines rather than in the open for-mations of the past. Gradually, the *gladius* gave way to the barbarian sword, the *spatha*. Derived from the Celtic long sword, the *spatha* had a blade sixty to seventy centime-ters in length and functioned as a cutting, not a stabbing, weapon. Its introduction to the legions was a response to changing tactics. It was also a function of the fact that more and more barbarian infantry were being used in the legions, infantry whose native weapon was the *spatha*. Training the soldier to use a cutting weapon required less time and less skill than was formerly the case with the *gladius*.

Roman cavalry underwent significant changes during the second century c.e. Although armored cavalry had been around for years in the Roman army, the emphasis on infantry had always relegated cavalry to a secondary role. It was during Hadrian's time that this began to change. The arrival of the Roxolani along the Danube introduced the Romans to a new type of cavalry first developed in the East. These *cataphracti* were heavy cavalry, where both the horse and cavalryman were armored and the cavalryman carried the lance, the *contus*. Hadrian was the first Roman emperor to introduce units of *cataphracti* into the Roman army. The introduction of these new units, however, did not change the traditional Roman emphasis on infantry. Most cavalry still consisted of hired foreigners, and the role of cavalry in Roman tactics was essentially unchanged.

Traditional Roman cavalry rode small horses, averaging fourteen hands high, and wore no armor. The cavalryman himself wore chain mail armor and a helmet that covered the whole head, except for the eyes and nose, and carried the long *spatha* as his main weapon. The standard cavalry shield was a flat oval or sometimes hexagonal-shaped device. The saddle appeared among Roman cavalry for the first time in the late first century along with the horseshoe, another Celtic innovation in warfare. There is no evidence of the stirrup by the Romans. The armament of the Roman cavalry during this period clearly reflected its limited tactical role in support of infantry.

THE IMPERIAL ARMY IN THE THIRD CENTURY

By the middle of the third century Roman military equipment underwent further significant changes and became more like that of the barbarian armies the Romans fought. By the time of the battle of Adrianople the *gladius* had disappeared from the kit of the Roman infantryman and was replaced by the barbarian *spatha*. As Roman infantry were expected more and more to act as a phalangeal barrier to barbarian cavalry charges, the thrown *pilum* gradually gave way to the stabbing spear, a weapon much more suited for use in a wall of pikes. The straight-sided cylindrical *scutum*, a shield designed to repel infantry attack, was replaced with the light oval shield characteristic of barbarian cavalry. The oval shield permitted the soldier more striking area with his spear. As Roman infantry increasingly became light infantry valued for their mobility more than their combat weight, body armor fell into disuse so that most Roman legionaires went into battle with little or no body armor. The characteristic Roman helmet finally gave way to the lighter, cheaper, barbarian helmet known as the Intercisa type, and even the military belt, the very symbol of the legionnaire, was discarded in favor of a single broad belt with a leather baldric for holding the sword.

From 235 to 297 C.E. Rome suffered through sixty years of civil war in which no fewer than sixteen emperors and more than thirty would-be emperors were felled by the dagger or the sword. The increased pressure on the frontiers revealed the shortcomings of a Roman army weakened by political war. The old preclusive defensive strategy was no longer possible and changed to a more elastic system of defense. The

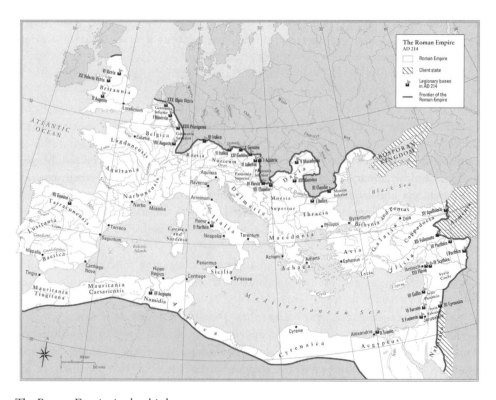

The Roman Empire in the third century.

frontier legions and border garrisons and strongpoints were retained, but it was now recognized that the quality of the legions and the multiplicity of highly mobile threats from penetrations by barbarian raiders required increased mobility on the part of the defensive forces to contain the penetrations. The legions acquired stronger cavalry components designed to run down enemy horsemen and engage them until the legion infantry could be brought to bear. Credit is usually given to Gallienus (253–268 c.e.) for creating the first large-scale Roman cavalry force that was used as a central reserve to reinforce the border infantry garrisons.

THE FOURTH-CENTURY MILITARY REFORMS OF DIOCLETIAN AND CONSTANTINE

Major reforms of the Roman army came during the reigns of Diocletian (284–305 c.e.) and Constantine (306–337 c.e.). Since it remains a matter of some debate as to which reforms were introduced by which emperor, the reigns of the two emperors are treated here as a single period in which to trace the outline of the reforms of the Roman army. Diocletian restored the imperial borders in a series of vigorous campaigns on several fronts. To manage the empire more efficiently, Diocletian created the post of Vice Emperor, to which he appointed Maximian. He and Maximian then took successors-designate (Caesars), appointing Galerius in the East and Constantius in the West. In 293 c.e. Diocletian reorganized the empire for administrative purposes, creating a number of smaller provinces out of the older provincial boundaries. The frontiers were reorganized into four military sectors, each sector assigned as the direct responsibility of one of the Caesars. Each sector had its own legions, cavalry detachments, and mobile cavalry reserves. To tie the system of forts and unit deployments together to make rapid reinforcement possible, Diocletian constructed roads, bridges, and strongpoints.

Under Diocletian, the army grew from 300,000 to about 400,000 men. The number of legions was doubled from thirty-three to almost seventy, but in some instances the number of men per legion was reduced to 1,000. This process of reducing the strength of the infantry legions was completed under Constantine. The increase in manpower came in the area of the *auxilia* and the creation of new types of specialized infantry units. The old legionary infantry became a smaller proportion of the overall army. At the same time Diocletian expanded the number of cavalry units, almost all of which were drawn from German and other barbarian tribes. A variety of these units—*cunei, alae, vexillationes*—were raised for all segments of the army. The old legionary cavalry disappeared and was replaced by these new units. Despite the increases in cavalry, it is important to note that the Roman army under both Diocletian and Constantine was still predominantly an infantry army. Whereas in the early empire the cavalry-to-infantry ratio was approximately one to ten or twelve, by the time of Adrianople it was one to three.

The larger armies were reorganized to make the strategy of elastic in-depth defense work properly. The remnants of the old legions were posted in fixed positions at key border or river points for frontier defense. Gradually, their quality declined. These remnants were designated as *limitanei* (border guards) and *riparienses* (river guards) and were usually deployed in "legions" of 1,000 men. Diocletian formed the *Comitatenses,* or a mobile imperial army, comprising largely provincials from Germany, Illyrium, Gaul, and the Danube, commanded by the emperor himself. It was stationed near the major cities and roads in the interior of the empire and functioned as a rapid reaction force to expel border penetrations. The contingents of infantry within this force were largely light infantry and of provincial and barbarian origin. The cavalry was divided into 500-strong horse regiments called *vexillationes*, and the infantry, although still called legions, were assembled in brigades of 1,000 men. There were a total of 170 legions at the end of the fourth century. Between the *comitatenses* and the field legions, there was another rapid reaction cavalry force, called the *pseudo-comitatenses*, that was used to fill in the gaps as the occasion arose.

Diocletian replaced the old Praetorian Guard with a large Imperial Guard loyal to the emperor. This new unit was called the *palatini*. It is not possible to say with accuracy how large the Imperial Guard was under Diocletian, but by the time of the battle of Adrianople the *palatini* comprised twenty-four horse regiments of 500 troopers each and twenty-five infantry legions of 1,000 men each. The Guard also comprised another 108 *auxilia* infantry regiments, each 500 strong. Constantine added a personal life guard, the *Scholae Palatinae*, comprising mostly Germans, to the Imperial Guard. By the end of the century the Imperial Guard consisted of 12,000 horse and 80,000 foot, nearly all cantoned around the provincial capitals of the empire.

The old strategy of static defense centered about the infantry legions was no longer successful against sporadic hit-and-run raids undertaken against thousands of miles of border. Roman strategy recognized that the entire frontier could not be made impenetrable, except at prohibitive cost. The mobile reaction strategy was based on the idea that the frontier infantry could defend the largest and most important sectors of the border. If a penetration occurred, infantry forts and border strongpoints served as pockets of resistance until larger forces could be rushed to the point of penetration. Since most of the raiders were horse-borne, Roman reaction forces were cavalry and light infantry. Behind the legion border, forts garrisoned by the *limitanei* were the provincial forces, comprising small infantry and cavalry units, capable of rapid reaction. Positioned at key points within the empire were segments of the large strategic field army, comprising cavalry and infantry forces, that functioned as the empire's strategic reserve.

Roman tactics changed to accommodate both the new strategy and the nature of the threat. Legion infantry now fought in smaller contingents (about 1,000 strong compared to the old 5,000-man legion) armed with the spear and light shield. Since their opponents were essentially cavalry forces and untrained light infantry, Roman infantry required flexibility and mobility to deal with the enemy infantry and had to be capable of stopping a barbarian cavalry charge. To accomplish the latter, Roman infantry deployed more in compact lines than in the old open infantry formation of the quincunx and functioned more like the old precohortal infantry phalanx, with a hedge of spears to stop enemy cavalry. The idea was to fix the enemy until the cavalry could engage and deal decisively with it. Infantry, still the largest and strongest combat arm of the Roman army by far, were gradually reduced to a tactical platform of maneuver for cavalry in much the same way as they had been for Alexander.

FURTHER READING

Ball, Warwick. *Rome in the East: The Transformation of an Empire.* New York: Routledge, 2000.

Burns, Thomas S. "The Battle of Adrianople: A Reconsideration." *Historia* 22 (1973): 336–345.

Campbell, J. B. *The Emperor and the Roman Army: 31 B.C.–A.D. 235.* New York: Oxford University Press, 1984.

———. *Warfare and Society in Imperial Rome.* London: Routledge, 2002.

Carcellinus, Ammianus. *Roman History of Ammianus Carcellinus.* Translated. Rolfe, 1939.

Dixon, Karen R. *The Roman Cavalry from the First Century to the Third Century A.D.* London: Routledge, 1997.

Ferrill, Arther. *The Fall of the Roman Empire: The Military Explanation.* New York: Thames and Hudson, 1986.

Fuller, J.F.C. *A Military History of the Western World.* 3 vols. New York: Funk and Wagnalls, 1954.

Goldsworthy, Adrian Keith. *The Roman Army at War: 100 B.C.–A.D. 200.* New York: Clarendon Press, 1996.

Holder, P. A. *Studies in the Auxilia of the Roman Army from Augustus to Trajan.* Oxford: B.A.R., 1980.

Le Bohec, Yann. *The Imperial Roman Army.* London: Routledge, 2002.

Luttwak, Edward. *The Grand Strategy of the Roman Empire from the First Century A.D. to the Third.* Baltimore: Johns Hopkins University Press, 1976.

Roth, Jonathan. *The Logistics of the Roman Army at War (264 B.C.–A.D. 235).* Boston: Brill, 1999.

BIBLIOGRAPHY

Acharya, A. M. "Military Medicine in Ancient India." *Bulletin of the Indian Institute of Medicine* 6 (1963): 50–57.

Adams, W. Lindsay. "In the Wake of Alexander the Great: The Impact of Conquest on the Aegean World." *Ancient World* 27 (1996): 29–37.

Adamson, P. B. "A Comparison of Ancient and Modern Weapons in the Effectiveness of Producing Battle Casualties." *Journal of the Royal Army Medical Corps* 123 (1977): 93–103.

———. "The Military Surgeon: His Place in History." *Journal of the Royal Army Medical Corps* 128 (1982).

Adcock, F. E. *The Roman Art of War Under the Republic.* Cambridge, MA: Harvard University Press, 1940.

———. *The Greek and Macedonian Art of War.* Berkeley: University of California Press, 1957.

Aldea, Peter A., and William Shaw. "The Evolution of Surgical Management of Severe Lower Extremity Trauma." *Clinics in Plastic Surgery* 13, no. 4 (October 1986): 554–562.

Alexander, Bevin. *How Great Generals Win.* New York: W. W. Norton, 1993.

Alexander, Franz G., and Sheldon T. Selesnick. *The History of Psychiatry: An Evaluation of Psychiatric Thought and Practice from Prehistoric Times to the Present.* New York: Harper and Row, 1966.

Alkim, U. Bahadir. *Anatolia.* London: Barrie and Rockliff, 1969.

Allen, Nick, and Ali Daud. *Ancient India.* Southwater, 2003.

Anderson, J. D. *Roman Military Supply in North East England.* British Series 224. Oxford: British Archeological Reports, 1992.

Anderson, J. K. *Ancient Greek Horsemanship.* Berkeley: University of California Press, 1961.

———. *Military Theory and Practice in the Age of Xenophon.* Berkeley: University of California Press, 1970.

Angold, M. *Byzantium 1025–1204: A Political History.* London: Longman, 1984.

Animal Management. London: British Army Veterinary Department, 1908.

Appian. *The Civil War.* Translated. New York: Loelo, 1964.

Arnold, Thomas. *The Second Punic War.* London: Macmillan, 1886.

Arrian. *The Campaigns of Alexander the Great.* Translated. New York: Penguin Classics, 1976.

Astour, Michael. *Hittite History and the Chronology of the Bronze Age.* New York: Coronet Books, 1989.

Austin, M. "Hellenistic Kings, War, and the Economy." *Classical Quarterly* 36 (1986): 450–466.

Bachrach, Bernard S, ed. *Armies and Politics in the early Medieval West.* Brookfield, VT: Variorum, 1993.

Bagnall, Nigel. *The Punic Wars 264–146 B.C.* New York: Routledge, 2003.

Baldson, J.P.V. *Julius Caesar and Rome.* London: English Universities Press, 1970.

Ball, Warwick. *Rome in the East: The Transformation of an Empire.* New York: Routledge, 2000.

Balmforth, Edmund. "A Chinese Military Strategist of the Warring States: Sun Pin." PhD diss., Rutgers University, 1979.

Barbieri-Low, Anthony Jerome. "Wheeled Vehicles in the Chinese Bronze Age, 2000–771 B.C.E." MA thesis, Harvard University, 1997.

Bar-Kochva, B. *The Seleucid Army: Organization and Tactics in the Great Campaigns.* New York: Cambridge University Press, 1976.

Baronowski, D. "Roman Military Forces in 225 B.C.E." *Historia* 42 (1993): 181–202.

Bartusis, Mark C. *The Late Byzantine Army: Arms and Society, 1204–1453.* Philadelphia: University of Pennsylvania Press, 1992.

Basham, A. L. *The Wonder That Was India: A Survey of the Culture of the Indian Sub-continent Before the Coming of the Muslims.* New York: Grove Press, 1959.

Bath, Tony. *Hannibal's Campaigns.* New York: Barnes and Noble Books, 1992.

"Battle of the Teutoburg Forest." *Archaeology* (September–October 1992): 26–32.

Battne, Bruce L. "Foreign Threat and Domestic Reform: The Emergence of the *Ritsuryo* State." *Monumenta Nipponica* 41, no. 2 (1986): 199–219.

Beal, Richard H. *The Organization of the Hittite Military.* Chicago: University of Chicago Press, 1992.

Berthold, Richard M. "The Army and Alexander the Great's Successors." *Strategy and Tactics* 152 (June 1992): 45–47.

Bishop, M. C., and J.C.N. Coulston. *Roman Military Equipment from the Punic Wars to the Fall of Rome.* London: Batsford, 1993.

Blankenship, K. Y. *The End of the Jihad State.* Albany: State University of New York Press, 1994.

Boak, Arthur. *Manpower Shortage and the Fall of the Roman Empire in the West.* Ann Arbor: University of Michigan Press, 1955.

Bonfante, G. "Who Were the Philistines?" *American Journal of Archaeology* 50 (1946): 251–262.

Bose, Partht Sarathi. *Alexander the Great's Art of Strategy.* New York: Gotham Books, 2003.

Bosworth, A. B. *Conquest and Empire: The Reign of Alexander the Great.* New York: Oxford University Press, 1988.

Bradford, Alfred S. *With Arrow, Sword, and Spear: A History of Warfare in the Ancient World.* Westport, CT: Praeger, 2001.

Bray, R. S. *Armies of Pestilence: The Effects of Pandemics on History.* New York: Lutterworth, 1996.

Breasted, James Henry. *The Battle of Kadesh: A Study in the Earliest Known Military Strategy.* Chicago: University of Chicago Press, 1903.

———. *Ancient Records of Egypt: Historical Documents from the Earliest Times to the Persian Conquest.* 5 vols. Chicago: University of Chicago Press, 1906.

Breeze, D. J. "The Organization of the Legion: The First Cohort and Equites Legionis." *Journal of Roman Studies* 59 (1969): 50–55.

Brunt, P. A. "Alexander's Macedonian Cavalry." *Journal of Hellenic Studies* 83 (1963): 27–46.

Bryant, Anthony. *Early Samurai: 200–1500 A.D.* London: Osprey, 1991.

Bryce, Trevor. *The Kingdom of the Hittites.* New York: Oxford University Press, 1998.

———. *Life and Society in the Hittite World.* New York: Oxford University Press, 2002.

Budiansky, Stephen. *The Nature of Horses.* New York: Free Press, 1997.

Burn, A. R. *Persia and the Greeks.* London: Arnold Press, 1962.

Burne, Alfred. "Some Notes on the Battle of Kadesh." *Journal of Egyptian Archaeology* (1921): 191–195.

———. *The Battle of Kadesh.* Harrisburg, PA: Military Service Press, 1947.

Burns, Thomas S. "The Battle of Adrianople: A Reconsideration." *Historia* 22 (1973): 336–345.

———. *Rome and the Barbarians, 100 B.C.–A.D. 400.* Baltimore: Johns Hopkins University Press, 2003.

Caesar, Julius. *Commentaries on the Gallic War.* Translated. New York: Penguin Books, 1982.

———. *The Civil War.* Translated. New York: Penguin Books, 1988.

Cambridge Ancient History. New York: Cambridge University Press, 1970–2005.

Cambridge History of India. New York: Cambridge University Press, 1922.

Campbell, J. B. *The Emperor and the Roman Army, 31 B.C.–A.D. 235.* New York: Oxford University Press, 1984.

Carcellinus, Ammianus. *Roman History of Ammianus Carcellinus.* Translated. Rolfe, 1939.

Cartwright, Frederick F. *Disease and History.* New York: Barnes and Noble Books, 1991.

Caven, Brian. *The Punic Wars*. New York: Barnes and Noble Books, 1992.

Cawkwell, G. *Philip of Macedon*. Boston: Faber and Faber, 1978.

Chadwick, John. *The Macedonian World*. New York: Cambridge University Press, 1976.

Chambers, James. *The Devil's Horsemen: The Mongol Invasion of Europe*. New York: Atheneum, 1979.

Chang, Kwang-chih. *The Archaeology of Ancient China*. New Haven, CT: Yale University Press, 1977.

———. *Shang Civilization*. New Haven, CT: Yale University Press, 1980.

Charvát, Peter. *Mesopotamia Before History*. New York: Routledge, 2002.

Childe, V. Gordon. "Horses, Chariots, and Battle-Axes." *Antiquity* 15 (1941): 196–199.

———. "War in Prehistoric Societies." *Sociological Review* 23 (1942): 126–38.

———. *What Happened in History*. London: Hammondsworth, 1950.

———. *New Light on the Most Ancient East*. London: Routledge and Paul, 1952.

Chopra, P.N.A. *A Comprehensive History of Ancient India*. 3 vols. London: Sterling, 2003.

Clay, A. T. *The Empire of the Amorites*. New Haven, CT: Yale University Press, 1919.

Clayton, Peter C. *Chronicle of the Pharaohs*. London: Thames and Hudson, 1994.

Connolly, Peter. *The Roman Army*. London: Macdonald Educational Press, 1975.

———. *Greece and Rome at War*. Englewood Cliffs, NJ: Prentice-Hall, 1981.

Contenau, Georges. *Everyday Life in Babylon and Assyria*. Translated by K. R. Maxwell-Hyslop and A. R. Maxwell-Hyslop. London: Edward Arnold, 1954.

Cook, J. M. *The Persian Empire*. London: Schocken, 1983.

Cornell, Tim. *The Beginnings of Rome: Italy and Rome from the Bronze Age to the Punic Wars*. New York: Routledge, 1995.

Cottrell, Leonard. *Hannibal: Enemy of Rome*. New York: Holt, Rinehart, Winston, 1960.

———. *The Warrior Pharaohs*. New York: Putnam, 1969.

Creasy, Edward S. *Fifteen Decisive Battles of the World*. New York: Dorsett, 1987.

Creel, Herlee G. "The Horse in Chinese History." In *What is Taoism? and Other Studies in Chinese Cultural History*. Chicago: University of Chicago Press, 1970.

———. *The Origins of Statecraft in China*. Chicago: University of Chicago Press, 1970.

Crone, Patricia. *Slaves on Horses: The Evolution of the Islamic Polity*. New York: Cambridge University Press, 1980.

———. "The Early Islamic World." In *War and Society in the Ancient and Medieval Worlds*, edited by Kurt Raaflaub and Nathan Rosenstein. Cambridge, MA: Harvard University Press, 1999.

Crossan, John Dominic. *The Historical Jesus: The Life of a Mediterranean Jewish Peasant*. San Francisco: Harper Collins, 1991.

Daly, Gregory. *Cannae: The Experience of Battle in the Second Punic War*. New York: Routledge, 2001.

Davies, Roy. *Service in the Roman Army*. New York: Columbia University Press, 1989.

Dayal, Raghubir. *An Outline of Indian History and Culture*. 2nd ed. Delhi, 1984.

De Beer, Gavin. *Hannibal: Challenging Rome's Supremacy.* New York: Viking Press, 1969.

Delbrück, Hans. *History of the Art of War within the Framework of Political History.* 4 vols. Westport, CT: Greenwood Press, 1975–1985.

Dennis, George T. *Three Byzantine Military Treatises.* Washington, DC: Dunbarton Oakes, 1985.

Devine, A. M. "Grand Tactics at the Battle of Issus." *Ancient World* 12 (1985): 39–59.

———. "The Strategies of Alexander and Darius III in the Issus Campaign." *Ancient World* 12 (1985): 25–38.

———. "The Battle of Gaugamela: A Tactical and Source Critical Study." *Ancient World* 13 (1986): 87–116.

———. "The Battle of the Hydaspes." *Ancient World* 16 (1987): 91–113.

Dien, Albert E. "The Stirrup and Its Effect on Chinese History." *Ars Orientalis* 16 (1986): 33–56.

Dikshitar, V. R. Ramachandra. *War in Ancient India.* Delhi: Motilil Banarsidass, 1987.

Dio Cassius. *Roman History.* Translated. New York: Penguin Books, 1972.

Dixon, K. R., and P. Southern. *The Roman Cavalry from the First to the Third Century* A.D. London: Batsford, 1992.

Dodge, Theodore A. *Hannibal: A History of the Art of War Among the Carthaginians and the Romans Down to the Battle of Pydna, 168* B.C. 2 vols. Boston: Houghton, 1891.

———. *Alexander: A History of the Origin and Art of War from Earliest Times to the Battle of Issus, 301* B.C., *with a Detailed Account of the Campaigns of Alexander the Great.* New York: Da Capo Press, 1966.

Doyle, R. J., and Nancy C. Lee. "Microbes, Religion, and Warfare." *Canadian Journal of Microbiology* 32, no. 3 (March 1986): 190–197.

Drews, Robert. "The Chariots of Iron of Joshua and Judges." *Journal for the Study of the Old Testament* 45 (1989): 15–23.

———. *The End of the Bronze Age: Changes in Warfare and the Catastrophe ca. 1200* B.C.E. Princeton, NJ: Princeton University Press, 1993.

Duffy, Christopher. *The Military Experience in the Age of Reason.* New York: Atheneum, 1988.

du Picq, Ardant. *Battle Studies: Ancient and Modern Battle.* Harrisburg, PA: The Military Service Publishing Company, 1947.

Dupuy, T. N. *Numbers, Predictions, and War.* New York: Bobbs-Merrill, 1979.

———. *The Evolution of Weapons and Warfare.* New York: Bobbs-Merrill, 1980.

Dupuy, T. N., and R. Ernest. *The Encyclopedia of Military History.* New York: Harper and Row, 1986.

Duus, Peter. *Feudalism in Japan.* New York: Knopf, 1969.

Dyer, Gwynne. *War.* New York: Crown, 1985.

Eadie, J. W. "The Development of Roman Mailed Cavalry." *Journal of Roman Studies* 57 (1967): 161–173.

Edgerton, Robert. *Like Lions They Fought.* New York: Free Press, 1988.

Edwards, Michael, and James L. Stanfield. "Lord of the Mongols: Genghis Khan." *National Geographic* 190, no. 6 (December 1966).

Engels, Donald W. *Alexander the Great and the Logistics of the Macedonian Army.* Berkeley: University of California Press, 1978.

Erman, Adolf. *Life in Ancient Egypt.* New York: Dover, 1971.

Erman, Adolf, and C. Blackman. *The Literature of Ancient Egypt.* Metheun, MA: Little, Brown, 1927.

Essin, Emmett M. "Mules, Packs, and Packtrains." *Southwestern Historical Quarterly* 74, no. 1 (1970): 49–55.

Fabricus, E. "Some Notes on Polibius' Description of Roman Camps." *Journal of Roman Studies* 22 (1932): 78–87.

Fairbank, John King. *China: A New History.* Cambridge, MA: Harvard University Press, 1992.

Farris, William Wayne. *Heavenly Warriors: The Evolution of Japan's Military, 500–1300.* Cambridge, MA: Harvard University Press, 1992.

Faulkner, R. O. "The Battle of Megiddo." *Journal of Egyptian Archaeology* 28 (1942): 43–49.

———. "Egyptian Military Organization." *Journal of Egyptian Archaeology* 39 (1953): 36–48.

Feest, Christian. *The Art of War.* New York: Thames and Hudson, 1980.

Ferrill, Arther. "Herodotus and the Strategy and Tactics of the Invasion of Xerxes." *American Historical Review* 72 (1966): 102–115.

———. *The Origins of War: From the Stone Age to Alexander the Great.* New York: Thames and Hudson, 1985.

Finley, M. I. *The Ancient Enemy.* Berkeley: University of California Press, 1973.

Frankfort, Henri. *More Sculpture from the Diyala Region.* Chicago: University of Chicago Press, 1943.

Friday, Karl. *Hired Swords: The Rise of Private Warrior Power in Early Japan.* Stanford, CA: Stanford University Press, 1992.

Frolich, H. *Die Militarmedicin Homers.* Stuttgart, 1897.

Frost, H. M. *Orthopaedic Biomechanics.* Springfield, IL: Charles C. Thomas, 1973.

Frye, Richard N. *The Heritage of Persia.* Cleveland, OH: World Publishing, 1963.

———. *The Golden Age of Persia.* London: Sterling Press, 2000.

Fuller, J.F.C. *A Military History of the Western World.* 3 vols. New York: Da Capo Press, 1954.

———. *The Generalship of Alexander the Great.* New Brunswick, NJ: Rutgers University Press, 1960.

———. *Julius Caesar: Man, Soldier, and Tyrant.* New Brunswick, NJ: Rutgers University Press, 1965.

Gabriel, Richard A. *The Antagonists: A Comparative Combat Assessment of the Soviet and American Soldier.* Westport, CT: Greenwood Press, 1984.

———. *Military Psychiatry: A Comparative Perspective.* Westport, CT: Greenwood Press, 1986.

———. *No More Heroes: Madness and Psychiatry in War.* New York: Hill and Wang, 1987.

———. *The Painful Field: The Psychiatric Dimension of Modern War.* Westport, CT: Greenwood Press, 1988.

———. "Armaments." In *Italian Encyclopedia of Social Sciences.* Rome: University of Rome, 1990.

———. *The Culture of War: Invention and Early Development*. Westport, CT: Greenwood Press, 1990.

———. *The Battle of Kadesh*. U.S. Army War College Ancient Battle Series. Carlisle, PA, 1991.

———. *Great Captains of Antiquity*. Westport, CT: Greenwood Press, 2001.

———. *Warrior Pharaoh*. New York: Iuniverse, 2001.

———. *Gods of Our Fathers: The Memory of Egypt in Judaism and Christianity*. Westport, CT: Greenwood Press, 2002.

———. *The Great Armies of Antiquity*. Westport, CT: Praeger, 2002.

———. *Lion of the Sun*. New York: Iuniverse, 2003.

———. *The Military History of Ancient Israel*. Westport, CT: Praeger, 2003.

———. *Empires at War: A Chronological Encyclopedia*. 3 vols. Westport, CT: Greenwood Press, 2005.

———. *Warrior Prophet: The Military Biography of Mohammed*. Norman: Oklahoma University Press, 2006.

Gabriel, Richard A., and Donald W. Boose, Jr. *The Great Battles of Antiquity: A Strategic and Tactical Guide to Great Battles That Shaped the Development of War*. Westport, CT: Greenwood Press, 1994.

Gabriel, Richard A., and Karen S. Metz. *From Sumer to Rome: The Military Capabilities of Ancient Armies*. Westport, CT: Greenwood Press, 1991.

———. *A History of Military Medicine*. 2 vols. Westport, CT: Greenwood Press, 1992.

Gabriel, Richard A., and Paul L. Savage. *Crisis in Command: Mismanagement in the Army*. New York: Hill and Wang, 1978.

Gale, Sir Richard. *Great Battles of Bible History*. New York: John Day, 1970.

Gardiner, Sir Alan. *The Kadesh Inscriptions of Ramses II*. Oxford: Griffith Institute, 1960.

———. *Egypt of the Pharaohs*. London: Oxford University Press, 1961.

Garrison, Fielding H. *The History of Medicine*. London: W. B. Saunders, 1968.

Gernet, Jacques. *A History of Chinese Civilization*. Cambridge: Cambridge University Press, 1996.

Gilliver, Catherine. *Caesar's Gallic Wars*. London: Routledge, 2003.

Goedicke, Hans. "Considerations on the Battle of Kadesh." *Journal of Egyptian Archaeology* 52 (1966): 71–80.

———. "Egyptian Military Actions in Asia in the Middle Kingdom." *Revue d'Egyptologie* 42 (1991): 89–94.

Goetz, A. "Warfare in Asia Minor." *Iraq* 25 (1963): 125–130.

Goffart, Walter A. *Barbarians and Romans, A.D. 418–584: The Techniques of Accommodation*. Princeton, NJ: Princeton University Press, 1980.

Goldsworthy, Adrian. *The Roman Army at War, 100 B.C.E.–200 C.E.* Cambridge: Cambridge University Press, 1996.

Gordon, D. H. "Fire and Sword: Techniques of Destruction." *Antiquity* 27 (1953): 159–162.

Gothic History of Jordanes. Princeton, NJ: Princeton University Press, 1915.

Graham, Philip. *Metal Weapons of the Early and Middle Bronze Age in Syria and Palestine*. 2 vols. Oxford: B.A.R., 1989.

Grant, Michael. *The Army of the Caesars*. New York: Charles Scribner, 1974.

———. *History of Rome*. New York: Charles Scribner, 1978.

———. *From Alexander to Cleopatra: The Hellenistic World*. New York: Charles Scribner, 1982.

———. *The History of Ancient Israel*. New York: Charles Scribner, 1984.

Grant, Michael, and Rachel Kitzinger, eds. *Civilization of the Ancient Mediterranean: Greece and Rome*. New York: Charles Scribner, 1988.

Green, Peter. *Alexander of Macedon: A Historical Biography*. Berkeley: University of California Press, 1991.

Greenblatt, Miriam. *Augustus and Imperial Rome*. Tarrytown, NY: Benchmark Books, 2000.

Greenhalgh, P. *Early Greek Warfare: Horsemen and Chariots in the Homeric and Archaic Ages*. Cambridge: Cambridge University Press, 1973.

Griffith, Guy. *Mercenaries of the Hellenistic World*. Cambridge: Cambridge University Press, 1935.

———. "Alexander's Generalship at Gaugamela." *Journal of Hellenistic Studies* 67 (1947): 77–89.

———. *Alexander the Great: The Main Problems*. Cambridge: Cambridge University Press, 1966.

Grimal, Nicolas. *A History of Ancient Egypt*. London: Blackwell, 1988.

Grossman, Dave. *On Killing: The Psychological Cost of Learning to Kill in War and Society*. Boston: Little, Brown, 1995.

Grousset, Rene. *The Empire of the Steppes: A History of Central Asia*. Translated by Naomi Wolford. New Brunswick, NJ: Rutgers University Press, 1970.

Gruen, Erich. *The Hellenistic World and the Coming of Rome*. Berkeley: University of California Press, 1984.

Gruen, Peter. *Alexander of Macedon*. Garden City, NJ: Doubleday, 1950.

Grundy, G. B. *The Great Persian War*. London: J. Murray, 1990.

Gurdjian, E. Stephen. "The Treatment of Penetrating Head Wounds of the Brain Sustained in Warfare: A Historical Review." *Journal of Neurosurgery* 39 (February 1974): 161–169.

Gurney, O. R. *The Hittites*. Baltimore: Penguin Books, 1952.

Guterbock, H. G. *The Hittite Instructions for the Royal Bodyguard*. Chicago: Oriental Institute, 1991.

Hackett, Sir John. *Great Battlefields of the World*. New York: Macmillan, 1984.

———. *Warfare in the Ancient World*. New York: Facts on File, 1989.

Halden, John. "The Byzantine World." In *War and Society in the Ancient and Medieval Worlds*, edited by Kurt Raaflaub and Nathan Rosenstein. Cambridge, MA: Harvard University Press, 1999.

Hammond, N., and G. T. Griffith. *A History of Macedonia*. 2 vols. Oxford: Oxford University Press, 1979.

Hammond, N.G.L. "The Two Battles of Chaeronea." *Klio* 33 (1938): 186–218.

———. "Training in the Use of the Sarissa and Its Effect in Battle." *Antichthon* 14 (1980): 53–63.

Hanson, Victor David. *The Western Way of War: Infantry Battle in Classical Greece*. New York: Knopf, 1989.

———. *Hoplites: The Classic Greek Battle Experience.* London: Routledge, 1993.

———. *The Wars of the Ancient Greeks.* London: Cassell, 1999.

———. *Carnage and Culture: Landmark Battles in the Rise of Western Power.* New York: Doubleday, 2001.

Hardy, E. G. "Augustus and His Legionnaires." *Classical Quarterly* 14 (1921): 187–194.

Harrak, Amir. *Assyria and Hanigalbat: A Historical Reconstruction of Bilateral Relations from the Middle of the Fourteenth to the End of the Twelfth Centuries* B.C. New York: G. Olms Verlag, 1987.

Harrison, Mark. *Viking Warrior.* London: Osprey, 1993.

Hastings, Max. *The Oxford Book of Military Anecdotes.* New York: Oxford University Press, 1985.

Hawkins, J. D. "Assyrians and Hittites." *Iraq* 36 (1974): 67–83.

Head, D. *The Achaemenid Persian Army.* Stockport: Montvert, 1992.

Healy, Mark. *Qadesh: Clash of the Warrior Kings.* London: Osprey, 1993.

Healy, Mark, and Angus McBride. *The Ancient Assyrians.* London: Osprey, 1992.

Heath, E. G. *Archery: A Military History.* London: Osprey, 1980.

Heckel, Waldemar. *The Wars of Alexander the Great.* London: Osprey, 2002.

Herzog, Chaim, and Mordechai Gichon. *Battles of the Bible.* Jerusalem: Steimatzky's Agency, 1978.

Hignet, C. *Xerxes' Invasion of Greece.* New York: Oxford University Press, 1963.

Hill, D. R. "The Role of the Camel and the Horse in Early Arab Conquests." In *War, Technology and Society in the Middle East,* edited by V. J. Parry and M. E. Yapp. London: Oxford University Press, 1975.

Historical Statistics of the United States: Colonial Times to 1970. Washington, DC: Bureau of the Census, 1975.

Hobbs, T. R. *A Time for War.* Wilmington, DE: Michael Glazier, 1989.

Hoffman, Michael A. *Egypt Before the Pharaohs.* New York: Knopf, 1979.

Hogg, O.F.G. *Clubs to Cannon.* London: Duckworth, 1968.

Holladay, A. J. "Hoplites and Heresies." *Journal of Hellenic Studies* 102 (1982): 97–103.

Holland, Tim. *Rubicon: The Last Years of the Roman Republic.* New York: Doubleday, 2003.

Homan, Michael M. "The Divine Warrior in His Tent: A Military Model for Yahweh's Tabernacle." *Bible Review* XX (December 2000).

Hopkins, Keith. "Taxes and Trade in the Roman Empire, 200 B.C.E. to C.E. 400." *Journal of Roman Studies* 70 (1980).

Hourani, Albert. *A History of the Arab Peoples.* New York: Warner Books, 1991.

Howarth, Anthony. "Zama: Triumph of the Roman Way of War." *Strategy and Tactics* (August 1992): 5–14.

Huber, Karen C. "Triumphant Over All People: Constantine the Great." *Military History* (October 1991): 9–13.

Hudson, Harris Gary. "The Shield Signal at Marathon." *American Historical Review* 42 (1936–1937): 443–359.

Huston, James A. *The Sinews of War: Army Logistics, 1775–1953.* Washington, DC: Office of the Chief of Military History, 1966.

Hyland, Ann. *Equus: The Horse in the Roman World*. New Haven, CT: Yale University Press, 1990.

Inalcik, H. *The Ottoman Empire: The Classical Age*. New York: Praeger, 1973.

Jackson, A. V. Williams. *History of India*. London: Grolier Society, 1906.

———. *Persia: Past and Present*. New York: Macmillan, 1966.

Jarcho, S. "A Roman Experience with Heatstroke in 24 B.C." *Bulletin of the New York Academy of Medicine* 43, no. 8 (August 1967): 767–768.

Jiménez, Ramon L. *Caesar against Rome: The Great Roman Civil War*. Westport, CT: Praeger, 2000.

Jones, Archer. *The Art of War in the Western World*. Urbana: University of Illinois Press, 1987.

Jones, Gwyn. *The Vikings*. London: Oxford University Press, 1968.

Junkelmann, Marcus. *The Legions of Augustus: The Roman Soldier in an Archeological Experiment* [in German]. Mainz, Germany: Philipp von Zabern, 1986.

Kaegi, W. E. *Byzantium and the Early Islamic Conquests*. Cambridge: Cambridge University Press, 1992.

Kagan, Donald. *The Fall of the Athenian Empire*. Ithaca, NY: Cornell University Press, 1991.

———. *The Archimedian War*. Ithaca: Cornell University Press, 1994.

———. *Pericles and Athens: The Birth of Democracy*. New York: Free Press, 1998.

———. *The Peloponnesian War*. New York: Viking, 2003.

Kar, H. C. *Military History of India*. Calcutta: Firma KLM, 1980.

Keay, John. *India: A History*. New York: Grove Press, 2001.

Keegan, John. *The Face of Battle*. New York: Vintage Books, 1994.

———. *The Book of War*. Baltimore: Penguin Books, 2000.

Kelly, Thomas. "Thucydides and the Spartan Strategy in the Archidamian War." *American Historical Review* 87 (1982): 399–427.

Kennedy, Paul. *The Rise and Fall of the Great Powers*. New York: Random House, 1987.

Keppie, L.J.F. *The Making of the Roman Army: From Republic to Empire*. Totawa, NJ: Barnes and Noble Books, 1984.

Kerstein, Morris, and Roger Hubbard. "Heat Related Problems in the Desert: The Environment Can Become the Enemy." *Military Medicine* 149 (December 1984): 650–656.

Kierman, Frank A., and John K. Fairbank, eds. *Chinese Ways in Warfare*. Cambridge, MA: Harvard University Press, 1974.

Kikuli Horse Training Manual. Translated by Gerhard Probst. Louisville, KY: Kings Library Press, 2001.

Kiss, Peter A. "Horsemen of Cruel Cunning." *Military History* (December 1986): 34–41.

Korfmann, Manfred. "The Sling As a Weapon." *Scientific American* 229, no. 4 (1973): 34–42.

Kramer, Samuel N. *The Sumerians*. Chicago: University of Chicago Press, 1963.

———. *Cradle of Civilization*. New York: Time, 1969.

Krige, E. J. "The Military Organization of the Zulus." In *Peoples and Cultures of Africa*, edited by E. Skinner. Garden City, NY: Natural History Press, 1973.

Laffont, Robert. *The Ancient Art of Warfare*. Vol. 1, *Antiquity*. New York: Time-Life Books, 1968.

Lamb, Harold. *Genghis Khan*. New York: Doubleday, 1927.

———. *Hannibal: One Man against Rome*. Garden City, NY: Doubleday, 1958.

Lancel, Serge, and Antonia Nevill. *Hannibal*. London: Blackwell, 1998.

Lawrence, A. W. "Ancient Fortifications." *Journal of Egyptian Archaeology* 51 (1965): 69–94.

———. *Greek Aims in Fortification*. New York: Oxford University Press, 1979.

Lazenby, J. F. *The Spartan Army*. Warminster, UK: Aris and Phillips, 1985.

Levy, Martin. "Some Objective Factors of Babylonian Medicine in Light of New Evidence." *Bulletin of the History of Medicine* 35 (January–February 1961): 63–68.

Lewis, Jon E., ed. *Ancient Egypt*. New York: Carroll and Graf, 2003.

Lewis, Mark Edward. *Sanctioned Violence in Early China*. Albany: State University of New York Press, 1990.

Liddell Hart, Basil Henry. *A Greater Than Napoleon, Scipio Africanus*. London: Blackwood and Sons, 1926.

Lister, R. P. *Genghis Khan*. New York: Dorsett Press, 1969.

Littauer, M. A., and J. Crouwel. *Wheeled Vehicles and Ridden Animals in the Ancient Near East*. Leiden: E. J. Brill, 1979.

Liver, Jacob, ed. *The Military History of the Land of Israel in Biblical Times* [in Hebrew]. Jerusalem: Israeli Defense Force, 1964.

Livy. *The History of Rome*. Translated. London: G. Bell and Sons, 1919.

———. *The War With Hannibal*. Translated by Aubrey de Selincourt. London: Penguin Books, 1965.

Lloyd, Alan, ed. *Battle in Antiquity*. London: Duckworth and Swansea, 1996.

Lloyd, Seton. *The Archaeology of Mesopotamia: From the Old Stone Age to the Persian Conquest*. London: Thames and Hudson, 1978.

Lu, David John. *Sources of Japanese History*. New York: McGraw-Hill, 1974.

Luckenbill, D. D. *Ancient Records of Assyria and Babylon*. 2 vols. Chicago: University of Chicago Press, 1926.

Luttwak, Edward N. *The Grand Strategy of the Roman Empire*. Baltimore: Johns Hopkins University Press, 1976.

Lynn, John A. *Battle: A History of Combat and Culture*. Boulder, CO: Westview Press, 2003.

Macqueen, J. G. *The Hittites and Their Contemporaries in Asia Minor*. Boulder, CO: Westview Press, 1975.

Majno, Guido. *The Healing Hand: Man and Wound in the Ancient World*. Cambridge, MA: Harvard University Press, 1975.

Major, Duncan K., and Roger S. Fitch. *Supply of Sherman's Army during the Atlanta Campaign*. Ft. Leavenworth, KS: Army Service Schools Press, 1911.

Majurmdar, R. C. *Ancient India*. Delhi: Motilal Banardissas, 1977.

Malinowski, Bronislaw. "An Anthropological Analysis of War." In *War: The Analysis of Armed Conflict and Aggression*, edited by Fred Harris and R. Murphy. Garden City, NY: Natural History Press, 1968.

Manitius, W. "The Army and Military Organization of the Assyrian Kings." *Zeitschrift für Assyriologie* 24 (1910): 90–107.

Manti, Peter A. "The Cavalry Sarissa." *Ancient World* 8 (1983): 75–83.

Manucy, Albert. *Artillery through the Ages*. Washington, DC: U.S. Government Printing Office, 1985.

Markle, M. "The Macedonian Sarissa, Spear, and Related Arms." *American Journal of Archaeology* 82 (1978): 483–497.

Markowitz, Michael C. "The Thousand-Year Garrison State: The Evolution of the Byzantine Army." *Command* 7 (November–December 1990): 42–61.

Marsden, E. W. *Greek and Roman Artillery*. Oxford: Clarendon Press, 1971.

Marshall, S.L.A. *The Soldier's Load and the Mobility of a Nation*. Washington, DC.: Combat Forces Press, 1950.

Martin, H. D. "The Mongol Army." *Journal of the Royal Asiatic Society* 1 (1943): 46–85.

Maspero, Henri. *China in Antiquity*. Boston: University of Massachusetts Press, 1978.

Mass, Jeffrey. *Warrior Government in Early Medieval Japan*. Stanford, CA: Stanford University Press, 1974.

McGeer, E. *Sowing the Dragon's Teeth: Byzantine Warfare in the Tenth Century*. Dumbarton Oaks Studies 33. Washington, DC: Dumbarton Oaks, 1955.

McGrew, Robert E. *Encyclopedia of Medical History*. New York: McGraw-Hill, 1985.

Mellaart, James. *The Neolithic of the Near East*. New York: Charles Scribner, 1975.

Mertz, Barbara. *Red Land, Black Land: Daily Life in Ancient Egypt*. New York: Peter Bedrick Books, 1990.

Milius, R. D. "Alexander's Pursuit of Darius thorough Iran." *Historia* 15 (1966): 249–257.

Misra, Ratnalal. *Military Architecture in Ancient India*. Delhi: B.R., 2002.

Moorey, P.R.S. "The Emergence of the Light, Horse-Drawn Chariot in the Near East, 2000–1500 B.C." *World Archaeology* 18 (1986): 196–215.

Morgan, David. *The Mongols*. Oxford: Blackwell, 1986.

Morris, Ivan. *The Nobility of Failure: Tragic Heroes in the History of Japan*. New York: Henry Holt, 1975.

Needham, Joseph. *Science and Civilization in China*. Cambridge: Cambridge University Press, 1954.

Nelson, Harold Hayden. *The Battle of Megiddo*. Chicago: University of Chicago Press, 1913.

Nesbit, J. "The Rate of March of Crusading Armies in Europe: A Study and Computation." *Traditio* 19 (1963): 176–181.

Newark, Timothy. *The Barbarians: Warriors and Wars of the Dark Ages*. London: Blandford Press, 1985.

Nicole, David, and Angus McBride, *The Armies of Islam*. London: Osprey, 1982.

———. *Armies of the Ottoman Turks, 1300–1774*. London: Osprey, 1983.

Nissen, Hans J. *The Early History of the Ancient Near East*. Chicago: University of Chicago Press, 1983.

Nutton, Vivian. "Medicine and the Roman Army: A Further Reconsideration." *Medical History* 13 (1969): 260–265.

Oakeshott, R. Ewart. *The Archaeology of Weapons*. New York: Praeger, 1960.

Oates, D. "Fort Shalamaneser: An Interim Report." *Iraq* 21 (1959): 98–129.

Ober, Josiah, and Barry S. Strauss. *The Anatomy of Error: Ancient Military Disasters and Their Lessons for Modern Strategists.* New York: St. Martins Press, 1990.

O'Connell, Robert L. "The Roman Killing Machine." *Quarterly Journal of Military History* 1 (Autumn 1988): 30–42.

———. *Of Arms and Men: A History of War, Weapons, and Aggression.* New York: Oxford University Press, 1989.

Olmstead, A. T. *History of the Persian Empire.* Chicago: University of Chicago Press, 1948.

———. *The History of Assyria.* Chicago: University of Chicago Press, 1951.

Oman, Sir Charles William Chadwick. *The Art of War in the Middle Ages: 378–1515.* Ithaca, NY: Cornell University Press, 1953.

Oppenheim, A. Leo. *Ancient Mesopotamia.* Chicago: University of Chicago Press, 1977.

Oughtred, Orville. "How the Romans Delivered Medical Care Along Hadrian's Wall Fortifications." *Michigan Medicine* 17 (February 1980): 56–59.

Park, Robert. "The Social Function of War." *American Journal of Sociology* 46 (1941): 551–570.

Parker, H.M.D. "The Legions of Diocletian and Constantine." *Journal of Roman Studies* 23 (1933): 175–189.

———. *The Roman Legions.* New York: Barnes and Noble Books, 1958.

Parrot, Andre. "The Excavations of Mari." *Syria* 16 (1935): 117–140.

Parry, V. J., and M. E. Yapp, eds. *War, Technology and Society in the Middle East.* London: Oxford University Press, 1975.

Patrick, Stephen B. "Byzantium: The Forgotten Empire." *Strategy and Tactics* 138 (October 1990): 16–19, 50–56.

———. "The Dark Ages: A Military Systems Profile, 500–1200." *Strategy and Tactics* (March 1993): 7–26.

Payne, Gallwey. "The Artillery of the Carthaginians, Greeks, and Romans." *Journal of the Royal Artillery* 58, no. 1 (April 1931): 34–40.

Peers, C. J., and Angus McBride. *Ancient Chinese Armies: 1500–200 B.C.E.* London: Osprey, 1990.

Piotrovsky, R. *The Ancient Civilization of the Urartu.* London: Cresset Press, 1969.

Plutarch. *Plutarch: The Lives of the Noble Grecians and Romans.* New York: Modern Library, 1992.

Pollock, Susan. *Ancient Mesopotamia.* Cambridge: Cambridge University Press, 1999.

Polybius. *The History of Rome.* Translated. London: William Heinemann, 1922.

Postgate, J. N. *Taxation and Conscription in the Assyrian Empire.* Rome: Biblical Institute Press, 1974.

Prasad, S. N., ed. *Historical Perspectives of Warfare in India.* Delhi: Motilal Banarsidass, 2002.

Prevas, John. *Hannibal Crosses the Alps: The Invasion of Italy.* New York: Da Capo, 2001.

Pritchard, James B. *Ancient Near Eastern Texts Relating to the Old Testament.* Translated by W. F. Albright. Princeton, NJ: Princeton University Press, 1955.

Pritchett, W. K. *The Greek State of War.* 4 vols. Berkeley: University of California Press, 1971.

Professional Guide to Diseases. Springhouse, PA: Intermed Communications, 1982.

Raaflaub, Kurt, and Nathan Rosenstein, eds. *War and Society in the Ancient and Medieval Worlds.* Cambridge, MA: Harvard University Press, 1999.

Rainey, A. F. "The Military Personnel of Ugarit." *Journal of Near Eastern Studies* 24 (1965): 17–27.

Rawlinson, George. *The Great Monarchies of the Ancient World: Babylonia, Media, and Persia.* London: Gorgias Press, 2002.

Reades, J. "The Neo-Assyrian Court and the Army: Evidence from the Sculptures." *Iraq* 34 (1972): 87–112.

Redford, Donald. *Akhenaten: The Heretic King.* Princeton, NJ: Princeton University Press, 1984.

———. *Egypt, Canaan, and Israel in Ancient Times.* Princeton, NJ: Princeton University Press, 1992.

Rice, Tamara Talbot. *Everyday Life in Byzantium.* New York: Putnams, 1967.

Riches, David, ed. *The Anthropology of Violence.* New York: Blackwell, 1986.

Risch, Erna. *Quartermaster Support of the Army: A History of the Corps, 1775–1939.* 2nd ed. Washington, DC: Center of Military History, 1989.

Robertson, J. I., Jr. *Tenting Tonight: The Soldier's Life.* Alexandria, VA: Time-Life Books, 1984.

Robinson, H. Russell. *The Armor of Imperial Rome.* London: Arms and Armor Press, 1975.

Rohl, David M. *Pharaohs and Kings: A Biblical Quest.* New York: Crown, 1995.

Rombauer, Irma S., and Marion Rombauer Becker. *The Joy of Cooking.* New York: Penguin Books, 1993.

Rossabi, Morris. *Khubilai Khan: His Life and Times.* Berkeley: University of California Press, 1988.

Roth, Jonathan P. *The Logistics of the Roman Army at War (264 B.C.–A.D. 235).* Boston: Brill, 1999.

Roux, Georges. *Ancient Iraq.* 3rd ed. New York: Penguin Books, 1992.

Roy, P. C. *The Mahabharata.* 2nd ed. Calcutta, 1919.

Rufus, Curtius Quintus. *The History of Alexander.* New York: Penguin Books, 1984.

Sage, Michael. *Warfare in Ancient Greece: A Sourcebook.* New York: Routledge, 1996.

Saggs, H.W.F. *The Greatness That Was Babylon: A Sketch of the Ancient Civilization of the Tigris-Euphrates Valley.* New York: Hawthorn Books, 1962.

———. "Assyrian Warfare in the Sargonid Period." *Iraq* 25, part 2 (1963): 141–149.

———. *The Might That Was Assyria.* London: Sidgwick and Jackson, 1984.

Salmon, E. T. "The Roman Army and the Disintegration of the Roman Empire." *Proceedings of the Royal Society of Canada* 52 (1958): 43–60.

Sandars, Nancy K. *The Sea Peoples: Warriors of the Ancient Mediterranean, 1250–1150 B.C.E.* London: Thames and Hudson, 1978.

Sandhu, Gurcharn Singh. *A Military History of Ancient India.* Delhi: Vision Books, 2000.

Sasson, Jack M., ed. *Civilizations of the Ancient Near East.* 3 vols. New York: Charles Scribner, 1995.

Sato, Kanzan. *The Japanese Sword.* Tokyo: Kodansha International, 1983.

Sawyer, Ralph D. *The Seven Military Classics of Ancient China.* Boulder, CO: Westview Press, 1993.

Schneider, Joseph. "On the Beginnings of Warfare." *Social Forces* 31 (1952): 68–74.

Schonberger, H. "The Roman Frontier Army in Germany." *Journal of Roman Studies* 59 (1969): 144–197.

Schulman, Alan Richard. *Military Rank, Title, and Organization in the Egyptian New Kingdom*. Berlin: Bruno Hessling Verlag, 1964.

———. "Chariots, Chariotry, and the Hyksos." *Journal of the Society for the Study of Egyptian Antiquities* 10 (1980): 105–153.

Scullard, Howard H. *Scipio Africanus in the Second Punic War*. Cambridge: Cambridge University Press, 1929.

———. *Scipio Africanus: Soldier and Politician*. Ithaca: Cornell University Press, 1970.

Sekunda, Nick. *The Army of Alexander the Great*. London: Osprey, 1988.

———. *The Persian Army, 560–330 B.C.E.* London: Osprey, 1988.

Seymour, Thomas D. *Life in the Homeric Age*. New York: Biblo and Tannen, 1963.

Shaughnessy, Edward L. "Historical Perspectives on the Introduction of the Chariot into China." *Harvard Journal of Asiatic Studies* 48, no. 1 (1988): 189–237.

Shaw, Ian. *Egyptian Warfare and Weapons*. Buckinghamshire, UK: Shire, 1991.

Shih, Yuan Chao. *The Secret History of the Mongols*. Translated by F. W. Cleaves. Cambridge, MA: Harvard University Press, 1982.

Shinoda, Minoru. *The Founding of the Kamakura Shogunate, 1180–1185*. New York: Columbia University Press, 1960.

Shoki, Nihon. *Nihongi: Chronicles of Japan from the Earliest Times to A.D. 697*. Translated by W. G. Aston. Rutland, VT: Charles E. Tuttle, 1972.

Shuckburgh, E. S. *Augustus Caesar*. New York: Barnes and Noble Books, 1997.

Simpson, William Kelly, ed. *The Literature of Ancient Egypt: An Anthology of Stories, Instructions, and Poetry*. New Haven, CT: Yale University Press, 1972.

Singh, Sarva Daman. *Ancient Indian Warfare*. Delhi: Motilal Banarsidass, 1997.

Sinor, D. "The Inner Asian Warriors." *Journal of the American Oriental Society* 101/102 (1981): 133–144.

Sippel, Donald V. "Some Observations on the Means and Costs of the Transport of Bulk Commodities in the Late republic and Early Empire." *Ancient World* 16 (1987).

Smith, R. E. *Service in the Post-Marian Roman Army*. Manchester, UK: Manchester University Press, 1958.

Smith, Vincent Arthur. *The Oxford History of India*. 3rd ed. Oxford: Clarendon Press, 1958.

Snodgrass, A. *Early Greek Armor and Weapons*. Edinburgh: Edinburgh University Press, 1964.

———. "The Hoplite Reform and History." *Journal of Hellenic Studies* 86 (1965): 110–122.

———. *Arms and Armor of the Greeks*. Ithaca, NY: Cornell University Press, 1967.

Spalinger, Anthony. *Aspects of the Military Documents of the Ancient Egyptians*. New Haven, CT: Yale University Press, 1982.

Starr, Chester G. *The Roman Imperial Navy*. Cambridge: Heffer, 1960.

Statistical Abstract of the United States. Washington, DC: U.S. Government Printing Office, 1988.

Steinman, Alan. "Adverse Effects of Heat and Cold on Military Operations." *Military Medicine* 152 (August 1987): 387–391.

Stillman, Nigel, and Nigel Tallis. *Armies of the Ancient Near East: 3000 to 539* B.C.E. Sussex, UK: Flexiprint, 1984.

Strabo. *The Geography of Strabo*. 8 vols. Translated by Horace Leonard Jones. London: Loeb Classical Library, 1922.

Strange, John. "The Transition from the Bronze Age to the Iron Age in the Eastern Mediterranean and the Emergence of the Israelite State." *Scandinavian Journal of the Old Testament* (1987): 1–19.

Sunzi. *Sun-Tzu: The Art of Warfare*. Translated by Roger T. Ames. New York: Ballantine Books, 1993.

Sykes, Sir Percy. *A History of Persia*. 2 vols. London: Macmillan, 1985.

Syme, R. "Some Notes on the Legions Under Augustus." *Journal of Roman Studies* 23 (1933): 14–33.

Tacitus. *The Annals*. Translated. New York: Penguin Books, 1972.

———. *Germania*. Translated. New York: Penguin Books, 1972.

———. *The Histories*. Translated. New York: Penguin Books, 1972.

Tadmor, H. "The Campaigns of Sargon II of Assur." *Journal of Cuneiform Studies* 12 (1958): 22–46.

Tarn, William W. *Hellenistic Military and Naval Developments*. London: Ares, 1975.

Thapar, Romila. *A History of India*. Middlesex, UK: Penguin Books, 1966.

Threadgold, Warren. *Byzantium and Its Army*. Stanford, CA: Stanford University Press, 1995.

Tien, Chen-Ya. *Chinese Military Theory: Ancient and Modern*. New York: Mosaic Press, 1992.

Toy, Sidney. *A History of Fortifications from 3000* B.C. *to 1700* A.D. London: Heinemann, 1955.

Tranquillus, Gaius Suetonius. *The Twelve Caesars*. Translated by Robert Graves. Baltimore: Penguin Books, 1957.

Tripathi, Ramashankar. *History of Ancient India*. Delhi: Motilal Banarsidass, 1999.

Turnbull, Stephen R. *The Samurai: A Military History*. New York: Macmillan, 1977.

———. *The Mongols*. London: Osprey, 1980.

———. *Battles of the Samurai*. London: Arms and Armour Press, 1987.

Turney-High, H. *Primitive War: Its Practice and Concepts*. 2nd ed. Columbia: University of South Carolina Press, 1971.

Tyldesley, Joyce A. *Judgement of the Pharaoh: Crime and Punishment in Ancient Egypt*. New York: Peartree, 2002.

Van Creveld, Martin. *The Art of War: War and Military Thought*. London: Cassell, 2000.

Varley, H. Paul. *Warriors of Japan as Portrayed in War Tales*. Honolulu: University of Hawaii Press, 1994.

Vaughn, P. Byron. "Local Cold Injury: Menace to Military Operations." *Military Medicine* 145 (May 1980): 304–307.

Vegetius, Renatus Flavius. *The Military Institutions of the Romans*. Harrisburg, PA: Military Service Publishing Company, 1944.

Venel, S. "War and Warfare in Archaeology." *Journal of Anthropology and Archaeology* 3 (1984): 116–132.

Vickers, Ralph. "The Siege of Constantinople: The End of the Middle Ages, 1453 A.D." *Strategy and Tactics* 66 (February 1978): 4–17.

———. "The Mongols and Their Impact on the Medieval West." *Strategy and Tactics* (March–April 1979): 23–28.

von Hagen, Victor W. *The Ancient Sun Kingdoms of the Americas: Aztec, Maya, Inca.* Cleveland, OH: World Publishing, 1961.

Wagner, Donald B. *Iron and Steel in Ancient China.* New York: Brill, 1993.

Wainwright, G. A. "Some Sea Peoples." *Journal of Egyptian Archaeology* 47 (1961): 71–90.

Waldbaum, Jane C. "From Bronze to Iron: The Transition from the Bronze Age to the Iron Age in the Eastern Mediterranean." *Studies in Mediterranean Archaeology* 54 (1978): 5–39.

Waldron, Arthur. *The Great Wall of China: From History to Myth.* Cambridge: Cambridge University Press, 1990.

Walker, Richard. *The Multi-State System of Ancient China.* Hamden, CT: Shoestring Press, 1953.

Wallbank, F. W. *Philip V of Macedon.* Cambridge: Cambridge University Press, 1940.

Warmington, B. H. *Carthage: A History.* New York: Praeger, 1960.

Warry, John. *Warfare in the Classical World: An Illustrated Encyclopedia of Weapons, Warriors, and Warfare in the Ancient Civilisations of Greece and Rome.* London, Salamander Books, 1980.

Watson, G. R. "The Pay of the Roman Army: The Republic." *Historia* 7 (1958): 113–120.

———. "The Pay of the Roman Army: The Auxiliary Forces." *Historia* 8 (1959): 372–378.

———. *The Roman Soldier: Aspects of Greek and Roman Military Life.* Ithaca, NY: Cornell University Press, 1969.

Webster, Graham. *The Roman Army: An Illustrated Study.* Chester, UK: Grosvenor Museum, 1956.

———. *The Roman Imperial Army of the First and Second Centuries A.D.* 3rd ed. Totawa, NJ: Barnes and Noble Books, 1985.

Weingartner, Steven. *Chariot Warfare in the Ancient World.* Westport, CT: Praeger, forthcoming.

———. "The Saga of Piyamaradu." *Military Heritage* (October 2001): 84–87.

———. "Chariot Tactics." *Military Heritage* XX (August 2002).

Wells, Peter. *The Barbarians Speak: How the Conquered Peoples Shaped the Roman World.* Princeton, NJ: Princeton University Press, 2001.

Wenke, Robert J. *Patterns of Prehistory: Man's First Three Million Years.* New York: Oxford University Press, 1980.

Werner, E.T.C. *Chinese Weapons.* Singapore: Graham Bush, 1989.

Whatley, N. "On Reconstructing Marathon and Other Ancient Battles." *Journal of Hellenic Studies* 84 (1964): 119–139.

White, K. D. *Roman Farming.* Ithaca, NY: Cornell University Press, 1970.

Wiesehofer, Josef. *Ancient Persia.* Teheran: Center for Arab Studies, 2001.

Wilcox, Peter, and Rafael Trevino. *Barbarians against Rome.* London: Osprey, 2000.

Wilson, David M. *The Vikings and Their Origins.* London: Thames and Hudson, 1989.

Winter, F. E. *Greek Fortifications*. Toronto: University of Toronto Press, 1971.

Wise, Terrence. *The Armies of the Carthaginian Wars, 265–146 B.C.* London: Osprey, 1988.

———. *Hannibal's War with Rome: The Armies and Campaigns*. London: Osprey, 1999.

———. *Ancient Armies of the Middle East*. London: Osprey, 2001.

Wiseman, Ann. *Julius Caesar: The Battle for Gaul*. London: Chatto and Windus, 1980.

Wolfram, Herwig. *History of the Goths*. Berkeley: University of California Press, 1990.

Wood, W. J. *Leaders and Battles: The Art of Military Leadership*. Novato, CA: Presidio Press, 1984.

Woolley, Sir Leonard. *Ur Excavations*. Vol. 2, *The Royal Cemetary*. London: Oxford University Press, 1934.

Wright, Quincy. *A Study of War*. 2nd ed. Chicago: University of Chicago Press, 1965.

Xenophon. *Anabasis*. Translated by Carleton I. Brownson. 2 vols. Cambridge: Loeb Classical Library, 1922.

———. *The Persian Expedition*. Translated by Rex Warner. Baltimore: Penguin Books, 1972.

———. *Hellenica*. Translated by E. C. Marchant. New York: Arno Press, 1979.

———. *Cyropaedia*. Translated by Wayne Ambler. Ithaca, NY: Cornell University Press, 2001.

Yadin, Yigael. "Hyksos Fortifications and the Battering Ram." *Bulletin of the American School of Oriental Research* 137 (1955): 23–32.

———. *The Art of Warfare in Biblical Lands in the Light of Archaeological Study*. 2 vols. Translated by M. Pearlman. New York: McGraw-Hill, 1963.

Yamada, Nakaba. *Ghenko: The Mongol Invasion of Japan*. New York: E. P. Dutton, 1916.

Yeivan, S. "Canaanite and Hittite Strategy in the Second Half of the Second Millennium, B.C.E." *Journal of Near Eastern Studies* 9 (1950): 101–107.

Zoka, Yaha. *The Imperial Iranian Army from Cyrus to Pahlavi*. Teheran: Ministry of Culture and Arts Press, 1970.

Zun, Ofer. "The Psychology of Warfare: The Evolution of Culture, Psyche, and the Enemy." *Journal of Peace Research* 24 (1987): 125–134.

INDEX

About the Author

RICHARD A. GABRIEL is a military historian and the author of numerous books. He was Professor of History and Politics at the U.S. Army War College and Professor of Humanities and Ethics at Daniel Webster College. Among his many books are *Empires At War: A Chronological Encyclopedia* (Greenwood, 2005), *The Great Captains of Antiquity* (2001) and *From Sumer To Rome: The Military Capabilities of Ancient Armies* (1991).

3/14/15 - 1.0 = 3/24/15 6/15/15

৭/১৫/১৬   ৭/১৫